Mindfulness in Organiz...... M000165275

Mindfulness techniques, having long played an important role in contemplative traditions around the world, are now recognized as having the potential to transform workplaces. As interest in the role of mindfulness in organizational settings continues to increase, this timely book fills a gap in the literature by providing an overview of the latest theoretical and empirical research on workplace mindfulness. It brings together world-leading scholars to explore the foundations, key discussions, diversity of approaches and applications of mindfulness in organizations. It acts as a catalyst for future research on the topic by suggesting research directions and stimulating organizational researchers to embark on new projects involving mindfulness. Furthermore, it provides valuable ideas for implementing mindfulness programs in organizations, for teaching mindfulness in business contexts, and for coaching with mindfulness. This must-read book will appeal to researchers and professionals in the fields of organizational behavior, organizational psychology, human resources and employee well-being.

JOCHEN REB is Associate Professor of Organisational Behaviour and Human Resources at the Lee Kong Chian School of Business, Singapore Management University (SMU), where he also serves as the Director of the SMU Mindfulness Initiative. He conducts research and training on mindfulness with a particular interest in interpersonal effects of mindfulness and mindful leadership.

PAUL W. B. ATKINS is a Senior Lecturer in the School of Psychology, Australian Catholic University and researcher with the ACU Institute for Positive Psychology and Education. He regularly teaches mindfulness courses, as well as conducting research on the effects of mindfulness, values and meditation training upon identity, perspective taking, empathy, and relationships.

CAMBRIDGE COMPANIONS TO MANAGEMENT

Cambridge Companions to Management provide an essential resource for academics, graduate students and reflective business practitioners seeking cutting-edge perspectives on managing people in organizations. Each *Companion* integrates the latest academic thinking with contemporary business practice, dealing with real-world issues facing organizations and individuals in the workplace, and demonstrating how and why practice has changed over time. World-class editors and contributors write with unrivalled depth on managing people and organizations in today's global business environment, making the series a truly international resource.

TITLES PUBLISHED:

FORTHCOMING IN THIS SERIES:

Mindfulness in Organizations

Foundations, Research, and Applications

Edited by

JOCHEN REB and PAUL W. B. ATKINS

CAMBRIDGE UNIVERSITY PRESS

CAMBRIDGE
UNIVERSITY PRESS

University Printing House, Cambridge CB2 8BS, United Kingdom

One Liberty Plaza, 20th Floor, New York, NY 10006, USA

477 Williamstown Road, Port Melbourne, VIC 3207, Australia

4843/24, 2nd Floor, Ansari Road, Daryaganj, Delhi - 110002, India

79 Anson Road, #06-04/06, Singapore 079906

Cambridge University Press is part of the University of Cambridge.

It furthers the University's mission by disseminating knowledge in the pursuit of education, learning and research at the highest international levels of excellence.

www.cambridge.org
Information on this title: www.cambridge.org/9781107683440

First published 2015
First paperback edition 2017

A catalogue record for this publication is available from the British Library

Library of Congress Cataloging in Publication data
Mindfulness in organizations : foundations, research, and applications / edited by Jochen Reb and Paul W. B. Atkins.
    pages   cm. – (Cambridge companions to management)
Includes bibliographical references and index.
ISBN 978-1-107-06480-5 (hardback)
1. Job stress.   2. Meditation.   3. Organizational behavior.   4. Psychology, Industrial.   5. Work–Psychological aspects.   6. Management–Psychological aspects.   I. Reb, Jochen, 1973–   II. Atkins, Paul W. B.
HF5548.85.M56 2015
158.7–dc23
2015003682

ISBN   978-1-107-06480-5   Hardback
ISBN   978-1-107-68344-0   Paperback

Contents

Figures

Tables

Contributors

HUGO J. E. M. ALBERTS is Assistant Professor at the Faculty of Psychology and Neuroscience, department of Clinical Psychological Science in Maastricht, the Netherlands. His field of expertise is mindfulness and self-regulation. His research is focused on the effects of mindfulness in different contexts as well as uncovering the underlying mechanisms responsible for the effects. Besides his role as Assistant Professor, Hugo is a mindfulness trainer and coach.

TAMMY D. ALLEN is Professor of Psychology at the University of South Florida. Her research interests include work-family issues, career development, and occupational health. She is Past President of the Society for Industrial and Organizational Psychology and former Associate Editor for the *Journal of Applied Psychology* and *Journal of Occupational Health Psychology*.

PAUL W. B. ATKINS teaches and conducts research with the Psychology Department and the Institute for Positive Psychology and Education at the Australian Catholic University. His research interests include studying the effects of mindfulness, values and meditation training upon identity, perspective taking, empathy and relationships. He regularly teaches both meditation and Acceptance and Commitment Training (ACT) courses. He is President-elect of the Australia and New Zealand Association for Contextual Behavioural Science.

DEVASHEESH P. BHAVE is Assistant Professor of Organisational Behaviour and Human Resources in the Lee Kong Chian School of Business at Singapore Management University. His research interests include dynamic processes of affect and performance, interpersonal relationships at work, and customer service. His research has been published in *Personnel Psychology*, *Journal of Applied Psychology*, *Academy of Management Journal*, and other outlets.

RICHARD E. BOYATZIS is Distinguished University Professor, and Professor in the Departments of Organizational Behavior, Psychology, and Cognitive Science at Case Western Reserve University and People and Organization at ESADE. Ranked ninth Most Influential International Thinker by HR Magazine in 2012 and 2014, he is the author of more than 150 articles on leadership, competencies, emotional intelligence, competency development, coaching, and management education.

MIRABAI BUSH is a Senior Fellow and Founding Director of the Center for Contemplative Mind in Society. Under her direction, the center introduced contemplative practices into the fields of higher education, law, business, journalism, social justice activism, and the military. A key contributor to Google's Search Inside Yourself curriculum, she has taught mindfulness in organizations including AMEX, Hearst Publications, Mind and Life Institute, Smith College, Amherst College, and Fetzer Institute.

MICHAEL CHASKALSON is an Honorary Lecturer in the Centre for Mindfulness Research and Practice at Bangor University and an Adjunct Professor at IE Business School in Madrid. His work mainly focuses on mindfulness training in organizations. He is the author of *The Mindful Workplace* and *Mindfulness in Eight Weeks* as well as various articles in peer-reviewed journals.

KRAIVIN CHINTAKANANDA is a Ph.D. student in the Organisational Behaviour and Human Resources area at Singapore Management University. He holds a Master's Degree in Organisational Behaviour from London School of Economics and Political Science and a Bachelor's Degree in Economics from the University of North Carolina at Chapel Hill. His research focuses on mindfulness, prosocial motivation and behavior, compassion, and ethics.

ELLEN CHOI is an organizational behavior doctoral student at the Ivey School of Business, University of Western Ontario. She completed her Master's Degree in Organizational Psychology at the London School of Economics. Ellen's research looks at the effects of mindfulness in the workplace. Specifically she studies mindfulness in conjunction with emotion regulation, resilience, self-regulation, productivity, and performance.

CHRISTIAN GÄRTNER is Assistant Professor of Organization Theory at Helmut Schmidt University, Germany. His research covers organizational design and change with a focus on mindful organizing and knowledge-intensive service work as well as the tools that are used to cope within these complex and uncertain work settings. He has authored articles in international and national academic journals as well as practitioner outlets.

SHARON GRACE HADLEY is a business manager and researcher working in the Centre for Mindfulness Research and Practice (CMRP) at Bangor University. Sharon is leading the CMRP's workplace research which is currently investigating the cost–benefit analysis of mindfulness training in the workplace. With an interest in government policy, Sharon contributes to various forums including a UK All Party Parliamentary Group set up to study the benefits of bringing mindfulness into public policy.

LIZ HALL is the Editor of *Coaching at Work* magazine and a Senior Practitioner coach (accredited by the European Mentoring & Coaching Council). She is the author of *Mindful Coaching* (Kogan Page, 2013). She runs mindfulness programmes for individuals and corporates. She is an award-winning journalist with 27 years' experience, writing for publications including *The Guardian*, *The Observer*, *The Financial Times*, and *People Management*.

CHRISTIAN HUBER is an assistant professor at the Helmut Schmidt University – University of the Federal Armed Forces – in Hamburg, Germany. His work has been published in journals such as *Human Relations*, *Management Accounting Research*, *Journal of Management Inquiry*, *Critical Perspectives on Accounting* and the *Journal of Business Ethics*. His research interests include management accounting, risk management, public sector organizations, financial regulation, valuation, and the use of literature in organizational theory.

UTE R. HÜLSHEGER is Associate Professor of Work and Organizational Psychology at the Faculty of Psychology and Neuroscience, Maastricht University, The Netherlands. Her research primarily focuses on occupational health-related topics, including emotional labor and employee mindfulness, as well as personnel selection and innovation in organizations. She serves on the editorial boards of the

Journal of Applied Psychology, *Journal of Personnel Psychology*, and *Journal of Business and Psychology*.

JEREMY HUNTER serves as Assistant Professor of Practice at the Peter F. Drucker Graduate School of Management at Claremont Graduate University. He has more than a decade's experience helping leaders to relentlessly develop themselves while retaining their humanity in the face of monumental change and challenge. He has been featured in the *Wall Street Journal*, *The Economist*, the *Los Angeles Times* and National Public Radio's *Morning Edition*.

NATALIA KARELAIA is an assistant professor of Decision Sciences at INSEAD where she teaches Managerial Decision Making and Negotiations. Her research, which focuses on how people make decisions and how their decision making can be improved, has been presented at numerous international conferences and published in leading academic journals including *Organization Science*, *Psychological Review*, *Management Science*, and *Organizational Behavior and Human Decision Processes*.

DEJUN TONY KONG PH.D. is Assistant Professor of Leadership Studies and Management in the Jepson School of Leadership Studies and the Robins School of Business at the University of Richmond, USA. His research largely focuses on trust in various contexts and the psychology of social relationships. His work has appeared in the *Academy of Management Journal*, the *Journal of Cross-Cultural Psychology*, the *Journal of Positive Psychology*, and *Small Group Research* among others.

RAVI S. KUDESIA is a doctoral candidate of Organizational Behavior at the Olin Business School at Washington University in St. Louis. His research focuses on attention, sensemaking, and managerial metacognition. Prior to joining academia, Ravi founded an Internet startup company and ran frequent mindfulness seminars for fellow entrepreneurs. His ideas have been featured on CNN.com, *Integral Yoga Magazine*, and the *Huffington Post*.

HANNES LEROY is a visiting assistant professor at Cornell University, Johnson Graduate School of Management. His research interests include the study of authenticity and its value to organizations, especially its leadership implications. He holds a Ph.D. in management from the University of Leuven in Belgium and was a visiting doctoral student at Cornell University.

E. LAYNE PADDOCK is Assistant Professor of Organisational Behaviour and Human Resources at Singapore Management University. She holds a B.S. and M.A. from the College of William & Mary and an M.Sc. and Ph.D. from the University of Arizona. Her research interests include organisational justice and gender at work, including the work-family interface. Her work on these topics is published in high-ranking, peer-reviewed journals.

EMILY H. PELTASON is a graduate student in counseling psychology at Santa Clara University. Prior to enrolling at Santa Clara, Emily was a member of the research and writing team at the Center for Research on Education Outcomes (CREDO) at Stanford University. She received her B.A. in political science from Stanford University.

JOCHEN REB is Associate Professor of Organisational Behaviour and Human Resources and Director of the Mindfulness Initiative @ SMU, Singapore Management University. His research focuses on the role of mindfulness in organizational contexts such as leadership and performance and on judgment and decision making in organizations He currently serves on the editorial boards of *Organizational Behavior and Human Decision Processes*, the *Journal of Management*, and the *Journal of Business and Psychology*.

SHAUNA L. SHAPIRO PH.D. is a professor at Santa Clara University, a licensed clinical psychologist, and an internationally recognized expert in mindfulness. Dr. Shapiro has conducted extensive clinical research investigating the effects of mindfulness training across a wide range of populations and has published over 100 peer-reviewed journal articles. Dr. Shapiro is the recipient of the American Council of Learned Societies teaching award, acknowledging her outstanding contributions to graduate education.

SAMANTHA SIM is a doctoral candidate in Organisational Behaviour and Human Resources at the Lee Kong Chian School of Business, Singapore Management University (SMU). Her research interests include mindfulness, compassion at the workplace and organizational justice. She is also part of the Mindfulness Initiative @ SMU, a group dedicated to research, education, and outreach to the SMU community and beyond on secular mindfulness in all spheres of life.

ROBERT STYLES is the Director of Organisational Leadership and Performance at ANUedge, the commercial arm of the Australian National University. He advises corporations and public sector agencies on mindfulness/wellbeing approaches in human capital development. His Ph.D. research focus is on self and identity in the field of Contextual Behavioural Science.

MARGARET C. WANG is a graduate student in the Counseling Psychology program at Santa Clara University. Her past research at the Harvard Psychology Department has included areas related to moral judgment, attraction, and culture. She holds a B.A. in Psychology from Harvard University.

Foreword

Scholarly and practical interest in mindfulness has exploded in recent years, bringing with it questions about what mindfulness is, how it differs from related concepts in organization and management, and on the effectiveness of organizational mindfulness interventions. Professors Jochen Reb and Paul W. B. Atkins have gathered together the leading scholars and practitioners into a collection that seeks to address these questions and to demonstrate the theoretical and practical richness of mindfulness. This collection is deeply based in scholarship, taking care to discuss the history of mindfulness research, methodological challenges and critical debates; yet, it also includes several chapters by mindfulness teachers and practitioners. Thus, scholars interested in mindfulness can read rich descriptions of mindfulness interventions, and practitioners can better understand the empirical and theoretical basis of mindfulness research.

While mindfulness has traditionally centered on stress reduction, here the concept is applied to new areas of management scholarship, helping to further our understanding of negotiation, decision making, work-life balance, creativity and leadership, among others. It is a resource for those already conducting research on mindfulness as well as those considering moving into this exciting new area of organizational scholarship. This collection will also be useful to practitioners and educators who would like to know what others have done that has been effective and what has not worked so well. Overall we anticipate that this collection will help establish mindfulness in organizations as an important topic within management research and practice.

Series editors:
Cary Cooper
Lancaster University Management School;
Jone L. Pearce
University of California, Irvine

Preface

This work started as the idea of bringing together pioneering scholars for a state-of-the-art edited volume on mindfulness in organizations. The goal was to help put this novel area of research "on the map" of organizational scholarship. Seeing the quality of the various chapters, we are hopeful that this goal will be achieved. Along the way, it has been a wonderful journey to help this book develop from a simple idea to reality. This journey would not have been possible without the help of our editorial team. We would like to thank Paula Parish for supporting the idea of this book from the beginning and offering crucial guidance throughout. We are also grateful to Claire Wood, Rob Wilkinson and Deborah Renshaw for their excellent editorial work.

For Jochen, it has been an extraordinary experience working with such a dedicated and professional group of contributors. I had been warned by experienced editors about uncooperative chapter authors and the need to chase after them. It turned out to be much easier than expected. I can only speculate that this was because of the passion the contributors have for mindfulness. I also feel fortunate that Paul came on board as editor; we complemented each other in a variety of ways. Many thanks go to Samantha Sim, Jocelyn Ho, and Jolylynn Tan for their help with formatting the chapters. The idea of this edited volume originally emerged from conversations with my colleague at National University of Singapore, Jayanth Narayanan. Jay, thank you for the many, many enjoyable conversations on mindfulness and related topics.

I believe that individuals, organizations, and societies can benefit from the practice of mindfulness in many ways. Research such as that presented in this book can support informed practice. Ultimately, I believe that the "miracle" of mindfulness needs to be experienced personally. This book will have served its purpose if it inspires more scholars and organizations to not only study, but also practically experiment with mindfulness.

For Paul, one of the great pleasures of conducting research and practice among the mindfulness community is that just about everybody I have met in the community is someone I would love to invite for dinner and count as a friend. Although Jochen and I hardly knew one another before starting this book, I have found working with him, and with all the contributors to this volume, to be a genuine pleasure. I love working in a field that produces this kind of collaboration.

I also feel a huge debt of gratitude to all the mindfulness teachers and scholars who have helped shape my understanding and practice of mindfulness. Most notably I would like to thank Tim Goddard, Sue Hayes, Patrick Kearney, Gregory Kramer, S. N. Goenka, Jon Kabat-Zinn and Steve Hayes. When I teach mindfulness, I feel a sense of ease that I do not feel teaching my university classes. I think that ease comes from knowing that in some other important way, all I need to do is get myself out of the way enough to allow the timeless wisdom and truth of the practice to work through me. So I would like to thank also the wise ones through the ages whose compassion for the human condition led to this great flowering of mindfulness we see in the world today.

PART I

Foundations

1 | Introduction

JOCHEN REB AND PAUL W. B. ATKINS

Hardly a day goes by without a new media report on the benefits of mindfulness. In the corporate world mindfulness training programs are becoming increasingly popular. This trend is fuelled by highly visible organizations such as Google offering mindfulness-based programs for their employees. At the same time, many leaders, human resources and wellbeing professionals in organizations are probably still wondering what mindfulness is and whether mindfulness training would work in their organization. Organizational scholars, having taken note of research on mindfulness conducted mostly in medical and clinical psychology, are also wondering whether mindfulness is a valid research area for the organizational sciences or some wishy-washy, esoteric, or religious topic not qualifying for serious scholarship.

It is for these reasons that this edited volume on mindfulness in organizations is needed. Now that we have assembled all the contributions, we know that this book provides a treasure trove of information, knowledge, and insights into the role of mindfulness in organizations. And perhaps even more importantly, the contributors raise fascinating questions about mindfulness, thus providing countless valuable directions for future research and exploration.

To our knowledge, this is the first edited, scholarly book on mindfulness in organizations. We think this book will be useful for three main audiences. First, if you are a scholar, or Ph.D. student, interested in mindfulness, particularly in organizations, you will find this volume valuable because the chapters provide the most contemporary account of empirical and theoretical research on mindfulness in organizations, as well as providing helpful suggestions for promising areas of future research. Our hope is that this volume will help scholars who are thinking of starting research in this relatively new area.

Second, and just as importantly, this volume will also help organizational practitioners and leaders who may be trying to incorporate mindfulness into their (work) lives or who may wonder whether they should make mindfulness training programs available to their employees. If this is you, you will find ideas about the design and implementation of mindfulness programs, traps to avoid, and ways to make such training relevant to staff who may never have heard of mindfulness.

Last but not least, we think this book will provide valuable material to those who work with mindfulness in other ways. These include mindfulness trainers offering mindfulness-based interventions (MBIs) in organizations, business school instructors wanting to incorporate mindfulness into their teaching, and coaches working with mindfulness for themselves or their clients. If you are in this group, having a sense of the range of different perspectives and approaches to mindfulness, as well as the extent and limits of the research supporting its use in organizations, will help support you in delivering effective interventions.

The authors have done an excellent job in clarifying foundations, describing current debates, highlighting critical issues, advancing theorizing and research on mindfulness in organizations, and laying out directions for future research. We feel very fortunate to have been able to assemble such an outstanding group of chapter authors including many of the leading scholars working on mindfulness in organizations. The result has been, we believe, a volume that presents the cutting edge of research and thinking on the topic of mindfulness in organizations.

The chapters are grouped into three parts. Part I addresses such foundational issues as the history and conceptualization of mindfulness and MBIs, an overview of the role of mindfulness in the workplace, and an introduction and critical discussion of methods used in mindfulness research. Part II contains chapters exploring the role of mindfulness in various areas of organizational life, including identity, decision making, negotiations, work-life balance, and leadership. These chapters illustrate the broad contribution mindfulness can make to organizational scholarship and practice. Part III is on applications. We were keen to include this section because work on mindfulness traditionally and ultimately has a very pragmatic orientation: improving the lives of mindfulness practitioners. Consistent with this aspiration, the chapters in this part discuss more applied issues, such as practical experiences in bringing mindfulness into organizations, teaching mindfulness to executives, and coaching with mindfulness.

In proposing this volume, we had the following goals in mind. First, to provide an overview of the theory and empirical research on mindfulness in an organizational context as well as situate this research into a broader context. Second, to provide an integration of different approaches to the study of mindfulness in organizations, as well as illustrate the diversity of approaches that have been pursued in order to remove some of the confusion that is created through the different approaches. Third, to act as a catalyst for future theoretical and empirical research on mindfulness in organizations. The book should suggest promising lines of future research, excite organizational researchers to embark on new projects involving mindfulness, and give confidence that the field is a legitimate and theoretically grounded area of investigation. And fourth, to inform the design of future research on mindfulness in organizations using methods such as mindfulness interventions, experiments, or surveys. We hope that readers will find these goals met.

Overview of chapters

In the next chapter, Shapiro, Wang and Peltason explore the foundational questions "What is mindfulness, and why should organizations care about it?" They unpack Shapiro and Carlson's (2009) now widely cited and very useful definition of mindfulness in terms of intention, attention, and attitude. After highlighting the terrible costs of workplace stress, Shapiro *et al.* briefly review evidence that mindfulness helps not only in alleviating stress but also in enhancing decision making, perspective taking, resilience, positive organizational relationships and self-care. A fascinating aspect of this chapter is the exploration of the possibility of "mindfulness-informed business" – where mindfulness-inspired concepts and practices such as impermanence, no-self and acceptance are integrated into organizations without formally teaching meditation. Mindfulness is deeply counter-cultural to many organizational practices. This chapter explores the possibility that, in a world where individual achievement is often emphasized at the expense of self or others' wellbeing, mindfulness offers the promise of radical, transformational culture change for organizations.

In the third chapter, Chaskalson and Hadley examine the Buddhist origins of arguably the most widely used approach to mindfulness training, Jon Kabat-Zinn's eight-week mindfulness-based stress reduction (MBSR) course. Their chapter explores the ways in which fundamental Buddhist language and techniques have been translated into Western contexts. This translation, they argue, has inevitably involved changes in emphasis and approach in order to accommodate a different cultural context. Three changes are notable. First, MBSR in the secular context aims to alleviate suffering, whereas Buddhism is a system for the complete elimination of suffering. Second, MBSR tends to emphasize mindfulness over concentrative states of absorption, and is taught within a different ethical framework than that offered by the Buddha. Finally, MBIs in organizations are demonstrating positive benefits even with lower-dose amounts of formal practice. Chaskalson and Hadley's chapter manages to skilfully blend an acknowledgement and honouring of the past with a recognition of the need for continual evolution and growth of mindfulness practices in the future.

In Chapter 4 Choi and Leroy address the question of *how* mindfulness is being studied in the workplace. Their chapter includes sections on conceptualization, operationalization, and construct validity issues related to mindfulness. They also review specific methods such as MBIs, and self-report scales of mindfulness (with a useful overview of such scales in Table 4.1), and directions for future research. Choi and Leroy provide not only a good overview of the major methods employed in mindfulness research, but also a thoughtful evaluation and critique of these methods. For example, they discuss limitations of different research designs as well as strengths and weaknesses in terms of internal and external validity. We believe that this chapter is an essential read not only for researchers, but also for intelligent consumers who want to be in a position to make judgments about the implications that can be drawn from mindfulness research.

In the fifth chapter, Alberts and Hülsheger provide a very thorough review and discussion of different MBIs with a special focus on application in the context of work. The chapter first examines MBIs from the perspective of their different elements including formal practices, such as body scan and sitting meditation, and informal practices, such as awareness of routine activities and impulsive or reactive thought and behavior patterns. It then examines differences among MBIs with respect to duration and delivery mode, reviewing and discussing empirical findings. One of the fascinating results from this review is that it appears that beneficial effects of MBIs have been found for various different programs. In the next section of the chapter, the authors review the effects of MBIs on a variety of work-relevant variables including task performance, stress, and emotion regulation. One of the particularly outstanding characteristics of this chapter is that Alberts and Hülsheger not only review the literature, but also provide a very insightful discussion of the (mindfulness-based) mechanisms through which MBIs have beneficial effects at the workplace.

In Chapter 6 Atkins and Styles explore how mindfulness can affect one's sense of identity at work. Identity can be seen as a kind of filter through which all organizational activity occurs. Atkins and Styles use a theory of language and cognition called relational frame theory (Hayes, Barnes-Holmes, and Roche 2001) to construct a three-tiered understanding of identity as a conceptualized self, a knowing self and a more transcendent, observing sense of self as awareness. In a small pilot study, they find that an eight-week MBSR intervention decreases rigid conceptualizations about the self while increasing the extent to which the self is seen as an observer of experience. This study is fascinating for three main reasons. First, relational frame theory and its associated therapy (acceptance and commitment therapy – ACT) define mindfulness in behavioural terms (Hayes and Shenk 2004). This approach offers clarity and precision that is sometimes lacking in the Buddhist-inspired practices and concepts discussed in most of the other papers in this volume. Second, the Atkins and Styles system for coding the extent to which participants displayed a sense of self as an observer represents the beginnings of an entirely new, behavioral approach to measuring mindfulness that could potentially avoid some of the pitfalls of self-report measures of mindfulness. Finally, Atkins and Styles highlight the way in which identity is a critical determinant of workplace behavior that has hardly been studied in relation to mindfulness. Perhaps the biggest effect of MBSR and similar courses is to cause participants to redefine themselves less closely tied to any particular categorization of the self, and more closely tied to a sense of self as a container for observing the unfolding of any experience.

It has been said that life is a matter of making choices. Accordingly, in Chapter 7, Karelaia and Reb explore the potential influence of mindfulness on the fundamental activity of making decisions. They organize their chapter around four stages of decision making: (1) framing the decision, (2) gathering and processing information, (3) coming to conclusions, and (4) learning from feedback; and explore for each stage how mindfulness may help (and sometimes interfere) with making good, and perhaps even wise, choices. Among other things, Karelaia and Reb discuss how being more mindful can lead to a greater awareness of choicefulness, of one's decision objectives, and of ethical conflicts; how it can reduce information processing-related judgment biases (de-biasing) and a better appreciation of uncertainty; how it can help in making tradeoffs and implementing decisions; and how mindfulness may support processes of learning from past decisions. Their chapter provides a wealth of ideas for anyone interested in studying mindfulness in workplace or leader decision making. It also provides many ideas for anyone trying to apply mindfulness with the intention of improving their own decision making.

In Chapter 8 Kudesia conducts a fascinating review of mindfulness and creativity in the workplace. He begins by describing contexts that support creativity and the cognitive processes involved. He then reviews a growing list of studies showing that mindfulness practice appears to improve the capacity to see problems in new ways, before speculating on how mindfulness "as a state characterized by decreased discursive thought, heightened meta-awareness, and goal-based regulation of attention" could feasibly improve creativity. Decreased discursive thought means relying more upon direct experience than one's conceptualizations of experience, heightened meta-awareness means being able to notice multiple aspects of one's own mental processes and goal-based regulation of attention simply means "the ability to modify the level of focus and breadth of attention to maximize goal-directed behaviour." To the extent that we can flexibly hold our pre-existing assumptions and categorizations in mind while broadening or narrowing our attention at will, we are likely to enhance creativity. Overall, this chapter is very exciting as it provides a platform for future research in an area of high importance for modern organizations.

In Chapter 9 Allen and Layne Paddock turn our attention to a hugely important aspect of modern life: tensions between work and family life. This might seem like a surprising area of study for a mindfulness researcher, and certainly research on the effects of mindfulness upon the work-family interface is scant. But Allen and Paddock do a tremendous job first reviewing what relevant evidence there is and then exploring why mindfulness might improve work-family balance. Allen and Kiburz (2012) found that those with higher trait mindfulness also reported greater work-family balance and that this relationship was mediated by sleep quality and by vitality. In subsequent research they showed that a relatively short mindfulness intervention reduced work interference with family life. Allen and Paddock detail four mechanisms whereby mindfulness might have positive effects. First, attentional training might, for example, reduce the time needed at work while also enhancing relations with significant others through enhanced connections. Second, improved emotion regulation might enhance wellbeing at work but also help people to not take negative emotional experiences home to their loved ones. Third, mindfulness might help people to optimize their allocation of resources to work and family; and, finally, mindfulness can alter perceptions of time such that more mindful individuals perceive that they have more time and thus appear to be less affected by time pressures. This is an entirely new area of study and so some of this is inevitably speculation. But such speculation is important to promote good research and suggest more effective interventions in this important aspect of modern life.

Chapter 10 is unique in that Boyatzis uses the real-life story of "Dimitrios", the CEO of a company, away from and back towards mindfulness as a way of vividly demonstrating several principles of mindfulness. In so doing, Boyatzis elaborates on four main causes that disrupt the natural processes of being mindful with self, others, and the environment: (1) chronic stress; (2) life and career stages and cycles; (3) antagonistic neural networks; and (4) living and working around mindless others. These are followed by a discussion of processes that can help leaders move back towards mindfulness, including working with a personal vision, coaching with compassion, and developing resonant relationships. What makes this chapter a particularly captivating read is the interweaving of theory and story as well as the diverse set of topics covered, ranging from the micro (neural networks) to the macro (life stages). Readers may also find themselves inspired to reflect on their own journey away from and towards mindfulness. Also, read this chapter if you are curious to find out about the real person behind "Dimitrios"!

In Chapter 11, the second chapter on mindfulness in leadership, Reb, Sim, Chintakandanda, and Bhave start from the observation that both leadership and mindfulness are positively laden, "hot" topics.

Against this backdrop, they set themselves the goal of exploring the bright *and* the dark sides of mindfulness in leadership. They suggest that "being open to the complexities of mindfulness in leadership, rather than painting a perhaps unrealistically positive picture, will increase the chances of mindfulness surviving beyond the current buzz as a valid construct and training intervention that has implications for leadership research and practice." For this purpose, they make three important distinctions: among several dimensions of mindfulness; between mindfulness as a construct and mindfulness as a practice; and finally between the more commonly researched *intrapersonal* effects of mindfulness and *interpersonal* effects that are particularly relevant in the context of leadership. Their exploration is organized around (1) leadership behaviors and outcomes, (2) leadership styles, and (3) leadership development. In each of the sections, they explore beneficial as well as detrimental effects. In so doing, they propose a number of interesting ideas for future research studies. One of the fascinating, albeit speculative, conclusions they draw is that mindfulness is often approached as a self-regulatory resource that could potentially be used in the service of both wholesome and unwholesome goals. They conclude that only a holistic approach to mindfulness, emphasizing not only focused attention but also witnessing awareness and other dimensions will allow leaders to realize the full potential of what mindfulness (practice) has to offer.

In Chapter 12, Kong takes on the topic of mindfulness in interpersonal negotiations. Negotiations are ubiquitous in organizations and some research suggests that being more mindful enables negotiators to achieve better outcomes (Reb and Narayanan 2014). Kong develops a mindful, relational self-regulation (MRSR) model of negotiation that views mindfulness as a moderating factor, influencing how negotiators "manage their relationships in negotiation settings." To do so, Kong first delineates mindfulness from four nomologically related concepts: absorption, flow, emotional intelligence (EI), and intuition. He then develops his MRSR model and discusses its implications for negotiation theory and practice. The chapter also provides several interesting ideas for future research on mindfulness in negotiations. One of the main contributions of this chapter is to illustrate the vast unexplored potential of studying mindfulness in interpersonal contexts such as negotiation, as well as the benefits of integrating mindfulness into existing theories, such as the Gelfand *et al.*'s relational negotiation theory(2006). The reader is both inspired and challenged to think in more complex ways about mindfulness.

Coming from a different theoretical tradition than most of the authors of this volume, Gärtner and Huber in Chapter 13 concern themselves with both individual mindfulness and mindful organizing. Mindful organizing refers to "fluid and fragile bottom-up processes of organizing" and, therefore, needs to be re-accomplished as an ongoing activity. Gärtner and Huber specifically examine the role of tools in this process of re-accomplishing mindfulness. Thereby, their chapter sheds light on how to understand the mechanisms that link individual and collective forms of mindfulness. In particular, they illustrate this process with the example of visual templates, such as those used in the ubiquitous PowerPoint presentations. In focusing on visual templates as *antecedents* of mindfulness, they provide a very welcome counterpart to the common focus on *consequences* of mindfulness. In addition, by examining both how such tools can induce and inhibit mindfulness, they provide an interesting, balanced discussion. Coming from a different theoretical perspective and linking mindfulness to visual templates – a very novel idea – this chapter challenges us to think more creatively and broadly about how processes of mindfulness can be enacted and enabled in organizations.

In Chapter 14, Bush invites us to reflect on her journey to bring mindfulness to organizations, with a particular emphasis on her experiences with Monsanto and Google. Her work was part of pioneering and path-breaking efforts by the Center for Contemplative Mind in Society to support the development of more *contemplative organizations*. Through her thoughtful reflections on these experiences, we learn not only about the benefits organizations derived from working with mindfulness, but also the obstacles faced, as well as the importance of being responsive to the context and culture of the organization in implementing MBIs. Acknowledging concerns about the instrumental use of mindfulness, Bush nevertheless concludes that "mindfulness and related practices can lead to insight and then to wisdom and compassion, encouraging new forms of inquiry and creativity, potentially taking organizations and their leaders from good to great and from great to wise and compassionate." This chapter will be useful for both mindfulness researchers as well as practitioners implementing mindfulness-based programs in organizations.

Hunter, in Chapter 15, generously shares with us his experiences of the Executive Mind/Practice of Self-Management courses he developed and taught at the Peter F. Drucker School of Management from the early 2000s. The chapter describes the origins, methods, and motivations of the courses. Being strongly influenced by Drucker's work, Hunter argues that "[j]ust as leaders need tools to manage external realities, they also need tools to manage the internal ones. Effectiveness starts inside." Hunter's courses are designed to help executives develop the ability to achieve greater balance and thus greater potential to "do well by doing good." An important role is given to "the map" (see Fig. 15.1) as a guide to working with and ultimately overcoming rigid automatic responding. Hunter does a wonderful job in illustrating his teaching method and approach through concrete examples, "drawing from the lives of working executives" and shares with us invaluable "lessons learned" from his experience. The chapter ends by taking a broader perspective and briefly explores the role of mindfulness in the future of management (education). The chapter should appeal particularly to those interested in teaching mindfulness in a business context but also to anyone working with mindfulness.

Finally, in Chapter 16, Hall explores the ways in which mindfulness can help improve coaching. Her chapter is organized around two main themes: 1) the ways in which coaches can use their own mindfulness to coach more effectively and 2) the ways in which mindfulness can be taught to coaching clients to enhance their own outcomes. Her FEEL model (Focus, Explore, Embrace, and Let go/Let in) reflects the move away from simple goal setting-based formulations of coaching (such as the GROW model) toward coaching based more upon the evolving needs of the client. Hall then raises the important and interesting question of whether practices oriented toward being or "non-doing" can be useful in a culture of doing, concluding that it is possible to mindfully engage in doing. Mindfulness can potentially help coaches be more present and compassionate in relationships with their clients. Hall then explores how helpful it can be for coaches to teach mindfulness skills to their clients. This chapter is relevant not just for professional coaches, but for managers wanting to adopt a more coaching approach with their staff. Hall's FEEL model could just as easily apply to a performance appraisal meeting as it could to a formal coaching relationship.

Reflections on tensions and open issues

We had originally intended to write a concluding chapter to this book. But when we had assembled all the chapters, we saw that they stood on their own as a multifaceted image of where mindfulness has been and where it is going with respect to the workplace. We do, however, see some key creative tensions and open issues that exist in the current literature reflected in this volume and it is to these tensions that we now wish to turn.

Tension between spirituality and typical workplace culture

The first tension we notice is between spirituality and typical workplace culture. Although there is an increasing recognition that people bring their "whole selves" to work, there is still deep reticence in most workplaces regarding mixing the spiritual with the professional. From our perspective, this reticence reflects many factors including but not limited to values conflicts between spiritual practices and typical workplaces, the growing secularization of society, and a deep desire by many to retain at least some separation between work life and personal life. All these factors are real and can be respected in their own right.

Partly to address such legitimate concerns, most organizational scholars and practitioners have framed mindfulness in a secular context. This is reflected, for example, in defining mindfulness as a state of mind, rather than a spiritual or religious/Buddhist practice, in replacing "spiritual words" such as meditation with more acceptable (in a workplace context) words such as "mind fitness", in conducting scientific research on mindfulness, and in developing MBIs that are adapted to the context. This, in turn, has led to concerns about losing the essence of mindfulness, as understood in contemplative traditions (see also Bush's interesting discussion of this issue in this volume).

Ultimately, we believe that facilitators of workplace MBIs play a crucial role in balancing this tension. For example, when I (Atkins) teach mindfulness in the workplace, I almost always begin by encouraging people to bring both personal and professional issues into the discussions, while at the same time making it clear that mindfulness training is not therapy but skills development. By doing this, I am trying to give permission to participants to be whole people, not just workers. But also I am aiming to build a kind of respectful boundary

where people remember the context in which they are learning mindfulness and decide for themselves how best to share with others in a
way that preserves their dignity and career.

Diversity of perspectives on mindfulness

Another tension that emerges from our reading of the chapters in this
volume is the way in which definitions of mindfulness get "pulled" in
different directions as the concept is applied in different ways. While
almost all the authors refer to mindfulness in terms similar to Shapiro
et al. (this volume) and Jon Kabat Zinn (1990), some focus more on the
attentional elements (Kudesia), some focus more upon aspects of self
and identity (Atkins and Styles), and yet others view it as an umbrella
term comprising a number of constructs (Reb *et al.*). While most authors
now see mindfulness as a state, some still appear to assume that meditation, and sometimes specifically meditation within the framework of
Buddhist understanding, is the only or best way to attain that state. This
perhaps reflects the fact that the Buddhist perspective has more profoundly influenced mindfulness in the West than any other perspective,
and also the way in which many practitioners and teachers of mindfulness (including ourselves) have experienced their most profound and
intimate moments of mindfulness in the context of Buddhist retreats.

   In our view the diversity of perspectives is as it should be, given that
mindfulness concerns something as centrally important as the way
human beings attend and relate to the world. Mindfulness is a multifaceted idea with a rich nomological network extending across history,
discipline, and areas of application. The tension here is not so much how
to agree on the *right* definition. This will never happen because mindfulness is a living and fundamentally disputed concept like "leadership," in
that part of its value is in the continual discussion and redefinition of its
nature. Instead, the tension is more about how to move forward productively in researching mindfulness and developing workplace MBIs against
the backdrop of ongoing discussion about the nature of mindfulness.

How can mindfulness and MBIs be translated into the workplace?

Historically mindfulness and MBIs have been studied from a clinical
perspective. This perspective is quite different to one derived from

the context of organizations. First, the clinical perspective focuses largely on the individual. This can be seen, for example, in that most research has examined intra-individual consequences of mindfulness, such as reduced stress and anxiety. In contrast, an organizational perspective places much more emphasis on interpersonal and organizational issues, such as conflict management, organizational culture, or processes of mindful organizing (Gärtner and Huber, this volume). We believe that organizational scholars are in a wonderful position to enrich our understanding of mindfulness by approaching the topic from various levels of analysis, something they are used to doing.

Second, the clinical perspective has focused largely on intentional mindfulness practice as the antecedent of mindfulness (probably influenced by its roots in contemplative traditions, in particular Buddhism). In contrast, from an organizational perspective, the view is broadened considerably and includes antecedents of mindfulness such as organizational constraints (Reb, Narayanan, and Ho 2015), visual templates (Gärtner and Huber, this volume), life and career stages (Boyatzis, this volume), and the design of workplaces. Such research also helps to counterbalance the overwhelming focus on studying the consequences, rather than causes of mindfulness. Overall, while we believe that intentional practice will always remain one of the pillars of developing mindfulness, a broadening to include other antecedents is welcome.

Finally, most MBIs have been developed to address clinical populations and health issues. As a result, there has been a focus on alleviating suffering. In organizations, while we also work with participants who suffer from clinically significant health issues, this is not the focus of our work and our approach must also appeal to people who would not identify themselves as "suffering" to any significant extent. So, while health and wellbeing remain important (e.g., stress, burnout, job satisfaction), this focus must be complemented by a focus upon functioning and performance (e.g., job performance, negotiation skills, leadership effectiveness).

Clearly, much research will have to be conducted in order to better understand the implications of these differences. These differences in perspective challenge us to think creatively about how to study and practice mindfulness in the organizational context. Despite the differences, however, we believe that mindfulness and mindfulness practice can and do already play an important role in organizational life, and the various chapters in this volume attest to this.

Adapting mindfulness with richness and integrity while avoiding the pitfalls of faddism

The final tension we would like to discuss lies in how researchers and practitioners can appropriately adapt and apply mindfulness to their contexts, without losing the richness, quality and nuance of the experience. We are already seeing the rise of a backlash against McMindfulness – mindfulness as a fad, just another commercial commodity. From our perspective, and the perspective of many authors in this volume, an important way to protect against this risk is for researchers, practitioners and anyone else advocating the use of mindfulness to be engaged in a sincere practice of their own. Engaging in a systematic, sustained and iterative practice will allow us to remain connected to mindfulness at the experiential level; and this experiential level crucially keeps all our conceptual efforts at understanding the nature, antecedents, and consequences grounded. In our experience, it helps to do good work in this area if one understands mindfulness not only from a conceptual vantage point. Researchers of mindfulness can gain much from being "in the soup" and making real attempts to be more mindful in their own lives, rather than standing outside the system and relating to mindfulness as just another concept to be studied or taught. We recognize that for organizational researchers in particular, this stance is deeply counter-cultural. We encourage you to plunge into this adventure!

At the same time, while we believe that an experiential approach to mindfulness is hugely important, we also recognize the need for researchers, in particular, to remain open and unbiased. Assuming that mindfulness is always a good thing actually runs counter to the open, curious, and nonjudgmental attitude of mindfulness. Furthermore, uncritical proclamations about the benefits of mindfulness as a kind of "cure all" will only contribute to a boom and bust of the mindfulness bubble. Both as researchers and practitioners, we can gain from utilizing witnessing awareness to remaining open and sensitive to both positives and negatives of mindfulness and mindfulness practice.

Conclusions

We hope this book will be a valuable resource for both researchers and practitioners. We further hope that it will inspire others to conduct much-needed research on mindfulness in a work context. We are only taking the first steps in understanding the role, processes and power of mindfulness in organizations. Much work also remains to be done to develop interventions tailored specifically to organizational contexts, such as leadership development or change management. We are encouraged by the passion of a growing number of, often young, researchers in taking on the challenge and joy of studying mindfulness in the workplace in creative and sincere ways. Developments such as the dedicated and well-attended symposia at the annual meeting of the Academy of Management and the formation of a mindfulness interest group at the same conference, provide both credibility and evidence of the growing interest in and acceptance of mindfulness as a valid topic of organizational scholarship. This volume contributes to enhancing the legitimacy of this area of scholarship by illustrating the immense theoretical and practical contributions offered by the study and practice of mindfulness at work.

References

Allen, T. D. and Kiburz, K. M. (2012). Trait mindfulness and work-family balance among working parents: the mediating effects of vitality and sleep quality. *Journal of Vocational Behavior*, 80, 372–9.

Gelfand, M. J., Major, V. S., Raver, J. L., Nishii, L. H., and O'Brien, K. (2006). Negotiating relationally: the dynamics of the relational self in negotiations. *Academy of Management Review*, 31, 427–51.

Hayes, S. C., Barnes-Holmes, D., and Roche, B. (2001). *Relational frame theory: a post-Skinnerian account of human language and cognition*. New York: Kluwer Academic/Plenum Publishers.

Hayes, S. C. and Shenk, C. (2004). Operationalizing mindfulness without unnecessary attachments. *Clinical Psychology: Science and Practice*, 11(3), 249.

Kabat-Zinn, J. (1990). *Full catastrophe living*. New York: Dell Publishing.

Reb, J. and Narayanan, J. (2014). The influence of mindful attention on value claiming in distributive negotiations: evidence from four laboratory experiments. *Mindfulness*, 5(6), 756–66.

Reb, J., Narayanan, J., and Ho, Z. W. (2015). Mindfulness at work: antecedents and consequences of employee awareness and absent-mindedness.
Mindfulness, 6(1), 111–22
Shapiro, S. L. and Carlson, L. E. (2009). *The art and science of mindfulness: integrating mindfulness into psychology and the helping professions*. Washington, DC: American Psychological Association
Publications.

2 | *What is mindfulness, and why should organizations care about it?*

SHAUNA L. SHAPIRO, MARGARET C. WANG
AND EMILY H. PELTASON

Introduction

Mindfulness offers the potential to transform internal and external environments in a way that nurtures growth, emotional intelligence, creativity, innovation and the capacity to respond to life with an open mind and a wise heart. In business, mindfulness may confer powerful advantages. Research suggests that fear-based, top-down hierarchies inhibit creativity and innovation, whereas attuned, empathic, and spacious environments catalyze human capacity. The thoughtful incorporation of mindfulness into a professional culture can evolve a work environment toward a richer and more creative state, where one's "work" arises from a state of being rather than reactive doing. This chapter offers a brief overview of mindfulness and its applications in workplace settings. We review the literature and explore mechanisms of action for its beneficial effects. We propose specific pathways of integrating mindfulness, as a self-care practice as well as a way to cultivate professional effectiveness. Finally, we explore future directions of integrating mindfulness in organizational settings, offering our aspirations for the modern promise of this ancient tradition.

* Passion

What is mindfulness?

Mindfulness is above all about presence. It is about inhabiting our lives fully, and bringing all of our awareness into the present moment. Mindfulness fundamentally is a way of being, a way of relating to experience, moment by moment. A simple, yet nuanced definition of mindfulness is "the awareness that arises through intentionally attending in an open, caring, and discerning way" (Shapiro and Carlson 2009). Mindfulness *practice* provides the framework through which we can sharpen and develop this state of consciousness. When we practice we cultivate mindfulness, and yet mindfulness is always already here within us (Shapiro, Carlson, Astin, and Freedman, 2006).

The definition of mindfulness can be unpacked into three core elements: intention, attention, and attitude (IAA). Intention, attention, and attitude are not separate processes or stages, but rather interwoven aspects of a single cyclic *process*, the three elements informing and feeding back into each other. *Intention* involves knowing why we are paying attention. It involves reflecting on our values, goals, and hopes, and consciously setting our heart's compass in the direction we want to head. As Shunryu Suzuki (1970) put it, "the most important thing is to remember the most important thing." Reflecting on our values, our motivations, and our intentions is an essential element of mindfulness.

*[handwritten margin note: *Intension is reflection of why]*

A second fundamental element of mindfulness is *attention*: attending to our experience in the present moment, right here and now. Mindfulness involves training and stabilizing the mind in the present moment. Often we experience life mindlessly, through a lens of conditioned reactivity and limited attentional focus (Langer 1992). And yet, if we are to meet the present moment with skill and grace, we must be present. The word mindfulness means to see clearly, to see clearly the nature of reality so that we can respond effectively. If we are not paying attention, we are unable to see clearly what is most needed As Germer (2009) notes, "an unstable mind is like an unstable camera; we get a fuzzy picture."

*[handwritten margin note: *Staying present in the moment]*

The third element of mindfulness is our *attitude: how* we pay attention. Mindfulness involves an attitude of curious open-heartedness. We do not try to change our experience; we simply observe it with an attitude of acceptance, openness, caring, and curiosity. For example, if while practicing mindfulness anger arises, the anger is noted with acceptance and kindness, but these qualities are not meant to be substituted for the anger or to make the anger disappear, they are simply the container. The attitudes are not an attempt to make things be a certain way; they are an attempt to relate to whatever *is* in a certain way, without judgment or manipulation.

*[handwritten margin note: *Attitude is how we pay attention + is to be met w/ Kindness + acceptance]*

Mindful awareness arises as we intentionally pay attention to our present moment experience with curiosity, acceptance and kindness. It is interesting to note that in Asian languages the words for mind and heart are interchangeable; thus *mindfulness* could also be translated as *heartfulness.* Mindfulness is a loving presence. It is embodied and not simply about cognitive "mind" training. It is a way of being, of inhabiting life fully, requiring us to connect with our heart, emotions and bodies.

This caring and relaxed, yet alert awareness offers something very unique to the corporate world. Mindfulness can create spacious, attuned, empathic internal and external environments that lead to productivity, creativity, and innovation. As Cangemi and Miller (2007) argue, the fear-based, top-down hierarchies with which we are so culturally familiar inhibit creativity and innovation. Integrating mindfulness into our personal experience as well as in the workplace may catalyze both the personal wellbeing and professional effectiveness of the workplace. The IAA model of mindfulness, in fostering this type of attuned present awareness, can aid in the evolution of the work environment toward greater health and wellbeing.

What is mindfulness practice?

Although mindfulness is an inherent human capacity, it is also a skill that can be cultivated and trained. Mindfulness is fundamentally a way of being; it is a way of inhabiting our bodies, our minds, and our moment-by-moment experience. Jon Kabat-Zinn (1990) suggests that mindfulness entails an attitude and commitment to non-judgment, patience, and trust in ourselves, such that we can relinquish ourselves from expectation and be receptive to this experience as if it were a new one.

To understand this experience more clearly, let us begin with a practice, for example, the awareness of simple breathing. Are you aware of your breathing right now? Can you simply experience breath going in and out of the body? This awareness can be an intellectual or conceptual knowing, but it can also be a felt sense, an integrated experience of one's thoughts, feelings, and bodily sensations. This deep knowing is mindfulness: as you breathe in, knowing with your whole being "breathing in." As you breathe out, knowing with your whole being "breathing out."

And yet, we are often not present for our breath, or our lives. Without mindfulness training, people spend much of their time engaged in "mind wandering." In fact, in a rigorous empirical study of over 650,000 people, Killingsworth and Gilbert (2010) found that people's minds wander approximately 47 percent of the time. That is almost half of our life! Rather than being present in the moment, we often lose ourselves in distracting thoughts or opinions about what is happening, what happened in the past, or what might happen in the future. When we are habitually pulled into the past or future, we miss the present moment, which is the only place where innovation, production, learning, and creating occur. Although each of us has the innate capacity to be mindful, it is also helpful to cultivate this capacity. Thus, mindfulness is both a way of being as well as a meditation practice.

Formal mindfulness meditation practice typically consists of setting aside a specific place and amount of time each day that will be devoted to explicitly cultivating mindfulness through formal practice. Mindfulness meditation practice can begin with setting an intention for the practice, and then focusing on an object of attention, such as the breath to calm and stabilize the mind. The practitioner, once stable, can expand the awareness to include all experience as it arises in the present moment. Each moment is met with an attitude of kind, curious, open-hearted attention. Through training our moment-to-moment awareness in this way, we strengthen the neural pathways of mindfulness, making it easier to be present in the next moment. What we practice becomes stronger. Our repeated experiences shape our brain. Thus, mindfulness meditation strengthens our capacity to be mindful in every moment of our lives.

Stress in the workplace

The experience of mindfulness offered above may seem anathema to the modern workplace setting, a realm in which efficiency, output, and impatience dominate. Indeed, workplace stress has emerged as a pressing concern of organizations globally (Burke 2010). Research clearly posits a link between workplace stress and numerous organizational consequences, including lost productivity, poor job performance, higher rates of worker absenteeism and turnover, increased accident frequency, and greater healthcare or legal spending (Quick, Quick, Nelson, and Hurrell 1997). More difficult to calculate, or perhaps even recognize, may be the indirect costs of stress to worker vitality, workplace communication, decision-making processes, and collegial relationships (Quick *et al.*, 1997).

Research has begun to shed light on the mechanisms underlying these indirect organizational costs. For example, we know now that stress decreases clinicians' attention and concentration (Bernstein-Bercovitz 2003; Mackenzie, Smith, Hasher, Leach, and Behl 2007; Skosnik, Chatterton, Swisher, and Park 2000), weakens decision making and communication skills (Shanafelt, Bradley, Wipf, and Back 2002), decreases empathy (Beddoe and Murphy 2004; Thomas, Dyrbye, Huntington, Lawson, Novotny, Sloan, and Shanafelt 2007), reduces trust (Meier, Back, and Morrison 2001), and reduces professionals' abilities to engage in meaningful relationships (Enochs and Etzbach 2004). Such findings suggest the profound cumulative impact of workplace stress on professional effectiveness and the collective health of the work environment.

Workplace stress also exacts a heavy toll of personal suffering. The annual representative survey of stress in the United States by the American Psychological Association (2013) reports that, after financial woes, job stress is the second most cited source of personal stress, leading to pervasive experiences of anxiety, depression, sleep disturbance, and general psychological distress. Research also demonstrates a strong relationship between stress in the workplace and physical health. Specifically, job stress has been associated with fatigue, insomnia, heart disease, obesity, hypertension, infection, carcinogenesis, diabetes, and premature aging (Melamed, Shirom, Toker, Berliner, and Shapira 2006; Melamed, Shirom, Toker, and Shapira 2006; Spickard, Gabbe and Christensen 2002). What stress does not cause, it may exacerbate.

At stake, then, is the wellbeing and healthy functioning of both individuals and organizations. If employees and their supervisors do not learn how to manage the stress induced by the modern, productivity-driven workplace, they risk their own health and compromise their professional effectiveness.

[handwritten margin note: ✳ If Stressed, compromise Professional effectiveness + health]

Mindfulness and the workplace

A growing body of research suggests that mindfulness training may function as a partial antidote to the epidemic of stress in the workplace. In particular, mindfulness may play a role in optimizing some of the workplace processes most vulnerable to the effects of stress: decision making, problem solving, and productivity (Butler and Gray

2006; Glomb, Duffy, Bono, and Yang 2011; Fiol and O'Connor 2003). Mindfulness also appears to create more effective team management and interpersonal communication (Sadler-Smith and Shefy 2007; Ucok 2006). In addition, mindfulness practice appears to enhance strategic decision making and intuition (Shapiro *et al.* 2006; Dane 2011; Thomas 2006). Further, mindfulness promotes both cognitive flexibility, open-mindedness, and response flexibility (Dane 2011; Thomas 2006).

Mindful awareness invites pause and reflection and helps us avoid the misuse of knowledge and attention to irrelevant factors that lead to judgment errors. Mindfulness focuses cognitive processes such that we can accurately assess the present moment and respond skillfully and effectively instead of reactively and habitually. Further, mindfulness helps us hone our internal compass, encouraging reflection on what we value and what is most important. This awareness of values and ethics helps organizations and individuals discern among options to make decisions that align with the organization's values and ethics. In fact, a recent study demonstrated that brief mindfulness training significantly increased ethical decision making in college students (Shapiro, Jazaieri, and Goldin 2012).

Similarly, mindfulness promotes prioritization of important assignments and appropriate attention to relevant knowledge. Managers may benefit from the increased capacity to process a situation from a variety of perspectives and to delegate decisions – rather than spend valuable resources attending to smaller, unrelated issues (Sadler-Smith and Shefy 2007). Given that mindfulness leads to the decreased use of automatic cognitive processes, mindfulness may have a role in inhibiting automatic habitual reactions and instead promoting action that is in accordance with conscious goals (Thomas 2006).

Additionally, mindfulness improves coping mechanisms and cultivates faster recovery from negative events (Keng, Smoski, and Robins 2011). Because of this connection to resilience, Jordan, Messner, and Becker (2009) proposed integrating mindfulness into organizations to promote learning, stating that mindfulness creates an environment for employees in which to reflect upon, address, and question expectations. Providing opportunities to voice employees' needs, and to predict and discuss potential uncertain situations, may not only facilitate open communication and awareness but also has the potential to increase employees' confidence in their own abilities and in their corporation. Employees can feel more in control and that their needs are being met. This promotes a collaborative and trusting environment.

Another way mindfulness enhances the work environment is through increasing interpersonal relations. Work-based interactions require employees to be fully present in order to facilitate effective communication. Mindfulness facilitates potent relationships within the workplace through enhancing presence, attunement, and empathy (Shapiro, Schwartz, and Bonner 1998, Shapiro, Astin, Bishop, and Cordova 2005). This state of awareness avoids instances of miscommunication, in which individuals are not fully present (Ucok 2006). One key aspect of interpersonal connection is emotional regulation and how one understands one's own and others' emotional experiences. In the absence of awareness of our own emotions we can become overwhelmed with negative emotions and react disruptively.

In contrast, mindfulness instills an awareness and increased tolerance for experiencing a variety of emotions via response flexibility, meaning the ability to slow down to pause before verbally or physically acting (Glomb *et al.* 2011). Response flexibility allows us to be present in the moment and to be aware of our own emotions, such that we can acknowledge the current emotional state without reacting to our own and others' negative internal states. Mindfulness teaches the capacity to be compassionate and nonjudgmental, which fosters authentic relationships with other clients and co-workers. The mindful process of perceiving experiences in new ways distinct from our expectations situates us in the present and has numerous implications for the workplace (Langer and Moldoveanu 2000). Langer and Moldoveanu (2000) suggest that openness to and awareness of the environment, new perspectives, and information translate to decision making and collaborative team efforts, permitting them to evaluate, interpret, and respond appropriately in these situations (Butler and Gray 2006).

In short, mindfulness training in the workplace may improve myriad aspects of workplace functioning, including decision making, productivity, interpersonal communication and relationships, consistency, and resilience. *Mindfulness helps with*

Mindfulness as self-care

Mindfulness training may also be useful as a self-care strategy. Mindfulness offers the dual benefit of teaching employees how to manage their own stress as well as teaching them basic and essential qualities necessary to professional effectiveness (Shapiro and Carlson 2009). Research demonstrates that mindfulness training significantly increases the capacity to cope with stress and increases one's sense of wellbeing (Newsome, Christopher, Dahlen, and Christopher 2006; Shapiro, Astin, Bishop, and Cordova 2005). And existing literature posits that the cultivation of mindfulness can enhance mental and physical health (Baer, 2003; Grossman, Niemann, Schmidt, and Walach 2004). Specifically, in a workplace setting, mindfulness training decreased employee stress, emotional exhaustion, and job burnout and increased mood and life satisfaction (Shapiro, Astin, Bishop, and Cordova 2005; Galantino, Baime, Maguire, Szapary, and Farrar 2005).

Another way in which mindfulness enhances self-care is that it teaches self-compassion, allowing professionals to accept themselves and their mistakes as natural and not desiring of shame or blame (Shapiro and Carlson 2009). A great deal of resources, time and energy are often spent in self-judgment of one's shortcomings. This lack of self-compassion and overly harsh self-criticism creates great harm and reduces innovation, productivity, and learning. Self-compassion, on the other hand, significantly increases wellbeing and the capacity to learn and change (Neff 2011). Controlled empirical research demonstrated that mindfulness training in the workplace significantly increases self-compassion (Shapiro, Astin, Bishop, and Cordova 2005).

It is important for employees to acknowledge that despite their best intentions, things will sometimes go wrong. Instead of becoming self-critical and condemning in these situations, mindfulness can help them to learn to treat themselves with the same care and compassion they seek to bring to their co-workers and clients. As Germer (2009) explains in his book on mindfulness and self-compassion, "the more openhearted we are with ourselves, the closer we feel toward the rest of life" and the more empathy we feel for others.

Though the mindfulness literature remains a young one, and researchers continue to debate optimal methods of measuring and defining mindfulness as a construct (see, for example, Bergomi, Tschacher, and Kupper 2012; Grossman 2011), interventions that target mindfulness training show tremendous promise in the workplace setting. In addition to helping professionals cope with stress and distress and enhance wellbeing, mindfulness may also cultivate the very skills needed for professional effectiveness and success (Shapiro and Carlson 2009).

Mechanisms of action

The beneficial and transformational effects of integrating mindfulness in the workplace may occur through a number of different pathways. Below, we explore potential mechanisms of action.

Mindfulness decreases stress. Direct and indirect stress-related costs to organizations are nearly incalculable and include poor job performance, lost productivity, high rates of employee turnover, and increased healthcare and workers' compensation costs (Quick *et al.* 1997; Hargrove, Quick, Nelson, and Quick 2011). Sixty-five percent of Americans cite the workplace as a major source of stress in their lives, leading many to experience a neverending cycle of psychological and physiological fight-or-flight (American Psychological Association 2013). Research demonstrates that mindfulness practice reduces states of anxiety or stress by invoking a state of related alertness from which a conscious skillful response can be made (for a conceptual and empirical review, see Baer (2003)).

Mindfulness creates a healthy learning environment. Chronically stressful environments filled with fear, threat, or shame inhibit learning. Deadlines, meetings with clientele: these high-pressure environments inevitably create stress and affect one's optimal learning process. The practice of awareness instigates a more efficient and effective learning process (Bandura 1986). The safe, nonjudgmental, and compassionate environment cultivated by mindfulness practice activates neural systems that allow the practitioner to learn and adapt to the demands of the situation (Fletcher, Schoendorff, and Hayes 2010).

Receiving news of failure can be debilitating to one's sense of self-efficacy and motivation. Self-efficacy is the perceived ability that one can perform a task (Bandura 1986). Belief in our own capabilities inspires the perseverance necessary to succeed, and in so doing mediates both performance and outcome (Bandura 1986). Yet recovery from failure is crucial in continuing the learning process.

Shame inhibits one's process in learning because one focuses on deficiencies, thereby inhibiting recovery from failure. Shame is defined as a negative evaluation of the self, derived from perceived failure to meet

personal standards (Lewis 1971). Shame significantly disrupts attention and motivation, such that having this negative evaluation lowers
standards, thereby hindering the process of recovering and learning
from failure (Turner and Schallert 2001).

Luoma, Kohlenberg, Hayes, and Fletcher (2012) demonstrate that
in substance-abuse patients, acceptance has a role in decreasing internalized shame. Mindfulness practice explicitly cultivates an attitude
of awareness and acceptance; it therefore has the potential to reduce
feelings of shame. Through mindfulness, one can cultivate the ability
to tolerate emotions – even negative, painful ones – thereby increasing
the capacity to endure through challenge (Shapiro, Carlson, Astin, and
Freedman 2006).

Mindfulness enhances innovation and creativity. Mindfulness practice improves the individual's perception of cues that allow a shift in
one's consciousness from the goal to the process (Butler and Gray
2006). This focus on the process opens up opportunities for creativity. Because mindful awareness encourages individuals to explore
multiple perspectives and attend to information holistically (Langer
and Moldoveanu 2000; Sadler-Smith and Shefy 2007), mindfulness
increases the possibilities that a new approach will be discovered,
thereby enhancing the potential for innovation (Vogus and Sutcliffe
2012; see also Chapter 8 of this volume on mindfulness and creativity).

Mindfulness improves attention and concentration. Whatever the
nature of one's professional endeavours, success typically demands the
ability to sustain attention. While it is ideal for us to experience, or be
mindfully present of, ourselves in the moment, systematic mindfulness
practice may be required to hone this skill. Existing research reveals
that mindful presence and attention develop through formal mindfulness meditation practice.

In one study, researchers found greater cortical thickening in
areas of the brain associated with sustained attention and awareness in practitioners experienced in mindful meditation, compared
to non-meditating participants (Lazar, Kerr, Wasserman, Gray, Greve,
Treadway, McGarvey, Quinn, Dusek, Benson, Rauch, Moore, and
Fischl 2005). In another, Jha, Krompinger, and Baime (2007) measured response times on the Attention Network Test after eight weeks
of mindfulness meditation training for novices and a month-long
retreat for more experienced meditators, and found significant
improvements in overall attention among participants. Specifically,

those who participated in the eight-week training were more able to direct focused attention when required, and those who attended the one-month retreat showed an increased ability to return their focus when faced with distractions.

Mindfulness reduces the negative effects of multitasking. At the office we are surrounded by distractions from email to text messages, and we have, as a culture, accepted and even rewarded multitasking in the workplace. Higher expectations and demands are placed on employees such that they are required to switch tasks and to respond immediately to meet the demands of the customer (Appelbaum and Marchionni 2008). However, multitasking, characterized by interruption in attention and performing two or more tasks concurrently reduces performance, decreases accuracy, increases stress and lowers overall productivity (Appelbaum and Marchionni 2008).

Mindfulness operates to control these automatic cognitive processes and to focus one's resources on the present task (Thomas 2006). Mindfulness allows one to prioritize competing tasks (conflict monitoring) and attend to a current task for a longer period of time before shifting attention to a new task (Levy, Wobbrock, Kaszniak, and Ostergren 2012; Jha *et al.*, 2007). In integrating a mindful approach, employees will be more productive and able to attend to what they were doing prior to the distraction.

In the informational age, practicing mindfulness is even more significant because it has been shown to improve attention, increase sensitivity, concentration, and openness to experience, and decrease the susceptibility to distraction (Valentine and Sweet 1999). For example, if too much attention is focused on one stimulus, another stimulus might be missed. Valentine and Sweet's study (1999) compared concentrative meditation with mindfulness meditation, in which the participants counted the number of tones that they heard during an auditory task as a measure of sustained attention. Concentrative meditation was defined as a type of meditation focused on a concrete image or source (e.g., an object, breath, or thought) in the context of everything else, whereas mindfulness meditation was based on the concept that one focuses on anything, whether physical and mental, within one's awareness. The fact that mindfulness meditators recorded these unexpected tones more adeptly than concentrative meditators suggests the important role of mindful awareness in sustaining attention and preventing distractions from causing vital information to be missed.

Mindfulness decreases reactivity. Emotional reactivity underlies much interpersonal conflict in the workplace. Mindfulness practice cultivates a process of reperceiving, or a shift in consciousness, in which the subjective becomes the objective, allowing us to observe and interpret our emotional experiences without judgment (Shapiro, Carlson, Astin, and Freedman 2006). Practicing mindfulness, then, helps manage highly reactive thoughts and feelings before they overtake behavior (Hede 2010). Hede further suggests that an enhanced ability to regulate emotions also enables individuals to recover from failure or criticism more quickly. Dunn, Hartigan, and Mikulas (1999) demonstrate that mindfulness meditation produces effects distinct from relaxation, suggesting a different state of consciousness. The reperceiving that accommodates mindfulness may serve as an escape from experiencing one's emotions.

The concept of mindfulness has a role in mitigating conflict and, therefore, applies to the interactive nature of the business world. Managers, too, may use the practice of mindfulness to aid employees in re-conceptualizing professional disappointments. In the right conditions, supervisors may assist people in regulating their emotions by emphasizing different aspects of the situation and augmenting their employees' sense of control over the experience (Boss and Sims 2008). This requires an effort to redefine the emotion-eliciting situation in non-emotional terms. Mindfulness practice has the potential to assist managers and employees in reperceiving the situation nonjudgmentally. This reframed perspective opens doors to providing more constructive feedback. By emphasizing employees' strengths and operational obstacles, managers affirm that each disappointment need not reflect on employees' essential worth or abilities. Therefore, the ability to reperceive influences our capacity to step back during stressful moments. A practice of mindfulness places this orientation toward defeat squarely in the hands of both managers and employees, enhancing the capacity of all professionals to identify and distance themselves from their emotions, so as to prevent painful – and possibly career-limiting – emotionality from interfering with constructive communication among team members and clients.

Mindfulness enhances interpersonal functioning, empathy, and self-awareness. Being compassionate toward oneself furthers one's ability to be compassionate toward others and has many consequences for enhancing levels of trust and creating a collaborative, safe work environment (Kanov, Maitlis, Worline, Dutton, Frost, and Lilius 2004). The ability to discern one co-worker's negative effect empowers the leader to take action before these negative emotions escalate and lead to counterproductive work behaviors or resentment in the organization (Riggio and Reichard 2008). This has implications for applying these attitudes to oneself and to others, thereby fostering positive, professional relationships. For example, when faced with an incomplete assignment, rather than judging this as a failure, one can attend to this situation with acceptance and be able to focus on the next assignment.

At every level of employment, communication among co-workers is necessary, and being aware of how one portrays oneself to others impacts the professional relationship. The enhanced interpersonal awareness garnered by mindfulness training may permit both manager and supervisee to emphasize encouragement and improvement rather than failure. A manager's trust in others is crucial, because it affects how one perceives oneself and builds rapport with other employees. For example, a manager who thoughtlessly communicates that he is unsure of another's ability to produce quality work may affect that employee's ability to trust his boss or himself.

Mindfulness practice increases empathy and self-awareness, which generates authenticity and concern for others (Shapiro, Carlson, Astin and Freeman 2006; Holt and Marques 2012). Multiple applications of empathy range from organizational commitment to employee connectedness. Empathy is defined as the ability to understand another's perspective and common experienced emotional responses are empathic concern and personal distress (Atkins 2013). Empathic concern consists of concern for another's welfare (Batson and Ahmad 2009; Atkins 2013), whereas personal distress is an orientation focused on one's own distress rather than the person experiencing it (Eisenberg 2010; Atkins 2013). Empathy differs from sympathy, which centers around one's own emotional experience, rather than another person's. In observing another's subjective experience, the neural structures are the same as those activated in the person experiencing the emotion (Gallese, Eagle, and Migone 2007). This evidence suggests that we are biologically programmed to communicate with and understand others' experiences.

The empathy cultivated through mindfulness practice may have broader applications for individuals' ability to relate to others. Riggio and Reichard (2008) suggest the importance of the leader's emotional sensitivity in setting the tone for all members of the team. Being compassionate toward employees and being able to assess others' emotions cultivate trust, such that each member feels valued in the organization. High-functioning work teams foster strong interpersonal relationships, which require leaders to be empathic toward other team members' moods, attitudes and needs (Riggio and Reichard 2008).

Leaders can use empathy to evaluate and share constructive values to maintain a positive range of emotions (Levine, 2007). Attunement revolves around the awareness of one's own and others' internal experiences, leading to self-compassion and compassion toward others. Attunement generated through mindfulness practice can inform us of emotional discord. By responding proactively to these negative reactions, individuals counter interpersonal conflict. However, because of our disparate capacities to understand others' perspectives, individuals may be limited in their ability to be empathic (Atkins 2013). Despite engagement in mindfulness practice, these limits in perspective-taking may hinder our ability to gauge others' emotions and prevent impending conflict. The management team has the potential to manage the emotional tone of the workplace and optimize attunement effectively to inspire, relate to employees, and create collective aspirations (Riggio and Reichard 2008).

Mindfulness training increases the social connectedness that follows from empathy (Shapiro, Schwartz, and Bonner 1998; Cohen and Miller 2009). Through the careful cultivation of moment-to-moment awareness and nonjudgmental acceptance, mindfulness practice specifically enhances the sensory, perceptual, and self-regulatory components that comprise emotional intelligence (Schutte and Malouff 2011). Because of its positive impact on emotion regulation and emotional intelligence, mindfulness training may support a shift from a relentless, depersonalizing focus on results to a shared emphasis between results and relationships (Baer, Smith, and Allen 2004; Baer, Smith, Hopkins, Krietemeyer, and Toney 2006; Brown and Ryan 2003; Feldman, Hayes, Kumar, Greeson, and Laurenceau 2007). This shift may lead to improved interpersonal and professional effectiveness.

Beyond formal meditation: mindfulness-informed business

Mindfulness-informed business refers to the integration of mindfulness-inspired teachings into organizations *without formally teaching meditation*. It is a potential framework for the integration of the accumulated wisdom and insight of Buddhist literature, the psychological mindfulness literature, and one's own mindfulness practice into the corporate world. To date, there are no explicit instructions for how to develop a mindfulness-informed business practice, nor is the concept itself well-suited to empirical scrutiny. The ideas presented here are not intended to be comprehensive or evidence-based, but instead to expand upon our clinical experience that the core themes of mindfulness have much to offer the work environment. To this end, we introduce several themes that organizations might draw upon as part of a mindfulness-informed approach.

Impermanence

Impermanence, or the reality of constant change, is central to Buddhism. As Bien (2006) explains, it is inevitable that we all to have to face impermanence. The real question is whether we will come to terms with it. When we resist reality, our suffering increases.

Learning to accept impermanence can have important implications for the stressful work environment, in which the sudden urgency of a rapidly approaching deadline or the pressure to produce the next deliverable can threaten to overwhelm employees' equanimity. Those structuring the mindfulness-informed organization can present examples of impermanence, using language that highlights the ever-changing nature of human experience. Employees can be invited to investigate the changing nature of their own lives and experiences, and to focus on their ever-changing thoughts, emotions, and sensations (Shapiro and Carlson 2009). In such an environment, the inevitable pressures of the workplace can be acknowledged and attended to, and yet not threaten to overwhelm or derail personal wellbeing or professional effectiveness.

No self

Buddhist psychology also emphasizes impermanence of the self. This does not mean that people are not real, but rather that there is no discrete entity which can be identified as the distinct self. Given the focus in much of the modern world on individualism, many people have difficulty with this idea. As Bien (2006) explicates, we typically think of ourselves as individual entities that move through time and space accumulating experiences, but remaining fundamentally the same. In reality, however, there is nothing solid for people to hold on to that they can call the self. One's body, feelings, thoughts, and perceptions are all flowing and shifting moment to moment. While at first hard to grasp, the idea of "no self" is liberating as it allows us to see that we are larger than any of our perceptions or experiences. Emotions are just emotions; thoughts are just thoughts. They are not "me." Similarly, difficult interactions with supervisors, negative client feedback, or even positive performance reviews do not reflect a distinct or indelible self, but only transient moments in the whole of our work history and professional identity. With practice, professionals can learn to internalize this idea by noticing that all emotions and thoughts are ephemeral, "like guests who visit and then leave" (Goodman and Greenland 2009).

Acceptance

Acceptance refers to a way of receiving experiences without judgment or preference, with kindness and curiosity. Buddhist teachings on acceptance suggest that suffering descends when people desire things to be different than they are. Physical and emotional suffering, we learn, is a function of two variables. The first of these is pain, which arises inevitably in the course of living, and which no being can avoid entirely. The second of these, however, is the degree to which we resist our pain – and this is something we can directly affect. The American meditation master Shinzen Young has offered the following useful equation: Suffering = Pain x Resistance. Simply put, when people resist rather than accept, they multiply their suffering.

Fortunately, acceptance is a skill that can be cultivated. With practice, people can be encouraged to "relax into" or "soften into" an experience of acceptance (Germer, Siegel, and Fulton 2005). Goldstein (1993) proposes using mantras such as "Let it be," or "It's okay, just let me feel this." Regardless of the specific verbiage employed, professionals can learn to embrace the full range of their emotions. Particularly in the workplace, where output may be emphasized at the expense of process or internal experience, it is tempting to dismiss negative thoughts and emotions as irrelevant to the task at hand. And yet, despite our best efforts, these thoughts and feelings can have a profound impact on our professional attitude and effectiveness. Mindfulness teaches us to acknowledge and attend to our pain so that we can respond consciously, with wisdom and clarity. When we can recognize and acknowledge our true experience in the moment, we are freed from our emotional suffering and empowered to respond deliberately and appropriately – whether that be to a client, colleague, employee, or supervisor.

Conscious responding

A central teaching of Buddhism is that suffering arises from habitual ways of reacting. Indeed, if we pay attention, it is possible to observe how often our experiences are followed by automatic reactions, thoughts, or actions. In the workplace, the necessarily cyclical nature of certain regular tasks or interactions can lead to simmering resentment or interpersonal conflict. Informed by mindfulness, we are granted the option to choose a healthier or more constructive response. When we are able to see clearly beyond our first instincts and automatic reactions, an appropriate response is more likely to arise. What is more, mindfulness ensures that when interpersonal conflicts do occur in the work environment, they may be seen clearly for what they actually are – fleeting and natural to the human experience – and not come to take on a larger or more lingering personal or professional significance.

Interdependence

A central Buddhist tenet is that all things are connected or interdependent. That means our happiness or unhappiness affects others, and their happiness or unhappiness affects us. This is why the particular energy of one project team member can so profoundly affect the collective experience of the group, or why time spent listening to a litany of stressors from an overwhelmed colleague can leave the listener feeling equally stressed or anxious. Indeed, we are not as separate as we generally think.

When people live their lives as though they are separate from others, confusion, despair, conflict, and loneliness can result (Shapiro and

Carlson 2009). This is as true globally as it is locally. For example, a country might adopt friendly relationships with oppressive, oil-rich Arab nations and consequently enjoy a cheap energy supply. Being on friendly terms with oppressive regimes, however, causes other nations to see this country as oppressive and therefore to direct hatred terrorist tactics against them (Bien 2006). Simply put, the global community, and the individuals who comprise it, are interdependent.

The concept of interdependence is keenly relevant to professional communities. Employees can learn to observe how workplace processes unfold in a mutually dependent web of complex interconnections. Colleagues' thoughts, ideas, and behaviors have consequences that inform future moments and interactions. Crucially, as individuals begin to uncover small examples of interconnectedness in their own lives, they will come to appreciate how everything in the universe is mutually interdependent, which will generate feelings of responsibility and connectedness to all beings. On a smaller scale, a growing awareness of interdependence in the work environment may also lead to a sense of connectedness and shared responsibility not only to other employees, but to the central mission or missions of the organization as a whole.

Conclusion

Mindfulness has a variety of useful applications for the workplace including enhancing personal care and wellbeing as well as professional effectiveness. There are a number of important future directions and research paths that warrant continued attention.

Research is needed to investigate the extent to which mindfulness can be used to help professionals develop core skills for professional success and effectiveness. Preliminary research suggests that mindfulness increases empathy, creativity, emotional regulation, and attention in individuals; however, rigorous scientific studies that explore the specific impact of mindfulness on professional effectiveness are sparse. Toward that end, we need research across a broad range of measures including self-reporting, behavioral observation, and objective productivity and effectiveness scales (Grepmair, Mitterlehner, Loew, Bachler, Rother, and Nickel, 2007; Grepmair, Mitterlehner, Loew, and Nickel 2006). Also important is research investigating the mechanisms through which these effects occur.

Further, we know that self-care is critical for professionals, both in terms of protecting practitioners' own health and wellbeing, and for optimizing their productivity, innovation, and professional effectiveness. Accordingly, it is important to expand existing research on how mindfulness affects professionals' mental and physical health. A more systematic approach to self-care and mindfulness training in workplace settings and in continuing education programs for professionals is needed. This includes directing attention toward the integration of mindfulness training into human resources and professional development curricula (Shapiro and Carlson 2009).

The potential applications of mindfulness for the workplace are far reaching. We believe the multifaceted nature of mindfulness combined with its inherent simplicity may offer a unique and powerful resource to the corporate setting. Mindfulness offers an approach that does not put self-care and wellbeing at odds with productivity and the bottom line. Instead, mindfulness teaches us that *wellbeing and corporate success go hand in hand.* The continued exploration of mindfulness requires great sensitivity and a range of methodological and clinical lenses to determine how best to integrate these teachings and practices into the workplace. However, the pioneering research and clinical applications are promising, and we are hopeful that continued research and exploration in this area will benefit individuals and society as a whole.

Appendix

Mindfulness at work: six practices

1. **Intention.** Begin each day by setting intention. Throughout the day, take a few moments before each new activity (e.g. a phone call, a meeting, a presentation) and set a specific intention for it.
2. **Pause.** Throughout the day set a bell to ring, pause, take three mindful breaths and renew your intention.
3. **Listen.** In the course of the workday, practice deeply listening to others. Feel the resonance of what they are sharing by listening with your whole being.
4. **Attend to the body.** Listen to the body's messages, attend to and honor them.
5. **Reflection.** Find some time at the end of the workday for self-reflection and discernment for what needs to be followed

up or inquired into. Write these reflections down and then let them go.

6. **Gratitude.** Practice gratitude for all that you have offered and received today. Take a moment of kind appreciation for yourself and those who have helped you.

References

American Psychological Association (2013). Stress in America: missing the health care connection. Retrieved from www.apa.org/news/press/releases/stress/2012/full-report.pdf.

Appelbaum, S. H., and Marchionni, A. (2008). The multi-tasking paradox: perceptions, problems and strategies. *Management Decision*, 46(9), 1313–25.

Atkins, P. W. B. (2013). Empathy, self-other differentiation and mindfulness. In K. Pavlovich and K. Krahnke (eds.), *Organizing Through Empathy*. New York: Routledge, pp. 49–70.

Baer, R. A. (2003). Mindfulness training as a clinical intervention: a conceptual and empirical review. *Clinical Psychology: Science and Practice*, 10, 125–43.

Baer, R. A., Smith, G. T., and Allen, K. B. (2004). Assessment of mindfulness by self-report: the Kentucky Inventory of Mindfulness Skills. *Assessment*, 11(3), 191–206.

Baer, R. A., Smith, G. T., Hopkins, J., Krietemeyer, J., and Toney, L. (2006). Using self-report assessment methods to explore facets of mindfulness. *Assessment*, 13(1), 27–45.

Bandura, A. (1986). *Social foundations of thought and action: a social cognitive theory*. Englewood Cliffs, NJ: Prentice Hall.

Batson, C. D., and Ahmad, N. Y. (2009). Empathy-induced altruism: a threat to the collective good. *Altruism and Prosocial Behavior in Groups*, 26, 1–23.

Beddoe, A. E., and Murphy, S. O. (2004). Does mindfulness decrease stress and foster empathy among nursing students? *Journal of Nursing Education*, 43(7), 305–12.

Bergomi, C., Tschacher, W., and Kupper, Z. (2012). The assessment of mindfulness with self-report measures: existing scales and open issues. *Mindfulness*, 4(3), 191–202.

Bernstein-Bercovitz, H. (2003). Does stress enhance or impair selective attention? The effects of stress and perceptual load on negative priming. *Anxiety, Stress and Coping: An International Journal*, 16, 345–57.

Bien, T. (2006). *Mindful therapy: a guide for therapists and helping professionals*. Boston, MA: Wisdom.

Boss, A. D., and Sims, H. P. (2008). Everyone fails! Using emotion regulation and self-leadership for recovery. *Journal of Managerial Psychology*, 23(2), 135–50.

Brown, K. W., and Ryan, R. M. (2003). The benefits of being present: mindfulness and its role in psychological wellbeing. *Journal of Personality and Social Psychology*, 84, 822–48.

Burke, R. J. (2010). Workplace stress and well-being across cultures: research and practice. *Cross Cultural Management*, 17(1), 5–9.

Butler, B. S., and Gray, P. H. (2006). Reliability, mindfulness and information systems. *MIS Quarterly*, 30(2), 211–24.

Cangemi, J., and Miller, R. (2007). Breaking-out-of-the-box in organizations: structuring a positive climate for the development of creativity in the workplace. *Journal of Management Development*, 26(5), 401–10.

Cohen, J., and Miller, L. (2009). Interpersonal mindfulness training for well-being: a pilot study with psychology graduate students. *The Teachers College Record*, 111(12), 2760–74.

Dane, E. (2011). Paying attention to mindfulness and its effects on task performance in the workplace. *Journal of Management*, 37(4), 997–1018.

Dunn, B. R., Hartigan, J. A., and Mikulas, W. L. (1999). Concentration and mindfulness meditations: unique forms of consciousness. *Applied Psychophysiology and Biofeedback*, 24(3), 147–65.

Eisenberg, N. (2010). Empathy-related responding: links with self-regulation, moral judgment, and moral behavior. In M. Mikulincer (ed.), *Prosocial motives, emotions, and behavior: the better angels of our nature*. Washington DC: American Psychological Association, pp. 129–48.

Enochs, W. K., and Etzbach, C. A. (2004). Impaired student counselors: ethical and legal considerations for the family. *Family Journal: Counseling and Therapy for Couples and Families*, 12, 396–400.

Feldman, G., Hayes, A., Kumar, S., Greeson, J., and Laurenceau, J. P. (2007). Mindfulness and emotion regulation: the development and initial validation of the Cognitive and Affective Mindfulness Scale–Revised (CAMS-R). *Journal of Psychopathology and Behavioral Assessment*, 29(3), 177–90.

Fiol, C. M., and O'Connor, E. J. (2003). Waking up! Mindfulness in the face of bandwagons. *The Academy of Management Review*, 28(1), 54–70.

Fletcher, L. B., Schoendorff, B., and Hayes, S. C. (2010). Searching for mindfulness in the brain: a process-oriented approach to examining the neural correlates of mindfulness. *Mindfulness*, 1, 41–63.

Galantino, M. L., Baime, M., Maguire, M., Szapary, P. O., and Farrar, J. T. (2005). Short communication: association of psychological and physiological measures of stress in health-care professionals during an 8-week mindfulness meditation program. Mindfulness in practice. *Stress and Health*, 21, 255–61.

Gallese, V., Eagle, M. N., and Migone, P. (2007). Intentional attunement: mirror neurons and the neural underpinnings of interpersonal relations. *Journal of the American Psychoanalytic Association*, 55(1), 131–76.

Germer, C. K. (2009). *The mindful path to self-compassion: freeing yourself from destructive thoughts and emotions*. New York: Guilford Press.

Germer, C. K., Siegel, R. D., and Fulton, P. R. (2005). *Mindfulness and psychotherapy*. New York: Guilford Press.

Glomb, T. M., Duffy, M. K., Bono, J. E., and Yang, T. (2011). Mindfulness at work. *Personnel and Human Resources Management*, 30, 115–57.

Goldstein, J. (1993). *Insight meditation: the practice of freedom*. Boston, MA: Shambhala.

Goodman, T. A., and Greenland, S. (2009). Mindfulness with children: working with difficult emotions. In F. Didonna (ed.), *Clinical handbook of mindfulness*. New York: Springer Science + Business Media, pp. 417–29.

Grepmair, L., Mitterlehner, F., Loew, T., Bachler, E., Rother, W., and Nickel, M. (2007). Promoting mindfulness in psychotherapists in training influences the treatment results of their patients: a randomized, double-blind, controlled study. *Psychotherapy and Psychosomatics*, 76(6), 332–8.

Grepmair, L., Mitterlehner, F., Loew, T., and Nickel, M. (2006). Promotion of mindfulness in psychotherapists in training and treatment results of their patients. *Journal of Psychosomatic Research*, 60(6), 649–50.

Grossman (2011). Defining mindfulness by how poorly I think I pay attention during everyday awareness and other intractable problems for psychology's re(invention) of mindfulness: comment on Brown et al. (2011). *Psychological Assessment*, 23(4), 1034–40.

Grossman, P., Niemann, L., Schmidt, S., and Walach, H. (2004). Mindfulness-based stress reduction and health benefits: a meta-analysis. *Journal of Psychosomatic Research*, 57(1), 35–43.

Hargrove, M., Quick, J., Nelson, D. L., and Quick, J. D. (2011). The theory of preventive stress management: a 33-year review and evaluation. *Stress and Health: Journal Of The International Society For The Investigation Of Stress*, 27(3), 182–93.

Hede, A. (2010). The dynamics of mindfulness in managing emotions and stress. *Journal of Management Development*, 29(1), 94–110.

Holt, S., and Marques, J. (2012). Empathy in leadership: appropriate or misplaced? An empirical study on a topic that is asking for attention. *Journal of Business Ethics*, 105(1), 95–105.

Jha, A. P., Krompinger, J., and Baime, M. J. (2007). Mindfulness training modifies subsystems of attention. *Cognitive, Affective, and Behavioral Neuroscience*, 7(2), 109–19.

Jordan, S., Messner, M., and Becker, A. (2009). Reflection and mindfulness in organizations: rationales and possibilities for integration. *Management Learning*, 40(4), 465–73.

Kabat-Zinn, J. (1990). *Full catastrophe living*. New York: Delta Publishing.

Kanov, J. M., Maitlis, S., Worline, M. C., Dutton, J. E., Frost, P. J., and Lilius, J. M. (2004). Compassion in organizational life. *American Behavioral Scientist*, 47(6), 808–27.

Keng, S., Smoski, M. J., and Robins, C. J. (2011). Effects of mindfulness on psychological health: a review of empirical studies. *Clinical Psychology Review*, 31(6), 1041–56.

Killingsworth, M. A., and Gilbert, D. T. (2010). A wandering mind is an unhappy mind. *Science*, 330(6006), 932.

Langer, E. J. (1992). Matters of mind: mindfulness/mindlessness in perspective. *Consciousness and Cognition*, 1, 289–305.

Langer, E. J., and Moldoveanu, M. (2000). The construct of mindfulness. *Journal of Social Issues*, 56(1), 1–9.

Lazar, S. W., Kerr, C. E., Wasserman, R. H., Gray, J. R., Greve, D. N., Treadway, M. T., McGarvey, M., Quinn, B. T., Dusek, J. A., Benson, H., Rauch, S. L., Moore, C. I., and Fischl, B. (2005). Meditation experience is associated with increased cortical thickness. *Neuroreport*, 16, 1893–7.

Levine, D. P. (2007). Keeping track of the self: empathy, recognition, and the problem of emotional attunement in organizations. *Journal of Organizational Psychodynamics*, 1(1), 26–45.

Levy, D. M., Wobbrock, J. O., Kaszniak, A. W., and Ostergren, M. (2012). The effects of mindfulness meditation training on multitasking in a high-stress information environment. *Proceedings of Graphics Interface*, 45–52.

Lewis, H. B. (1971). Shame and guilt in neurosis. *The Psychoanalytic Review*, 58, 419–38.

Luoma, J. B., Kohlenberg, B. S., Hayes, S. C., and Fletcher, L. (2012). Slow and steady wins the race: a randomized clinical trial of acceptance and commitment therapy targeting shame in substance use disorders. *Journal of Consulting and Clinical Psychology*, 80(1), 43–53.

Mackenzie, C. S., Smith, M. C., Hasher, L., Leach, L., and Behl, P. (2007). Cognitive functioning under stress: evidence from informal caregivers of palliative patients. *Journal of Palliative Medicine*, 10(3), 749–58.

Meier, D. E., Back, A. L., and Morrison, R. S. (2001). The inner life of physicians and care of the seriously ill. *The Journal of the American Medical Association*, 286(23), 3007–14.

Melamed, S., Shirom, A., Toker, S., Berliner, S., and Shapira, I. (2006). Burnout and risk of cardiovascular disease: evidence, possible causal paths, and promising research directions, *Psychological Bulletin*, 132, 327–53.

Melamed, S., Shirom, A., Toker, S., and Shapira, I. (2006). Burnout and risk of type 2 diabetes: a prospective study of apparently healthy employed persons, *Psychosomatic Medicine*, 68, 863–9.

Neff, K. D. (2011). Self-compassion, self-esteem, and well-being. *Social and Personality Psychology Compass*, 5, 1–12.

Newsome, S., Christopher, J. C., Dahlen, P., and Christopher, S. (2006). Teaching counsellors self-care through mindfulness practices. *Teachers College Record*, 108, 1881–900.

Quick, J. C., Quick, J. D., Nelson, D. L., and Hurrell, J. J. (1997). *Preventive stress management in organizations*. Washington, DC: American Psychological Association.

Riggio, R. E., and Reichard, R. J. (2008). The emotional and social intelligences of effective leadership: an emotional and social skill approach. *Journal of Managerial Psychology*, 23(2), 169–85.

Sadler-Smith, E., and Shefy, E. (2007). Developing intuitive awareness in management education. *Academy of Management Learning and Education*, 6(2), 186–205.

Schutte, N. S., and Malouff, J. M. (2011). Emotional intelligence mediates the relationship between mindfulness and subjective well-being. *Personality and Individual Differences*, 50(7), 1116–19.

Shanafelt, T. D., Bradley, K. A., Wipf, J. E., and Back, A. L. (2002). Burnout and self-reported patient care in an internal medicine residency program. *Annals of Internal Medicine*, 136, 358–67.

Shapiro, S. L., Astin, J. A., Bishop, S. R., and Cordova, M. (2005). Mindfulness-based stress reduction for health care professionals: results from a randomized trial. *International Journal of Stress Management*, 12(2), 164–76.

Shapiro, S. L., and Carlson, L. E. (2009). *The art and science of mindfulness: integrating mindfulness into psychology and the helping professions*. Washington, DC: American Psychological Association Publications.

Shapiro, S. L., Carlson, L. E., Astin, J. A., and Freedman, B. (2006). Mechanisms of mindfulness. *Journal of Clinical Psychology*, 62(3), 373–86.

Shapiro, S. L., Jazaieri, H., and Goldin, P. R. (2012). Mindfulness-based stress reduction effects on moral reasoning and decision making. *Journal of Positive Psychology*, 7(6), 504–15.

Shapiro, S. L., Schwartz, G. E., and Bonner, G. (1998). Effects of mindfulness-based stress reduction on medical and premedical students. *Journal of Behavioral Medicine*, 21, 581–99.

Skosnik, P. D., Chatterton, R. T., Swisher, T., and Park, S. (2000). Modulation of attentional inhibition by norepinephrine and cortisol after psychological stress. *International Journal of Psychophysiology*, 36, 59–68.

Spickard, A., Gabbe, S., and Christensen, J. (2002). Mid-career burnout in generalist and specialist physicians. *The Journal of the American Medical Association*, 288, 1447–50.

Suzuki, S. (1970). *Zen mind, beginner's mind*. New York: Weatherhill.

Thomas, D. C. (2006). Domain and development of cultural intelligence: the importance of mindfulness. *Group and Organization Management*, 31(1), 78–99.

Thomas, M. R., Dyrbye, L. N., Huntington, J. L., Lawson, K. L., Novotny, P. J., Sloan, J. A., and Shanafelt, T. D. (2007). How do distress and well-being relate to medical student empathy? A multicenter study. *Journal of General Internal Medicine*, 22(2), 177–83.

Turner, J. E., and Schallert, D. L. (2001). Expectancy-value relationships of shame reactions and shame resiliency. *Journal of Educational Psychology*, 93, 320–9.

Ucok, O. (2006). Transparency, communication and mindfulness. *Journal of Management Development*, 25(10), 1024–8.

Valentine, E. R., and Sweet, P. L. (1999). Meditation and attention: a comparison of the effects of concentrative and mindfulness meditation on sustained attention, *Mental Health, Religion and Culture*, 2(1), 59–70.

Vogus, T. J., and Sutcliffe, K. M. (2012). Organizational mindfulness and mindful organizing: a reconciliation and path forward. *Academy of Management Learning and Education*, 11(4), 722–35.

3 Mindfulness: historical and contemplative context and recent developments

MICHAEL CHASKALSON AND
SHARON GRACE HADLEY

Introduction

The world is all-abuzz nowadays about mindfulness. This is a wonderful thing because we are sorely lacking, if not starving for some elusive but necessary element in our lives.

(Kabat-Zinn 2011 p. 9).

The buzz Kabat-Zinn referred to shows no sign of dying down. If anything, it is growing and more and more large organizations appear to be including one or more elements of mindfulness training in their offering to employees (Gelles 2012). What an extraordinary journey the practice of mindfulness has made from the monasteries of Asia where it resided almost exclusively for 2,500 years to the "Mindful Leadership" sessions led by Janice Marturano at the World Economic Forum in Davos (Marturano 2013).

The concept of mindfulness as it is being used in this chapter emerges from the Buddhist tradition, but the mindfulness-based approaches and interventions that are found in organizational contexts today generally take an entirely secular approach. The aim of this chapter is to explore how mindfulness training has evolved from being set within traditional religious contexts to a more secular and modern approach. Emphasis is given to mindfulness programs derived from Buddhist teachings, in particular the mindfulness-based stress reduction (MBSR) course, which is currently the most prevalent and well-researched mindfulness intervention used in organizational contexts. A brief overview of major current theories and programs on mindfulness is provided along with suggestions for future research. Our aim is to provide a description of the most widely used approach to mindfulness training and to help the reader understand why it is designed as it is. We contend that it is critical to understand where ideas and practices associated with mindfulness have come from in order to understand where the mindfulness movement might be going, particularly in relation to organizational life.

The word "mindfulness" can be used to describe both an outcome – mindful awareness; and a process – mindful practice (Shapiro and Carlson 2009). The first of these, mindful awareness, consists in an abiding presence or awareness, a deep knowing that manifests, to some degree, as an increased freedom from reflexive conditioning and delusion. The second, mindful practice, consists of a systematic practice of intentionally attending in an open, caring, and discerning way, which involves both knowing and shaping the mind.

By what trajectory has a training that aims to bring about a way of intentionally attending in an open, accepting, and discerning way come to be used in the context of contemporary organizational life? What does this training look like? And what kind of outcomes might one expect from applying it? To address these questions, we need to begin with history in order to understand the original intentions and conceptual basis of mindfulness training in the Buddhist tradition and how those intentions and concepts have evolved over time.

Historical overview and context: from the Buddha to the boardroom

In this section we briefly review the Buddhist history of mindfulness and examine some key terms that informed the conceptual framework within which mindfulness was historically taught. The Buddha – who lived some 2,600 years ago in North-Eastern India – was not the first spiritual teacher to prescribe meditation: descriptions of meditation exist in pre-Buddhist Brahmanical literature such as the Chandogya Upanishad (Zaehner 1992). But so far as we know, the Buddha was the first person in history to prescribe sustained mindfulness as a key component in a path to spiritual liberation (Wynne 2007).

The language spoken by the Buddha has died out. His early teachings were preserved in two Indian languages that have survived: Pāli and Sanskrit. The most comprehensive surviving body of the Buddha's teachings in an early Indian language is that which was preserved in Pāli (Gombrich 2009). In terms of its literary origins, the word "mindfulness" may be broadly taken to translate a compound of Pāli words: *sati* and *sampajañña*.

Sati is related to the verb *saratti* – to remember. "it is due to the presence of *sati* that one is able to remember what is otherwise only too easily forgotten: the present moment." (Anālayo 2003, pp. 47–8). It is not clear what led T. W. Rhys Davids to render *sati* as "mindfulness" in 1881 (Gethin 2011), but the term has stuck.

Sampajañña, on the other hand, may be rendered as "Clarity of Consciousness" or "Clear Comprehension" (Nyanatiloka, 1972). The compound, then, *sati-sampajañña*, may be rendered as "remembering to pay attention to what is occurring in your immediate experience with care and discernment" (Shapiro and Carlson 2009) and that seems to capture much of what is spoken about in the general literature around secular mindfulness training.

Although the secular approach to mindfulness training that is generally found in organizations today emerges from, and has many significant intersections with, the traditional Buddhist approach, there are also differences between them. Perhaps the most important of these differences consists in the overall goal that underlies the two approaches. Broadly speaking, secular mindfulness-based approaches, especially those that have a clinical background, seek to *alleviate* distress. The explicit goal of Buddhism is to *eliminate* it altogether.

Secular mindfulness-based approaches seek to alleviate suffering by training clients or patients in more skillful ways of "coping" with stress (Grossman *et al.* 2004), "managing" chronic pain (Kabat-Zinn 1996), "treating" depression relapse (Segal, Williams and Teasdale 2013). The goal of Buddhism is more explicitly all-encompassing. "Awakening", *Bodhi*, the goal of the Buddhist path, involves "the deepest understanding of the nature of suffering, its cause, its cessation, and the way leading to its cessation" (Gethin 1998, p. 15).

And yet it is a part of the Buddha's genius, and why his teachings are so relevant to people in general, that he saw that "the patterns of mind that keep people trapped in emotional suffering are, fundamentally, the same patterns of mind that stand between all of us and the flowering of our potential for a more deeply satisfying way of being" (Teasdale and Chaskalson 2011a, p. 90). Whether we are working to free ourselves from emotional distress, or to awaken to a new way of being, we are dealing with fundamentally the same patterns of mind.

One key to understanding the patterns of mind in question is the Pāli word *dukkha*, for which there is no really adequate English translation. It is often translated as suffering, but that can be misleading. Etymologically connected with the idea of an ill-fitting cart wheel (Anālayo 2003), it covers a wide range of experience – from the anguish of physical or emotional pain, to the sense of world weariness or existential unease that drove the Buddha himself to abandon his life of pleasure and to search for another way of being. All forms of *dukkha* share this sense of unsatisfactoriness, a sense that we are somehow missing out on life's full potential. Loy (2000) translates *dukkha* in this sense as "lack", and that captures some of the sense of it very well. So long as we have that sense of lack, so long as we do not have a sense of complete peace, contentment, ease, and wholeness, then *dukkha* is present (Teasdale and Chaskalson 2011a). Given there is no single adequate word to translate *dukkha*, we will leave the term untranslated.

The Buddha's classic account of *dukkha*, its cause and its elimination is found in his teaching of the Four Noble Truths (Bodhi 2000; Sumedho 1992). Following Garfield in Gutting (2014), we can render this teaching as follows:

1) Life is fundamentally *dukkha*, permeated by suffering of various types, including pain, aging and death and the inability to control one's own destiny.
2) This sense of *dukkha* is caused by attraction and aversion – attraction to things one cannot have, and aversion to things one cannot avoid, and this attraction and aversion is in turn caused by primal confusion about the fundamental nature of reality and a consequent egocentric orientation to the world.
3) If one extirpates these causes by eliminating attraction and aversion through metaphysical insight, one can eliminate suffering.
4) There is a set of domains and concerns – the eightfold path – attention to which can accomplish that.

We will describe the eightfold path below, but before then it is important to recognize and emphasize that from the perspective of both Buddhism and secular mindfulness-based approaches, the key issue is not the fact that life is often fraught with pain and difficulty. Rather, it is that the strategies we often employ to deal with difficulty often make things worse, not better.

All un-Awakened human beings experience *dukkha* and it is the Buddha's unique insight that the unpleasant or uncomfortable physical sensations or emotional feelings that are inherent in life are not *in themselves* our problem. Rather, *dukkha* is the suffering we add to unpleasant feelings by the way we relate to them. Most often, it is this suffering, rather than the unpleasant feelings themselves, that is the main source of our unhappiness (Teasdale and Chaskalson 2011a).

In the "Sallatha Sutta" (2010) the Buddha put it like this:

When an untaught worldling is touched by a painful (bodily) feeling, he worries and grieves, he laments, beats his breast, weeps and is distraught. He thus experiences two kinds of feelings, a bodily and a mental feeling. It is as if a man were pierced by an arrow and, following the first piercing, he is hit by a second arrow. So that person will experience feelings caused by two arrows.

But in the case of a well-taught noble disciple, when he is touched by a painful feeling, he will not worry nor grieve and lament, he will not beat his breast and weep, nor will he be distraught. It is one kind of feeling he experiences, a bodily one, but not a mental feeling. It is as if a man were pierced by an arrow, but was not hit by a second arrow following the first one. So this person experiences feelings caused by a single arrow only.

The message of this teaching is that whereas unpleasant and uncomfortable feelings are unavoidable, *dukkha* in the sense of suffering is optional. It is optional because we actually fire the second arrow at ourselves.

In the case of depression, for example, the first arrow of a simple feeling of sadness is transformed into a more intense and persistent state of depression when those who suffer from it add the second arrow of ruminative thinking (Teasdale and Chaskalson 2011a). In the case of anxiety, very often the second arrow is catastrophization (Vasey and Borkovec 1992). In the workplace, especially for decision makers, one instance of the second arrow might be thought of as the stream of mental proliferation that clouds our judgment when we are called upon to make decisions under pressure, or it might be the unnecessary additional mental stressors that our inner dialogues can add to existing stressful situations (Chaskalson 2011).

A key intersection between Buddhism and secular mindfulness-based approaches, then, is that they both suggest that by cultivating mindfulness it is possible to experience difficulty without (in different degrees) the unnecessary addition of *dukkha*.

Teasdale and Chaskalson (2011b) suggest that there are three strategies by way of which mindfulness training can reduce *dukkha*. Mindfulness training transforms suffering through changes in *what* the mind is processing, changes in *how* the mind is processing it, and changes in the *view* of what is being processed.

To illustrate these, consider a workplace scenario: imagine that you have been working on a key presentation for a week, fitting that into an already packed schedule. That has called on you to work late into the night and at the weekend at home. You send the presentation to your boss for review. He drops by your desk and, without preamble, draws attention to a few small failings in your work, suggests corrections, and returns to his office. You make a point of always treating your own subordinates with care and courtesy and you're angered by his apparent insensitivity. You find yourself upset and irritable, constantly dwelling on the thoughts about that interaction that force their way into your mind.

Participants in mindfulness-based programs often report a reduction in rumination and distress following such upsetting events. In the example above, they might describe how, as a result of practicing mindfulness, an interaction such as this, which could have upset them for hours, now only leads to disturbance and dwelling on the experience for a matter of minutes, or even seconds. How does that come about?

The first, and simplest, strategy for altering the conditions that sustain or create suffering is to change the *content* the mind is processing. This involves intentionally redirecting the focus of attention to aspects of experience less likely to support the arising and continuation of configurations that create suffering. For example, when we find ourselves upset and irritable, constantly dwelling on the thoughts about that interaction that force their way into our mind, we can intentionally focus and sustain our attention on the bodily sensations as the breath moves in and out. This relatively neutral focus provides less "fuel" for the maintenance of problematic configurations than emotion-laden thoughts following the difficult interaction.

The first strategy changes *what* is processed. The second strategy changes *how* material is processed, for example by intentionally allowing and attending *to* the unpleasant feelings created by the upsetting interaction with interest and curiosity – seeing them as objects of experience, rather than becoming "lost" *within* them in the automatic reaction of aversion.

The third strategy is to change the *view* we have of the material being processed. From the Buddha's perspective, the configurations that keep us stuck in suffering are rooted in our fundamental ignorance. This ignorance is marked by a failure to recognize three essential characteristics of existence. This teaching of the Buddha on "The Three Characteristics" (Bodhi 2012, AN III 134) asserts that all phenomena are impermanent; they are *dukkha*; and they are ultimately insubstantial (Kulananda 2003). Instead, un-Awakened human beings share a basic misperception in which we see the impermanent as permanent, the unreliable as reliable, what is "not-self" as "self," and in which we do not see clearly the nature and origins of *dukkha*, nor the way to end it.

If, on the other hand, we can see things clearly as they are, and let go of our tendency to identify personally with experience, then we remove a basic condition for the arising of the configurations that support *dukkha*. With the difficult interaction, this might involve, for example, a change from the perception "my boss really hurt me by being so insensitive" to the perception "unpleasant thoughts, feelings and body sensations are here in this moment."

The practice of mindfulness cultivates meta-awareness – the capacity to know, directly and intuitively, our experience as it arises in each moment. That meta-awareness is a key contributor to each of the three strategies outlined above.

Whereas research suggests that mindfulness-based approaches can play a significant part in helping participants to reduce their levels of stress, anxiety, or depression (Chiesa and Serretti 2009; 2010), we have noted above that Buddhism seeks to eliminate these and all other forms of *dukkha* altogether. To that end, the Buddha concluded his teaching of the Four Noble Truths by advocating an approach to life described as the Noble Eightfold Path.

The path begins with a reorientation to one's approach to life in a stage known as right vision, and then consists in seven further stages: right emotion, speech, action, livelihood, effort, mindfulness and concentration. This is not a path to be traversed sequentially, rather one works in different ways on different aspects all the time (Kulananda 2003).

There are two immediately striking differences between the approach advocated by the secular mindfulness-based approaches and that of the eightfold path. Firstly, the eightfold path culminates in concentration, *samādhi*, a state of deep calm and one-pointedness that many Buddhist texts suggest is a necessary precondition to Awakening. A classic approach, found throughout the Pāli literature, for instance, suggests that the path to Awakening typically proceeds via states of deep meditative absorption – the *jhānas* (*Aṅguttara Nikāya* 5.28). For some Buddhist scholars, such as B. Alan Wallace and Bhikkhu Bodhi (2006), the failure of secular mindfulness-based approaches to incorporate such states of deep absorption into their teachings marks a significant failure and a departure from the tradition.

At the other end of the scale, the fact that secular approaches take as their focus mindfulness (*sati*), the seventh limb of the eightfold path without the explicit context of ethical training implied by the rest of the path, gives rise to considerable questioning of these approaches by some contemporary Buddhists, who have dubbed the approach "McMindfulness":

Uncoupling mindfulness from its ethical and religious Buddhist context is understandable as an expedient move to make such training a viable product on the open market. But the rush to secularize and commodify mindfulness into a marketable technique may be leading to an unfortunate denaturing of this ancient practice, which was intended for far more than relieving a headache, reducing blood pressure, or helping executives become better focused and more productive.

(Purser and Loy 2013)

Set against this are comments by contemporary researchers such as Willoughby Britton, who is quoted by Heuman (2014) as suggesting that the main delivery system for Buddhist meditation in the modern West is not Buddhism – it is science, medicine, and schools (and we might hopefully add workplaces); and that mindfulness-based stress reduction (MBSR) practitioners, who currently account for the majority of new meditators, will soon be the vast majority. She therefore calls for Buddhists to stop criticizing and start collaborating with those teaching mindfulness through secular approaches.

In answer to both the scholars such as Wallace and Bodhi, who wish that secular mindfulness-based approaches focused more upon one-pointed concentration, and to the critics such as Purser and Loy, who question their "de-naturing" of the Buddhist teachings, stands the concept of *upāya* "skilful means":

What Jon Kabat-Zinn did is in line with a long-standing Buddhist approach called upāya, usually translated as "skilful means". Buddhism is not dogmatic, it is not a creed. It is a practice to be learned and when we read the oldest texts, closest to the historical Buddha, we see that he was an excellent teacher. The Buddha always addresses the person he is talking to in the language and frame of reference of that person ... Kabat-Zinn has done nothing else but continue that tradition and restate the tradition in a way that makes it acceptable to the medical and scientific world ... All this is very traditionally Buddhist, the product of upāya.

(Maex 2011, p. 167)

Mindfulness-based approaches: an overview

By far the most common form of secular mindfulness-based training is the MBSR programme referred to by Maex and developed by Kabat-Zinn and his colleagues at the University of Massachusetts Medical Center in 1979. This approach is implicitly informed by several strands of Buddhist thought. Kabat-Zinn (2011) references Theravada Buddhism, Soto and Rinzai Zen (including the earlier Chinese and Korean streams) alongside currents from the Indian yogic traditions, including Vedanta, the teachings of J. Krishnamurti and Ramana Maharshi. Because MBSR has had such an influence upon mindfulness-training in organizations, in this section, we describe its methodology and origins.

Upon examining the MBSR methodology, as well as that of mindfulness-based cognitive therapy (MBCT) that emerged from it and is closely allied to it, two aspects stand out in particular: inquiry and the four foundations of mindfulness.

The "inquiry" process in MBSR and MBCT consists in "interactive moment-by-moment exchanges in the classroom between teacher and participants in which they explore together in great and sometimes challenging detail first-person experience of the practice and its manifestations in everyday life" (Kabat-Zinn 2011, p. 289). This approach Kabat-Zinn attributes to his primary Zen teacher, Seung Sahn, whose teaching method made extensive use of koans[1] and koan-based "Dharma combat" exchanges between teacher and student. Within

---

[1] Koan – noun: a paradoxical anecdote or riddle without a solution, used in Zen Buddhism to demonstrate the inadequacy of logical reasoning and provoke enlightenment (*Oxford English Dictionary*).

the MBSR approach, such inquiry is seen as an important way of helping MBSR course participants to develop a greater curiosity about
their inner experience. By being invited to describe their experience
of any practice soon after doing it, a deeper quality of reflection is
encouraged. Participants may also be invited to turn toward what is
difficult for them in the moment. That can help people to see that
what they ordinarily avoid may in fact be tolerable – or even positively
interesting.

The four foundations of mindfulness

Another crucial component of MBSR is the attention given in the
training to four aspects of mindful awareness: thoughts, feelings,
sensations and "experiences". This categorization comes from the
Pāli *Satipaṭṭhāna Sutta*, or "Discourse on the Four Foundations of
Mindfulness." In the *Satipaṭṭhāna Sutta*, the Buddha recommends four
contemplations as "the direct path for the purification of beings, for
the surmounting of sorrow and lamentation, for the disappearance
of *dukkha* [suffering] and discontent, for acquiring the true method,
for the realisation of *Nibbāna* [release of suffering], namely the four
satipaṭṭhānas." (Anālayo 2003, p. 3). These four consist in turn of contemplations of the body (*kayānupassanā*), feelings (*vedānupassanā*),
the mind (*cittānupassanā*) and experiences in terms of the teachings
(*dhammānupassanā*).

It isn't obvious on first reading what the Buddha meant in detail by
his admonition to pay mindful attention to each of these domains and
any exegesis very rapidly runs into translation difficulty. Not only do
the Pāli terms not always have simple English equivalents, but in order
for the teaching to make sense to the modern reader much of it needs
first to be set in the wider context of early Buddhist thought.

That said, there are one or two particularly salient issues here that
shed important light on the early Buddhist approach to mindfulness.
What follows is a necessarily partial account. This is not intended as a
detailed commentary on the *Satipaṭṭhāna Sutta*, nor is this piece written in a Buddhist studies context. We have therefore left out those
elements in the teaching that are not obviously relevant to secular
approaches to mindfulness training in order to have the space to highlight and further discuss those that do.

In the *Satipaṭṭhāna Sutta* the Buddha first of all admonishes his followers to pay detailed attention to their bodies. Starting with the breath, in a meditation somewhat similar to the "mindfulness of breathing meditation" that is taught in MBSR and MBCT, they go on to practice awareness of the body in all of its postures: walking, standing, sitting, and lying down. That touches on several other secular mindfulness practices, as we shall see below.

With the second *satipaṭṭhāna*, the Buddha calls on his followers to pay mindful attention to *vedanā*, often translated as "feelings," but that does not quite capture it. *Vedanā* is a difficult term to translate. It refers to the initial hedonic response (like, don't like, or don't care) to sense contacts. In that respect it lies somewhere between the English terms "sensation" and "feeling." It does not imply "emotions," which come under the third and fourth applications of mindfulness. It may be that a term like "affective quality" comes closer to its meaning inasmuch as *vedanā* refers to the constantly changing but continuously present affective tone of every moment of experience.

This *satipaṭṭhāna* has a particular relevance to secular approaches to mindfulness training, as one of the key skills participants learn in the context of their training is the capacity to "be with" what is difficult or unwanted without reacting to it. In Buddhist terms, this is the ability to maintain a simple awareness of pleasant or unpleasant *vedanā* without being tipped by that experience into states of craving or aversion. That is a key move. In terms of the Four Noble Truths it involves the capacity to "stay with" a sense of unsatisfactoriness, "lack," pain, or discomfort – in other words *dukkha*, the First Noble Truth – without being tipped by that experience into the states of craving or aversion that mark the Second Noble Truth (Teasdale and Chaskalson 2011a).

With the third *satipaṭṭhāna*, the Buddha admonishes his followers to pay mindful attention to mental activity. The suggestion of the *Sutta* is that the meditator simply "knows" from moment to moment what is moving in the mind at any time. He or she does not adopt a judgmental attitude to the contents of their mind, but they *do* "know" it. From the perspective of secular approaches to mindfulness training, the capacity for that kind of nonjudgmental metacognition is a key component in the capacity of mindfulness to transform suffering (Teasdale and Chaskalson 2011b).

Finally, the fourth *satipaṭṭhāna*, the contemplation of experiences in terms of the teachings, calls upon the meditator to notice how some of the key teachings of the Buddha – including, for example, the Four Noble Truths that we discussed above – play out in their lived experience. This *satipaṭṭhāna* has considerable resonance with the psycho-educational aspects of, for example, MBSR or MBCT. In Session Four of MBSR, for instance, participants might learn about the neuro-biology of stress in order to equip them better to manage it and they learn how to spot signs of stress in their lived experience. The same is true of Session Four of MBCT, although there the focus is depression. Wisdom based upon insight into the nature of the world is a key part of mindfulness training.

In the mindfulness-based approaches, the *Satipaṭṭhāna* approach to mindfulness training is often contracted for teaching purposes to the admonition to pay attention to thoughts, feelings, and body sensations. Williams (2008) describes how the process of attending with mindfulness to such elements of our experience can be therapeutically valuable:

Bringing awareness to the elements of events gives more degrees of freedom than is offered by those same events once they have assembled into habitual patterns. In particular, people who are vulnerable to depression discover, often to their great surprise, that bringing an open and friendly curiosity to how unpleasant experiences can be "felt" experientially in patterns of ever-changing physical sensations in the body creates a sense of greater freedom and choice than they had ever experienced when they had been ruminating about or trying to avoid the experience.

(p. 730)

One effect of attending to one's thoughts, feelings, body sensations, and experiences with mindful attention is the emergence of what Segal, Williams, and Teasdale (2013) refer to as a "decentered" perspective. That is, participants on mindfulness training courses come to see their thoughts, feelings, sensations, and experiences to some extent from the perspective of an observer. Segal, Williams, and Teasdale (2013) quote Kabat-Zinn's *Full Catastrophe Living*:

It is remarkable how liberating it feels to be able to see that your thoughts are just thoughts and that they are not "you" or "reality" ... The simple act of recognising your thoughts as thoughts can free you from the distorted reality they often create and allow for more clear-sightedness and a greater sense of manageability in your life.

(p. 66)

The *Satipaṭṭhāna Sutta* approach to mindfulness training enables participants to develop a degree of distance from their experience. But this is not about disconnection or dissociation. Instead, it allows participants to experience the changing flow of their mental and physical experiences without over-identifying with these or cling-ing strongly to such experiences. Rather than leading to a cold detachment, this lets participants connect more intimately with their moment-to-moment experience, allowing it to rise and fall and change naturally. Participants begin to experience *what is* instead of a commentary or story *about* what is. Rather than creating apathy or indifference, this helps participants to experience greater rich-ness, texture, and depth – from moment to moment. Shapiro *et al.* (2006) speak of this as a form of "intimate detachment" that cap-tures both sides of the experience.

From the perspective of the *Satipaṭṭhāna Sutta*, that "intimate detachment," pursued with rigor over time, leads to the complete eradication of "all identifications with, and corresponding attach-ments to, a sense of self" (Anālayo 2003, p. 210). As taught in organizational contexts, the approach is generally less ambitious. Below, we describe one approach to teaching MBSR in organiza-tional contexts.

MBSR outlined

The eight-week MBSR program is deliberately not manualized in order to promote flexibility in response to individual contexts:

There are many different ways to structure and deliver mindfulness-based stress reduction programs. The optimal form of its delivery will depend crit-ically on local factors and on the level of experience and understanding of the people undertaking the teaching. Rather than "clone" or "franchise" one cookie cutter approach, mindfulness ultimately requires effective use of the present moment as the core indicator of the appropriateness of particular choices.

(Kabat-Zinn 1996, p. 165)

While bearing that caveat in mind, McCown, Reibel, and Micozzi (2010) have published what they see as the template MBSR program, based on Kabat-Zinn's (1990) *Full Catastrophe Living*. McCown, Reibel and Micozzi's MBSR "template" program describes an eight-week, nine-session course. Participants attend two-and-a-half-hour sessions once a week for eight weeks with an additional seven-hour (all-day) session between the sixth and seventh sessions.

Although we have no hard data to support this assertion, anecdotal evidence from our own conversations with human resources and learning and development departments in organizations in different parts of the world suggests that it is unlikely that the MBSR program described above would be offered in many workplaces. The session length of two and a half hours would be more than many employers could fit into a working day, to say nothing of the seven-hour session between weeks six and seven. What is more, based on our experience of teaching in organizations, we believe that the 45 minutes per day of home practice that is called for in "classic" MBSR training is more than most busy people feel they can spare.

In *Mindfulness in Eight Weeks* (2014), Chaskalson has published an eight-week programme based on MBSR and incorporating elements of Segal, Williams, and Teasdale's (2013) MBCT, which can be delivered in one-and-a-half-hour sessions and which asks participants to undertake twenty minutes of home practice each day. This "low mindfulness dose" type of program is fast becoming favored in the workplace. Klatt, Buckworth and Malarkey (2009) have published early research with promising findings and a web search conducted in May 2014 reveals several training organizations in the United Kingdom now offering workplace specific mindfulness curriculums. "Low dose" workplace programs tend to dispense with the "classic" program's single seven-hour session, although this can sometimes be an "optional extra".

Below is a week-by-week outline from Chaskalson's (2014) program, showing how some of the elements from the historical Buddhist background to mindfulness training continue to play out in contemporary contexts.

Week 1: automatic pilot. The rationale for this session is that mindfulness begins when we recognize our tendency not to be mindful. We go about our days in a kind of "automatic-pilot mode," doing what we know how to do without a great deal of awareness of ourselves, others, and the world around us. In this session, participants come to see that fact to some extent. They also take the first steps towards some kind of commitment to learn how regularly to step out of automatic-pilot mode and become more aware.

Two key practices bring these ideas to light. The "raisin exercise," in which participants are guided in mindfully eating a single raisin and "the body scan," in which they are guided in systematically moving their attention around their bodies, exploring in detail whatever sensations (or none) they find as they do so.

In respect of the Buddhist historical background to mindfulness training, these practices introduce the idea of mindfulness, *sati*, a form of awareness that many participants will not consciously have experienced before, and they begin the process of learning to pay nonjudgmental attention to their body sensations as well as to any thoughts and feelings that arise as they do so. The instructor will suggest that when their minds wander away from attention to the body in the body scan – as minds inevitably do – they simply acknowledge where their attention went and, gently and kindly, return the attention to the body.

In this way, three of the four *satipaṭṭhānas* are introduced (attention to sensations, feelings, and thoughts) as well as the implicit attitude of kindness and care that informs all of Buddhist teaching. Germer (2009, p. 133) references a Zen Buddhist saying that aptly captures this idea: "Kindness is the fruition of awareness and awareness is the foundation of kindness." From a psycho-educational perspective (the fourth *satipaṭṭhāna*), participants are introduced to the idea of nonjudgmental attention:

This doesn't mean that we don't make judgements when we're mindful, or that we stop discerning what is appropriate at any time from what is inappropriate. That would be simple foolishness. But think of what we mean when we speak of someone being "judgemental". A thesaurus gives these synonyms: critical, hypercritical, condemnatory, negative, disapproving, disparaging, pejorative. Quite a list.

The non-judgemental attitude of mindfulness, on the other hand, is neither condemnatory nor prejudicial.

(Chaskalson 2014, p. 8)

Week 2: mindfulness of the breath. In addition to the body scan, this week sees the introduction of "mindfulness of breathing meditation."

Participants are invited to sit in meditation, allowing their attention simply to rest with the sensations that come with each breath. As well as introducing a practice that aids calm to some extent, this meditation exposes more clearly the extent of chatter in the mind. Participants begin to see the extent to which their center of attention tends to be located in their thinking processes. Through discussion, they also come to see the way that mental chatter tends to control their reactions to everyday events.

In this way, all four *satipaṭṭhānas* are practiced. Participants are guided in paying attention to sensations and feelings in the mindfulness of breathing and the body scan; in the process they become more aware of the extent of their (unwanted) mental activity; and in psycho-educational discussion the idea that such unwanted mental activity controls much of their reactive behavior is introduced.

Week 3: mindfulness of the body moving. Participants discover this week how they can work with difficulties, even intense difficulties, by maintaining a present-moment awareness, especially by way of bringing deliberate attention to their bodies at times of difficulty. Sitting meditation is further developed and participants are introduced to simple mindful-movement practices (mindful stretching, yoga, qigong or some combination of these) as well as mindful walking and a three-step breathing space (a three-minute meditation).

In learning to bring kindly curiosity to the "feeling tone" of experience, noticing the layers that we add to our experience – especially difficult experience – participants further develop their experience of the second satipaṭṭhāna, mindfulness of "feeling." And in learning more about how to deconstruct experience: coming to see how it is made up of thoughts, feelings, and body sensations, they further practice their awareness of the first three *satipaṭṭhānas*. By deepening an understanding of the attitudinal qualities of mindfulness – such as non-judgment, non-attachment, acceptance, kindness, openness, curiosity, trust, and non-reactivity; and by learning more about the habitual and automatic patterns of their minds, they also practice the fourth satipaṭṭhāna.

Week 4: managing reactions. In this session participants learn how attempts to cling on to desirable experiences and push undesirable ones away color our minds and drive our behavior. They see how this can scatter and fragment our attention, or narrow it too sharply. Instead, they now begin to learn to allow what is the case simply to be the case. By taking a wider view on their experience, they learn to relate to it differently. They also learn about the neurophysiology of stress and begin to develop more resourceful ways of dealing with stressful situations. Participants learn more about how to use mindfulness skills to reduce reactivity. They continue to deepen their meditation practice and to learn more about stress, its causes, and its neurophysiology.

As well as further building on participants' experience of the four *Satipaṭṭhānas*, this session implicitly draws out the ideas contained in the Four Noble Truths: that our reactive tendencies towards aversion and craving exacerbate *dukkha*.

Week 5: letting things be. In this session participants learn that although it is important to change things that need to be changed when that is possible, there are also parts of our lives that can't be changed and they learn the value of allowing such things simply to be as they are without judging them or trying to make them different. Unless we can accept that what we are currently experiencing is simply what we are experiencing, and we learn just to be with it, we have little choice in relation to it. Choice begins when we can accept – in an open and kindly way – that what is here right now is simply what is here now. When we can do that, we may have some choice about what to do next.

As well as further developing and extending the sitting meditation, in this session there is a discussion of Rumi's poem "The Guest House" (Barks 2004) to explore the value of allowing oneself to experience without judgment. Again, this session further develops participants' experience of all four *satipaṭṭhānas*.

Week 6: recognizing thoughts and emotions as mental events. In this session the skills of reperceiving are drawn out and made more explicit. Here participants learn to see that thoughts are just thoughts and that, in the case of stress, catastrophizing thoughts can strongly colour the nature of their experience. They learn to see such thoughts for what they are – just thoughts – and to step back from them, without necessarily needing to question them or to seek alternatives. If such thoughts still have a strong pull on our awareness, one can choose to work with them more directly, with an attitude of investigation, curiosity, and kindness.

The main practices taught this week are sitting meditation practice – mindfulness of breathing, mindfulness of breath and body, mindfulness of sounds and thoughts; the three-step breathing space – especially as a way of taking a wider view on thoughts. As well as that there is a moods and thoughts exercise that illustrates how moods color thoughts, feelings, and attendant sensations in a self-perpetuating cycle.

This session further develops participants' experience of all four *satipaṭṭhānas*, with a particular emphasis on the third *satipaṭṭhāna* – mindfulness of mental activity.

Week 7: taking good care of yourself. In this session participants explore the relationship between activities and stress. They each develop a "map" of their own stress signatures, explore behaviors that generally accentuate their stress and what they can do to diminish stress. They begin to create strategies for recognizing and dealing with stress in the moment and they do a longer sitting meditation.

In terms of the *satipaṭṭhānas*, the fourth gets most attention here as participants begin to reflect more deeply on the nature of their lived experience and on how, by applying what they have learned on the course, they might change that experience in the future. As well as that, the overall attitude of kindness discussed above, especially kindness to oneself, gets a particular emphasis this week.

Week 8: living mindfully. The rationale of this session is that regular mindfulness practice can support a sustainable balance in life that makes for greater effectiveness and higher levels of satisfaction and wellbeing. The good intentions that have been generated on the course are now strengthened by linking the practices with positive reasons for taking better care of oneself.

As well as either an extended sitting meditation or a body scan, participants are supported in planning how to keep their practice going.

Home practice: a core component. Home practice of meditation is widely considered to be a core requirement of secular mindfulness-based approaches. In the "classic" course taught at the Center for Mindfulness at the University of Massachusetts Medical School, participants are asked to commit to formal home practice, supported by recorded audio instruction, of around forty-five minutes a day. But participants on the course generally do less than they are asked to and the reported average practice time ranges from sixteen to twenty minutes per day for sitting meditation and mindful movement, to thirty-one to thirty-five minutes per day for the body scan practice (Carmody and Baer 2008). Participants on a workplace course typically are asked to do a similar style of home practice but the time commitment is less, For example, body scans can be reduced from forty-five minutes to twenty to twenty-five minutes, depending on the program and tutor.

What the relationship is between what participants are *asked* to do, what they *say* they do, and what they *actually* do is hard to determine. Interestingly, MBSR programs requiring shorter home practices, ranging from fifteen to thirty-five minutes, have yielded health outcomes consistent with those of the "classic" Center for Mindfulness program (Jain *et al.* 2007; Reibel *et al.* 2001; Rosenzweig *et al.* 2003; Roth and Calle-Mesa 2006).

There is no consensus in the research to date on the relationship between home practice duration and frequency and the outcomes for participants. Some studies show no significant correlations (Astin 1997; Carmody and Baer 2008; Davidson *et al.* 2003). Other studies find significant correlations between practice time and specific outcomes (Carmody and Baer 2008; Jha *et al.* 2010; Speca *et al.* 2000).

"We know this much," say McCown, Reibel, and Micozzi (2010, p. 144), "participants who *have* a six-day-a-week, 45 minutes-a-day meditation practice, and participants who simply *are* mindful at some moment, ... [can both] change their lives."

How is MBSR typically adapted to organisational settings? Emerging workplace programmes range in session numbers and time frames. They are most commonly four to eight weeks in duration with sessions lasting anywhere from one to two and a half hours. Several studies report differences of class frequency and duration. There are studies reporting course lengths of between four and ten weeks (Jain *et al.* 2007; Rosenzweig *et al.* 2003; and Speca *et al.* 2000). Class durations of between one and a half to two hours are also reported (Astin 1997; Jain *et al.* 2007; Rosenzweig *et al.* 2003; Roth and Calle-Mesa 2006). The changes to the MBSR core template needed to make these timing adaptations are primarily in the extent and type of didactic material presented and in the opportunities allowed for group discussion and inquiry. From a review of the literature thus far, there appears to be much less variation in the presentation and practice of the core meditations (McCown, Reibel, and Micozzi 2010) – although clearly one cannot know what is happening in unreported programs or in those not yet reviewed.

Klatt, Buckworth and Malarkey's (2009) study suggested good outcomes such as substantial reductions in perceived stress and increases in mindfulness from a program referred to as "Low-Dose MBSR". This program was delivered to staff from all functions in a university setting. Although there were only six sixty-minute sessions, one session per week, and they were asked to do only twenty minutes per day of home practice, participants in the study demonstrated positive improvements in terms of perceived stress and increased mindfulness. This paves the way for future research on practice requirements for effective mindfulness training.

There is some difficulty in keeping track of curriculums and trainers within the mindfulness field as currently there are no governing or regulating bodies, although there are various guides such as *The Good Practice Guidance for Mindfulness Teachers* from the UK Network for Mindfulness-Based Teacher Training Organisations. Taking this into consideration it is almost impossible to give an accurate account of programs and training available for workplace-based settings.

We know from observation that the number of organizations offering workplace programs is growing and what all of these workplace programs seem to have in common is that they ask for a shorter duration of daily home practice. Several are based on shorter session times and some have fewer taught sessions.

Other workplace mindfulness-based programs not based on MBSR

In addition to the main approaches such as MBSR and MBCT there are other permutations of mindfulness training in organizational contexts. Research indicates that "Emotional Resilience Training" is successful in reducing perceived stress for military personal (Stanley *et al.* 2011). Corporate-based mindfulness training is another approach tailored to organizational needs. Mindfulness in schools programs are being introduced to educational intuitions via teacher training (Kuyken *et al.* 2013). "Search Inside Yourself" is a program originally developed at Google, which is now being offered to other organizations.[2] As there is no central collection point or recording requirement for this type of information, it is impossible to measure what is

[2] See http://siyli.org/.

being offered in the workplace, but what is clear is that mindfulness training is becoming more accepted with businesses such as Google and Transport for London integrating mindfulness in their workplace (Crossland-Thackray 2012).

Conclusion

We have explored the path that mindfulness-based interventions have taken thus far in coming to be used in the context of contemporary organizational life and also what that training might look like. Overall we conclude that, while secular approaches to mindfulness training in the workplace differ markedly from approaches to mindfulness training adopted historically in the context of Buddhism, this process of evolution is a natural and necessary feature of promoting mindfulness to populations disinterested in Buddhism. The workplace outcomes one might expect from applying these types of intervention are still very much the focus of discussion and research globally. The body of research into mindfulness is heavily weighted in the clinical setting and workplace research is limited although growing, for example, Klatt *et al.* (2009), Levy *et al.* (2012), and Wolever *et al.* (2012) have all reported on workplace research around mindfulness-based interventions and findings are promising.

The aspiration is that the proven psychosocial changes resulting from mindfulness training can translate into a cost-effective way of improving tangible workplace variables such as productivity, sickness absence, leadership styles, and employee wellbeing. Although not as copious as the clinical base an evidence base for this is gradually emerging.

The possibilities of change are immense, as greater mindfulness appears to correlate with a variety of desirable outcomes such as a reduction in depression (NICE 2009); reduced stress and anxiety (Cohen and Miller 2009), or increased patience and gratitude (Rothaupt and Morgan 2007). The ways in which the changes in thinking, feeling, and behaviour taught by the Buddha might translate into changes in practice in the modern workplace opens an exciting new frontier for research and debate.

References

Anālayo, V. (2003). *Satipatthana: the direct path to realization.* Birmingham: Windhorse.

Astin, J. (1997). Stress reduction through mindfulness meditation: effects on psychological symptomology, sense of control, and spiritual experience. *Psychotherapy and Psychosomatics*, 66, 97–106.

Barks, C. (ed.) (2004). The guest house. In *The Essential Rumi*. New York: HarperOne, p. 109.

Bodhi, B. (2000). *The connected discourses of the Buddha: a new translation of the Samyutta Nikaya*. Boston, MA: Wisdom Publications.

Bodhi, B. (trans.) (2012) The Three Characteristics. In *The Numerical Discourses of the Buddha: A New Translation of the Anguttara Nikaya*. Boston, MA: Wisdom Publications, AN III, p. 134.

Carmody, J., and Baer, R. A. (2008). Relationships between mindfulness practice and levels of mindfulness, medical and psychological symptoms and well-being in a mindfulness-based stress reduction program. *Journal of Behavioural Medicine*, 31, 23–33.

Chaskalson, M. (2011). *The mindful workplace: developing resilient individuals and resonant organisations with MBSR*. Chichester: Wiley-Blackwell.

Chaskalson, M. (2014). *Mindfulness in eight weeks: the revolutionary 8-week plan to clear your mind and calm your life*. London: Harper Thorson.

Chiesa, A., and Serretti, A. (2009). Mindfulness-based stress reduction for stress management in healthy people: a review and meta-analysis. *The Journal of Alternative and Complementary Medicine*, 15(5), 593–600.

Chiesa, A., and Serretti, A. (2010). A systematic review of neurobiological and clinical features of mindfulness meditations. *Psychological Medicine*, 40, 1239–52.

Cohen, J., and Miller, L. (2009). Interpersonal mindfulness training for well-being: a pilot study with psychology graduate students. *The Teachers College Record*, 111(12), 2760–74. Retrieved from www.tcrecord.org.

Crossland-Thackray, G. (2012). Mindfulness at work: what are the benefits? *The Guardian*, December 21. Retrieved from http://careers.theguardian.com/careers-blog/mindfulness-at-work-benefits.

Davidson, R. J., Kabat-Zinn, J., Schumacher, J., Rosenkrantz, M., Muller, D., Santorelli, S. F., … Sheridan, F. S. (2003). Alterations in brain and immune function produced by mindfulness meditation. *Psychosomatic Medicine*, 65, 564–70.

Gelles, D. (2012). The mind business. *The Financial Times*, August 24. Retrieved from www.ft.com/cms/s/2/d9cb7940-ebea-11e1-9 85a-00144feab49a.html#axzz30sT9d7FR.

Germer, C. K. (2009). *The mindful path to self-compassion: freeing yourself from destructive thoughts and emotions*. New York and London: The Guilford Press.

Gethin, R. (1998). *The foundations of Buddhism.* Oxford University Press.

Gethin, R. (2011). On some definitions of mindfulness. *Contemporary Buddhism*, 12(1), 263–79.

Gombrich, R. (2009). *What the Buddha thought.* London: Equinox Publishing.

Grossman, P., Niemann, L., Schmidt, S., and Walach, H. (2004). Mindfulness-based stress reduction and health benefits: a meta-analysis. *Journal of Psychosomatic Research*, 57(1), 35.

Gutting, G. (2014). What does buddhism require? *The New York Times*, April 27. Retrieved from http://mobile.nytimes.com/blogs/opinionator/2014/04/27/what-does-buddhism-require/.

Heuman, L. (2014). Meditation nation: how convincing is the science driving the popularity of mindfulness meditation? *Tricycle*, April 25. Retrieved from www.tricycle.com/blog/meditation-nation.

Jain, S., Shapiro, S. L., Swanick, S., Roesch, S. C., Mills, P. J., Bell, I., and Schwartz, G. E. (2007). Randomized controlled trial of mindfulness meditation versus relaxation training: effects on distress, positive states of mind, rumination, and distraction. *Annals of Behavioral Medicine*, 33(1), 11–21.

Jha, A. P., Stanley, E. A., Kiyonaga, A., Wong, L., and Gelfand, L. (2010). Examining the protective effects of mindfulness training on working memory capacity and affective experience. *Emotion*, 10(1), 54–64.

Kabat-Zinn, J. (1990). *Full catastrophe living.* New York: Delta Publishing.

Kabat-Zinn, J. (1996). Mindfulness meditation. What it is, what it isn't, and its role in health care and medicine. In Y. Haruki and M. Suzuki (eds.), *Comparative and psychological study on meditation.* Delft: Eburon Publishers, pp. 161–70.

Kabat-Zinn, J. (2011). Some reflections on the origins of MBSR, skillful means, and the trouble with maps. *Contemporary Buddhism*, 12(01), 281–306.

Kabat-Zinn, J. (2013) *Full catastrophe living: how to cope with stress, pain and illness using mindfulness meditation*, 2nd edn. London: Piatkus.

Klatt, M. D., Buckworth, J., and Malarkey, W. (2009). Effects of low-dose mindfulness-based stress reduction (MBSR-ld) on working adults. *Health Education and Behaviour*, 36, 601–14.

Kulananda (2003). *Principles of Buddhism.* Birmingham: Windhorse Publications.

Kuyken, W., Weare, K., Ukoumunne, O. C., Vicary, R., Motton, N., Burnett, R., ... and Huppert, F. (2013). Effectiveness of the mindfulness in schools programme: non-randomised controlled feasibility study. *The British Journal of Psychiatry*, 203(2), 126–31.

Levy, D. M., Wobbrock, J. O., Kaszniak, A. W., and Ostergren, M. (2012). The effects of mindfulness meditation training on multitasking in a high-stress information environment. In *Proceedings of Graphics Interface 2012*. Canadian Information Processing Society, pp. 45–52.

Loy, D. R. (2000) Anglo American Civil Society: a Buddhist perspective. Unpublished.

Maex, E. (2011). The buddhist roots of mindfulness training: a practitioner's view. *Contemporary Buddhism*, 12(1), 165–75.

Marturano, J. L. (2013). Mindful leadership receives warm welcome at Davos. *Huffington Post*, January 24. Retrieved from www.huffingtonpost.com/janice-l-marturano/mindful-leadership-receiv_b_2543151.html.

McCown, D., Reibel, D. K., and Micozzi, M. S., (2010) *Teaching mindfulness: a practical guide for clinicians and educators*. New York: Springer.

NICE (2009) *Depression: The treatment and management of depression in adults*. A partial update of NICE clinical guideline 23. Retrieved from www.nice.org.uk/nicemedia/pdf/cg90niceguideline.pdf.

Nyanatiloka (1972). *Buddhist dictionary: manual of buddhist terms and doctrines*. Colombo: Frewin and Co. Ltd.

Purser, R., and Loy, D. R. (2013). Beyond McMindfulness. *Huffington Post*, January. Retrieved from www.huffingtonpost.com/ron-purser/beyond-mcmindfulness_b_3519289.html.

Reibel D. K., Greeson, J. M., Brainard, G. C., Rosenzweig, S. (2001). Mindfulness-based stress reduction and health-related quality of life in a heterogeneous patient population. *General Hospital Psychiatry*, 23(4), 183–92.

Rosenzweig, S., Reibel, D., Greeson, J., Brainard, G., and Hojat, M. (2003). Mindfulness-based stress reduction lowers psychological distress in medical students. *Teaching and Learning in Medicine*, 15(2), 88–92.

Roth, B., and Calle-Mesa, L. (2006). Mindfulness-based stress reduction (MBSR) with Spanish and English-speaking inner-city medical patients. In R. Baer (ed.), *Mindfulness-based treatment approaches: clinicians guide to evidence base and applications*. Boston, MA: Elsevier Academic Press.

Rothaupt, J. W., and Morgan, M. M. (2007). Counselors' and counselor educators' practice of mindfulness: A qualitative inquiry. *Counseling and Values*, 52, 40–54.

"Sallatha Sutta: The Dart" (SN 36.6), translated from the Pāli by Nyanaponika Thera. *Access to Insight (Legacy Edition)*, June 13, 2010. Retrieved from www.accesstoinsight.org/tipitaka/sn/sn36/sn36.006.nypo.html.

Segal, Z. V., Williams, J. M. G., and Teasdale, J. D. (2013). *Mindfulness-based cognitive therapy for depression* 2nd edn. New York and London: The Guilford Press.

Shapiro, S. L., and Carlson, L. E. (2009). *The art and science of mindfulness: integrating mindfulness into psychology and the helping professions*. Washington, DC: American Psychological Association.

Shapiro, S. L., Carlson, L. E., Astin, J. A., and Freedman, B. (2006). Mechanisms of mindfulness. *Journal of Clinical Psychology*, 62(3), 373–86.

Speca, M., Carlson, L. E., Goodey, E., and Angen, M. (2000). A randomized, wait-list controlled clinical trial: the effect of a mindfulness meditation-based stress reduction program on mood and symptoms of stress in cancer outpatients. *Psychosomatic Medicine*, 62, 613–22.

Stanley, E., Schaldach, J. M., Kiyonaga, A., and Jha, A. P. (2011). Mindfulness-based mind fitness training: a case study of a high-stress predeployment military cohort. *Cognitive and Behavioral Practice*, 18, 566–76.

Sumedho, A. (1992). *The four noble truths*. Amaravati. Retrieved from www.buddhanet.net.

Teasdale, J. D., and Chaskalson, M. (2011a). How does mindfulness transform suffering? I: The nature and origins of dukkha. *Contemporary Buddhism*, 12(01), 89–102.

Teasdale, J. D. and Chaskalson, M. (2011b). How does mindfulness transform suffering? II: The transformation of dukkha. *Contemporary Buddhism*, 12(01), 103–24.

UK Network For Mindfulness-based Teacher Training Organisations. *The Good Practice Guidance for Mindfulness Teachers*. Retrieved from http://mindfulnessteachersuk.org.uk.

Vasey, M. W., and Borkovec, T. D. (1992). A catastrophizing assessment of worrisome thoughts. *Cognitive Therapy and Research*, 16(5), 505–20.

Wallace, B. A., and Bodhi, B.(2006). The nature of mindfulness and its role in buddhist meditation: a correspondence between B. Alan Wallace and the venerable Bhikkhu Bodhi. Retrieved from https://sbinstitute.com/isp/sites/default/files/Bhikkhu_Bodhi_Correspondence.pdf.

Williams, J. M. G. (2008). Mindfulness, depression and modes of mind. *Cognitive Therapy and Research*, 32, 721–33.

Wolever, R. Q., Bobinet, K. J., McCabe, K., Mackenzie, E. R., Fekete, E., Kusnick, C. A., and Baime, M. (2012). Effective and viable mind-body stress reduction in the workplace: a randomized controlled trial. *Journal of Occupational Health Psychology*, 17, 246–58.

Wynne, A. (2007). *The origin of Buddhist meditation*. Abingdon: Routledge.

Zaehner, R. C. (1992). *Hindu scriptures*. New York: Everyman's Library.

4 Methods of mindfulness: how mindfulness is studied in the workplace

ELLEN CHOI AND HANNES LEROY

Introduction

Interest in mindfulness in the workplace has been on the rise. A recent surge of research has built a compelling case for mindfulness and its potential benefits continue to attract the attention of organizational scholars. To name but a few, in the past years we have seen research linking mindfulness to work-family balance (Allen and Kiburz 2012), work engagement (Leroy, Anseel, Dimitrova, and Sels 2013), negotiation outcomes (Reb and Narayanan 2014), job burnout (Roche and Haar 2013), resilience to bias (Hafenbrack, Kinias, and Barsade 2013), working memory (Mrazek *et al.* 2013) and performance (Dane and Brummel 2014; Reb, Narayanan, and Chaturvedi 2014). While mindfulness was initially studied as a method of treating ailing clinical populations (Kabat-Zinn 1990), today its application has expanded to executive boardrooms, elementary school classrooms, professional sports, and military Special Forces. The rapid expansion of mindfulness studies in non-clinical populations, particularly work environments, is exciting for practitioners but also raises a series of methodological concerns. It is to this end that we focus this chapter: a review and analysis of the study of mindfulness in the workplace. We hope this chapter will offer a roadmap to scholars new to mindfulness by summarizing prevailing methods and their areas for improvement. We also aim to offer innovative insights for more established researchers by reflecting on directions for further research.

This chapter discusses the study of workplace mindfulness in three sections. First, we review how researchers have studied the various conceptualizations of mindfulness and the major issues concerning the construct of mindfulness altogether. Clearly operationalizing mindfulness is an important precursor to any other step in the research process for it stands to help define the scope and boundaries of the topic under investigation. In the second section, we review the most commonly used methods in mindfulness research such as experiments, surveys, and mindfulness-based interventions (MBIs). We also discuss several key methodological limitations including self-report measures, and internal and external validity. Understanding the limitations of existing designs may help mindfulness researchers to refine their own research designs and contribute to this growing body of literature.

The final section discusses some exciting avenues for future mindfulness research. These include areas of research that are being pursued by contemporary researchers in mindfulness, but have yet to find their way into published formats. Here we encourage the development of a mindfulness taxonomy that distinguishes between the different types, elements, dosages, and effects of mindfulness and meditation. Additionally we discuss the promise of multi-level mindfulness research and contextual influences to advance our understanding of workplace mindfulness. Lastly, we urge researchers to expand the breadth of their existing methodologies to incorporate experiential sampling methods, qualitative research, and neuroscientific approaches. Building on existing methodologies, integrating new techniques may help paint a more comprehensive picture of mindfulness in the workplace.

The construct of mindfulness: navigating conceptual waters

Mindfulness has a wide variety of conceptualizations. While we applaud the diversity of definitions researchers have applied to advance the study of mindfulness, the vast range of mindfulness constructs may confuse rather than enlighten researchers. Workplace mindfulness has been studied at both the individual and collective level through a number of depictions. In the simplest form, individual mindfulness is anchored by present-moment awareness and by the nonjudgmental observation of thought (e.g. Brown and Ryan 2003; Dane 2011). Collective mindfulness departs from individual mindfulness by focusing on a group's overall cognitive processes of organizing instead of individual characteristics. In this chapter, we focus on individual mindfulness; however, for a more extensive review of collective mindfulness research, see Gärtner's chapter in this book.

At the individual level alone, mindfulness has been depicted as: 1) as a state of mind, 2) an enduring dispositional trait, 3) an attitude, 4) a cognitive or affective process, 5) a set of behaviors, 6) a type of meditation, and 7) an intervention program (Vago and Silbersweig 2012).

Not only can it be easy to get lost amongst so many conceptualizations, the wide variability of the term raises several construct validity flags. Construct validity is an estimate of the degree to which a measure consistently assesses the construct it intends to (Jarvis, MacKenzie, and Podsakoff 2003). Below, we visit some of the main concerns related to construct validity from a methods perspective.

Construct validity of mindfulness scales

Depending on how one chooses to define mindfulness, careful scale selection may strengthen construct validity. One aspect to consider is face validity; which refers to the extent to which a measure appears to capture the construct it purports to assess (Mosier 1947). If mindfulness is depicted as attention and awareness (e.g. Brown and Ryan 2003) it may hold low face validity for those that consider mindfulness to include facets such as attitude (e.g. Bishop *et al.* 2004) or intention (e.g. Shapiro *et al.* 2004). Relatedly, a second aspect of content validity refers to the extent to which a measure represents the entire construct (Lawshe 1975). In this case, some scales may not adequately represent the entire domain of mindfulness, or they may be measuring different aspects of the construct.

We, like others before us (Grossman and Van Dam 2011; Kudesia and Nyima, in press; Lutz *et al.* 2007), suggest that understanding the traditional context of "mindfulness" may enrich the study of mindfulness in the workplace. Nomological validity describes the relationships between the construct in question and other constructs within the theoretical context (Cronbach and Meehl 1955). Mindfulness has a profound nomological network and scholars would be remiss to simply pluck one concept from these ancient eastern traditions, in particular Buddhism, without considering the broader context. When mindfulness is considered within its original context and in relation to other contemplative constructs, it is a means to enlightenment; yet mindfulness in the workplace has primarily been studied as a form of attention (Grossman 2008). Without accounting for the contemplative context, mindfulness research may be at risk of misconstruing the original meaning of the word. Indeed, several scholars have expressed concern that some mindfulness scales actually assess behavior, which is a departure from the original Buddhist conceptualization where mindfulness is reflected by attentional, cognitive, and affective qualities

(Chambers *et al.* 2009; Mikulas 2011; Rapgay and Bystrisky 2009). There is a balance to be struck by scholars between understanding the nomological framework of mindfulness and framing research in such a way that many audiences, those familiar with Buddhism or otherwise, can still appreciate the value of their contribution. We encourage researchers to consider the differences in definitions, contexts, populations, and outcomes when selecting their mindfulness instruments.

In workplace mindfulness research, the Mindful Attention Awareness Scale (MAAS: Brown and Ryan 2003) tends to be most often cited. Prior research has validated the MAAS with clinical and non-clinical populations (Brown and Ryan 2003; MacKillop and Anderson 2007) suggesting it is an appropriate measure for general work populations. Indeed, the widespread use of the MAAS by organization scholars is a credit to the instrument. Although the MAAS is frequently applied, it has received some criticism (e.g. Grossman 2008). For example, the MAAS has been found to be insufficient for those who prefer mindfulness to be operationalized as more than a one-dimensional construct centered around attention and awareness (Baer *et al.* 2006; Chiesa 2013; Walach *et al.* 2007). Further, as an individual's attention improves, the measure may depict them as less mindful as they become acutely aware of their mind wandering (Chiesa 2013; Grossman 2008).

Presently there are over ten different scales that assess mindfulness (see Table 4.1). Another scale that is often referenced in the literature is the Five-Facet Mindfulness Questionnaire (FFMQ; Baer *et al.* 2006). Baer and colleagues (2006) created the FFMQ based on five key mindfulness skills: observing, acting with awareness, describing, non-reactivity and non-judgment of inner experience. The FFMQ is conceptually distinct from the MAAS as it includes an attitudinal aspect in addition to attention and awareness. Although these two scales measure different facets of mindfulness, both purport to measure "mindfulness" without any distinction. When multiple measures of mindfulness are in agreement, these measures are said to possess high convergent validity (Cunningham *et al.* 2001). Of the many mindfulness scales, there is evidence to suggest that these measures exhibit little or even no correlation with each other (Thompson and Waltz 2007). Baer and colleagues (2006) compared five of these mindfulness scales and examined the correlations of mindfulness with other constructs such as openness to experience, self-compassion, and neuroticism.

They found that in most cases, correlations were significant and in predicted directions but that they varied widely. This is hardly surprising given the many conceptualizations of mindfulness.

In sum, mindfulness scales can be distinguished along five dimensions. First, as discussed above, scales differ by the particular facets of mindfulness they seek to measure. Additionally, scales differ by how mindfulness is scored. Some produce multiple scores for the different elements of mindfulness, and others generate a single total uni-dimensional score. For example, the Cognitive and Affective Mindfulness Scale (CAMS; Feldman *et al.* 2007) assesses several facets of mindfulness but represents them with one total score whereas the Kentucky Inventory of Mindfulness Skills (KIMS; Baer *et al.* 2004) produces four separate subscale scores for each facet of the construct. A third distinction lies in the state or trait assessment of mindfulness. The MAAS (Brown and Ryan 2003) and the Toronto Mindfulness Scale (TMS; Lau *et al.* 2006; Davis, Lau, and Cairns 2009) have both a state and trait version of their scales. Fourth, some scales were developed under the guidance of experts with long-term mindfulness practices and may thereby reflect a more traditional contemplative conceptualization of mindfulness. For example, the Freiburg Mindfulness Inventory (FMI; Buchheld, Grossman, and Walach 2001) was developed with input from Buddhist experts at a Vipassana meditation retreat. A last point of differentiation is the audience the scale is intended for: clinical or non-clinical, and novice or experienced meditators. For example, the FMI (Buchheld, Grossman, and Walach 2001) was created specifically for experienced meditators whereas the Southampton Mindfulness Questionnaire (SMQ; Chadwick *et al.* 2008) and the TMS (Lau *et al.* 2006) distinguish between novice and experienced meditators. The CAMS (Feldman *et al.* 2007) was developed for and tested only on clinical populations but other scales (e.g. the MAAS) were tested on both clinical and non-clinical populations. These and other self-report measures of mindfulness are summarized in Table 4.1 (see also Baer *et al.* 2006; Bergomi, Tschacher, and Kupper 2013b; Chiesa 2013; Sauer *et al.* 2013).

Organizing multiple conceptualizations of mindfulness

What we, in line with others (e.g. Chiesa 2013), are attempting to convey is that mindfulness is a complex construct lacking scholastic

Table 4.1 *Mindfulness scales*

Scale	Description	Example
Mindful Attention Awareness Scale (MAAS; Brown and Ryan 2003)	A 15-item trait measure rated on a 6-point Likert-type scale assessing the awareness and attention to internal and external events.	"I do jobs or tasks automatically, without being aware of what I'm doing"; "I find myself preoccupied with the future or the past"
Five-Facet Mindfulness Questionnaire (FFMQ ; Baer *et al.* 2006)	A 39-item trait measure rated on a 5-point Likert-type scale encompassing five facets of mindfulness: 1) observing, 2) describing, 3) acting with awareness, 4) non-judgment of inner experience, and 5) non-reactivity to inner experience.	"I perceive my emotions and feelings without having to react to them"; "I rush through activities without being really attentive to them"
Mindfulness/Mindlessness Scale (MMS; Bodner and Langer, 2001)	A 21-item Western, trait measure rated on a 5-point Likert-type scale assessing four factors (novelty seeking, engagement, flexibility, and novelty producing). One of the original measures of mindfulness, this scale examines cognitive flexibility and avoidance of mindless or habitual behavior.	"I try to think of new ways of doing things"; "I am rarely aware of changes"; "I make many novel contributions"
Freiburg Mindfulness Inventory (FMI; Buchheld, Grossman, and Walach 2001)	A 30-item trait measure rated on a 4-point Likert scale (the short form uses 14 items) assessing nonjudgmental present moment awareness, openness to (negative) experience, and distinguishes meditator experience.	"When I notice an absence of mind I gently return to the here and now"; "I notice how emotions express themselves through my body"

Scale	Description	Example items
Kentucky Inventory of Mindfulness Skills (KIMS; Baer et al. 2004)	A 39-item trait measure rated on a 5-point Likert-type scale assessing four aspects of mindfulness (observing, describing, acting with awareness, and accepting without judgment).	"I'm good at finding the words to describe my feelings"; "I make judgments about whether my thoughts are good or bad"; "I notice the smells and aromas of things"
Cognitive and Affective Mindfulness Scale (CAMS; Feldman et al. 2007)	A 12-item trait measure rated on a 4-point Likert-type scale that assesses four elements of mindfulness (attention, present focus, awareness, acceptance/non-judgment) to yield a single total score.	"I am preoccupied with the future"; "I am easily distracted"; "I am able to accept the thoughts and feelings I have"
The Toronto Mindfulness Scale (TMS; Lau et al. 2006)	A 10-item state and trait measure rated on a 5-point Likert-type scale that can distinguish levels of meditation expertise and non-meditators.	"I experience myself as separate from my changing thoughts and feelings"; "I was curious what my mind was up to from moment to moment"
Southampton Mindfulness Questionnaire (SMQ; Chadwick et al. 2008)	A 16-item trait measure on a 7-point Likert-type scale that assesses mindful responses to negative thoughts, and distinguishes meditation experience and psychosis.	Each question starts with: "Usually when I have distressing thoughts and images:" "I am able just to notice them without reacting"; "I am able to accept the experience"
Philadelphia Mindfulness Scale (PMS; Cardaciotto et al. 2008)	A 20-item trait measure on a 5-point Likert-type scale along two sub-scales of mindfulness (acceptance and present moment awareness).	"I try and distract myself when I feel unpleasant emotions"; "I tell myself I shouldn't feel sad"

Table 4.1 (*cont.*)

Scale	Description	Example
Developmental Mindfulness Survey (DMS: Solloway and Fisher 2007)	A 30-item trait measure rated on an 8-point Likert-type scale assessing one dimension of mindfulness development to capture the additive qualities of a mindfulness practice. Scale development was created through both qualitative (thematic analysis of journal entries) and quantitative approaches.	"I notice more of my body sensations"; "I feel like I'm seeing for the first time"; "Mindfulness makes me feel thankful for things I usually take for granted"
Self-Other Four Immeasurables (SOFI; Kraus and Sears 2009)	A 16-item trait measure rated on a 5-point Likert-type scale that evaluates 8 thoughts, feelings, and behaviors towards one's self and others (friendly, hateful, angry, joyful, accepting, cruel, compassionate, mean).	"Indicate to what extent you have thought, felt, or acted this way toward yourself and others during the past week: Hateful – toward myself Hateful – toward others"
Comprehensive Inventory of Mindfulness Experiences beta (CHIME-β; Bergomi, Tschacher, and Kupper 2013a)	A 28-item trait measure designed for general populations to assess 4 main factors of mindfulness: 1) present awareness; 2) accepting, nonreactive, and insightful orientation; 3) describing of experiences; and 4) open, non-avoidant orientation.	"I can accept myself as I am"; "I rush through my activities without paying much attention to them"; "I find it hard to put my thoughts into words"; "I tend to suppress unpleasant feelings and thoughts"

consensus and in need of some organizing framework. One simple suggestion is to re-label the many mindfulness questionnaires to reflect the specific characteristics of interest (Grossman 2011). On a theoretical level, the various conceptualizations of individual mindfulness can perhaps be better understood through Vago and Silbersweig's (2012) S-ART framework for understanding the effects of mindfulness training. They suggest that mindfulness is cultivated through 1) self-awareness; 2) self-regulation; and 3) self-transcendence. Respectively, each of these three parts is said to enhance meta-awareness, modulation of behavior, and relationships with oneself so that one can focus on the needs of others. S-ART draws on six further mechanisms through which mindfulness training works: "(1) intention and motivation; (2) attention regulation; (3) emotion regulation; (4) memory extinction and reconsolidation; (5) prosociality; (6) non-attachment and de-centering" (p. 15).

This framework may provide the scaffolding to integrate the different facets of mindfulness and facilitate a broader understanding of the term. For example, researchers could study the self-awareness aspect of mindfulness through the mechanism of attention regulation with the MAAS (Brown and Ryan 2003). Alternatively, self-regulation could be studied through memory extinction and reconsolidation drawing on Langer's (1989) form of mindfulness. Here mindfulness is a cognitive process that interprets phenomena in new ways from multiple perspectives, without the automaticity of habitual mental processes that rely on past information (Langer 1989; Langer and Moldoveanu 2000; Weick *et al.* 1999; Weick and Sutcliffe 2006). Self-transcendence could be studied through non-attachment and de-centering, or through prosociality to illuminate the aspects of mindfulness that cultivate empathy and other-orientation.

The S-ART provides a helpful map for the study of mindfulness, yet, with its wide scope, it may be at risk of covering so many elements of mindfulness that outcomes and mediators become intertwined. A critical first step for scholars is to clearly define mindfulness to establish the boundaries of the populations and relationships under study, distinguishing the antecedents and outcomes from the measures themself. Gaining more clarity around the operationalization of the construct may strengthen methodological design (Chambers *et al.* 2009) and ultimately lead to the development of more finely tuned measures (Rapgay and Bystrisky 2009). This in turn may allow for more precise measurement of the essential active ingredients of mindfulness.

In this section we addressed various conceptualizations of individual and collective mindfulness in organizational research along with several construct validity issues permeating the study of mindfulness. In doing so, we reviewed existing scales used to assess mindfulness and five ways to categorize them. Further, we suggested that the S-ART might be a helpful framework for researchers to organize and integrate these varying definitions and scales when designing their methodological approaches. In the next section we review the common methodological methods and instruments used in empirical studies of organizational mindfulness: surveys, experiments, and intervention designs. We also discuss the major concerns and areas of improvement for these methods.

Existing research methods

Survey research

Surveys are a widely applied method of studying mindfulness, particularly trait mindfulness. New researchers might ask themselves three general questions to bolster the overall validity of their survey studies. First, what measures are best suited to address the population and context? As discussed in the section above, mindfulness scales assess different conceptualizations of mindfulness thus some measures may fit one's research question better than others. If a researcher does not consider their audience, they may confuse novice meditators struggling with item miscomprehension or offend seasoned meditators that may be skeptical of the recent popular upsurge or 'McDonaldization' of mindfulness. Choosing language that resonates with both novice and advanced meditators may be one way to subdue skepticism related to the introduction of an ancient monastic practice to a corporate environment.

A second consideration is the temporal logistics (i.e. when and how often) around implementing surveys. A common process is to conduct pre- and post-surveys flanking an intervention, followed by a last survey several months after intervention completion. When to conduct follow-up surveys deserves some reflection as they help shed light on how long effects can be detected, and in what form they manifest.

Lastly, both timing and frequency of data collection decisions are of course subject to real world boundaries of access to participants, non-response rates, compliance, and attrition.

Surveys often rely on self-report scales that have been developed to measure personality traits and/or emotional and psychological states related to mindfulness. The third survey consideration is to reflect on how and if multi-source data can be incorporated to address the limitations of self-reported data. Clearly social desirability and objectivity can confound perception of some contexts. Multi-source data strengthens the overall study design and provides a first line of defense to the criticisms of self-report methods. These three considerations may offer researchers some respite from the limitations restricting survey methods. Such limitations are discussed below.

Limitations of survey methods

Self-report. Self-report measures have contributed greatly to furthering mindfulness research. Such psychometric scales are convenient, widely accepted, and empirically supported (Baer *et al.* 2004; Chiesa and Malinowski 2011; Sauer *et al.* 2013). Yet, it is widely recognized that there are methodological concerns related to self-report methods (Bergomi, Tschacher, and Kupper 2013a; Grossman 2008; Thompson and Waltz 2007; Van Dam, Earleywine, and Borders 2010). For instance, mindless behaviors have been associated with a lack of meta-awareness (e.g. Smallwood, McSpadden, and Schooler 2007), such that individuals unaware of their stream of consciousness may not be able to estimate their mind-wandering patterns (Cheyne, Carriere, and Smilek 2006). Self-report methods presume that an individual is self-aware enough to accurately respond (Grossman 2008; Grossman and Van Dam 2011; Van Dam, Earlywine, and Borders 2010). This may trigger a "construct representationalism" issue (Van Dam, Earleywine, and Borders 2010) where the construct validity of mindfulness may be weakened if subjects are not aware of the psychological processes supporting their task response. This line of thought exposes self-report survey research to greater vulnerability: discrepancies between actual and reported mindfulness; item miscomprehension; biased ratings from variable levels of respondent experience; scale construction; and inconsistencies from interrelationships among scales meant to distinguish the multiple facets of mindfulness (Baer 2011; Grossman 2008).

When relying on self-reported mindfulness, self-enhancement biases should be accounted for. Defensiveness, or a desire to protect one's individual self-concept, may restrict participants from accurately reporting, even unconsciously, behavior they are not proud of or that is socially devalued. In this vein, studies show there is a tendency toward bias in rejecting survey items associated with mindless behavior (Van Dam, Earleywine, and Danoff-Burg. 2009). One way to mitigate these effects is to recruit a third party to assess the individual when object-ivity is a concern (i.e. obtain supervisor assessments in addition to a self-report) or use unobtrusive methods such as content analysis of digital information (i.e. emails).

Internal validity. Internal validity refers to the extent to which researchers can be confident that mindfulness is the variable respon-sible for the measured effects, or, in other words, if there might be an alternative rationale that could explain results (Bachrach, Bendoly, and Podsakoff 2001). Particularly with cross-sectional surveys, the extent to which mindfulness causes the observed effects may be question-able (Chiesa and Malinowski 2011). In studies comparing meditators to non-meditators, the process of sample selection and demographic considerations may influence results and thus, should be clearly stated (Lykins, Baer, and Gottlob 2012). For example, if the type of medi-tation practiced by experienced meditators differs from techniques used by novice meditators, there may be further doubt cast on the reli-ability of findings (Chiesa and Malinowski 2011). One well-designed study matched their participants on age and education (Chan and Woollacott 2007) but not all studies follow suit (e.g. Jha *et al.* 2010; Valentine and Sweet 1999).

Common method bias. Common method bias is a further threat to internal validity. It refers to "variance that is attributable to the measurement method rather than to the constructs the measures represent" (Podsakoff *et al.* 2003, p. 879). Surveys, self-report data, and cross-sectional data are susceptible to method effects related to a long list of response biases such as halo effects, leniency effects, and timing effects (Fiske 1982). Cross-sectional assessments are at risk of variability that may arise from any ephemeral moodiness of one par-ticularly optimistic or despondent day. A further consideration is that assessments immediately following program completion may exagger-ate the acute effects of the intervention itself without accounting for longitudinal effects. Longitudinal outlooks are an integral component of mindfulness research, given research confirming the compounding nature of positive day-to-day experiences (Fredrickson *et al.* 2008). Mindfulness research should consider accounting for increased daily experiences resulting from a sustained meditation practice (Fredrickson *et al.* 2008). Researchers might also consider systematically collecting data at similar temporal checkpoints to allow for direct comparisons across studies, and staggering wait-list control groups to allow for a more long-term study of effects (de Vibe *et al.* 2012).

External validity. In general, survey research has good potential to exhibit strong external validity. For high external validity in mindfulness research in the workplace, choosing scales that are designed for general populations and all meditation levels is likely most appropriate. For example, the KIMS (Baer *et al.* 2004) was designed to measure mindfulness based on the dialectical behavior therapy (DBT; Linehan 1993) definition of mindfulness, but DBT uses shorter exercises in therapeutic contexts that are not necessarily rooted in meditation (Baer *et al.* 2006). The KIMS, then, may be a good fit for non-meditators in clinical populations. Lastly, selecting scales that are grounded in either information processing theory or contemplative traditions may further strengthen external validity by selecting the commensurate scale to match the context

Survey alternatives. The interrelationships of mindfulness and mindlessness are said to operate on subtler, non-conscious levels that may not be easily detected by introspection alone (Levinthal and Rerup 2006). As such, methods used to measure explicit phenomena may not be appropriate in mindfulness methodology. Implicit measures are advantageous in several contexts: 1) when the construct lies outside conscious awareness; 2) if evaluations are impacted by social desirability; 3) when there is a risk of disengaged participants; and 4) when participants are reluctant to reveal their attitudes (Uhlmann, Poehlman, and Nosek 2012). In situations where evaluation apprehension may occur, implicit or unobtrusive measures are especially appropriate to overcome any non-conscious posturing of the participant (e.g. an employee self-reporting job satisfaction in a survey distributed by their organization) (Leavitt, Fong, and Greenwald 2011).

One study indirectly measured mindfulness by assessing the disparity between implicit and explicit levels of self-esteem (Koole *et al.* 2009). They postulated that individuals higher in mindfulness would have less divergence between the two levels. Grossman (2011) suggests that mindfulness self-reports would benefit more from asking individuals to report how much they value characteristics and behaviors associated with mindfulness instead of how skilled they are in these respects. Another implicit measure might involve observing the level of self-criticism a participant expresses while completing a difficult, present-moment oriented task. Other alternatives include Frewen *et al.*'s (2014) method of Meditation Breath Attention Scores, which counts the number of times an individual is on task when meditating. Sauer *et al.* (2013) suggest researchers embrace alternatives like qualitative approaches, biological and neurological feedback, assessment from others in addition to self-report measures, language-based measures, or content analysis (e.g. Collins *et al.* 2009). Given the noted difficulties with self-report mindfulness, common method bias, construct validity and the complexities of measuring mindfulness altogether, incorporating alternative measures may benefit future research.

Experimental and intervention research

State mindfulness tends to be studied using experimental and intervention designs. The majority of mindfulness experiments employ MBIs that are largely based on a variation of Kabat-Zinn's (1994) Mindfulness-Based Stress Reduction (MBSR) program (Chiesa and Serretti 2009; Grossman *et al.* 2004) or a selective portion of it. As such, Chapter 5 in this book has been dedicated to MBIs. In general, there are three categories of experimental designs used in mindfulness studies: pre-experiments, quasi-experiments, and pure experiments.

Pre-experiments are experiments without control groups that use pre- and post-comparisons to capture the effects of a particular treatment (Campbell 1975). Some have suggested that a lack of control groups is too common in current mindfulness practices (Chiesa and Serretti 2011). We maintain that incorporating control groups is advisable wherever possible. There are various types of control groups a mindfulness study could incorporate: no-treatment controls, wait-list controls (e.g. Fredrickson *et al.* 2008); passive controls (e.g. mind-wandering exercises, Arch and Craske 2006; Kiken and Shook 2011; and mental silence, Manocha *et al.* 2011); active controls (e.g. relaxation training, Josefsson, Lindwall and Broberg 2014; and yoga, Sauer-Zavala *et al.* 2013); or perhaps a placebo where a group of participants nap in lieu of treatment.

Quasi-experiments use control groups, but not random assignment (Mark and Reichardt 2004). A lack of random assignment threatens the internal validity of the study since it is possible that groups are not comparable at baseline (Boruch *et al.* 2004) or that some bias may compromise the objectivity of the study. A recent meta-analytic review (de Vibe *et al.* 2012) examined thirty-one MBSR studies and found that the overall risk of bias was high for almost one third of the studies and urged authors to better report randomized controlled trial procedures (i.e. randomization, allocation, blinding). To suggest that randomization is important would be trite; however, in many cases, random assignment is not possible given participants are self-selecting into the study. Despite this issue, quasi-experiments provide reasonable estimates as to the causal impact of the intervention on the population under study (Mark and Reichardt 2004).

Pure experiments are those that are fully randomized between an experimental group and a control group (Boruch *et al.* 2004). In many disciplines randomized controlled studies mark the gold standard of experiments and mindfulness scholars should strive for such designs. An example of a well-executed intervention experiment conducted in the workplace is a study on the effects of meditation on work stress and anxiety (Manocha *et al.* 2011). The authors employed a three-arm randomized controlled trial designed to compare relaxation techniques, mental silence, and a no-treatment control group using a blindfolded lottery allocation system. Participants were instructed not to disclose their method of meditation to other participants or researchers involved in the study. Classes were held in similar rooms within the same institution, and at the same time. All meetings were matched for duration, breaks, and periods of time between sessions. Results found a significant improvement for the meditation group compared to both the relaxation and the wait-list control group in psychological strain and depression scores.

Systematic variation and standardization of interventions

Given the frequency with which interventions are used, researchers might consider invoking some standardization and systematic variation of intervention components in their design to ensure greater internal validity. Calculated attention to the content and duration of experimental design would do just that. An ordered approach to intervention procedures is thought provoking as there are endless conceivable permutations. Here we discuss three key areas: systematic study of temporal variation, meditation type, and mode of program delivery.

Temporal variation. Temporally, an intervention may be as long as eight weeks (e.g. MBSR training), or as brief as five days (e.g. Tang *et al.* 2007). Presently it is unclear why some interventions are more effective than others, or what components of an intervention – content, level of interaction, program duration, amount of class contact or home practice hours – have the most impact on participants. One study suggested that interventions intended to boost wellbeing and reduce psychological symptoms in a working population would be more effective if they were longer than four weeks and spanning at least seven sessions (Josefsson, Lindwall, and Broberg 2014). While there is evidence that actual time spent practicing mindfulness techniques is commensurate with enhanced affective experiences (Carmody and Baer 2008; Shapiro *et al.* 2008), it remains inconclusive what the optimal length of a program should be.

Presently, the relationships between in-class contact hours and mean effect sizes are unclear (Carmody and Baer 2009). More data is required to understand why some studies find significant positive associations between practice time and outcomes (Carmody and Baer 2008), and others do not (Davidson *et al.* 2003). Similarly, short mindfulness inductions in some studies have had success in manipulating mindfulness levels (Reb and Narayanan 2014; Reb, Narayanan, and Ho 2015) whereas others (Ruedy and Schweitzer 2010) have not. Systematically categorizing mindfulness interventions and identifying temporal checkpoints would allow for apple-to-apple comparisons. In this way, differences in mindfulness programming and any emergent or aggregate effects of a sustained practice could be better understood.

Type of meditation. Meditation practices differ widely by origin, for example, Tibetan Buddhist, Zen Buddhist, Taoist Buddhist, Vedic, and Chinese traditions. Lutz and colleagues (2008) argue that it is essential to distinguish the type of meditation practice, for neglecting to do so would be like using the word "'sport' to refer to all sports as if they were essentially the same" (p. 163). Deciding which type of meditation tradition, program, or technique to use is another point of variability as different approaches may yield varying effects (e.g., Baer 2003; Chiesa and Serretti 2011). Using mindfulness as an all-encompassing construct makes poor use of prior research that has distinguished that there are measurable differences among the multiple aspects of mindfulness.

Mindfulness-based stress reduction is mainly based on three techniques: hatha yoga, sitting meditation and body scan (Kabat-Zinn 1990); yet, even these three practices may have different outcomes. Sauer-Zavala and colleagues (2013) divided 141 undergraduates into three mindfulness conditions: yoga, body scan, and sitting meditation. Psychological wellbeing was enhanced most in the yoga condition; emotion regulation improved for both the yoga group and the body scan; and those in the sitting meditation condition were associated with the greatest increases in non-evaluative perspectives.

A further distinction among meditation practices is whether they can be categorized as focused attention (a voluntary focusing of attention on a chosen object) or open monitoring, a practice of non-reactive monitoring of experience as it unfolds (Lutz *et al.* 2008). Automatic self-transcending has been proposed as a third category, which involves techniques encouraging transcendence, in other words a meta-experience, of one's own activity (Travis and Shear 2010). We know that different parts of the brain are engaged in open monitoring compared to focused attention meditation (Lutz *et al.* 2008) and that these three meditation categories can be characterized by different brain wave patterns (Travis and Shear 2010). Mindfulness researchers should make efforts to understand the implications of these differences when designing their own studies.

The experiences that a participant has in an intervention and the study's ensuing outcomes may vary by the participant's level of expertise (Baer 2011; Grossman 2008). While unguided meditations may have powerful effects for advanced practitioners, even ten minutes of breath meditation may be excruciating for a beginner. As such, body scans, characterized by their frequent instruction, may be more practical for wider audiences (Koole *et al.* 2009). Since the measurement of mindfulness may be confounded by the individual experiences of the population (Masicampo and Baumeister 2007), considering the participants and their level of expertise will help guide the experimental design process.

Mode of delivery. In contrast to MBSR programs where participants meet weekly, other recent approaches use online or self-guided interventions (e.g. Hülsheger *et al.* 2012). The convenience of a self-guided intervention is considerable given the contrast to lengthy, facilitated studies. Logically it follows that different modes of program delivery will have associated benefits and limitations. Consider the differences between guided meditations that are experienced online versus in-person: autonomy, interaction levels, compliance, and attrition to name a few. The mode of program delivery will affect facilitator credibility, group dynamics, and other context effects (home vs. office practice). Studying the effects of such components as the time, length and location of sessions, intervals of data collection, facilitator skills, online or in-person sessions, and support materials used (e.g. handouts, home practice exercises, DVDs) is a worthy endeavor. Additional considerations when designing experimental or intervention studies are discussed below.

Limitations of experimental and intervention research

Experimental design and comparison groups. When structuring comparison groups, the research question and context should drive the study design. Wait-list controls may be attractive to researchers in instances where recruiting sufficient numbers of participants for long studies is arduous. Wait-list controls may also appeal to those conscious of ethical and face-validity concerns with using placebo controls or "sham meditations" (Fredrickson *et al.* 2008, p. 1047) on participants that have been attracted to the study with expectations to receive some form of mindfulness training. Passive controls, like mental silence or mind wandering exercises, allow for a comparison of multiple states of mind. Another option is the use of active control groups (e.g. yoga, relaxation training). Indeed, research from clinical literature strongly advocates the use of active controls in mindfulness research (MacCoon *et al.* 2012) in the event that other factors (i.e. social gatherings) are confounding effects. When evaluating the efficacy of mindfulness, matching as many conditions with an active control will aid in testing and isolating the active ingredient in the intervention (MacCoon *et al.* 2012). Although active controls require more resources and add another layer of complexity to experimental designs, they may help to circumvent experimental confounds related to the influence of other mental, emotional, and physiological benefits associated with mindfulness.

Internal validity. In experiments, even though an effect can be attributed with considerable confidence to the intervention, attributing causality specifically to mindfulness can nevertheless be difficult. Some argue that the effects of an intervention may be a result of other factors (e.g. self-control exercises) and any effects may result from an innumerable list of other causes (Masicampo and Baumeister 2007; Nyklicek and Kuijpers 2008). Consider, for example, the possibility that participants appear to be more mindful because they are more rested, and consequently alert, in the period of testing following the intervention. Or, in another case, perhaps participants show improved focus simply from harnessing their will power.

A recent meta-analysis on the effects of mindfulness meditation found that the MBSR curriculum had a larger positive effect on psychological wellbeing compared to solely practicing meditation training techniques (Eberth and Sedlmeier 2012). They theorized that the psychosocial nature of MBSR group meetings, the educational component, and expectations that the program could reduce stress – as its name implies – might amplify its effects. When designing an induction then, the methodology should distinguish between meditation types along with a rationale as to why that particular type was selected to show the linkages between cause and effect and potential confounds. Pinpointing the mechanisms of interest and systematically varying the elements in a mindfulness intervention is one way to choose the type of mindfulness practice and establish a stronger case for causality.

External validity. Findings from laboratory experiments may be criticized for their applicability to broader situations. Methodologically, intervention studies in the field exhibit stronger external validity by bringing experimental aspects out into the natural environment. While it has been said that field experiments in organizational mindfulness research are scarce (Dane and Brummel 2014), they appear in the literature more often than in other areas of organizational research, which largely feature laboratory experiments. Presently, any scarcity of mindfulness field interventions may be related more to the overall nascence of mindfulness research. Indeed, we find the relatively frequent use of field interventions in workplace mindfulness research laudable. As with any field intervention, there are challenges related to accessing organizations, recruitment, compliance, and attrition. Furthermore, complications ensue when coordinating schedules and garnering sufficient executive-level and management buy-in to support individuals taking time to practice mindfulness.

Suggestions for future research

In a short time, research on mindfulness in the workplace has built a compelling case for the impact of mindfulness in organizational settings. In this section we put forward suggestions for further research that we hope will refine what is currently known, and guide researchers as they advance this body of literature. We present four areas to organize such pursuits: 1) developing a taxonomy of mindfulness and meditation to distinguish their key elements; 2) understanding the interactions of mindfulness across individuals, groups and organizations; 3) neuroscientific approaches; and 4) applying mixed method approaches to capture the complexity and dynamism of mindfulness in the workplace.

Workplace mindfulness research would benefit greatly from the systematic analysis of mindfulness practices and their varying effects, potencies, and optimal configurations within organizations. Understanding the active ingredients, the expected outcomes of mindfulness practices, and the length of time such observed effects last is a worthy endeavor. Along these lines, it remains unclear if different mindfulness techniques (e.g. mindfulness meditation vs. transcendental meditation) have unique mechanisms specific to each practice (Chiesa and Malinowski 2011; Tanner *et al.* 2009). In contrast to the MBSR lengthy eight-week program(Kabat-Zinn 1994), it would be interesting to systematically catalogue the efficacy of alternative programs in the workplace (e.g. dialectical behavior therapy, Linehan 1993; acceptance and commitment therapy, Hayes, Strosahl, and Wilson 1999; integrative body-mind training, Tang 2009). Future research might study the use of different mindfulness exercises and programs as intervention techniques and their effectiveness in manipulating mindfulness levels to yield specific outcomes in the workplace (Carmody and Baer 2009).

A second area of future research might be to explore how mindfulness manifests in response to the context and the interactions between individuals, groups, and organizations. Empirical studies that describe contextual or group level antecedents of mindfulness in the workplace are critical for advancing the case for mindfulness practices at work. Yet, we know little about the contexts where low mindfulness might be preferable (Dane 2011), and whether such conditions are consciously induced or are a result of automatic processes. For example, can online clicking behavior be manipulated by a website to induce a mindful (or mindless) state that impacts purchasing patterns or task performance? Can mindfulness be induced to circumvent errors caused by automaticity in repetitive work settings? Should mindlessness be induced to help managers cope with the duress of impending layoffs? In addition to the impact that context may have on mindfulness in the workplace, research that examines the bottom-up and top-down effects of mindfulness in individuals, teams, and organizations offers exciting areas for new insight.

It appears that aggregating a group of individuals high in mindfulness does not necessarily have additive properties (Chan 1998) such that the group is also mindful (Leroy *et al.* 2013) but we know little about how a mindful organization might affect individual mindfulness, or how one very mindful team member might impact the group. One of the only multi-level studies we are aware of examined mindfulness at the individual and organizational level and the performance of financial advisors (Hensler, Lingham and Perelli 2013). They found that more mindful advisors in more mindful organizations performed better in dynamic markets. The overall dearth of multi-level mindfulness research in the workplace leaves many questions unanswered. If an individual undergoes mindfulness training, is there a mindfulness effect that ripples over into the team or firm level? Would a mindful workgroup simply be a group of present-moment oriented and accepting individuals or would higher mindfulness levels alter group dynamics, communication patterns, and shared mental models that result in higher functioning teams? At the group level, can mindfulness practices be used to enhance team effectiveness and cohesion? Additionally, in the wake of globalization, how might cross-cultural differences affect mindfulness in individuals and processes within multi-national corporations? We encourage future research to pursue the validation of mindfulness as a multi-level construct (e.g. Chen, Matthieu, and Bliese 2005) and examine how mindfulness operates at and between different levels of analysis.

A promising method for future research rests in neuroscientific approaches. The neurological effects of mindfulness and meditation have been examined in medical and psychological research for several decades. Neuroscientific studies may further ground mindfulness research in the workplace by offering insight into the mechanisms of mindfulness via neural correlates. Neuroscience has produced numerous findings that demonstrate patterns in neural activity showing how meditation affects cognitive functioning in the brain (Cahn and Polich, 2006; Lazar *et al.* 2005; Lutz *et al.* 2007; 2008). For instance, key cognitive mechanisms of breath-focused meditation can be directly mapped onto modern neuropsychology (Kudesia and Nyima, in press). In many cases, brain activity data is obtained using electroencephalography (EEG) or function magnetic resonance imaging (fMRI) to establish a brain profile. The EEG measures cortical and subcortical electrical activity by applying sensors either on the scalp or directly on the cortex. EEG metrics can be used to describe the frequency of the brain waves in different states (mindful vs. mindless) and in some studies, to categorize mental states during different types of meditation (Travis and Shear 2010). Takahashi and colleagues (2005), for example, studied the effects of Zen meditation by observing brain frequencies on EEG and heart-rate variability. Function magnetic resonance imaging uses high-resolution imaging to compare reliable snapshots of different regions of the brain. This method measures brain activity by capturing images of blood flow in the brain that represent neuronal activation. Thus, fMRI can be used to study which parts of the brain are being used and in what capacity. In this way Luders and colleagues (2009) compared the brain images of meditators against a group of non-meditators, controlling for demographics such as age, gender, or length of time maintaining meditative practices.

We appreciate that the field of neuroscience lends credibility to the advent of organizational mindfulness; however, we have two general cautions with fMRI and EEG methodologies. First, the complexity of fMRI technology and interpreting neuroimaging data can make it prone to false positives. The infamous study by Bennett and colleagues (2009) demonstrated that failure to correct for multiple comparisons in datasets could result in, astonishingly, finding brain activity in a dead fish. Second, relying on fMRI images presumes that the localized activation of a particular region of the brain can be conclusively associated with a particular behavior – a gross over-simplification of the brain's complex operating system (Menon and Uddin 2010); to explain behavior using neuronal activation explanations alone would be remiss.

Our final area of future research advocates the use of mixed method approaches to study mindfulness in the workplace. Mindfulness is a rich and dynamic construct that makes research on the topic endlessly complex. Mindfulness can be depicted as attention and awareness but even attention can be categorized into ten developmental stages when drawing from contemplative texts (e.g. Wallace 2006). Just as a caterpillar can take the form of an insect, cocoon or butterfly, depending on the individual and its context, mindfulness may also appear in different forms. To this end, we encourage industrial and organizational scholars to integrate qualitative and longitudinal approaches, and biofeedback data with traditional methods wherever possible.

Mindfulness stands to impact multiple facets of the human experience and conceivably, may take time to manifest. As such, quantitative data may not provide a comprehensive understanding of mindfulness in the workplace. Surveys and experiments conducted over shorter periods of time may not capture the valleys and peaks of meditation experiences (e.g. boredom, itchiness, anxiety, relaxation, tranquility, or interconnectedness). Interviews, open-ended questions, and journaling are effective ways in which researchers could collect qualitative data. Surveys may be complemented with qualitative approaches (e.g. background and follow-up interviews) that capture the individual differences and phenomenological experience of participants (e.g. Atkins and Parker 2012; Dane and Brummel 2014) or experiential sampling methods that draw on many data points over time. Applying multiple approaches over time would allow for a more comprehensive understanding of mindfulness and capture any curvilinear, non-polar aspects of mindfulness that can only be seen through frequent and extended observation. We fear that short-term studies using only quantitative data may miss the butterflies by fixating solely on cocoons.

As biofeedback technology becomes increasingly accessible, an exciting union between mindfulness research and cutting-edge technology is upon us. Whereas monitoring EEG signals was once a complex and costly process only feasible in laboratories, now thought-computing devices powered by EEG signals are available for mass consumption (e.g. Muse by InteraXon.ca). Such devices work by using sensors to pick up brain waves, which are then translated into data that can be processed to, for example, turn on lights or close the blinds. We urge future research to consider the integration of neuroscience along with other biological data where psychologists hold a history of expertise (e.g. rapid eye movement, electrocardiogram, skin testing, blood chemistry, and vital signs) into their data collection. Along these lines, Lutz and colleagues (2008) have suggested a *neurophenomenological* approach (Varela, Thompson, and Rosch 1991) to mindfulness research where individual accounts of firsthand experience are paired with quantitative neural methods. Smart phones present another fascinating point of access for researchers to apply experiential sampling methods. Consider the possibilities of combining smart phones with thought computing devices to collect neural data. Worthy of note are the ethical issues that may accompany the monitoring and harvesting of brain wave activity in the workplace. As mass amounts of neural data are acquired, organizational mindfulness scholars should stay aware of who is collecting the data, intended objectives, and the implications associated with research findings. In sum, we put forth that mixed method approaches may offer a richer means of studying the different depths and forms of mindfulness.

Conclusion

The study of mindfulness is in its infancy and the pioneers of the field have contributed compelling findings that have demonstrated potentially far-reaching benefits. As interest from organizational scholars grows and this body of literature develops, we urge researchers to take heed that the study of mindfulness is as complex as it is alluring. This chapter began by reviewing how organizational scholarship has studied the different conceptualizations of mindfulness, and the related construct validity issues. Next we discussed the common methods of analysis and their limitations. Lastly, we proposed three general directions for further research that we believe hold great promise. We hope this chapter has helped describe the prevailing methodologies and their limitations to offer researchers a guide that leads to a more rigorous study of mindfulness in the workplace. In this way, together we can advance the impact of mindfulness research in both theory and practice.

References

Allen, T. D. and Kiburz, K. M. (2012). Trait mindfulness and work-family balance among working parents: the mediating effects of vitality and sleep quality. *Journal of Vocational Behavior*, 80(2), 372–9.

Arch, J. J. and Craske, M. G. (2006). Mechanisms of mindfulness: Emotion regulations following a focused breathing induction. *Behavior Research and Therapy*, 44, 1849–58.

Atkins, P. W. B. and Parker, S. K. (2012). Understanding individual compassion in organizations: the role of appraisals and psychological flexibility. *Academy of Management Review*, 37(4), 524–46.

Bachrach, D. G., Bendoly, E., and Podsakoff, P. G. (2001). Attributions of the "Causes" of Group Performance as an Alternative Explanation of the Relationship Between Organizational Citizenship Behavior and Organizational Performance. *Journal of Applied Psychology*, 86, 1285–93.

Baer, R. A. (2003). Mindfulness training as a clinical intervention: a conceptual and empirical review. *Clinical Psychology: Science and Practice*, 10, 125–43.

   (2011). Measuring mindfulness. *Contemporary Buddhism*, 12, 241–61.

Baer, R. A., Smith G. T., and Allen, K. B. (2004). Assessment of mindfulness by self-report: the Kentucky Inventory of Mindfulness Skills. *Assessment*, 11, 191–206.

Baer, R. A., Smith, G. T., Hopkins, J., Krietemeyer, J., and Toney, L. (2006). Using self-report assessment methods to explore facets of mindfulness. *Assessment*, 13, 27–45.

Bennett, C. M., Baird, A. A., Miller, M. B., and Wolford, G. L. (2009). Neural correlates of interspecies perspective taking in the post-mortem Atlantic Salmon: an argument for multiple comparisons correction. *Neuroimage*, 47, S125.

Bergomi, C., Tschacher, W., and Kupper, Z. (2013a). Measuring mindfulness: first steps towards the development of a comprehensive mindfulness scale. *Mindfulness*, 4, 18–32.

Bergomi, C., Tschacher, W., and Kupper, Z. (2013b). The assessment of mindfulness with self-report measures: existing scales and open issues. *Mindfulness*, 4, 191–202.

Bishop, S. R., Lau, M., Shapiro, S., Carlson, L., Anderson, N. D., Carmody, J., ... Devins, G. (2004). Mindfulness: a proposed operational definition. *Clinical Psychology: Science and Practice*, 11(3), 230–41.

Bodner, T. E. and Langer, E. J. (2001). Individual differences in mindfulness: The Mindfulness/Mindlessness Scale. Poster presented at the 13th annual American Psychological Society Conference, Toronto, Ontario, Canada.

Boruch, R. F., Wesiburd, D., Turner, H. M., Karpyn, A., and Littell, J. (2004). Randomized controlled trials for evaluation and planning. In L. Bickman and D. Rog (eds.). *The SAGE Handbook of Applied Social Research*. 2nd edn. Thousand Oaks, CA: SAGE Publications, Inc., pp. 147–81.

Brown, K. W. and Ryan, R. M. (2003). The benefits of being present: mindfulness and its role in psychological wellbeing. *Journal of Personality and Social Psychology*, 84, 822–48.

Buchheld, N., Grossman, P., and Walach, H. (2001). Measuring mind-fulness in insight meditation (Vipassana) and meditation-based psycho-therapy: the development of the Freiburg Mindfulness Inventory (FMI). *Journal for Meditation and Meditation Research*, 1, 11–34.

Cahn, B. R. and Polich, J. (2006). Meditation states and traits: EEG, ERP, and neuroimaging studies. *Psychological bulletin*, 132(2), 180.

Campbell, Donald T. III. (1975). "Degrees of Freedom" and the case study. *Comparative political studies*, 8(2), 178–93.

Cardaciotto, L., Herbert, J. D., Forman, E. M., Moitra, E., and Farrow, V. (2008). The assessment of present-moment awareness and accept-ance: the Philadelphia Mindfulness Scale. *Assessment*, 15(2), 204.

Carmody, J. and Baer, R. (2008). Relationships between mindfulness prac-tice and levels of mindfulness, medical and psychological symptoms and well-being in a mindfulness-based stress reduction program. *Journal of Behavior Medicine*, 2, 23–33.

Carmody, J., and Baer, R. A. (2009). How long does a mindfulness-based stress reduction program need to be? A review of class contact hours and effect sizes for psychological distress. *Journal of Clinical Psychology*, 65(6), 627–38.

Chadwick, P., Hember, M., Symes, J., Peters, E., Kuipers, E., and Dagnan, D. (2008). Responding mindfully to unpleasant thoughts and images: reli-ability and validity of the Southampton mindfulness questionnaire (SMQ). *British Journal of Clinical Psychology*, 47, 451–5.

Chambers, R., Gullone, E., and Allen, N. B. (2009). Mindful emotion regulation: an integrative review. *Clinical Psychology Reviews*, 29, 560–72.

Chan, D. (1998). Functional relations among constructs in the same content domain at different levels of analysis: a typology of composition mod-els. *Journal of Applied Psychology*, 83(2), 234–46.

Chan, D. and Woollacott, M. (2007). Effects of level of meditation experi-ence on attentional focus: is the efficiency of executive or orientation networks improved? *The Journal of Alternative and Complementary Medicine*, 13(6), 651–8.

Chen, G., Matthieu, J. E., and Bliese, P. D. (2005). A framework for conduct-ing multi-level construct validation. *Research in Multi Level Issues*, 3, 273–303.

Cheyne, J. A., Carriere, J. S. A., and Smilek, D. (2006). Absent-mindedness: lapses of conscious awareness and everyday cogni-tive failures. *Consciousness and Cognition*, 15, 578–92.

Chiesa, A. (2013). The difficulty of defining mindfulness: current thought and critical issues. *Mindfulness*, 4(3), 255–68.

Chiesa, A. and Malinowski, P. (2011). Mindfulness-based approaches: are they all the same? *Journal of Clinical Psychology*, 67(4), 404–24.

Chiesa, A. and Serretti, A. (2009). Mindfulness-based stress reduction for stress management in healthy people: a review and meta-analysis. *Journal of Alternative and Complementary Medicine*, 15(5), 593–600.

Chiesa, A. and Serretti, A. (2011). Mindfulness based cognitive therapy for psychiatric disorders: a systematic review and meta-analysis. *Psychiatry Research*, 187(3), 441–53.

Collins, S. E., Chwala, N., Hsu, S. H., Grow, J., Otto, J. M., and Marlatt, G. A. (2009). Language-based measures of mindfulness: initial validity and clinical utility. *Psychology of Addictive Behaviors*, 23, 743–9.

Cronbach, L. J. and Meehl, P. E. (1955). Construct validity in psychological tests. *Psychological Bulletin*, 52(4), 281.

Cunningham, W. A., Preacher, K. J., and Banaji, M. R. (2001). Implicit attitude measures: consistency, stability, and convergent validity. *Psychological Science*, 12(2), 163–70.

Dane, E. (2011). Paying attention to mindfulness and its effects on task performance in the workplace. *Journal of Management*, 37(4), 997–1018.

Dane, E. and Brummel, B. J. (2014). Examining workplace mindfulness and its relations to job performance and turnover intention. *Human Relations*, 67(1), 105–28.

Davidson, R. J., Kabat-Zinn, J., Schumacher, J., Rosenkrantz, M., Muller, D., Santorelli, S. F., ... Sheridan, F. S. (2003). Alterations in brain and immune function produced by mindfulness meditation. *Psychosomatic Medicine*, 65, 564–70.

Davis, K. M., Lau, M. A., and Cairns, D. R. (2009). Development and preliminary validation of a trait version of the Toronto Mindfulness Scale. *Journal of Cognitive Psychotherapy*, 23(3), 185–97.

De Vibe, M., Bjorndal, A., Tipton, E., Hammerstrom, K., and Kowalski, K. (2012). Mindfulness Based Stress Reduction (MBSR) for improving health, quality of life, and social functioning in adults. *Campbell Systematic Reviews*, 8(3), 1–128.

Eberth, J. and Sedlmeier, P. (2012). The effects of mindfulness meditation: a meta-analysis. *Mindfulness*, 3, 174–89.

Feldman, G., Hayes, A., Kumar, S., Greeson, J., and Laurenceau, J. P. (2007). Mindfulness and emotion regulation: the development and initial validation of the cognitive and affective mindfulness scale–revised (CAMS-R), *Journal of Psychopathology and Behavioral Assessment*, 29, 177–90.

Fiske, S. T. (1982). Schema-triggered affect: applications to social perception. In M. S. Clark and S. T. Fiske (eds.), *Affect and Cognition: 17th Annual Carnegie Mellon Symposium on Cognition*. Hillsdale, MI: Lawrence Erlbaum, pp. 55–78.

Fredrickson, B. L., Cohn, M. A., Coffey, K. A., Pek, J., and Finkel, S. M. (2008). Open hearts build lives: positive emotions, induced through loving-kindness meditation, build consequential personal resources. *Journal of Personality and Social Psychology*, 95, 1045–62.

Frewen, P. A., Unholzer, F., Logie-Hagan, K. R. J., and MacKinley, J. D. (2014). Meditation Breath Attention Scores (MBAS): test-retest reliability and sensitivity to repeated practice. *Mindfulness*, 5, 161–9.

Grossman, P. (2008). On measuring mindfulness in psychosomatic and psychological research. *Journal of Psychosomatic Research*, 64, 405–8.

Grossman, P. (2011). Defining mindfulness by how poorly I think I pay attention during every-day awareness and other intractable problems for psychology's (re)invention of mindfulness: comment on Brown et al. (2011). *Psychological Assessment*, 23(4), 1034–40.

Grossman, P. and Van Dam, N. T. (2011). Mindfulness, by any other name ...: trials and tribulations of *sati* in western psychology and science. *Contemporary Buddhism*, 12(1), 219–39.

Grossman, P., Niemann, L., Schmidt, S., and Walach, H. (2004). Mindfulness-based stress reduction and health benefits. A meta-analysis. *Journal of Psychosomatic Research*, 57(1), 35–43.

Hafenbrack, A., Kinias, Z, and Barsade, S. G. (2013). Debiasing the mind through meditation: mindfulness and the sunk cost bias. *Psychological Science*, 25 (2), 369–76.

Hayes, S. C. Strosahl, K. D., and Wilson, K. G. (1999). *Acceptance and commitment therapy: an experiential approach to behavior change*. New York: Guilford Press.

Hensler, P., Lingham, T., and Perelli, S. (2013). Learning from disruptive market events: a study of financial advisor behavior. *The International Journal of Management and Business*, 4(1), 12–27.

Hülsheger, U. R., Alberts, H. J. E. M., Feinholdt, A., and Lang, J. W. B. (2012). Benefits of mindfulness at work: on the role of mindfulness in emotion regulation, emotional exhaustion, and job satisfaction. *Journal of Applied Psychology*, 98(2), 310–25.

Jarvis, C. B., MacKenzie, S. B., and Podsakoff, P. M. (2003). A critical review of construct indicators and measurement model misspecification in marketing and consumer research. *Journal of Consumer Research*, 30(2), 199–218.

Jha, A. P., Stanley, E. A., Kiyonaga, A., Wong, L., and Gelfand, L. (2010). Examining the protective effects of mindfulness training on working memory capacity and affective experience. *Emotion*, 10, 54–64.

Josefsson,T., Lindwall, M., and Broberg, A. G. (2014). The effects of a short-term mindfulness based intervention on self-reported mindfulness, decentering, executive attention, psychological health, and coping style: examining unique mindfulness effects and mediators. *Mindfulness*, 5, 18–35.

Kabat-Zinn, J. (1990). *Full catastrophe living: using the wisdom of your mind to face stress, pain and illness*. New York: Dell Publishing.

    (1994). *Wherever you go, there you are: mindfulness meditation in everyday life*. New York: Hyperion.

Kiken, L. and Shook, N. (2011). Looking up: mindfulness increases positive judgments and reduces negativity bias. *Social Psychological and Personality Science*, 2, 425–31.

Koole, S. L., Govorun, O., Cheng, C. M., and Gallucci, M. (2009). Pulling yourself together: meditation promotes congruence between implicit and explicit self- esteem. *Journal of Experimental Social Psychology*, 45, 1220–6.

Kraus, S. and Sears, S. (2009). Measuring the immeasurables: Development and initial validation of the self-other four immeasurables (SOFI) scale based on Buddhist teachings on loving kindness, compassion, joy, and equanimity. *Social Indicators Research*, 92(1), 169–81.

Kudesia, R. S. and Nyima, T. (in press). Mindfulness contextualized: a review and integration of Buddhist and neuropsychological approaches to cognition. *Mindfulness*.

Langer, E. (1989). *Mindfulness*. Reading, MA: Addison-Wesley.

Langer, E. J. and Moldoveanu, M. (2000). The construct of mindfulness. *Journal of Social Issues*, 56(1), 1–9.

Lau, M. A., Bishop, S. R., Segal, Z. V., Buis, T., Anderson, N. D., Carlson, L., Devins, G. (2006). The Toronto mindfulness scale: development and validation. *Journal of Clinical Psychology*, 62, 1445–68.

Lawshe, C. H. (1975). A quantitative approach to content validity. *Personnel Psychology*, 28, 563–75. doi:10.1177/0748175612440286.

Lazar, S. W., Kerr, C. E., Wasserman, R. H., Gray, J. R., Greve, D. N., Treadway, M. T., ... Fischl, B. (2005). Meditation experience is associated with increased cortical thickness. *NeuroReport*, 16, 1893–7.

Leavitt, K., Fong, C. T., and Greenwald, A. G. (2011). Asking about well-being gets you half an answer: intra-individual processes of implicit and explicit job attitudes. *Journal of Organizational Behavior*, 32, 672–87.

Leroy, H, Anseel, F., Dimitrova, N., and Sels, L. (2013). Mindfulness, authentic functioning, and work engagement: a growth modeling approach. *Journal of Vocational Behavior*, 82(3), 238–47.

Levinthal, D. and Rerup, C. (2006). Crossing an apparent chasm: bridging mindful and less-mindful perspectives on organizational learning. *Organization Science*, 17(4), 502–13.

Linehan, M. M. (1993). *Cognitive-behavioral treatment of borderline personality disorder*. New York: Guilford Press.

Luders, E., Toga, A. W., Lepore, N., and Gaser, C. (2009). The underlying anatomical correlates of long-term meditation: larger hippocampal and frontal volumes of gray matter. *Neuroimage, 45*, 672–8.

Lutz, A., Dunne, J. D., and Davidson, R. J. (2007). Meditation and the neuroscience of consciousness. In P. Zelazo, M. Moscovitch, and E. Thompson (eds.), *Cambridge handbook of consciousness*. New York: Cambridge University Press, pp. 480–551.

Lutz, A., Slagter, H. A., Dunne, J. D., and Davidson, R. J. (2008). Attention regulation and monitoring in meditation. *Trends in Cognitive Science, 12*(4), 163–9.

Lykins, E. L. B., Baer, R. A., and Gottlob, L. R. (2012). Performance-based tests of attention and memory in long-term mindfulness meditators and demographically matched non-meditators. *Cognitive Therapy and Research, 36*, 103–14.

MacCoon, D. G., Imel, Z. E., Rosenkranz, M. A., Sheftel, J. G, ... and Lutz, A. (2012). The validation of an active control intervention for Mindfulness Based Stress Reduction (MBSR). *Behavior Research and Therapy, 50*(1), 3–12.

MacKillop, J. and Anderson, E. J. (2007). Further psychometric validation of the mindful attention and awareness scale. *Journal of Psychopathology and Behavioral Assessment, 29*, 289–93.

Manocha, R., Black, D., Sarris, J., and Stough, C. (2011). A randomized, controlled trial of meditation for work stress, anxiety and depressed mood in full-time workers. *Evidence-based Complementary and Alternative Medicine*. eCAM 2011, 2011:960583. Epub 2011 Jun7.

Mark, M. M. and Reichardt, C. S. (2004). Quasi-experimentation. In L. Bickman and D. Rog (eds.), *The SAGE Handbook of Applied Social Research*. 2nd edn. Thousand Oaks, CA: SAGE Publications, Inc, pp. 182–213.

Masicampo, E. J. and Baumeister, R. F. (2007). Relating mindfulness and self-regulatory processes. *Psychological Inquiry, 18*, 255–8.

Menon, V. and Uddin, L. Q. (2010). Saliency, switching, attention and control: a network model of insula function. *Brain Structure and Function, 214*(5–6), 655–67.

Mikulas, W. L. (2011). Mindfulness: significant common confusions. *Mindfulness, 2*, 1–7. DOI 10.1007/s12671-010-0036-z.

Mosier, C. I. (1947). A critical examination of the concepts of face validity. *Educational and Psychological Measurement, 7*(2), 191–205.

Mrazek, M. D., Franklin, M. S., Phillips, D. T., Baird, B., and Schooler, J. W. (2013). Mindfulness training improves working memory capacity and GRE performance while reducing mind wandering. *Psychological Science*, 24, 776–81.

Nyklicek, I. and Kuijpers, K. F. (2008). Effects of mindfulness-based stress reduction intervention on psychological well-being and quality of life: is increased mindfulness indeed the mechanism? *Annals of Behavioral Medicine*, 35(3), 331–40.

Podsakoff, P. M., MacKenzie, S. B., Lee, J. Y., and Podsakoff, N. P. (2003). Common method biases in behavioral research: a critical review of the literature and recommended remedies. *Journal of Applied Psychology*, 88(5), 879–903.

Rapgay, L. and Bystrisky, A. (2009). Classical mindfulness: an introduction to its theory and practice for clinical application. *Annals of the New York Academy of Science*, 1172, 148–62.

Reb, J. and Narayanan, J. (2014). The influence of mindful attention on value claiming in distributive negotiations: evidence from four laboratory experiments. *Mindfulness* 5(6), 756–66.

Reb, J., Narayanan, J., and Chaturvedi, S. (2014). Leading mindfully: two studies on the influence of supervisor trait mindfulness on employee well-being and performance. *Mindfulness*, 5(1), 36–45.

Reb, J., Narayanan, J., and Ho, Z. W. (2015). Mindfulness at work: Antecedents and consequences of employee awareness and absent-mindedness. *Mindfulness*, 6(1), 111–22.

Roche, M. and Haar, M. J. (2013). Leaders life aspirations and job burnout: a self-determination theory approach. *Leadership and Organization Development Journal*, 34(6), 515–31.

Ruedy, N. and Schweitzer, M. (2010). In the moment: the effect of mindfulness on ethical decision making. *Journal of Business Ethics*, 95, 73–87.

Sauer, S., Walach, H., Schmidt, S., Hinterberger, T., Lynch, S., Büssing, A., and Kohls, N. (2013). Assessment of mindfulness: review on state of the art. *Mindfulness*, 4, 3–17.

Sauer-Zavala, S. E., Walsh, E. C., Eisenlohr-Moul, T. A., and Lykins, E. L. B. (2013). Comparing mindfulness-based intervention strategies: differential effects of sitting meditation, body scan, and mindful yoga. *Mindfulness*, 4, 383–8.

Shapiro, S. L., Katz, J., Wiley, S. D., Capuano, T., and Baker, D. M. (2004). The effects of mindfulness-based stress reduction on nurse stress and burnout. *Holistic Nursing Practice*, 18(6), 302–8.

Shapiro, S. L., Oman, D., Thoresen, C. E., Plante, T. G., and Flinders, T. (2008). Cultivating mindfulness: effects on well-being. *Journal of Clinical Psychology*, 64, 840–62.

Smallwood, J., McSpadden, M., and Schooler, J. W. (2007). The lights are on but no one's home: meta-awareness and the decoupling of attention when the mind wanders. *Psychonomic Bulletin and Review*, 14, 527–33.

Solloway, S. G. and Fisher, W. P. (2007). Mindfulness practice: a Rasch variable construct innovation. *Journal of Applied Measurement*, 8(4), 359–72.

Takahashi, T., Murata, T., Hamada, T., Omori, M., Kosaka, H., Kikuchi, M., ... Wadaa, Y. (2005). Changes in EEG and autonomic nervous activity during meditation and their association with personality traits. *International Journal of Psychophysiology*, 55(2), 199–207.

Tang, Y. Y. (2009). *Exploring the brain, optimizing the life.* Beijing: Science Press.

Tang Y. Y., Ma, Y., Wang, J., Fan, Y., Feng, S., Lu, Q., ... Posner, M. I (2007). Short term meditation training improves attention and self regulation. *Proceedings of the National Academy of Sciences*, 104(43), 17152–6.

Tanner, M. A., Travis, F., Gaylord-King, C., Haaga, D. A., Grosswald, S., and Schneider, R. H. (2009). The effects of the transcendental meditation program on mindfulness. *Journal of Clinical Psychology*, 65, 574–89.

Thompson, B. L. and Waltz, J. (2007). Everyday mindfulness and mindfulness meditation. Overlapping constructs or not? *Personality and Individual Differences*, 43, 1875–85.

Travis, F. and Shear, J. (2010). Focused attention, open monitoring and automatic self-transcending: categories to organize meditations from Vedic, Buddhist and Chinese traditions. *Cognition and Consciousness*, 19(4), 1110–18.

Uhlmann, E. L., Poehlman, T. A., and Nosek, B. A. (2012). Automatic associations: personal attitudes or cultural knowledge? In J. Hanson (ed.), *Ideology, Psychology, and Law.* Oxford University Press, pp. 228–60.

Vago, D. R. and Silbersweig, D. A. (2012). Self-awareness, self-regulation, and self-transcendence (S-ART): a framework for understanding the neurobiological mechanisms of mindfulness. *Frontiers in Human Neuroscience*, 6(296), 1–30.

Valentine, E. R. and Sweet, P. L. (1999). Meditation and attention: a comparison of the effects of concentrative and mindfulness meditation on sustained attention, *Mental Health, Religion and Culture*, 2(1), 59–70.

Van Dam, N. T., Earleywine, M., and Borders, A. (2010). Measuring mindfulness? An item response theory analysis of the Mindful Attention Awareness Scale. *Personality and Individual Differences*, 49, 805–10.

Van Dam, N. T., Earleywine, M., and Danoff-Burg, S. (2009). Differential item function across meditators and non-meditators on the Five Facet Mindfulness Questionnaire. *Personality and Individual Differences*, 47, 516–21.

Varela, F. J., Thompson, E., and Rosch, E. (1991). *The embodied mind: cognitive science and human experience*. Cambridge, MA: MIT Press.

Walach, H., Nord, E., Zier, C., Dietz-Waschkowski, B., Kersig, S., Schubach, H. (2007). Mindfulness-Based Stress Reduction as a method for personnel development: a pilot evaluation. *International Journal of Stress Management*, 14, 188–98.

Wallace, B. A. (2006). *The attention revolution: unlocking the power of the focused mind*. Boston, MA: Wisdom Publications Inc.

Weick, K. E. and Sutcliffe, K. (2006). Mindfulness and the quality of organizational attention. *Organization Science*, 17(4), 514–24.

Weick, K. E., Sutcliffe, K. M., and Obstfeld, D. (1999). Organizing for high reliability: processes of collective mindfulness. *Research in Organizational Behavior*, 21, 81–123.

5 Applying mindfulness in the context of work: mindfulness-based interventions

HUGO J. E. M. ALBERTS AND UTE. R. HÜLSHEGER

Introduction

Since its introduction to the mainstream of western medicine and society in the late 1970s (Kabat-Zinn 1990), mindfulness has received considerable scholarly attention. Over the last decade, scientific research on mindfulness has increased strongly, approaching the concept from both a practical and theoretical angle. For instance, different mindfulness training programs have been developed and tested, using a wide range of target populations. Training programs such as mindfulness-based stress reduction (MBSR; Kabat-Zinn 1982), mindfulness-based cognitive therapy (MBCT; Segal, Williams, and Teasdale 2002), and mindfulness-based eating awareness training (Kristeller, Baer, and Quillian Wolever 2006), have been used successfully to treat emotional and behavioral disorders, such as borderline personality disorder, major depression, chronic pain, or eating disorders (cf. Bishop *et al.* 2004). A growing body of empirical research has found evidence for the effectiveness of mindfulness-based interventions (MBIs) (a) to reduce symptoms in clinical samples (for meta-analytic reviews, see Bohlmeijer *et al.* 2010) and (b) to promote psychological wellbeing in non-clinical samples (Collard, Avny, and Boniwell 2008). Besides its practical application, different studies have attempted to uncover the underlying mechanisms of mindfulness, aiming to understand the construct in terms of processes such as self-regulation, impulsivity, executive functioning, and memory (see, for instance, Fetterman *et al.* 2010).

While mindfulness has achieved an undeniable position in the field of clinical and personality psychology, it has only recently started to gain attention in the field of industrial and organizational (IO) psychology and organizational scholarship. Theoretical papers have discussed the role of mindfulness for performance (Dane and Brummel 2014), employee wellbeing (Glomb *et al.* 2011), and relationships (Atkins and Parker 2012). Furthermore, a number of empirical studies have recently been published, focusing mostly on trait mindfulness and MBIs. These studies have provided initial evidence for the beneficial effects of mindfulness in the context of leadership (Reb, Narayanan, and Chaturvedi 2014), in the context of recovery (Marzuq and Drach-Zahavy 2012), for work-family balance (Allen and Kiburz 2012), for employee engagement (Leroy *et al.* 2013), for sleep quality and stress reduction (Klatt, Buckworth, and Malarkey 2009), for emotion regulation at work (Hülsheger, Alberts, Feinholdt, and Lang, 2013), for job satisfaction (Hülsheger *et al.* 2013), and job performance (Dane and Brummel 2014). This line of research is still in its infancy and many questions remain unanswered.

The role of mindfulness in the context of work can be studied from different perspectives. One can focus on natural (i.e., independent of training) between-person differences in mindfulness (trait), on natural within-person fluctuations in mindfulness (state), or on the effect of MBIs. In the present chapter we aim to contribute to the integration of mindfulness into the field of IO psychology by focusing on MBIs. Specifically, we will describe various forms of MBI, provide a detailed account of the different elements used in these interventions, and finally discuss how they might affect work-related outcomes. In doing so, we draw on findings and interventions from clinical as well as IO psychology, including our own recent intervention (Hülsheger *et al.* 2013).

Learning more about the elements of mindfulness interventions may be of interest not only for practitioners – who may wish to integrate them into occupational health promotion programs – but also for researchers. Studying the relation between mindfulness and work-related outcomes using MBIs bears certain advantages: first, finding an effect of MBIs on the outcomes of interest helps to draw causal conclusions. This is usually difficult when mindfulness is assessed with self-report measures in cross-sectional or diary designs, making it difficult to assess whether mindfulness truly is the causal agent in the mindfulness-outcome relationship. Second, findings will have direct practical implications in that they show whether or not MBIs may be effective and useful in organizations.

Elements of MBIs

Mindfulness entails a way of relating to oneself and reality. The goal of mindfulness interventions is to teach participants to become aware of body sensations, thoughts, and emotions and to relate to them with an open, nonjudgmental attitude (Shapiro, Astin, Bishop, and Cordova 2005). Such an open state of mind can be cultivated by repeated practice. It is important to note that mindfulness is related to, but does not equal meditation. Although mindfulness is often predominantly associated with meditation, the range of practical mindfulness exercises vastly extends beyond formal meditational practice. In other words, "sitting on a cushion" is merely one way of cultivating "an openhearted, moment-to-moment, nonjudgmental awareness" (Kabat-Zinn 2005, p. 24). Especially in the context of work, in which time pressure, deadlines, and tight schedules are often the order of the day, the integration of mindfulness in daily life routines and working habits is an important consideration.

The aim of this section is to briefly discuss the most commonly used mindfulness practices, both formal and informal, that are well documented and researched and are part of the MBSR program, developed by Kabat Zinn (Kabat-Zinn 1982; 1990). Formal exercises include meditation practices as well as movement practices, such as mindful yoga or mindful walking. Informal exercises, on the other hand, involve paying full attention in a mindful way to what one is doing or experiencing at a given moment.

Formal meditation exercises

In the following, three formal mindfulness meditation exercises are described. These are an inherent part of mindfulness interventions and performed during group sessions, guided by the mindfulness trainer. Participants are also encouraged to perform them at home on a daily basis. To help them do so, participants usually receive audio files in which the trainer guides them through the respective meditations.

Body scan. The body scan, as the name suggests, entails bringing awareness to each part of the body. Participants are first instructed to pay attention to their posture and then direct attention to their breathing. After this, attention is brought to different body parts, starting with the feet and moving up from there. During the exercise, participants pay attention to different physical sensations present in a specific area of the body. After attention has been briefly focused on a particular region of the body, one is instructed to move on to the next region. During the exercise, many find themselves easily distracted by thoughts, bodily sensations, or sounds. When distraction occurs, the participant is instructed to gently return attention to the body part at hand. Participants are encouraged to do so without blaming themselves or reacting in frustration, as the occurrence of distracting thoughts or sensations is inevitable and it requires extensive practice to reduce them. In addition, when paying attention to the body, one might become aware of painful or unpleasant sensations (e.g. neck or back pain). Instead of altering, ignoring, or suppressing these sensations, one simply notices them on a moment-by-moment basis.

Sitting meditation. Whereas the body scan uses the body as an object of attention, the sitting meditation takes the breath as the main focus of attention. Participants are instructed to sit in an upward position with a straight back, preferably with their eyes closed. After becoming briefly aware of current posture, the participant directs attention to the breathing. He or she notices the physical sensations of the breathing, such as the air moving into the nostrils and the chest expanding. As soon as the mind begins to wander, the participant simply notices the distracting thought without evaluation, and returns his or her attention to the breath in a kind way.

Three-minute breathing space. The three-minute breathing space is a very brief mindfulness meditation that can help to integrate mindfulness into everyday life. It enables one to disrupt automatic patterns of thinking and behavior and increase acceptance-based coping. The exercise commonly involves the following three steps. The first step is asking oneself "Where am I?" "How am I?" "What am I thinking?" In this way, one steps outside the "doing mode" for a moment, disrupts habitual patterns and introduces awareness of the current experience. The second step involves a single focus of attention. Attention is directed away from thinking and focused on the breath. During the third and last step, attention is expanded so that it also includes awareness of body sensations. The focus here is on the body as a whole. The three-minute breathing space involves a direct way of coping, characterized by awareness and willingness to experience what is present.

Obstacles and practical advice. Especially in a work context where performance, achievements, and evaluations are salient, mindfulness exercises can be (mis-)perceived as something one must become good at. Therefore, before and during formal mindfulness exercises it is important to emphasize that it is not the goal of the practice to monitor and evaluate one's performance as being good or bad. Quite the contrary, participants are encouraged to be kind and compassionate to themselves. This means that they are encouraged not to negatively evaluate or punish themselves if they were distracted by thoughts, but to simply observe and accept what happened. Perceiving mindfulness exercises in terms of success and failure will negatively interfere with the ability to be present and will increase the likelihood of negative emotions and thoughts. In a similar way, experiencing boredom or negative emotions can stimulate thoughts supporting the belief that one is not able to meditate. This can be prevented by stressing that the goal of the exercise is not to experience a certain state or to stay focused all the time, but rather to become aware of what is happening in the present. Participants are informed that being distracted or experiencing difficult emotions are not signs of failure, but rather natural processes.

Obviously, during working hours, it is often difficult, if not impossible, to spend fifteen minutes lying down performing a body scan or focusing on our breath with our eyes closed. However, formal exercises can be adapted. While the body scan is most often carried out in a lying position, it is possible to use a sitting position as well. Moreover, the duration can be altered. Both longer (e.g. forty-five minutes) and shorter versions (e.g. fifteen minutes) of the sitting meditation and body scan have been used in practice and research. In our own intervention (Hülsheger *et al.* 2013), an eight-minute body scan was performed twice. For some people, starting with shorter meditations and building from there is more effective in terms of adherence than starting with full fifteen-minute meditation sessions. The three-minute breathing space may be particularly useful in this respect because of its short duration. First, in order to build a habit, participants can be asked to use the breathing space at three fixed times during a day. Next, when participants are used to the exercise, they can use the exercise whenever they feel the need. In the latter case, the exercise is used as a way of coping with emotions, thoughts, feelings, or sensations. For instance, when an employee experiences stress at work, he may pause for a moment and use the exercise to disrupt the negative cycle of stress-related thoughts. By taking some time to connect to the body, he may also become aware of bodily stress responses, allowing for appropriate measurements (e.g. taking a break).

Often, integrating more extensive formal mindfulness practices in an already busy daily life requires careful planning and communication. It is advisable to let people find out themselves what time and which location for performing the exercises works best for them. While some people find it more feasible to practice in the morning before going to work, others may benefit more from practice in the evening after work. Moreover, informing family members about the practice can help to minimize interruptions during practice. Repeating a practice on a regular basis using the same time and location is likely to result in a habit, which will lead to increased effects.

Informal exercises

Above and beyond these formal exercises, mindfulness interventions also involve informal exercises that aim at enhancing mindful awareness during everyday activities. They require a single focus of attention and the ability to gently turn back to the object of attention. The object of attention can be anything, ranging from a conversation with a colleague to eating lunch. We predict that these exercises are particularly useful when attempting to integrate mindfulness at the workplace, because they do not necessarily require additional time or environmental changes. There are virtually endless examples of informal practices, making it impossible to list and describe them all. We have attempted to categorize the most important informal exercises and briefly explain them in the context of work.

Awareness of routine activities. Routine activities are activities performed regularly, often on a daily basis. Most routine activities require little conscious attention, because they are highly automatized. Examples include taking a shower, driving or walking to the workplace, or eating lunch. The idea is to focus attention fully on the activity; the body movements, the sight, the sensations. When thoughts or other distractions emerge, one notices them and brings back attention to the task at hand. For instance, when eating mindfully, one eats slowly and attention is mainly directed at the experience in the present moment, which includes physical movements and the taste and smell of the food. Thus, rather than doing multiple things at the same time (such as reading while eating, talking on the phone while driving home, thinking about work while taking a shower), one adopts a single focus of attention. As part of mindfulness training programs, participants are encouraged to pick a few of these routine activities and to practice performing them in a mindful way. Since it is not time consuming and involves activities that are performed on a daily basis, this exercise can easily be implemented into one's workday. Participants may pick activities such as being mindful while having lunch, being mindful while walking to the copy machine, or being mindful while driving home from work.

Body awareness. The awareness of the body that is cultivated through the body scan can be implemented in daily life by regularly paying attention to the body throughout the day in various circumstances. One can pay attention to the posture and become aware of physical sensations such as pain or tension. Jobs requiring lifting, monotonous work tasks, uncomfortable work postures, repetitive movements, and prolonged periods at computer terminals have been found to be associated with physical problems such as neck/back pain and occupational repetitive strain injuries (Aaras, Horgen, and Ro 2000). Mindful awareness of these sensations is likely to enhance early detection and prevention of physical complaints. One can, for instance, implement daily moments of mindful awareness by setting an alarm at random intervals in order to disrupt repetitive movements or become aware of one's posture.

Awareness of impulsive and reactive patterns. Many daily patterns of thinking and behavior are habitual (unconscious) reactions to experiences or events. Failing to perform well at work may immediately trigger negative self-critical thoughts and judgments. The experience of sadness can result in a direct attempt to push away the unwanted feeling. Receiving a snide remark from a colleague may cause us to raise our voice and say things we regret afterwards. In all these examples, behavior is guided by automatic patterns. Mindfulness requires awareness of these patterns as they arise during the day. While it may sometimes be difficult to become aware before the onset of an impulsive reaction, becoming aware afterwards can also be beneficial because it may enhance detection of similar patterns in the future.

Awareness during social interaction. Practicing mindfulness in a social context involves using the interaction with the other person(s) as a single point of focus. Instead of multitasking during a conversation with a colleague or thinking about what to say next, attention is directed at the current conversation. In contrast to identifying with one's own assumptions and reacting impulsively, mindfulness requires an open, nonjudgmental attitude during the conversation characterized by deep listening, perspective taking and allowing room for the other to respond. Moreover, mindfulness during social interaction can involve speaking with awareness. Examples include pausing before speaking, monitoring one's thoughts and considering the impact of speaking them out loud. Most jobs require social interaction and regular communication with clients, colleagues, and supervisors. Practicing awareness during social interaction is therefore another exercise that can easily be implemented into one's everyday working life.

Differences among MBIs

Research on mindfulness interventions started by investigating Kabat Zinn's MBSR program (Kabat-Zinn 1982; 1990). Today, a variety of different programs and interventions, varying in duration, target population, and delivery mode have been developed and tested. Moreover, several clinical therapeutic approaches have integrated mindfulness components into the treatment procedure, for instance Dialectical Behavior Therapy (Linehan 1993) and Acceptance and Commitment Therapy (Hayes, Strosahl, and Wilson 1999). This section will focus on the differences among interventions that are primarily concerned with the cultivation of mindfulness, rather than exploring the aforementioned therapeutic approaches.

Duration

Long-term mindfulness interventions. Most clinically oriented mindfulness interventions involve eight weeks of practice. For instance, MBSR (Kabat-Zinn 1982), MBCT (Segal, Williams, and Teasdale 2002) and mindfulness-based relapse prevention (Witkiewitz, Marlatt, and Walker 2005) include eight weekly meetings and daily practice. Jean Kristeller's mindfulness-based eating awareness training (Kristeller, Baer, and Quillian Wolever 2006) is a ten-week course. Participants of these programs meet on a weekly basis. Typically, the weekly sessions take two hours or more and consist of mindfulness practices (e.g., breath awareness or mindful yoga) and discussing the homework, exercises, and experiences of the last week. In between weekly meetings, participants are encouraged to conduct formal mindfulness practices at home on a daily basis for about forty-five minutes.

The rationale behind this high level of practice is that mindfulness cannot be regarded as a quick solution to problems. The primary aim of mindfulness is to cultivate a mindset that is characterized by open awareness and observation. Instead of occasionally using mindfulness techniques to cope with setbacks or stress, the goal is to achieve an overall change in one's relationship with thoughts, emotions, and sensations. Mindfulness involves (continual) awareness of automatic processes and maintaining open and focused awareness, in all kinds of situations, both easy and difficult, and in both one's private as well as work life. In other words, increasing mindfulness involves a continual process that relates to a profound and ongoing change in perception, behavior, and cognition, rather than a temporary employment of strategies that help one to "become present in the now" again.

In order to change (problematic) automatic patterns of behavior and thinking, continual awareness may be required. Changing a habit that has been active for many years takes time (Baumeister *et al.* 1994). For instance, an employee who strongly identifies with his negative, judgmental thoughts, will need time to become aware of the various manifestations and consequences of these thoughts, both at work and at home, and practice coping with them in a mindful way as soon as they are noticed. In a similar vein, an employee who is almost constantly in the "doing mode," rushing through activities and experiencing difficulties with psychological detachment from work, will need time and practice to restore the balance with the "being" mode again. Because a "mindful" mindset involves an *overall* tendency to pay "complete attention to the experience on a moment-to-moment basis" (Marlatt and Kristeller 1999, p. 68), it is not solely represented in the domain of work, but operational in various domains of life, demanding a rather profound change.

This notion is supported by research showing that structural changes often do not emerge until several weeks of training have passed. For instance, a study by Baer, Carmody, and Hunsinger (2012) showed that significant improvements in perceived stress did not occur until week four of the mindfulness intervention. Further support is offered by research comparing expert meditators to novice meditators, revealing that after extensive meditation training, minimal effort is needed to sustain attentional focus (Brefczynski-Lewis *et al.* 2007). In addition, some studies have found that the total duration of formal home mindfulness practice, also referred to as mindfulness "dose effects," predicts positive outcomes like psychological symptom reduction, psychological wellbeing, and perceived stress (Carmody and Baer 2008; Speca *et al.* 2000). However, this relationship has not been reported by all studies (see, for instance, Carmody, Reed, Kristeller, and Merriam 2008). Besides practice duration, practice *quality* has been found to contribute to improvements in psychological symptoms as well (Del Re *et al.* 2012).

Low-dose mindfulness interventions. While most clinical mindfulness programs have adopted the above described eight-week duration, the expansion of mindfulness in non-clinical fields has led to the development of interventions characterized by a different duration. Examples of variations in duration include four fifty-minute sessions within a three-week period (Jennings and Jennings 2013), three weekly forty-five-minute sessions of meditation exercises (Call, Miron, and Orcutt 2014), and four forty-five-minute sessions four times a week for two weeks (Mrazek *et al.* 2013). While the MBSR program requires participants to commit to about 45 minutes of daily mindfulness practice, low-dose interventions typically require less time for home practice, such as ten minutes (Mrazek *et al.* 2013) or even no home practice at all (Call, Miron, and Orcutt 2014; Jennings and Jennings 2013).

Especially in the context of work, a common barrier for participants in long-term, time-consuming interventions concerns the integration of daily practices into their workday and busy lives. Researchers have therefore adapted traditional mindfulness interventions, tailoring them to the needs of working adults. For instance, Klatt and colleagues (2009) developed a low-dose mindfulness intervention, involving weekly one-hour group meetings and twenty minutes of daily formal mindfulness practice over eight weeks. Furthermore, group meetings were held at the worksite during lunchtime, thereby facilitating participation for employees. Similarly, Wolever and colleagues (2012) adapted the MBSR into a program consisting of twelve weekly one-hour group meetings that can be delivered at worksites.

In an attempt to examine the effect of session time on outcomes, a review by Carmody and Baer (2009) revealed no evidence for reduced effectiveness of low-dose interventions compared to standard eight-week interventions. The correlation between mean effect size and number of session hours was nonsignificant for both clinical and nonclinical samples. Although this review only addressed outcome measures related to psychological distress, the findings suggest that low-dose interventions can be considered as an effective alternative to the more extensive programs.

Experimentally induced mindfulness. Very brief mindfulness interventions are most frequently used in lab settings to investigate the immediate effects and tackle the underlying mechanisms of mindfulness practice. In most studies, participants are instructed to apply mindfulness exercises for a brief period of time. For instance, in a study by Mohan and colleagues (2011), a control group waited quietly whereas a meditation group was exposed to an audio-guided twenty-minute meditation session. After this, all participants were exposed to a stress induction during which physiological stress responses were recorded. Sympathetic nervous system responses to the stress of the meditation group were found to be significantly lower compared to the control group. A study by Campbell-Sills, Barlow, Brown, and Hofmann (2006) addressed the short-term effects of mindfulness on coping with emotions. More specifically, participants were either instructed to mindfully accept or suppress their emotions while viewing a distressing film. Results indicated that the acceptance group reported greater recovery after the film and had a decreased heart rate during the film. In sum, previous studies have revealed that short-term mindfulness practice can temporarily have an impact on emotion, mood, stress physiology, and cognitive performance (see also Erisman and Roemer 2010; Feldman *et al.* 2010), thereby contributing to the understanding of the direct impact of mindfulness practice.

When comparing brief mindfulness manipulations to the earlier described long-term interventions, important questions concern the transferability of the observed effects. Is it possible to induce or increase mindfulness using fifteen-minute manipulations? And if so, can the results obtained from this induction be generalized or compared to the effects observed in long-term training? First, it should be noted that brief mindfulness inductions increase state mindfulness (the degree to which one is fully immersed in the present moment), rather than trait mindfulness (the general tendency of being mindful). State mindfulness can be measured with the Toronto Mindfulness Scale (TMS; Lau *et al.* 2006), a scale that addresses the extent to which participants were aware and accepting of their experiences during a former meditation exercise. Experimental studies have indeed found that brief mindfulness instructions can increase state levels of mindfulness, as reflected by higher scores on the TMS (see for instance Garland *et al.* 2013). Obviously, state and trait mindfulness are strongly related. Individuals with a high trait mindfulness or individuals engaging in regular meditation practice are likely to experience higher daily levels of state mindfulness; they experience mindfulness more intensely, more often, and over longer periods of time (Brown and Ryan 2003). Thus, although a temporary state of mindfulness is not necessarily related to the tendency to be mindful in ordinary daily life, the behavioral and cognitive effects that follow from such a state may form an accurate reflection of the behavior and cognition of a person with a high level of trait mindfulness.

Delivery mode

Not only the duration, but also the mode of delivery of mindfulness interventions has been adapted in recent years and mindfulness interventions have obtained a position in the rapidly expanding domain of e-coaching and e-mental health programs. For instance, a number of self-guided, online mindfulness interventions have appeared and research on their effectiveness has, so far, yielded promising results (Krusche *et al.* 2012; Wolever *et al.* 2012). Moreover, e-coaching has been used as an addition to face-to-face mindfulness training. For instance, a study by Van Berkel and colleagues (2013) tested an intervention aimed at improving work engagement and energy balance, added eight sessions of e-coaching to eight weeks of in-company mindfulness training. These recent online developments may be particularly interesting in the context of work. Self-administered online interventions are a cost-effective way to reach a large group of employees. In addition, gaining insight in the progress and effectiveness of an intervention by incorporating online measurement tools is interesting from both a scientific and organizational point of view. Detailed feedback on the progress of employees may provide useful information for further enhancement of the intervention and may at the same time prevent drop out by enabling monitoring of employees who are in need of extra attention (for instance because of early signs of burnout symptoms).

In our own study (Hülsheger, Alberts, Feinholdt, and Lang 2013), we investigated the effectiveness of a self-guided two-week mindfulness intervention, involving daily practice of formal and informal mindfulness exercises. In a diary booklet, participants received background information on mindfulness and instructions on when and how to perform formal mindfulness meditation exercises and informal exercises. Furthermore, participants received a CD with guided mindfulness meditations and daily reminders via email. Results were promising and revealed that participants in the intervention group experienced less emotional exhaustion, more job satisfaction, and better emotion regulation abilities than participants in the wait-list control group.

A downside of such fully self-administered interventions concerns the inability to directly discuss exercises with a trained professional and share experiences with and learn from other participants; a process that may not only increase conceptual understanding but enhance connectedness to other employees as well.

Linking MBIs to work-related outcomes

In the following section, some work-related consequences of mindfulness practice will be discussed. The emphasis is on the aspects of mindfulness practice responsible for different work-related outcomes, rather than the outcomes per se. The beneficial effects of mindfulness in the context of work are manifold and it is beyond the scope and feasibility of the present chapter to provide an exhaustive overview of all potential work-related consequences of mindfulness. We will therefore focus on emotion regulation, stress, and performance as some key outcomes and use these to illustrate how both informal and formal mindfulness practices may influence these outcomes.

Emotion regulation

Many jobs require the ability to successfully cope with difficult emotions and researchers have argued that the positive effects of mindfulness may be especially strong in emotionally demanding jobs (cf. Glomb *et al.* 2011).

Employees working in occupations involving interactions with the public are confronted with high emotional demands on a daily basis; specifically they have to comply with emotional display rules that are prescribed by the work role, occupation, or organization and that govern the expression of emotions, a work situation that has been described as emotional labor (Hochschild 1983). For instance, a flight attendant is required to appear happy and friendly, irrespective of what her true feelings are. Whenever actually felt emotions do not coincide with emotional display rules, employees need to regulate their emotions (Holman, Martinez-Iñigo, and Totterdell 2008). In this type of situation, employees frequently engage in surface acting, a form of emotion regulation that has been shown to be negatively related to employee health and wellbeing (Hülsheger and Schewe 2011). When employees engage in surface acting, they change the outward emotional expression without changing the underlying feeling. Most jobs have positive display rules; they consequently require employees to display positive and hide negative emotions. Surface acting consequently involves suppressing negative and faking positive emotional expressions (Grandey 2000). It has been argued that surface acting impairs employee health and wellbeing because it is effortful and depletes mental resources, it undermines employees' sense of authenticity, and it hinders positive social interactions (Côté 2005; Grandey 2003; Hülsheger and Schewe 2011).

Surface acting can be regarded as a form of experiential avoidance (Hayes, Strosahl and Wilson 1999) which is the very opposite of mindfulness-based emotional coping. Mindfulness theory suggests that mindfulness facilitates affect and emotion regulation (Shapiro, Carlson, Astin, and Freedman 2006) and it can therefore be expected to help employees deal with high emotional demands without engaging in detrimental forms of emotion regulation such as surface acting (Hülsheger *et al.* 2013). The following elements of MBIs promote adaptive coping with emotionally demanding situations and difficult emotions.

Exposure. Mindfulness exercises such as the three-minute breathing space foster the willingness to experience current (emotional) states without judgment or avoidance, even if these are negative. For instance, receiving a snide remark by a customer or receiving negative feedback at work may cause an employee to experience anger and may trigger the impulse to react aggressively. Mindful regulation requires awareness of the anger and willingness to stay in contact with it, without giving in to the impulse to act aggressively.

Observation. By intentionally focusing in a nonjudgmental way on the experience and content of the emotion, the "observing self" (Deikman 1982) is strengthened. This allows one to dis-identify from the emotion, thereby decreasing the chance that behavior will be guided by the emotion. In other words, mindful awareness creates room between the aggressive impulse and the reaction to the customer, enabling a more flexible emotional response (Shapiro, Carlson, Astin, and Freedman 2006). Through repeated exercise of this technique, the employee may cultivate a different *relationship* with difficult emotions. Instead of perceiving them as unwanted, which will trigger attempts to avoid or suppress the emotion, one can accept them as an inevitable, but transient part of the human experience. This element of acceptance and non-judgment is also cultivated during the body scan and sitting meditation, in which distractions and feelings are simply noticed and observed, without judging them or the self for experiencing them.

Awareness of emotions. A pre-requisite for the acceptance-based way of coping is awareness of the emotion. Emotional responses are represented on both a mental and physical level. Repeated exercise of the body scan and three-minute breathing space increases recognition of physical signals that accompany emotions, such as tension or restlessness (Creswell, Way, Eisenberger and Lieberman 2007). The three-minute breathing space exercise is a literal pause that enables observation of the current situation and experience. It may help to increase clarification of emotional experiences, making early detection (and appropriate acting) in the future more likely. Similarly, the cognitive aspects of emotions, i.e. thoughts that are triggered by the emotions ("I should not feel this" or "he is disrespecting me") are more likely to be recognized when observation is trained.

It is important to note that observing and accepting negative emotions does not mean that employees act them out. Quite the contrary, by accepting them rather than trying to suppress them, difficult emotions fade away more quickly (Siegel 2010). Accordingly, research has revealed that mindfulness-based coping with negative thoughts and emotions is more effective in dissolving them than control-based strategies such as suppression (Alberts, Schneider, and Martijn 2012; Marcks and Woods 2005). Similarly, mindfulness has been shown to be negatively related to verbal aggression, hostility, and anger (Borders, Earleywine, and Jajodia 2010).

Previous research addressing the link between mindfulness and general emotion regulation has revealed promising results. For example, research has shown that mindfulness displays negative links with thought suppression (one element of surface acting; Baer *et al.* 2006).

Also, a series of studies by Fetterman and colleagues (2010) revealed that trait mindfulness was negatively related to impulsivity and positively to self-control, supporting the notion that mindfulness promotes self-regulation by interrupting automatic thought and behavior patterns. Recently, we investigated the effectiveness of a brief mindfulness self-training intervention for emotion regulation in the context of work (Hülsheger *et al.* 2013). Results revealed that participants in the mindfulness group displayed significantly lower levels of surface acting and, in consequence, also experienced less emotional exhaustion and higher levels of job satisfaction.

Stress

Stress involves an internal and subjective state. From a social-cognitive perspective, stress emerges from the perception of a situation as overwhelming and the belief that one lacks the resources needed to address the situation adequately (Lazarus and Folkman 1984). When exceeding an optimal level, perceived work-related stress has been found to negatively affect learning performance and physical and mental health (Crawford, LePine, and Rich 2010; LePine, LePine, and Jackson 2004; Podsakoff, LePine, and LePine 2007). The detrimental effects of stress are even more apparent in cases of sustained stress, which have been linked with sleep disturbances (Williams *et al.* 2006), an increased risk of burnout (Rosenberg and Pace 2006) and depression (Tennant 2002).

The previously described MBIs promote awareness of thoughts, awareness of bodily sensations, and self-compassion, three elements which may help employees deal with stress adaptively.

Awareness of thoughts. Coping with work-related stress can involve minimization or elimination of the stressor (the event that causes stress) or adjustment of one's own affective responses to the stressor. In either case, awareness of stressors is a pre-requisite for effective coping with stress. Mindfulness practice aims at increasing awareness of stressful experiences and cultivating a different relationship with them. First of all, practical exercises like the three-minute breathing space require taking a break and they help to disrupt habitual patterns of responding to the stressor. Instead of getting absorbed by and reacting upon stressful thoughts ("I will never finish this in time" or "I am completely losing it") one becomes aware of these thoughts by simply noticing them. This helps to trigger the realization that thoughts are just thoughts and to make a distinction between what is actually happening, and one's own (biased) interpretation or appraisal of the situation. Exercises like the sitting meditation facilitate detachment from stress-related thoughts in that they cultivate the ability to let go of thoughts by directing attention to a neutral anchor, the breath.

Awareness of bodily sensations. Moreover, stress appraisal can trigger changes in body arousal and activity, such as increased blood pressure and heart activity, which in turn may increase stress-related thoughts and responses. Mindfulness exercises such as the body scan may disrupt this process by training non-reactive awareness of body sensations. The body scan encourages participants to notice and acknowledge bodily sensations, without reacting upon them or blaming oneself for experiencing them.

Self-compassion. Lastly, mindfulness practices cultivate self-compassion. Neff (2003) defines self-compassion as "being open to and moved by one's own suffering, experiencing feelings of caring and kindness toward oneself, taking an understanding, non-judgmental attitude toward one's inadequacies and failures, and recognizing that one's experience is part of the common human experience" (p. 224). Instead of blaming oneself for experiencing negative emotions or states such as stress, the mindfulness practitioner is instructed and continually reminded to be kind to oneself; difficult experiences such as stress indicate suffering and require him to take care of himself, for instance by taking a break or engaging in positive and forgiving self-talk. Self-compassion may help to disrupt the interplay between stress-enhancing thoughts and emotions. Increased levels of self-compassion have indeed been found to be negatively related to negative thoughts (e.g. "I am a loser") and self-related generalization ("my life is messed up") after failure (Leary *et al.* 2007) and positively associated with greater personal initiative to make needed changes in one's life (Neff, Rude, and Kirkpatrick 2007).

Through the above processes, the recognition of stress reactions is enhanced, and by disrupting habitual patterns of (ineffective) responding, absorption in stress enhancing thoughts decreases and room is created for reflection, planning, and problem solving in the presence of the current demands and challenges (Davidson and McEwen 2012). In support of this notion, research has revealed that mindfulness practice relates negatively to perceived stress. Whereas the vast majority of studies on MBIs and stress have involved clinical populations, a number of studies have revealed that mindfulness practice also reduces work-related stress (Klatt *et al.* 2009; Roeser *et al.* 2013; Wolever *et al.* 2012).

Other studies have provided evidence that mindfulness interventions positively affect physiological stress responses: in a study by Nyklicek and colleagues (2013), participants either received an eight-week mindfulness intervention or were assigned to a wait-list control group. Before and after the period of the intervention, all participants were exposed to a laboratory stress protocol. Those in the mindfulness group showed larger pre- to post-intervention decreases in overall blood pressure reactivity to stress. Importantly, mental stress has also been found to impair cognitive functions and reduce task performance (De Kloet 2000), an issue that will be discussed in the following section.

Task performance

Mindfulness interventions may be relevant to various aspects of work performance as discussed below.

Mind wandering. Mind wandering – a shift of attention from a task to unrelated concerns (Smallwood and Schooler 2006) – has been identified to negatively affect task performance. For instance, mind wandering has been related to diminished capacity for sustained attention (Farrin *et al.* 2003; Watts, Macleod, and Morris 1988), reduced awareness of task stimuli and the external environment (Barron *et al.* 2011), lower fluid intelligence and lower SAT performance (Mrazek, Smallwood, Franklin, *et al.* 2012).

A core component of mindfulness practices is *focused attention*. The practitioner uses one object of attention, for instance the breath or a body region, and attempts to stay connected to this object. This process has also been referred to as "alerting," sustained attention, or vigilance (Posner and Petersen 1990). Moreover, as soon as one gets distracted by thoughts, feelings, or sounds, attention is focused back on the initial object of attention, a process referred to as orienting or selective attention (Posner and Petersen 1990). In other words, mindfulness practices can help to learn to detect when attention wanders and thus strengthen the capacity to monitor thoughts and behavior, a crucial aspect of successful self-regulation (e.g. Carver 2004). Thus, mindfulness can be considered as the opposite process of mind wandering and thus can be expected to promote performance in jobs that require sustained attention and concentration on work tasks.

Research has confirmed that high dispositional mindfulness is associated with less mind-wandering (Mrazek, Smallwood and Schooler 2012). Research has also established a causal link between both constructs. For instance, a study by Mrazek, Franklin, Phillips, Baird, and Schooler (2013) found that two weeks of mindfulness training resulted in a decrease in mind wandering and improved cognitive performance. In a similar vein, a study by Lutz and colleagues (2009) showed that three months of intensive meditation training resulted in an improved ability to sustain attention during a task with distractors. These findings support the idea that practicing mindfulness can help to enhance task concentration and reduce performance decrements due to task-unrelated distractions.

Multitasking. In our current work environment, technological developments have greatly facilitated multitasking. Computers allow running several programs at the same time and mobile phones have become portable computers able to provide constantly updated information. Research shows an increase in media-related multitasking since the beginning of this century (Rideout, Foehr, and Roberts 2010) and has addressed its impact on both mental health and cognitive processes. Increased media multitasking has been found to be associated with higher depression and social anxiety symptoms (Becker, Alzahabi, and Hopwood 2013), lower academic performance in college students (Junco and Cotton 2011), and decreased ability to effectively filter irrelevant information (Ophir, Nass, and Wagner 2009). In terms of processes, multitasking often involves cognitive shifts of context. If one is writing a report and answering emails at the same time, every incoming email is an interruption of the writing task and requires reorientation. As a result of increased interruption due to multitasking, stress and effort have been found to increase (Mark, Gudith, and Klocke 2008).

Mindfulness has sometimes been referred to as "single tasking" and can be considered the antithesis of multitasking. Many mindfulness practices require the participant to use a single focus and thereby promote *single focused attention*. This aim is clearly demonstrated by the daily routine exercise, in which one is instructed to focus on only one specific task at hand. Thus, instead of talking to a client and at the same time checking one's phone for new messages, mindfulness cultivates attention for the conversation with the client only. In this example, the conversation with the client is the main and only object of attention and is therefore similar to the breath or body in formal practices.

A study by Levy and colleagues (2012) examined the relationship between mindfulness and multitasking. They found that participants who received an eight-week mindfulness training switched less frequently between competing tasks, experienced fewer negative emotions and spent more time on each individual task (without increasing total time investment) than those in the relaxation or control groups. The meditation and relaxation group also exhibited improved memory for the details of the work they performed. In sum, these findings support the idea that mindfulness practice enhances skills that can counteract the negative consequences of multitasking.

Paradoxical goal achievement. Goals are a keyword in almost every organization. Goals can serve as an essential ingredient necessary for effective task performance by enhancing detailed planning, motivation, confidence, and well-being (Manderlink and Harackiewicz 1984, McGregor and Little 1998; Sheldon and Krieger 2007). While there is a wealth of research providing evidence for the positive effects of goal setting (Latham and Locke, 2007) and goal-focused regulation (Shah, Higgins, and Friedman 1998) researchers have also acknowledged that an excessive striving for goals and concern with avoiding mistakes in pursuing goals can be counterproductive (Hrabluik, Latham, and McCarthy 2012). In some cases, too much focus on achieving a goal can paradoxically lead to a decreased likelihood of achieving the desired goal, a phenomenon known as the ironic process of control (Wegner 1994).

In a well-replicated classic study by Wegner, Schneider, Carter, and White (1987), participants were told that the goal of a task was to not think of a white bear. Every time participants did think of a white bear they were instructed to ring a bell. Participants who attempted to reach the goal of not thinking of a white bear, rang the bell significantly more often than participants who were not instructed to reach this goal. Similar findings have been found in the context of sleep (Harvey 2003) and eating behavior (McFarlane, Polivy, and McCabe 1999). Thus, while many self-regulation models assume that the cause of not reaching a goal state concerns the inability to monitor one's progress toward the goal, these findings illustrate that in some cases, too much focus on the progress towards the goal can result in decreased performance. For example, an employee whose goal is to meet a deadline and write a report by the end of the day, may fail to do so when he is not consciously thinking about the deadline (e.g. because he forgets to start or continue the process of writing). At the same, however, the performance of an employee who is constantly focused on the deadline while writing the report is likely to be hindered by an excessive focus on the goal, because it interferes with the process of writing. Especially when he notices that his progress is not as intended, he may experience stress or frustration, which may further decrease performance (Boekaerts 1999). In the latter case, deliberate attention to the goal is counterproductive, because it distracts the employee from the task at hand, creates both stress and frustration, and interferes with the present-oriented process of writing. Even complex tasks, such as writing a report, do not require continuous, conscious monitoring of progress (Bargh and Chartrand 1999).

Mindfulness has been argued to prevent decreased task performance due to an excessive goal focus (Leary, Adams and Tate 2006). Compared to goal-driven self-regulation models, mindfulness involves a fundamentally different process, since it does not involve the reduction of a discrepancy between a current state and a goal state. Instead, mindfulness requires attention to be directed at the present state, the present moment. In the example of the employee, mindfulness would enable the employee to notice when goal-related thoughts are attracting too much attention and help him to bring attention back to the task at hand. In other words, we posit that mindfulness would facilitate the restoration of the balance between the goal and the task-related process.

An orientation on processes rather than on specific goals is a central element of the mindfulness practices presented above, which promote a *present-moment orientation*. Before starting the exercise, participants are informed that it is important to let go of the desire to reach a certain state, such as relaxation, or to acquire a certain level of performance when doing the exercise, such as being free of thoughts and negative emotions. Rather than reaching these states, mindfulness aims to cultivate the ability to observe, allow, and accept whatever sensation, thought, or emotion is present in the current moment. A potential pitfall of mindfulness practice is that positive states often emerge during or after practice, which can increase the desire and expectancy to reach those states in the future. Paradoxically, as discussed above, this can reduce the chance of experiencing the desired or expected state.

Interestingly, mindfulness has been found to be associated with higher levels of self-regulation (Fetterman *et al.* 2010) and paradoxical effects of self-control have been found to be less likely when mindful regulation is employed (Alberts, Schneider, and Martijn 2012; Marcks and Woods 2005). In an attempt to investigate the direct impact of mindfulness on self-regulatory performance, Friese, Messner, and Schaffner (2012) exposed participants to a series of self-control tasks. One group received a brief mindfulness meditation in between two tasks. Participants whose self-regulatory resources were depleted by the first task exhibited a decreased performance on the second task. However, participants who were exposed to the mindfulness intervention kept self-regulatory performance stable. In sum, preliminary findings from basic research suggest that while mindfulness does not cultivate goal orientation (a process often considered necessary for successful self-regulation), goal achievement through self-regulation is more likely when higher levels of mindfulness are present.

Conclusion

The aim of this chapter was to provide a deeper understanding of MBIs for the work context. Specifically, we have discussed different types of interventions, described various practical exercises, and have addressed potential mechanisms underlying the effects of these practices.

Apparently, mindfulness is a multi-component process, which influences many factors related to human functioning, both psychological and biological. Whereas many of these factors have already been addressed in research, more remain to be uncovered. The scope and complexity of mindfulness is also illustrated by the fact that mindfulness has been applied and investigated in many different areas, such as eating behavior, depression, anxiety, stress, academic performance, and executive functioning (Alberts, Thewissen and Raes 2012; Beauchemin, Hutchins, and Patterson 2008; Heeren, Van Broeck, and Philippot 2009; Hofmann *et al.* 2010). This suggests that the mechanisms underlying mindfulness, rather than being domain specific, affect human functioning on a very profound and essential level. Given this complexity, the present chapter can best be considered as an attempt to integrate several aspects of mindfulness in the context of work. Evidently, the selection of work-related outcomes presented here is far from complete. For instance, we did not address the impact of mindfulness on factors directly related to quality of life, such as job satisfaction, psychological detachment, and sleep quality. Although these factors were not addressed here, preliminary findings in the field of IO psychology do support the link between mindfulness and quality of life. For instance, in a recent study we found that employees' levels of mindfulness during working hours were significantly related to their sleep quality the following night and that this relationship was mediated by the ability to psychologically detach from work in the afternoon (Hülsheger, Alberts, Lang, Depenbrock, Fehrmann, and Zijlstra 2014).

Moreover, although the mechanisms underlying mindfulness practice were discussed separately, in reality, they most likely operate together synergistically. For instance, the ability to stay focused on a task during work is likely to increase the chance of finishing it in time, which will contribute to self-efficacy and reduce the identification with thoughts relating to self-doubt. The ability to become aware of body sensations associated with enthusiasm and joy are a pre-requisite for accurate self-knowledge because they provide feedback regarding one's personal strengths and values. This self-knowledge may enhance the match between personal skills and task demands (Kasser 2002). In turn, the enhanced autonomy that is experienced through this match may act as a buffer against burnout or stress-related symptoms. In order to gain more insight into the interacting processes underlying mindfulness, future research in the field of IO psychology should not limit itself to field studies testing the effects of long-term mindfulness interventions or trait and state mindfulness, but will benefit from lab studies isolating separate components and processes as well. By exposing participants to mindfulness inductions under controlled lab settings, working mechanisms can be uncovered, contributing to the generalizability of the results to the work floor. In addition, this may also contribute to the development of new practical interventions tailored to the work context.

Future research on the effectiveness and utility of mindfulness interventions in the context of work may build upon interventions that have been developed specifically for the work context (Hülsheger *et al.* 2013; Klatt *et al.* 2009; Wolever *et al.* 2012) and try to answer questions that have not been addressed up until now. For instance, how do mindfulness interventions compare to traditional workplace health intervention programs in terms of effectiveness? How long do the effects of mindfulness interventions persist after the intervention has been completed? To what extent do participants continue to engage in (daily) mindfulness practice after the intervention has been completed? How can participants be encouraged to maintain daily mindfulness practice? Which participants are more likely to voluntarily participate in mindfulness programs and how can those who show less interest be encouraged to participate? Are there individual differences variables that explain who profits more or less from mindfulness interventions? Is there an optimal level of daily practice of mindfulness (dosage effects)? Are some practices more effective than others? These are just some examples of questions that may be addressed in future research in order to advance both research and practice in this area.

Most psychological studies since the 1980s have focused on the identification of factors that precede or relate to human suffering and decreased (employee) wellbeing, such as burnout, stress, and emotional exhaustion. These studies have mainly started from the question: "what is wrong with people/employees?" Attempts to answer this question have not revealed many insights into ways to *prevent* serious problems. These insights were provided by studies using a more positive perspective, attempting to uncover human qualities that act as buffers against problems. Findings suggest that mindfulness can be considered such a quality, and research on mindfulness at work therefore contributes to the positive occupational health psychology literature (Bakker and Derks 2010). An important future mission of IO psychology is therefore to understand and learn how to enhance and train positive qualities like mindfulness in order to prevent, rather than cure, work-related problems and enhance employee wellbeing, rather than reduce illness.

References

Aaras, A., Horgen, G., and Ro, O. (2000). Work with the visual display unit: health consequences. *International Journal of Human-Computer Interaction*, 12, 107–34.

Alberts, H. J. E. M., Schneider, F., and Martijn, C. (2012). Dealing efficiently with emotions: acceptance-based coping with negative emotions requires fewer resources than suppression. *Cognition and Emotion*, 26, 863–70.

Alberts, H. J. E. M., Thewissen, R., and Raes, L. (2012). Dealing with problematic eating behaviour. The effects of a mindfulness-based intervention on eating behaviour, food cravings, dichotomous thinking and body image concern. *Appetite*, 58, 847–51.

Allen, T. D. and Kiburz, K. M. (2012). Trait mindfulness and work-family balance among working parents: the mediating effects of vitality and sleep quality. *Journal of Vocational Behavior*, 80, 372–9.

Atkins, P. W. B. and Parker, S. K. (2012). Understanding individual compassion in organizations: the role of appraisals and psychological flexibility. *Academy of Management Review*, 37, 524–46.

Baer, R., Carmody, J., and Hunsinger, M. (2012). Weekly changes in mindfulness and perceived stress in a mindfulness-based stress reduction program. *Journal of Clinical Psychology*, 68, 755–65.

Baer, R. A., Smith, G. T., Hopkins, J., Krietemeyer, J., and Toney, L. (2006). Using self-report assessment methods to explore facets of mindfulness. *Assessment*, 13, 27–45.

Bakker, A. B. and Derks, D. (2010). Positive occupational health psychology. In S. Leka and J. Houdmont (eds.), *Occupational health psychology: A key text*. Oxford: Wiley-Blackwell.

Bargh, J. A. and Chartrand, T. L. (1999). The unbearable automaticity of being. *American Psychologist*, 54, 462–79.

Barron, E., Riby, L. M., Greer, J., and Smallwood, J. (2011). Absorbed in thought: the effect of mind wandering on the processing of relevant and irrelevant events. *Psychological Science*, 22, 596–601.

Baumeister, R. F., Todd, F., Heatherton, T. F., and Tice, D. M. (1994). *Losing control: How and why people fail at self-regulation*. San Diego, CA: Academic Press.

Beauchemin, J., Hutchins, T. L., and Patterson, F. (2008). Mindfulness meditation may lessen anxiety, promote social skills, and improve academic performance among adolescents with learning difficulties. *Comlementary Health Practice Review*, 13, 34–45.

Becker, M. W., Alzahabi, R., and Hopwood, C. J. (2013). Media multitasking is associated with symptoms of depression and social anxiety. *Cyberpsychology, behavior and social networking*, 16, 132–5.

Bishop, S. R., Lau, M., Shapiro, S., Carlson, L., Anderson, N. D., Carmody, J. ... and Devins, G. (2004). Mindfulness: a proposed operational definition. *Clinical Psychology: Science and Practice*, 11, 230–41.

Boekaerts, M. (1999). Self-regulated learning: where we are today. *International Journal of Educational Research*, 31, 445–57.

Bohlmeijer, E., Prenger, R., Taal, E., and Cuijpers, P. (2010). The effects of mindfulness-based stress reduction therapy on mental health of adults with a chronic medical disease: a meta-analysis. *Journal of Psychosomatic Research*, 68, 539–44.

Borders, A., Earleywine, M., and Jajodia, A. (2010). Could mindfulness decrease anger, hostility, and aggression by decreasing rumination? *Aggressive Behavior*, 36, 28–44.

Brefczynski-Lewis, J. A., Lutz, A., Schaefer, H. S., Levinson, D. B., and Davidson, R. J. (2007). Neural correlates of attentional expertise in long-term meditation practitioners. *Proceedings of the National Academy of Sciences*, 104, 11483–8.

Brown, K. W. and Ryan, R. M. (2003). The benefits of being present: Mindfulness and its role in psychological well-being. *Journal of Personality and Social Psychology*, 84, 822–48.

Call, D., Miron, L., and Orcutt, H. (2014). Effectiveness of brief mindfulness techniques in reducing symptoms of anxiety and stress. *Mindfulness*, 5, 658–68.

Campbell-Sills, L., Barlow, D. H., Brown, T. A., and Hofmann, S. G. (2006). Effects of suppression and acceptance on emotional responses on individuals with anxiety and mood disorders. *Behavior Research and Therapy*, 44, 1251–63.

Carmody, J. and Baer, R. A. (2008). Relationships between mindfulness practice and levels of mindfulness, medical and psychological symptoms and well-being in a mindfulness-based stress reduction program. *Journal of Behavioral Medicine*, 31, 23–33.

(2009). How long does a mindfulness-based stress reduction program need to be? A review of class contact hours and effect sizes for psychological distress. *Journal of Clinical Psychology*, 65(6), 627–38.

Carmody, J., Reed, G., Kristeller, J., and Merriam, P. (2008). Mindfulness, spirituality, and health-related symptoms. *Journal of Psychosomatic Research*, 64, 393–403.

Carver, C. S. (2004). Self-regulation of action and affect. In R. F. Baumeister and K. D. Vohs (eds.), *Handbook of self-regulation: research, theory, and applications*. New York: Guilford Press, pp. 13–39.

Collard, P., Avny, N., and Boniwell, I. (2008). Teaching Mindfulness Based Cognitive Therapy (MBCT) to students: the effects of MBCT on the levels of mindfulness and subjective well-being. *Counselling Psychology Quarterly*, 21, 323–36.

Côté, S. (2005). A social interaction model of the effects of emotion regulation on work strain. *The Academy of Management Review*, 30, 509–30.

Crawford, E. R., LePine, J. A., and Rich, B. L. (2010). Linking job demands and resources to employee engagement and burnout: a theoretical extension and meta-analytic test. *Journal of Applied Psychology*, 95, 834–48.

Creswell, J. D., Way, B. M., Eisenberger, N. I., and Lieberman, M. D. (2007). Neural correlates of dispositional mindfulness during affect labeling. *Psychosomatic Medicine*, 69, 560–5.

Dane, E. and Brummel, B. J. (2014). Examining workplace mindfulness and its relations to job performance and turnover intention. *Human Relations*, 67, 105–28.

Davidson, R. J. and McEwen, B. S. (2012). Social influences on neuroplasticity: stress and interventions to promote well-being. *Nature Neuroscience*, 15, 689–95.

De Kloet, E. R. (2000) Stress in the brain. *European Journal of Pharmacology*, 405(1), 187–98.

Del Re, A. C., Fluckiger, C., Goldberg, S., and Hoyt W. T. (2012). Monitoring mindfulness practice quality: an important consideration in mindfulness practice. *Psychotherapy Research*, 23, 54–66.

Deikman, A. J. (1982). *The observing self: mysticism and psychotherapy*. Boston, MA: Beacon Press.

Erisman, S. M. and Roemer L. (2010). A preliminary investigation of the effects of experimentally induced mindfulness on emotional responding to film clips. *Emotion*, 10, 72–82.

Farrin, L., Hull, L., Unwin, C., Wykes, T., and David, A. (2003). Effects of depressed mood on objective and subjective measures of attention. *Journal of Neuropsychiatry and Clinical Neuroscience*, 15, 98–104.

Feldman, G., Greeson, J., and Senville, J. (2010). Differential effects of mindful breathing, progressive muscle relaxation, and loving-kindness meditation on decentering and negative reactions to repetitive thoughts. *Behaviour Research and Therapy*, 48, 1002–11.

Fetterman, A. K., Robinson, M. D., Ode, S., and Gordon, K. H. (2010). Neuroticism as a risk factor for behavioral dysregulation: a mindfulness-mediation perspective. *Journal of Social and Clinical Psychology*, 29, 301–21.

Friese, M., Messner, C., and Schaffner, Y. (2012). Mindfulness meditation counteracts self-control depletion. *Consciousness and Cognition*, 21, 1016–22.

Garland, E. L., Hanley, A., Farb, N. A., and Froeliger, B. (2013). State mindfulness during meditation predicts enhanced cognitive reappraisal. *Mindfulness*, 1–9. doi: 10.1007/s12671-013-0250-6.

Glomb, T. M., Duffy, M. K., Bono, J. E., and Yang, T. (2011). Mindfulness at work. In J. Martocchio, H. Liao, and A. Joshi (eds.), *Research in personnel and human resource management.* Bingley: Emerald Group Publishing Limited, pp. 115–57.

Grandey, A. A. (2000). Emotional regulation in the workplace: a new way to conceptualize emotional labor. *Journal of Occupational Health Psychology,* 5, 95–110.

 (2003). When "the show must go on": surface acting and deep acting as determinants of emotional exhaustion and peer-rated service delivery. *Academy of Management Journal,* 46, 86–96.

Harvey, A. G. (2003). The attempted suppression of presleep cognitive activity in insomnia. *Cognitive Therapy and Research,* 27, 593–602.

Hayes, S. C., Strosahl, K., and Wilson, K. G. (1999). *Acceptance and commitment therapy: an experiential approach to behavior change.* New York: Guilford Press.

Heeren, A., Van Broeck, N., and Philippot, P. (2009). The effects of mindfulness training on executive processes and autobiographical memory specificity. *Behaviour Research and Therapy,* 47, 403–9.

Hochschild, A. R. (1983). *The managed heart.* Berkeley, CA: University of California Press.

Hofmann, S. G., Sawyer, A. T., Witt, A. A., and Oh, D. (2010). The effect of mindfulness-based therapy on anxiety and depression: a meta-analytic review. *Journal of Consulting and Clinical Psychology,* 78, 169–83.

Holman, D., Martinez-Iñigo, D., and Totterdell, P. (2008). Emotional labour, well-being and performance. In C. L. Cooper and S. Cartwright (eds.) *The Oxford Handbook of Organizational Well-being.* Oxford University Press, pp. 331–55.

Hrabluik, C., Latham, G. P., and McCarthy, J. M. (2012). Does goal setting have a dark side? The relationship between perfectionism and maximum versus typical employee performance. *International Public Management Journal,* 15, 5–38.

Hülsheger, U. R., Alberts, H. J. E. M., Feinholdt, A., and Lang, J. W. B. (2013). Benefits of mindfulness at work: the role of mindfulness in emotion regulation, emotional exhaustion, and job satisfaction. *Journal of Applied Psychology,* 98, 310–25.

Hülsheger, U. R., Lang, J. W. B., Depenbrock, F., Fehrmann, C., Zijlstra, F., and Alberts, H. J. E. M. (2014). The power of presence: The role of mindfulness at work for daily levels and change trajectories of psychological detachment and sleep quality. *Journal of Applied Psychology,* 99, 1113–28.

Hülsheger, U. R. and Schewe, A. F. (2011). On the costs and benefits of emotional labor: a meta-analysis spanning three decades of research. *Journal of Occupational Health Psychology,* 16, 361–89.

Jennings, S. J. and Jennings, J. L. (2013). Peer-directed, brief mindfulness training with adolescents: a pilot study. *International Journal of Behavioral Consultation and Therapy*, 8, 23–5.

Junco, R. and Cotton, S. (2011). Perceived academic effects of instant messaging use. *Computers and Education*, 56, 370–8.

Kabat-Zinn, J. (1982). An out-patient program in behavioral medicine for chronic pain patients based on the practice of mindfulness meditation: theoretical considerations and preliminary results. *General Hospital Psychiatry*, 4, 33–47.

(1990). *Full catastrophe living: using the wisdom of your body and mind to face stress, pain and illness*. New York: Delacorte.

(2005). *Coming to our senses*. New York: Hyperion.

Kasser, T. (2002). Sketches for a self-determination theory of values. In E. L. Deci and R. M. Ryan (eds.), *Handbook of self-determination research*. Rochester, NY: University of Rochester Press, pp. 123–40.

Klatt, M. D., Buckworth, J., and Malarkey, W. B. (2009). Effects of low-dose mindfulness-based stress reduction (MBSR-ld) on working adults. *Health Education and Behavior*, 36, 601–14.

Kristeller, J. L., Baer, R. A., and Quillian Wolever, R. (2006). Mindfulness-based approaches to eating disorders. In R. Baer (ed.) *Mindfulness-based treatment approaches: clinician's guide to evidence base and applications (Practical resources for the mental health professional)*. San Diego, CA: Elsevier Academic Press.

Krusche, A., Cyhlarova, E., King, S., and Williams, J. M. G. (2012). Mindfulness online: a preliminary evaluation of the feasibility of a web-based mindfulness course and the impact on stress. *BMJ Open*, 2. http://dx.doi.org/10.1136/bmjopen-2011-000803.

Latham, G. P. and Locke, E. A. (2007). New developments in and directions for goal-setting research. *European Psychologist*, 12, 290–300.

Lau, M. A., Bishop, S. R., Segal, Z. V., Buis, T., Anderson, N. D., Carlson, L., Shapiro, S., and Carmody, J. (2006). The Toronto mindfulness scale: development and validation. *Journal of Clinical Psychology*, 62, 1445–67.

Lazarus, R. S. and Folkman, S. (1984). *Psychological stress and the coping process*. New York: Springer.

Leary, M., Adams, C., and Tate, E. (2006). Hypo-egoic self-regulation: exercising self-control by diminishing the influence of the self. *Journal of Personality*, 74, 1803–31.

Leary, M. R., Tate, E. B., Adams, C. E., Batts Allen, A., and Hancock, J. (2007). Self-compassion and reactions to unpleasant self-relevant events: the implications of treating oneself kindly. *Journal of Personality and Social Psychology*, 92, 887–904.

LePine, J. A., LePine, M. A., and Jackson, C. L. (2004). Challenge and hindrance stress: relationships with exhaustion, motivation to learn, and learning performance. *Journal of Applied Psychology*, 89, 883–91.

Leroy, H., Anseel, F., Dimitrova, N. G., and Sels, L. (2013). Mindfulness, authentic functioning, and work engagement: a growth modeling approach. *Journal of Vocational Behavior*, 82, 238–47.

Levy, D. M., Wobbrock, J. O., Kaszniak, A. W., and Ostergren, M. (2012). The effects of mindfulness meditation training on multitasking in a high-stress information environment. Proceedings of Graphics Interface, Toronto, Ontario (May 28–30 2012). Toronto: Canadian Information Processing Society, pp. 45–52.

Linehan, M. M. (1993). *Cognitive-behavioral treatment of borderline personality disorder*. New York: Guilford Press.

Lutz, A., Slagter, H. A., Rawlings, N. B., Francis, A. D., Greischer, L. L., and Davidson, R. J. (2009). Mental training enhances attentional stability: neural and behavioral evidence. *Journal of Neuroscience*, 29, 13418–27.

McFarlane, T., Polivy, J., and McCabe, R. E. (1999). Help, not harm: psychological foundation for a nondieting approach toward health. *Journal of Social Issues*, 55, 261–76.

McGregor, I. and Little, B. R. (1998). Personal projects, happiness, and meaning: on doing well and being yourself. *Journal of Personality and Social Psychology*, 74, 494–512.

Manderlink, G. and Harackiewicz, J. M. (1984). Proximal versus distal goal setting on intrinsic motivation. *Journal of Personality and Social Psychology*, 47, 918–28.

Marcks, B. A. and Woods, D. W. (2005). A comparison of thought suppression to an acceptance-based technique in the management of personal intrusive thought: a controlled evaluation. *Behaviour Research and Therapy*, 43, 433–45.

Mark, G. J., Gudith, D., and Klocke, U. (2008). The cost of interrupted work: more speed and stress. In M. Burnett, M. F. Costabile, T. Catarci, B. De Ruyter, D. Tan, and M. C. A. Lund (eds.),. *Proceedings of the SIGCHI conference on human factors in computing systems.* New York: ACM Press, pp. 107–10.

Marlatt, G. A. and Kristeller, J. L. (1999). Mindfulness and meditation. In W. R. Miller (ed.), *Integrating spirituality into treatment*. Washington, DC: American Psychological Association, pp. 67–84.

Marzuq, N. and Drach-Zahavy, A. (2012). Recovery during a short period of respite: the interactive roles of mindfulness and respite experiences. *Work and Stress*, 26, 175–94.

Mohan, A., Sharma, R., and Bijlani, R. L. (2011). Effect of meditation on stress induced changes in cognitive functions. *Journal of Alternative and Complementary Medicine*, 17, 207–12.

Mrazek M. D., Franklin M. S., Phillips D., Baird B., and Schooler J. (2013). Mindfulness training improves working memory and GRE performance while reducing mind-wandering. *Psycholical Science*, 24, 776–81.

Mrazek, M. D., Smallwood, J., Franklin, M. S., Baird, B., Chin, J. M., and Schooler, J. W. (2012). The role of mind-wandering in measurements of general aptitude. *Journal of Experimental Psychology*, 141, 788–98.

Mrazek, M. D., Smallwood, J., and Schooler, J. W. (2012). Mindfulness and mind-wandering: finding convergence through opposing constructs. *Emotion*, 12, 442–8.

Neff, K. D. (2003). Self-compassion: an alternative conceptualization of a healthy attitude toward oneself. *Self and Identity*, 2, 85–102.

Neff, K. D., Rude, S. S., and Kirkpatrick, K. L. (2007). An examination of self-compassion in relation to positive psychological functioning and personality traits. *Journal of Research in Personality*, 41, 908–16.

Nyklicek, I., Mommersteeg, P. M. C., van Beugen, S., Ramakers, C., and van Boxtel, G. J. M. (2013). Mindfulness-based stress reduction and physiological activity during acute stress: a randomized controlled trial. *Health Psychology*, 32, 1110–13.

Ophir, E., Nass, C., and Wagner, A. D. (2009). Cognitive control in media multitaskers. *Proceedings of the National Academy of Sciences*, 106, 15583–7.

Podsakoff, N. P., LePine, J. A., and LePine, M. A. (2007). Differential challenge stressor-hindrance stressor relationships with job attitudes, turnover intentions, turnover, and withdrawal behavior: a meta-analysis. *Journal of Applied Psychology*, 92, 438–54.

Posner, M. I. and Petersen S. E. (1990). The attention system of the human brain. *Annual Review of Neuroscience*, 13, 25–42.

Reb, J., Narayanan, J., and Chaturvedi, S. (2014). Leading mindfully: two studies on the influence of supervisor trait mindfulness on employee well-being and performance. *Mindfulness*, 5, 36–45.

Rideout, V. J., Foehr, U. G., and Roberts, D. F. (2010). Generation M2: media in the lives of 8–18 year olds. Menlo Park, CA: Kaiser Family Foundation. Retrieved from: www.kff.org/entmedia/upload/8010.pdf.

Roeser, R. W., Schonert-Reichl, K. A., Jha, A. P., Cullen, M., Wallace, L., Wilensky, R., Oberle, E., Thomson, K., Taylor, C., and Harrison, J. (2013). Mindfulness training and reductions in teacher stress and burnout: results from two randomized, waitlist-control field trials. *Journal of Educational Psychology*, 105(3), 787–804.

Rosenberg, T. and Pace, M. (2006). Burnout among mental health professionals: special considerations for the marriage and family therapist. *Journal of Marital and Family Therapy*, 32, 89–99.

Segal, Z. V., Williams, J. M. G., and Teasdale, J. D. (2002). *Mindfulness-Based Cognitive Therapy for depression*. New York: Guilford Press.

Shah, J., Higgins, E. T., and Friedman, R. S. (1998). Performance incentives and means: how regulatory focus influences goal attainment. *Journal of Personality and Social Psychology*, 74, 285–93.

Shapiro, S. L., Astin, J. A., Bishop, S. R., and Cordova, M. (2005). Mindfulness-based stress reduction for health care professionals: results from a randomized trial. *International Journal of Stress Management*, 12, 164–76.

Shapiro, S. L., Carlson, L. E., Astin, J. A., and Freedman, B. (2006). Mechanisms of mindfulness. *Journal of Clinical Psychology*, 62, 373–86.

Sheldon, K. M. and Krieger, L. K. (2007). Understanding the negative effects of legal education on law students: a longitudinal test of self-determination theory. *Personality and Social Psychology Bulletin*, 33, 883–97.

Siegel, R. D. (2010). *The mindful solution: everyday practices for everyday problems*. New York: Guilford Press.

Smallwood, J. and Schooler, J. W. (2006). The restless mind. *Psychological Bulletin*, 132, 946–58.

Speca, M., Carlson, L. E., Goodey, E., and Angen, M. (2000). A randomized, wait-list controlled clinical trial: the effect of a mindfulness meditation-based stress reduction program on mood and symptoms of stress in cancer outpatients. *Psychosomatic Medicine*, 62, 613–22.

Tennant, C. (2002). Life events, stress and depression: a review of recent findings. *Australian and New Zealand Journal of Psychiatry*, 36, 173–82.

Van Berkel J., Boot C. R. L., Proper, K. I., Bongers, P. M., and Van der Beek, A. J. (2013). Process evaluation of a workplace health promotion intervention aimed at improving work engagement and energy balance. *Journal of Occupational and Environmental Medicine*, 55, 19–26.

Watts, F. N., MacLeod, A. K., and Morris, L. (1988). Associations between phenomenal and objective aspects of concentration problems in depressed patients. *British Journal of Psychology*, 79, 241–50.

Wegner, D. M. (1994). Ironic processes of mental control. *Psychological Review*, 101, 34–52.

Wegner, D. M., Schneider, D. J., Carter, S. R., and White, T. L. (1987). Paradoxical effects of thought suppression. *Journal of Personality and Social Psychology*, 53, 5–13.

Williams, A., Franche, R. L., Ibrahim, S., Mustard, C. A., and Layton, F. R. (2006). Examining the relationship between work-family spillover and sleep quality. *Journal of Occupational Health Psychology*, 11, 27–37.

Witkiewitz, K., Marlatt, G. A., and Walker, D. (2005). Mindfulness-based relapse prevention for alcohol and substance use disorders. *Journal of Cognitive Psychotherapy*, 19, 211–28.

Wolever, R. Q., Bobinet, K. J., McCabe, K., Mackenzie, E. R., Fekete, E., Kusnick, C. A., and Baime, M. (2012). Effective and viable mind-body stress reduction in the workplace: a randomized controlled trial. *Journal of Occupational Health Psychology*, 17, 246–58.

PART II

Research

6 | Mindfulness, identity and work: mindfulness training creates a more flexible sense of self

PAUL W. B. ATKINS AND ROBERT STYLES

Introduction

In this chapter we explore the effects of mindfulness training upon individual identity. We aim to show that mindfulness training extends beyond improving emotional self-regulation. Our work shows that over time it changes how we respond to the questions 'Who am I?' and 'Am I really separate from you?' In turn, these changes have profound implications for wellbeing, effectiveness and relationships at work. Our identity shapes both our individual and relational responding. In this sense, identity underpins many other aspects of organisational behaviour. Indeed, it has been argued that identity has become central to organisational studies and the social sciences more broadly (Alvesson, Ashcraft, and Thomas 2008). In recent years, identity has been linked to issues as diverse as change management (Beech *et al.* 2011), leadership development (Carroll and Levy 2010; DeRue and Ashford 2010; Hannah, Woolfolk, and Lord 2009), motivation (Osborne and Jones 2011), career development (Petriglieri and Petriglieri 2010), and emotions at work (Atkins and Parker 2012).

In this chapter we explore theoretically and empirically how mindfulness training affects identity and thereby affects work-related outcomes and wellbeing. We adopt the view that mindfulness involves the four processes of: knowing oneself as the observer of experience; flexibly attending to the present moment; willingly accepting experience as it is without trying to change its frequency or intensity, and defusion from the literality of verbal cognitions (Hayes, Strosahl, and Wilson

2011). This approach is based on a contextual-behavioural account of language and human cognition where identity is understood to be the ongoing behaviour of constructing descriptions of one's own behaviours and characteristics (Hayes, Barnes-Holmes, and Roche 2001). When mindful, such personal descriptions are not held as literal truths but rather are held flexibly as passing verbal constructs. We are particularly interested in the shift from treating self-referential statements as literal truths to flexibly engaging with them as constructs that serve varying degrees of usefulness. Mindfulness training appears to facilitate such a shift.

In the work context, a more flexible and mindful orientation to the self can reduce unproductive behaviours that occur as people act in defence of the stories they tell about themselves, who they are, and what they did or will do. Mindfulness in the workplace, we believe, curbs ineffective social behaviour that results from rigid self-conceptualisations. For example, when people are unable to interrupt default inflexible and defensive responses in challenging situations, they continue to do things that do not work, believing (treating verbal constructs as literal truths) that they should. They argue for certain positions based on underlying philosophies, rationalistic traditions and beliefs (all verbal constructs) even though they do not take them in the direction intended (Bennett and Howlett 1992; Colebatch 2002; Dolowitz and Marsh 2000). They struggle with the resulting aversive experience and yet continue to justify and use the same strategies that yield this limiting and ineffective experience (Thacher and Rein 2004). By this analysis, we suggest that entrenched and intractable social, environmental, and economic problems are maintained as individuals in governments, organisations and communities adhere literally and rigidly to a sense of their own identity that they believe and wish to protect.

Because other chapters within this volume have focused upon the nature of mindfulness training (Alberts and Hülsheger), we will focus our initial literature review on individual identity change. We then present a contextual-behavioural account of identity development that we believe is a helpful alternative to the more sociological and constructivist models offered in the organisational literature to date. In order to validate this account, we then describe the development of a new qualitative measure of the way in which people dynamically construct a sense of self that is applicable to studying the effects of mindfulness training. Lacking a theory of the psychological processes underpinning identity development, the impact of mindfulness training upon identity change has been difficult to measure. Our approach has been to develop a behavioural measure based upon the way people talk about themselves in interviews. We conclude by applying the measure to demonstrate individual identity change resulting from a mindfulness-based stress reduction (MBSR) course, and exploring the implications of these results for mindfulness training at work.

Individual identity change

There is a growing body of research on individual identity change in organisations, usually referred to as identity work (Beech 2008; 2011; Beech *et al.* 2011; Ibarra and Petriglieri 2010; Pratt, Rockmann, and Kaufmann 2006). Sveningsson and Alvesson define identity work in the following terms: 'identity work refers to people being engaged in forming, repairing, maintaining, strengthening or revising the constructions that are productive of a sense of coherence and distinctiveness' (2003, p. 1165). The extent to which people engage in identity work within organisations appears to be dependent upon the complexity and rates of change of contexts, with identity work being more continuous in complex and dynamic contexts and more sporadic in simple or stable contexts. In more complex and dynamic situations, people must continuously redefine and reframe themselves in order to maintain a sense of coherence and direction. In stable contexts, such continual reframing of identity is unnecessary. Identity work can also be occasioned by conflicts with others (Fiol, Pratt, and O'Connor 2009) or formal events such as leadership development (Carroll and Levy 2010). As we demonstrate below, mindfulness training may well be one of the most powerful ways of influencing and developing identity.

Unfortunately most of the organisational research on identity has been conducted without reference to a broader understanding of the processes of identity development across the lifespan. If we are to understand identity change at work, we need a comprehensive theory of the characteristics and dynamics of identity beyond simple labelling of personal characteristics, roles, or group memberships. And we need an approach to measuring identity that both captures the richness of idiosyncratic identities while also allowing comparison between people. Next we present a more comprehensive contextual-behavioural approach (Hayes and Gregg 2000) to the development of identity that informed the design of our qualitative measure. Our primary aim was to create a standardised and precise, but still semantically rich, measure of identity that could be used to investigate how mindfulness training impacts upon identity in the workplace and beyond.

A contextual-behavioral account of identity development

When a person reports on their own identity, they are essentially reflecting upon and describing their own behaviour either currently or in the past. For example, if a person describes themselves as an introvert, they are abstracting from remembered experiences of not enjoying attending parties, having little to say when in the company of others, and so on. In behavioural terms, identity is thus self-discrimination. Similar ideas have a long history in social psychology (e.g. Bem 1967). A prototypical form of this behaviour can be found in animals where, for example, a pigeon is able to 'report' on its previous behaviour by differentially pecking keys. For humans who have verbal capabilities, self-discrimination is a complex behaviour involving symbolic representations of ourselves in the world. As children we receive a massive amount of training in reporting our own behaviour. We are continually reinforced for being able to appropriately report 'I want …', 'I am …', 'I know …' and for appropriately differentiating between 'I' and 'you'. From this behavioural perspective, self is the behaviour of reporting one's own behaviour. It is a verb not a noun.

Further from a behavioural perspective the self is functional: It is 'a repertoire of behaviour imparted by an organized set of contingencies" (Skinner 1976, p. 164). We construct a sense of self in response to the functional demands of social interactions. This process is inherently social and linguistic – our 'knowing' is a function of environmental contingencies rather than any internal 'force' or 'drive': 'In arranging conditions under which a person describes the public or private world in which he lives, a community generates that very special form of behavior called knowing. It is only when a person's private world becomes important to others that it is made important to him' (Skinner 1976, p. 35). However, Skinner's conceptualisation of self relied entirely upon operant processes that were unable to adequately account for the complexity of language. A more recent contextual-behavioural approach, known as relational frame theory (Hayes *et al.* 2001), provides a more adequate account of the verbal behaviours associated with creating and maintaining identity.

Relational frame theory views all human cognition as the behaviour or ongoing activity of relating events or experiences. When we learn to use language, we learn to relate. Indeed, the process of learning language is a process of being continually reinforced for bringing things and events into appropriate relationships with the arbitrary cues we call words. After enough direct training of relationships (e.g. A 'is bigger than' B, B 'is bigger than' C) we learn to derive relations between words and events (e.g. A 'is bigger than' C, C 'is smaller than' B), where 'events' are any experience of the world (including other words) or of the self. The infinite generativity of human language arises from our capacity to infer relations between anything, even arbitrary symbols, and to make use of many different types of relation, such as evaluative (better/worse), hierarchical (part of/includes), conditional (causal/if … then) and temporal (before/after) relations. This unique human ability to relate arbitrary cues allows us to step outside the realm of direct sensory experience, formulate a past and a future, and abstract a sense of self.

From the perspective of relational frame theory, the evolution of a sense of self corresponds to learning to appropriately use the relational frames I/you, here/there and now/then. Consistent with Skinner's account, these 'deictic' (Barnes-Holmes, McHugh, and Barnes-Holmes 2004) frames are thought to be abstracted from naturalistic multiple exemplar training responding to questions such as 'What are you doing now?', 'Where are you going then?', 'What do you want?' and so on. Deictic, in this instance, denotes relational terms where the meaning of that expression is dependent on the context and point of view from which it is used. Unlike the other types of relating described in the previous paragraph, deictic relational frames must be abstracted from a particular point of view. The individual child must begin to notice and abstract the experience of the I/here reporting on experience that is distinct from you/there. There is anywhere other than here and here is always from this point of view (Hayes 1984). It is easy to see how difficult it is to learn this sort of deictic relational framing by noticing how young children frequently make errors of perspective taking. A young child might mistakenly report what they ate for breakfast when asked what their brother ate (Hayes 1984) or they may mistakenly believe an absent observer would know where a hidden doll is located because they themselves know (Kegan 1994). It takes repeated exposure to social contingencies to successfully apply the terms I and you.

Relational frame theory thus sees the evolving self as the process of bringing one's verbal constructions of self into increasingly complex verbal relations with other aspects of experience (Barnes-Holmes, Hayes, and Dymond 2001). This approach has a number of resonances with modern social constructionist thinking on identity, particularly with regard to an emphasis on the processes of construction of self through social, dialogical processes (Beech 2008). However, there are also important differences. Most notably, relational frame theory provides a more complete account of the social contingencies that give rise to the acquisition of a sense of self through language. Most social constructionist accounts do not adequately describe language acquisition in childhood. Furthermore, social constructionist accounts often rely upon vague metaphors that rest on intuitions that the self is a thing not a process. Identity is thought to be 'constructed', having a 'structure' (Hannah *et al.* 2009) that can be 'patched' or 'splinted' (Pratt *et al.* 2006). By contrast, the relational frame theory account of identity development provides a precise, naturalistic description of the socio-linguistic basis of these effects.

One key element of this approach is to distinguish between three functional uses of the term 'self': self-as-story, self-as-process and self-as-perspective (Torneke 2010), each of which we now describe in turn.

Self-as-story: the conceptualised self

Self-as-story is the conceptualized self (Torneke 2010). It is any self-description of characteristic preferences, capabilities, and experiences; the sort of behaviour we engage in when we meet someone new and wish to describe ourselves. In the workplace, self-as-story might refer to conceptualisations of our job attitudes, the things we characteristically say we like and dislike. It might refer to our descriptions of our roles and responsibilities and our place in a network of social relationships.

As children, we learn very quickly that it is helpful to be able to describe ourselves to others. The social environment provides numerous reinforcers for being able to consistently describe characteristic preferences, capabilities, and experiences. Mature forms of self-as-story include personal philosophies, traditions, loyalties, and beliefs. Such descriptions allow others to predict our behaviour, and provide a concise and greatly simplified summary of our history of experience. Over time we learn to internalise our conceptualised self-discrimination. The contextual behavioural approach sees this behaviour as functionally identical to talking about the self except that, once internalised, we can have a different, private conceptualised self to that which we publicly display. We may say to others that we feel confident in order to save face while privately we acknowledge to ourselves we are not.

In order to allow ourselves and others to predict our behaviour it is critical that our conceptualised self is a) coherent, b) accurate, and c) reasonably stable over time. While some unpredictability in behaviour may enhance relationships, relationships with others are built on a sense of knowing the other, including their preferences and likely behaviours in a certain situation. A conceptualised self that is incoherent is less predictive or reliable. For example, if a child says they do not like broccoli but they do like vegetables, we are quick to point out that broccoli is a vegetable and that their preferences (qualities of themselves) are inconsistent and unhelpful for the person providing a meal. Similarly, if at one meal the child says they like broccoli and at the next they say they do not, it is equally unhelpful in terms of predicting the child's behaviour – consistent preferencing is reinforced. Verbal relating can easily support even such relatively simple behaviours becoming complex conceptualisations of self. For example, over time, parents may describe broad patterns of eating behaviour as either healthy or unhealthy and quite rapidly children learn (through derivation of relations as described above) to describe *themselves* as either healthy or unhealthy and, by extension, good or bad. In the same way, performance management and effective team leadership requires that leaders and members discriminate and communicate their preferences consistently and track broader patterns of behaviour over time. Inaccurate or inconsistent self-reporting makes it difficult to predict and manage performance in order to achieve important personal and team outcomes.

But while having a conceptualised self is functional and reinforcing, it can also be very limiting. The internalisation of the need for coherence provides stability through time, but it also provides significant limits on what a person feels they can say or do. For example, a person who sees themselves as an introvert may avoid social situations that they believe they will find stressful, living in an increasingly insular world. Furthermore, our conceptualised self is just a tiny, abstracted remnant of the totality of our experience. As such, it tends to be vastly simplified and does not capture the full richness of our life history. It refers to the sense of self that a person has abstracted from their experience over time, either through noticing their own behaviour or through listening to others' descriptions of their behaviour.

In summary, our self-as-story is our verbal (private or public) description of who we are – our labels of self, memories, plans, experiences, and descriptions. Self-as-story is less about the experience of the present moment, and more about an abstraction of past experiences or current qualities and characteristics as the result of past experiences. Self-as-story is more or less synonymous with the 'remembering self' (Kahneman and Riis 2005).

The entire field of identity research within organisational studies appears to focus upon this sense of self. Identity is conceptualised as the abstracted, linguistic responses offered to the question 'Who am I?' But our identity is not just the relatively rigid and abstracted labels we use to describe ourselves. Research and practice regarding mindfulness makes it clear that we also have a more dynamic, present-moment sense of self to which we now turn.

Self-as-process: the experiencing self

Self-as-process refers to the continuous and more flexible verbal self-knowledge of the present moment (Hayes *et al.* 2011), the description of experience of self in this present moment. It is the continuous unfolding dynamic of thoughts, feelings, sensations, and images occurring here-now, which is emphasised in mindfulness practice. Kahneman and Riis (2005) refer to it as the 'experiencing self' and note that it has hardly been studied in psychology because almost all instruments call for retrospective report and thus invoke remembered abstractions regarding the self.

Self-as-process behaviour is also highly socially useful. Statements like 'I am happy', 'My stomach is hurting' or 'I don't understand what I am meant to do' provide useful and predictive information to others. Over time, such statements about the self also serve useful private functions. Being able to monitor our current state is the basis of successful self-regulation. For example, identifying how one feels in the present moment is predictive of the contextual changes that might produce desired changes in feeling.

Self-as-process descriptions refer to the here and now of experience. They are still verbal descriptions of experience rather than the experience itself, and are thus somewhat abstracted. But compared with self-as-story, self-as-process is more about particular experiences within particular contexts than general responses over multiple instances and contexts. As such, self-as-process descriptions are socially predictive but in a different way than self-as-story. To say 'I am happy' may be highly predictive of what will happen in the next instance or in a very similar context in the future. To say 'I am generally a happy person' provides broad predictability across contexts. So self-as-process descriptions are more flexible and dynamic than self-as-story because they describe one's current state in context. This makes them less rigid.

Self-as-perspective: the transcendent self

Mindfulness practice in addition emphasises the cultivation of a third sense of self where the self is seen as an observer of experience. Unlike both self-as-story and self-as-process, self-as-perspective refers to the perspective from which experience is observed rather than the content that is observed. In relational frame theory, self-as-perspective is understood as the point of view or locus from which events are experienced and, as such, self-as-perspective is constant despite changing experiential content. A person aged forty-five witnesses experience from the same point of view as they did at the age of five. It is the bare awareness, the context of our experiencing (Hayes 1984) and the knowing that exists even before we are verbal. Metaphorically, we can understand self-as-perspective as a torch that shines a beam of light (self-as-process) on objects in our visual field (self-as-story) (Harris 2009). In this metaphor, self-as-perspective is the source of light (i.e. awareness itself).

Torneke (2010, p. 107) provides a vivid description of the content-free nature of self-as-perspective:

We cannot observe this perspective in itself. It can never become an object for us to observe. We can talk or write about it, just as I am doing now, and we can observe the consequences of being able to take this perspective. We can make observations from a specific perspective or locus, but we can never observe this locus or perspective as such. Of course, this is rather obvious, because from which perspective would we observe it? All we have is I-here-now. And whatever we observe, it simply cannot be this locus, as that is the vantage from which we observe it.

In summary, we have described three senses in which we engage in 'self-discrimination' behaviour. We describe our abstracted qualities and experiences as story, we describe our current here-and-now experience as process, and we have a sense of the continuity of a point of view from which we experience the world. From a contextual, behavioural perspective, identity is a behaviour (that we refer to as 'self-discrimination') and is a functional response to social contingencies. The way a person talks about the self *is* the act of creating an identity, it is not a reflection of some underlying true self. We learn to report our preferences, history, and characteristics because the social world values reliability and coherence. Similarly, we learn to report on our current experience because it allows social communication and cooperation. And while most verbal environments (with the exception of meditation retreats and philosophy seminars) do not explicitly reinforce talking about ourselves as bare awareness or perspective, we *are* continuously reinforced for correctly discriminating our 'own' experience (I/here) from that of others (you/there) and for having a stable perspective from which we view experience.

This theoretical framework provides a new way of understanding identity work in the organisational context. From this perspective (see Figure 6.1), our self-as-story is the abstracted, linguistic product of the experience of a continuous flow of events (self-as-process), witnessed from the perspective of a point of view (self-as-perspective). Whereas historically identity has referred almost exclusively to self-as-story, this framework offers an expanded notion of identity to include our awareness of present moment experience and also of awareness itself, a key requirement if one is to understand mindfulness. This approach provides an account of identity formation and change that is founded on precise theories of learning and language rather than vague naturalistic metaphors of construction.

In the study described in the next section, we use this theoretical approach to inform the design and validation of a behavioural

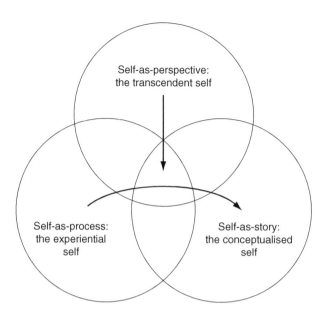

Figure 6.1 The relationships between the three functional senses of self

measure of self-discrimination as a behaviour. We examine changes in self-discrimination behaviour as the result of an MBSR course. Mindfulness training directly targets this process of identity construction: encouraging people to hold their self-conceptualisations (including evaluations) less rigidly, and focus more on the process of ongoing experience (self-as-process) and the point of view from which experience is observed (self-as-perspective). We thus make the following propositions:

1. Mindfulness training decreases the frequency of self-as-rigid-story statements as participants learn to de-identify from their experience.
2. Mindfulness training increases the frequency of self-as-process statements as participants learn to attend more to the experience of the present moment.
3. Mindfulness training increases the frequency of self-as-perspective statements as participants self-discriminate their own noticing of private mental experience and learn to see themselves as observers of their experience.

To date no measures of self-discrimination behaviour exist. Consistent with self-discrimination having its origins in verbal relating, the qualitative measure described next was designed to provide a behavioural measure of talking about the self and others.

Method

Participants and intervention

Seven participants from a community sample taking part in an MBSR course volunteered to participate in the research following a request by the course facilitator at an initial familiarisation session. This course emphasised learning mindfulness practices, and thus was expected to have some impact upon the way in which people saw themselves and discussed aspects of their experience. All but one of the participants were women. The average age was 40 (Min = 27, Max = 53). All participants were educated to at least senior high school level and all but one were university educated.

Interview

Interviewees were told the purpose of the study was to better understand their hopes and aims for the course and to gather examples of how they made sense of their experience. Interviews based on the subject-object interview technique (Lahey *et al.* 1988) were conducted before and after the course. The seven pre-course interviews commenced with the question 'What are you hoping to get out of the course?' while the post-course questions commenced with the question 'What did you get out of the course?'. Questioning within the interviews was semi-structured with the primary intention of the interviewer being to explore how different life experiences were understood in relation to meaning, what consequences were perceived as influencing behaviour and how the interviewee knew about and evaluated their experience.

Coding

The interviews were transcribed and analysed in NVivo using codes for eight main verbal acts: five for self-statements and three for statements about others. The coding of statements about others was part of our research examining the ways in which identity shapes our judgments and categorisations concerning others. However, here we describe only the coding of self-statements.

Each sentence was coded for any occurrence of a particular form of self-discrimination. Thus, sentences could be coded with multiple overlapping codes but each code could only appear once for a given sentence. The sentence (rather than individual words or phrases) was chosen as the unit of analysis because a) 'self-discrimination' behaviours are expressed most coherently at this level (Styles and Atkins, in preparation), b) it reduced the coding burden, and c) it allowed calculation of inter-rater reliability.

From a contextual-behavioural perspective, the way a person talks about the self *is* the act of creating an identity, it is not a reflection of some underlying true self causing a secondary behaviour. In the remainder of this section we define and give examples for each of the codes that we used in our behavioural measure of self-discrimination.

Self-as-story. We distinguished between rigid and flexible self-conceptualisations because these had different implications for identity change.

[SRS] = Self-as-rigid-story. As described previously, all self-as-story statements involve abstracted conceptualisations of experience. Self-as-rigid-story refers to instances where that abstracted story is expressed in a way that is relatively inflexible. It refers to literal (i.e. held as the truth) descriptions regarding who I am or could be; either qualities or characteristics, or evaluations of those qualities and characteristics. There is usually a strong sense of identification with the quality or characteristic: the 'I' is seen as being 'the same as' the quality or the characteristic. In the relational frame theory literature, this identification with an abstracted term is called 'fusion' (Hayes *et al.* 2011).

The prototypical self-as-rigid-story statement is a self-categorisation in terms of role, personal characteristics or beliefs about oneself, such as:

• 'I am not that sort of person; I am more of an introvert.'
• 'I am a lawyer.'
• 'I find I'm not judgmental about it now either.'
• '… I think it's God in me or God being in me or God working with what's in me.'

Self-as-story is often evaluative and involves comparison to a set of personal or social standards, for example:

- 'I'm not good enough in their eyes.'
- 'I've got a renewed focus perhaps of a set of values that I've probably had in the background for many years of really valuing or admiring or holding up a standard ...'

Sometimes it is difficult to tell if a self-as-story statement functions in a rigid or flexible way without taking account of the sentences around it. For example, the following statement could be either self-as-rigid-story or self-as-flexible-story depending upon whether it is a) identified with and b) is seen as influencing current behaviour:

- 'I was very much brought up to just try to figure out how to make it all right around me.'

[SFS] = Self-as-flexible-story. This code refers to descriptions of past and possible future behaviours and inner experiences that are seen as part of the conceptualised self but are not rigidly influencing behaviour (Hayes *et al.* 2011). Flexibility arises from either a) the person holding these statements somewhat more tentatively as a provisional interpretation rather than the literal truth, or b) the person not identifying with the qualities, characteristics, or experiences being described. In other words, these statements are less about defining 'who I am' in terms of qualities and characteristics, and more about describing 'what I have experienced or might experience in the future'. Prototypical examples of self-as-flexible-story are statements about memories held in a way that does not rigidly shape current behaviour:

- 'Each day I pick up my child, and we usually talk all the way home in the car.'
- 'On Wednesday I went to the dentist.'
- 'I will finish that in the morning.'

Other self-as-flexible-story components involve descriptions of self-characteristics that are offered in such a way that alternatives are possible:

- 'Most of the time I like it when that happens.'
- 'I don't think I would have been able to do that before.'

SFS statements are distinguished from self-as-process because they are more abstracted and story-like than a description of immediate experience.

[SP] = **Self-as-process**. This refers to any description of the current experience of the self. The standard form is a description of a current thought, feeling, image, or sensation. For example:

- 'I can't remember.'
- 'I don't really know what I mean.'
- 'I don't know if I'm answering your question.'
- 'It's hard to describe.'
- 'I want to take my daughter to school next week.'

Self-as-process describes the ongoing experience of the present moment here and now (Foody, Barnes-Holmes, and Barnes-Holmes 2012).

[SX] = **Self-as-perspective**. Technically, self-as-perspective is not observable in text because it refers to a point of view from which experience arises, rather than the content of the experience. Anything that we can describe is, by definition, *not* self-as-perspective but the content that perspective observes. However, for the purposes of this measure, we have used this label to refer to points where we could reasonably infer awareness of a self that is able to witness experience, an observing self. Based on empirical work with interventions to enhance perspective taking (Foody, Barnes-Holmes, Barnes-Holmes, and Luciano, 2013; Luciano *et al.* 2011), we distinguished between two forms of self-as-perspective which we labelled SX1 and SX2.

SX1. This code represents instances where a person clearly de-identifies from their private mental experience (thoughts, feelings, and sensations). That is, they make a statement recognising that they are not the same thing as their private mental experiences. This process of recognising private experiences as passing mental events rather than literal truths is called 'defusion' (Hayes *et al.* 2011):

- 'I noticed I was angry but I didn't want to lash out.'
- 'I've tended to give my emotions little personalities.'
- 'It is all just stupid thoughts that I look at afterwards and go "What was I thinking?"'
- 'But what's happened is I have thought those things but then I've thought, "No hang on, why are you thinking that, you weren't thinking that at all before this person approached you out of the blue".'
- 'And sometimes I think "Hang on, just take a step back from this, you're a person who's lying in bed, you [laughs] should be asleep

and you're thinking this set of thoughts, you can't do anything about them right now".'

Self-as-perspective statements can combine self-as-rigid-story with self-as-perspective.

- 'Once I started learning to get over stuff and letting things go I became really good at it, but throw a whole bunch of pain on there and I'm reverting back to my old self which I don't like, which is the scared anxious teary person, obviously that I used to be.'

SX2. Luciano *et al.* (2011) suggested a second form of self-as-perspective as when the person not only notices that they are not the same thing as their private mental experience, but that they are the 'container' for their experience. In a sense, SX1 focuses on what private mental experiences are not, while SX2 focuses on what they are – i.e. a transitory aspect of a more stable awareness of experience. The following quotes all illustrate ways in which the mind, brain, or 'I/me' are offered as 'containers' for the experience rather than identifying with the experience:

- '… recognising the unhelpful things that my mind does, because understanding that it'll latch on to an idea and then stick to it, being able to recognise that that's what I'm doing …'
- 'So my brain just goes, "Right let's find something to pick on" and it is whoever is making the most noise at the time usually.'
- 'Like, being able to recognise what I do in my head and what happens to me physically when I'm starting to get frustrated.'
- '… part of me has negative thoughts and gives me these, part of me is giving negative messages and another part of myself is criticising those and analysing that and saying, "Well that can't be wholly true".'

Results

Reliability

After initial discussions and comparisons of coding, a subset of interviews was selected for coding by both authors independently to establish a reliability score. At the time of writing, inter-rater reliability is adequate to excellent for the various codes and overall (Table 6.1). Fleiss (1981) recommended kappa of 0.4 to 0.75 be considered

Table 6.1 *Inter-rater reliability for the functional self-discrimination coding scheme*

	Cohen's Kappa
Self-as-rigid-story [SRS]	0.43
Self-as-flexible-story [SFS]	0.58
Self-as-process [SP]	0.49
Self-as-perspective 1 [SX1]	0.67
Self-as-perspective 2 [SX2]	0.53
Self-as-perspective overall	0.80
Mean overall Kappa	0.54

fair to good, while kappa > 0.75 be considered excellent. Table 6.1 reveals that the code used for self-as-rigid-story was the least reliable. Discussion of this result between raters revealed slight differences in the way in which 'rigid' was being interpreted. Subsequent coding is expected to produce higher inter-rater agreement.

Frequencies

The total frequency of each code was divided by the total number of sentences to obtain the proportion of sentences with each code. These do not necessarily add up to 100 per cent as sentences without a self-reference received no code and other sentences were given multiple codes. We calculated frequency of codes as a proportion of the total number of sentences in the interview to control for the effects of interview length. Figure 6.2 presents the mean frequencies of occurrence for each of the five codes across the seven participants. As expected, self-as-rigid-story (SRS) declined significantly following the course $(t(6) = 5.3, p = .002)$. Although we report significance tests throughout, we recognise that the n is very small for this pilot study and the results are therefore both conservative and should be interpreted cautiously. Unexpectedly, self-as-flexible-story increased following the intervention $(t(6) = 2.7, p = .035)$ and self-as-process did not systematically change $(t(6) = 0.7, p = \text{n.s.})$. As expected, self-as-perspective statements increased for both SX1 $(t(6) = 3.4, p = .015)$ and SX2 $(t(6) = 2.1, p = .078)$. The latter result was only marginally significant using a two-tailed significance test, but this was a conservative interpretation

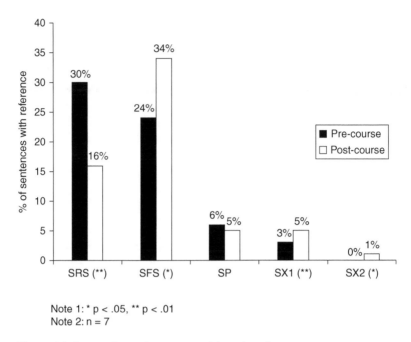

Note 1: * p < .05, ** p < .01
Note 2: n = 7

Figure 6.2 Proportions of sentences with each code

given that the change was in the direction predicted. Examination of frequencies for each individual revealed that all participants displayed the same pattern of results with the exception of one participant who demonstrated a slight decrease in SFS.

Qualitative analysis

Examination of the patterns of codes within the texts also supported the overall conclusion that participants were demonstrating more flexible self-discrimination behaviour. For example, participant PT, a 53-year-old female partner in a law firm, discussed in the pre-course interview how she experienced feelings of panic when she discovered that she had made a mistake in preparing a contract:

So a year later I could see a contract and see a mistake, and that triggers a reaction of anxiety that is far beyond the ... mistake [SRS] ... I can feel myself going into this panic and then it's like a veil comes down in front of my eyes... [SRS] It's like a whole physical reaction to the fear that I've made a mistake and that it's going to cause problems for a client [SRS]. ... And once I go into that state, I can stay in that place for three days, where I kind of can't really function [SRS]. If I have to come to work, I'll come in [SFS]. I'll deal with my work, but every minute that I'm not having to deal with other things, I'll be dealing with it in my head, and at night it'll be raging, uncontrollable kind of anxiety [SRS]. ... It's about being found out and knowing that I'm not perfect [SRS]...

[INTERVIEWER]: And what's the worst thing about [thinking 'I'm not perfect']?

I think that challenges my whole way I deal with my life [SRS]. ... if I can manage and control my life, then I'll be safe [SRS]. And if I don't manage and control my life, then I have a more catastrophic view of my – of how my life will be [SRS]...

If I've made that mistake, how do I trust myself to do what I do [SRS]? How can I be a lawyer? [SRS] ... I always felt like I was a fake, and that I probably – they'd made a mistake and I shouldn't have got into law school [SRS]. So the first year of law school was about proving that I could be there and they hadn't made a mistake [SFS]...

For PT, making a mistake was not just a matter of failing, it was a threat to her very identity that challenged the whole way she dealt with her life. In the post-course interview, she again reflected upon the experience of making a mistake, this time in a personal relationship. She still experiences some of the same thoughts and feelings, but there is also the beginning of a new way of understanding her identity in relation to those thoughts and feelings, a way of identifying herself as something different to, and bigger than, the mistake she has made:

A friend of mine rang me up and said to me that I'd said something to them that had hurt them, and I hadn't, of course, intended what – they had heard something I hadn't intended [SFS]. And my instant reaction was to pick up the phone and ring, which I did ...[SFS] So I cleaned it up really quickly, whereas previously I would have just stewed and made a big deal of it for the whole day ... [SFS] But then I was left all day thinking, a little bit, 'well how could they think that of me?' ... [SFS] I felt a little bit hurt that they had assumed the worst of what I had said, rather than tried to look for the good in it [SFS]. I talked to myself aloud by saying that that's my stuff, whatever they've got going on for them is their stuff, but I'm now getting my stuff into it by acting hurt myself, feeling hurt [SX2]. And so, I guess that I did get to the point where I didn't have to identify with it any more [SX2].

... And then I just thought, this is a friend and I don't want to spend time trying to dwell on this because it's all fixed up now and it doesn't – I don't have to make it a big deal if I choose not to [SFS][SX1]. So I felt I had a choice [SFS]. That's, I think, the difference [SP]. I had a choice in either staying with – locking into that or letting it go, and I was able to tell myself I had a choice [SRS][SX1].

Another participant, BC, a 50-year-old female pastoral care coordinator in a high school, had been in a new job for two months and was very concerned about maintaining a good reputation with other teachers. She had come to the MBSR course primarily to manage and reduce her stress. During the pre-course interview she discussed an evaluative and potentially embarrassing situation at school. She had been talking about how her father had been a Protestant minister and she believed this created a need for perfection within her, what she referred to as her 'good-girl voice'. She continually evaluated whether others approved of what she was doing, whether she was accepted and the fear she felt that she might be rejected by others if she made a mistake. Her pre-course interview was characterised by a great deal of self-as-rigid-story or self-as-flexible-story. Much of the interview was spent describing her anxiety regarding being observed by others at work:

So for me once I … start to become accountable and visible, I really have a reaction of over reacting really negatively in terms of myself [SRS]. … I could be going along fine managing something and if [I am perceived] by people as at all negative the impact is awful [SRS]… Both the physical feelings and the mental thoughts and sometimes it is all I can nearly do to try and keep going along when that happens [SFS]. And as I've got older, … it's got a stronger reaction … [SRS].

After the course, BC reflected on how her perspective had changed on her fear of being evaluated by others:

I feel like I'm starting to be able to have some peaceful time [SFS]. So it's not that, for example, at school it's not that things aren't sometimes difficult, it's being able to let them go and not be constantly caught up in this thinking and thinking and worrying about how I'm going to make that all right [SX1] … It's just being able to stop and step outside [the] physical effects of the anxiety or the worrying about other people [SX1]. [These physical effects] would always send me straight into my head [to work out] how to fix it, how to make it all right [SFS[1]]. And as long as those sensations stayed I would be trying to do that [SFS]. And really hating those sensations – so it's really meant that I don't have to fly into that [SFS]. It's just stopped that part of the conscious process of automatically [reacting], I mean I would be doing that without even knowing in the past [SFS]... So that's a really enormous shift for me [SRS]... My relationships are becoming strengthened, particularly my professional relationships, by not carrying that reaction to people of trying to fix everything [SRS] ... I'm finding (that) voice is still there, I'm very much aware that it is there [SX1], it's just not running the show any more.

What is so fascinating about this quote is that it is not the content of her experience that has changed as a result of the mindfulness course, but her response to her automatic thoughts regarding how she ought to be. No longer do thoughts carry the same power to hurt, they are relative, subsumed by a larger sense of self that can contain but not be constituted by the thoughts.

In summary, both cases illustrate the way in which personal dilemmas that were constituted by a particular way of viewing the self became less rigid and more flexible following the course. These examples illustrate how the coding scheme revealed qualitative, behavioural differences in the way that people were constructing a sense of themselves in the act of describing their experience. Both examples also powerfully illustrate the impact of positive identity work upon relationships. In both cases, after the course the participants demonstrated considerably more flexible perspective taking evidenced by less rigid and more flexible self-as-story statements, and also bigger perspectives on themselves as observers of their experience. In the organisational context, we might expect that this bigger perspective would be likely to lead to more positive and supportive relationships.

Discussion

Overall the pattern of these preliminary results provides strong support for both our approach to coding for flexibility of perspective taking

---

[1] Coding depends partially upon the tense. This and the next two sentences would have been coded SRS were it not for the fact that she subsequently says that she offers these examples only to say that they are patterns of behaviour that are no longer true for her.

and also for the efficacy of the MBSR course in fostering more flexible perspective taking. Our approach provides a new way of quantifying and evaluating changes in identity resulting from identity work interventions such as mindfulness training at work. It also potentially provides the beginning of a qualitative measure of mindfulness that could be used to overcome the many limitations of self-report measures of mindfulness. The functional approach to understanding self could also be useful for understanding other 'transformational' staff development initiatives. Leadership requires not just skills but also more complex ways of perceiving and understanding the self in context (Heifetz, Grashow, and Linsky 2009; Snook, Nohria, and Khurana 2012). But to date, little research has been conducted on the mechanisms underpinning such changes in perspective taking. In thinking about optimal states of functioning in the workplace and more generally, some theorists emphasise the acquisition of increasingly complex beliefs about the constructive nature of the self (Kegan and Lahey, 2009) while others emphasise the importance of an ongoing sense of awareness and/or self-endorsement of experience (Glomb *et al.* 2012; Ryan and Deci 2000). Our approach seems likely to contribute to a better understanding of the relative contributions of self-as-story, process and perspective in understanding and effectively engaging with self and other.

The relative frequency of different forms of self-discrimination behaviour could be expected to influence the capacity of the person to flexibly respond to different contexts. Self-as-story provides coherence and predictability, but it can create rigidity of response. Self-as-process and self-as-perspective increase contact with the direct contingencies of experience rather than one's verbal abstractions regarding experience, and thus increase context sensitivity and flexibility. Alvesson and Willmott eloquently noted the growing importance of a more flexible and open sense of self:

In conditions of late modernity, however, identities are comparatively open and achieved rather than given or closed ... Roles are improvised rather than scripted. Given the accomplished and sometimes precarious nature of contemporary identity, much, if not all activity involves active identity work: people are continuously engaged in forming, repairing, maintaining, strengthening or revising the constructions that are productive of a precarious sense of coherence and distinctiveness. Specific events, encounters, transitions, experiences, surprises, as well as more constant strains, serve to heighten awareness of the constructed quality of self-identity and compel more concentrated identity work. (2002, p. 626)

A similar point has also been made by constructive-developmental theorists exploring changes in perspective taking occasioned by changes in society (Commons and Ross 2008; Kegan 1994). The behaviour of talking about the self and its experiences is at the very core of organisational behaviour and psychology. Indeed, over recent decades, popular media and discourse has increasingly emphasised the importance of developing a strong sense of an authentic self. Global culture increasingly emphasises self-determination with a strong normative belief in most Western countries at least that more choice is better and that we should be able to decide for ourselves between more and more alternatives (Schwartz 2004). In parenting, therapy, and even gender roles, we are asked to actively construct meaning, be comfortable in ·our own skin and decide for ourselves instead of relying upon tradition or authorities (Kegan 1994).

The workplace makes identity demands that are at least as powerful as other contexts because it contains strong and sustained reinforcers and punishers for particular ways of making meaning and deciding. Employees are increasingly expected to demonstrate leadership that is authentic to their 'core selves' (Avolio and Gardner 2005), to be proactive (Parker, Bindl, and Strauss 2010), empowered (Argyris 1998; Campbell 2000), autonomously motivated (Deci and Ryan 2000), and agentic in pursuing their goals. In all these contexts, people are socially reinforced by being able to clearly state their preferences and values; and for being able to act assertively in the pursuit of those preferences even in the face of the social disapproval of others.

These changes amount to a broad trend towards being socially reinforced for being able to articulate one's *own* preferences and act in ways to obtain those preferences. But the push towards knowing 'who I am' may have unintended consequences as the 'me generation' has increasing difficulty reconciling its own needs with the needs of others (Gergen 2009). Modern society is increasingly making an even more complex identity demand upon us to move beyond reliance upon others for approval, while also recognising the extent to which every aspect of our being is inherently social (Kegan 1994). People are asked to 'transcend their egos' (Bauer and Wayment 2008) and be more 'dialectical' (Basseches 2005), 'postmodern' (Johnson and Cassell 2001), and systemic (Johnston and Atkins 2005) in their thinking – not just deciding for themselves but observing the processes of their unfolding sense-making (Kegan and Lahey 2010). For example, in managing conflict, people are requested to hold their interests and beliefs in suspension while they deeply appreciate multiple alternative perspectives and meanings regarding the situations in which they find themselves (Isaacs 1999). And complex ethical dilemmas often demand that we transcend simple self-interest and have the capacity to understand the systemic interactions of self and other. Taken together, these forces constitute tremendous demands to engage in identity work in organisations and in society more generally. Mindfulness training may provide an important avenue for organisations to assist staff to develop a sense of self that moves beyond a strong sense of a conceptualised self to a more flexible, authentic, and responsive sense of self experiencing in the present moment.

Limitations and further research

Our measure assesses how people talk about themselves. Mindfulness courses teach, among other things, a new way of talking about the self. Novice participants may never have previously even thought of talking about their mind or thoughts as something other than themselves (e.g. 'notice your mind wandering'). And they may never have heard experience being referred to as process rather than content. Is it possible that participants in such a course, or indeed in any training involving new ways of *talking* about the self, might simply learn to talk in a particular way rather than change their broader behaviours? It is an empirical issue to determine whether this measure correlates appropriately with other measures of interest such as wellbeing, engagement, and performance. However, we have argued that the way people *talk* about the self either internally or publically, *is* the process of constructing and maintaining a self. From our perspective, if people have learned a new way of talking this is the very essence of a new way of creating a sense of self and participants will continue to learn new ways of relating to the self if a more expansive way of talking is maintained over time.

More research using this approach is required. This was an exploratory study and, as such, it suffered from a number of limitations. An obvious concern here was that the authors were the coders and were not blind to the hypotheses or whether the interview was before or after training. Obviously a key stage in the evolution of this approach to understanding identity is to train others in coding in order to more thoroughly test reliability. Furthermore, future studies may employ sources of text that do not discuss the intervention so that it will be easier to blind the coder to whether the interview was before or after the course. Ultimately it will be important to compare more standardised interviews where similar questions are asked pre- and post-intervention so that the effects of interviewer questions upon self-discriminative statements can be parcelled out. We are currently finalising analysis of a larger study looking at the relationships between flexibility of self-discrimination behaviour and wellbeing in a workplace sample. Furthermore, we need to explore different ways of eliciting talk about the self. Currently all our data stems from a self-reflective interview but it is possible that this technique might be applicable to a broader range of natural language texts such as group discussions.

Finally we intend to explore relationships between talking about the self and talking about others. There is considerable evidence that the extent to which we are able to accept our own identities is predictive of the extent to which we are able to accept the identities of others (Williams and Lynn 2010). Atkins and Parker (2012) explored how changing relations to the self appears to mediate the relationship between compassion for self and others. Increasing awareness of one's own characteristic patterns of responding, both good and bad, may increase empathy for others.

Conclusion

In summary, we have argued that mindfulness training may have its effects through changes in identity. Specifically we have presented an account of identity change that goes beyond a conceptualised sense of self to include both a sense of moment-to-moment experience and also a sense of self as an observer. When we coded for occurrence of these different, more flexible and dynamic senses of self in natural language texts, we found that a mindfulness intervention significantly reduced the amount of rigid conceptualising among course participants while also increasing the use of terms reflecting a sense of self as an observer of experience. These changes may well be implicated in the changes in wellbeing and performance resulting from mindfulness training as discussed in other chapters in this volume.

While this approach to measuring the rich, natural expression of identity in organisations has obvious applications for mindfulness researchers wanting to move beyond the limitations of self-report measures of mindfulness (Grossman and Van Dam 2011), it may also have other practical applications in the workplace. In conducting the interviews for this study, we were struck by the extent to which participants enjoyed and appeared to benefit from these interviews. Talking about the self, and then learning about the three forms of self could be a coaching intervention in its own right (Berger and Atkins 2009). At the same time, our approach may provide a way of measuring and quantifying deeper elements of identity during the process of staff selection and development than is possible using other measures.

References

Alvesson, M., Ashcraft, K. L., and Thomas, R. (2008). Identity matters: reflections on the construction of identity scholarship in organization studies. *Organization*, 15(1), 5–28. doi: 10.1177/1350508407084426.

Alvesson, M. and Willmott, H. (2002). Identity regulation as organizational control: producing the appropriate individual. *Journal of Management Studies*, 39(5), 619–44. doi: 10.1111/1467–6486.00305.

Argyris, C. (1998). Empowerment: the emperor's new clothes. *Harvard Business Review*, 76 (May/June), 98–105.

Atkins, P. W. B. and Parker, S. K. (2012). Understanding individual compassion in organizations: the role of appraisals and psychological flexibility. *Academy of Management Review*, 37(4), 524–46.

Avolio, B. J. and Gardner, W. L. (2005). Authentic leadership development: getting to the root of positive forms of leadership. *Leadership Quarterly*, 16(3), 315–38.

Barnes-Holmes, D., Hayes, S. C., and Dymond, S. (2001). Self and self-directed rules. In S. C. Hayes, D. Barnes-Holmes and B. Roche (eds.), *Relational frame theory: a post-Skinnerian account of human language and cognition*. New York: Kluwer Academic/Plenum Publishers, pp. 119–39.

Barnes-Holmes, Y., McHugh, L., and Barnes-Holmes, D. (2004). Perspective-taking and theory of mind: a relational frame account. *The Behavior Analyst Today*, 5, 15–25.

Basseches, M. (2005). The development of dialectical thinking as an approach to integration. *Integral Review*, 1(1), 47.

Bauer, J. J. and Wayment, H. A. (2008). The psychology of quieting the ego. In H. A. Wayment and J. J. Bauer (eds.), *Transcending self-interest: Psychological explorations of the quiet ego*. Washington, DC: American Psychological Association, pp. 7–19.

Beech, N. (2008). On the nature of dialogic identity work. *Organization*, 15(1), 51–74. doi: 10.1177/1350508407084485.

(2011). Liminality and the practices of identity reconstruction. *Human Relations*, 64(2), 285–302. doi: 10.1177/0018726710371235.

Beech, N., Kajzer-Mitchell, I., Oswick, C., and Saren, M. (2011). Barriers to change and identity work in the swampy lowland. *Journal of Change Management*, 11(3), 289–304. doi: 10.1080/14697017.2011.564591.

Bem, D. J. (1967). Self-perception: an alternative interpretation of cognitive dissonance phenomena. *Psychological Review*, 74(3), 183–200. doi: http://dx.doi.org/10.1037/h0024835.

Bennett, C. J. and Howlett, M. (1992). The lessons of learning: reconciling theories of policy learning and policy change. *Policy Sciences*, 25(3), 275–94.

Berger, J. G. and Atkins, P. W. B. (2009). Mapping complexity of mind: using the subject-object interview in coaching. *Coaching: An International Journal of Theory, Research and Practice*, 2(1), 23–36.

Campbell, D. J. (2000). The proactive employee: managing workplace initiative. *The Academy of Management Executive*, 14 (Aug), 52–66.

Carroll, B. and Levy, L. (2010). Leadership development as identity construction. *Management Communication Quarterly*, 24(2), 211–31. doi: 10.1177/0893318909358725.

Colebatch, H. K. (2002). *Policy*. 2nd edn. Buckingham: Open University Press.

Commons, M. L. and Ross, S. N. (2008). What postformal thought is, and why it matters. *World Futures: Journal of General Evolution*, 64(5), 321–9.

Deci, E. L. and Ryan, R. M. (2000). The "what" and "why" of goal pursuits: human needs and the self-determination of behavior. *Psychological Inquiry*, 11(4), 227–68.

DeRue, D. S. and Ashford, S. J. (2010). Who will lead and who will follow? A social process of leadership identity construction in organizations. *The Academy of Management Review*, 35(4), 627–47.

Dolowitz, D. P. and Marsh, D. (2000). Learning from Abroac: the role of policy transfer in contemporary policy-making. *Governance: An International Journal of Policy and Administration*, 13(1), 5–24.

Fiol, C. M., Pratt, M. G., and O'Connor, E. J. (2009). Managing intractable identity conflicts. *Academy of Management Review*, 34(1), 32–55.

Fleiss, J. L. (1981). *Statistical methods for rates and proportions*. 2nd edn.. New York: John Wiley.

Foody, M., Barnes-Holmes, Y., and Barnes-Holmes, D. (2012). The role of self in acceptance and commitment therapy. In L. McHugh and I. Stewart (eds.), *The self and perspective taking: contributions and applications from modern behavioral science*. Oakland, CA: Context Press, pp. 125–42.

Foody, M., Barnes-Holmes, Y., Barnes-Holmes, D., and Luciano, M. C. (2013). An empirical investigation of hierarchical versus distinction relations in a self-based ACT exercise. *International Journal of Psychology and Psychological Therapy*, 13(3), 373–85.

Gergen, K. J. (2009). *Relational being: beyond self and community*. Oxford University Press.

Glomb, T. M., Duffy, M. K., Bono, J. E., and Yang, T. (2012). Mindfulness at work. *Research in Personnel and Human Resource Management*, 30, 115–57.

Grossman, P. and Van Dam, N. T. (2011). Mindfulness, by any other name: trials and tribulations of sati in western psychology and science. *Contemporary Buddhism: An Interdisciplinary Journal*, 12(1), 219–39.

Hannah, S., Woolfolk, R., and Lord, G. (2009). Leader self-structure: a framework for positive leadership. *Journal of Organizational Behavior*, 30(2), 269.

Harris, R. (2009). *ACT made simple*. Oakland, CA: New Harbinger Publications.

Hayes, S. C. (1984). Making sense of spirituality. *Behaviorism*, 12(2), 99–110.

Hayes, S. C., Barnes-Holmes, D., and Roche, B. (2001). *Relational frame theory: a post-Skinnerian account of human language and cognition*. New York: Kluwer Academic/Plenum Publishers.

Hayes, S. C. and Gregg, J. (2000). Functional contextualism and the self. In C. Muran (ed.), *Self-relations in the psychotherapy process*. Washington, DC: American Psychological Association, pp. 291–307.

Hayes, S. C., Strosahl, K. D., and Wilson, K. G. (2011). *Acceptance and commitment therapy: the process and practice of mindful change*. 2nd edn. New York: The Guilford Press.

Heifetz, R., Grashow, A., and Linsky, M. (2009). *The practice of adaptive leadership: tools and tactics for changing your organisation and the world*. Cambridge, MA: Harvard Business Press.

Ibarra, H. and Petriglieri, J. L. (2010). Identity work and play. *Journal of Organizational Change Management*, 23(1), 10–25.

Isaacs, W. (1999). *Dialogue and the art of thinking together.* New York: Doubleday.

Johnson, P. and Cassell, C. (2001). Epistemology and work psychology: new agendas. *Journal of Occupational and Organizational Psychology,* 74(2), 125–43.

Johnston, K. and Atkins, P. W. B. (2005). An exploration of the complexity of thinking and consciousness required to sustainably 'manage' the environment. Paper presented at the Australia and New Zealand Systems Thinking Conference, Christchurch, New Zealand, December 5–7, 2005.

Kahneman, D. and Riis, J. (2005). Living, and thinking about it: two perspectives on life. In F. A. Huppert, N. Baylis, and B. Keverne (eds.), *The science of well-being.* Oxford University Press, pp. 285–304.

Kegan, R. (1994). *In over our heads: the mental demands of modern life.* Cambridge, MA: Harvard University Press.

Kegan, R. and Lahey, L. (2009). *Reconceiving the challenge of change immunity to change.* Boston, MA: Harvard Business Press.

Kegan, R. and Lahey, L. (2010). Adult development and organisational leadership. In N. Nohria and R. Khurana (eds.), *Handbook of leadership theory and practice.* USA: Harvard Business School Publishing Corporation.

Lahey, L., Souvaine, E., Kegan, R., Goodman, R., and Felix, S. (1988). *A guide to the subject-object interview: its administration and interpretation.* Cambridge, MA: Harvard Graduate School of Education.

Luciano, C., Ruiz, F. J., Torres, R. M. V., Martin, V. S., Martinez, O. G., and Lopez, J. C. L. (2011). A relational frame analysis of defusion interactions in Acceptance and Commitment Therapy: a preliminary and quasi-experimental study with at-risk adolescents. *International Journal of Psychology and Psychological Therapy,* 11(2), 165–82.

Osborne, J. W. and Jones, B. D. (2011). Identification with academics and motivation to achieve in school: how the structure of the self influences academic outcomes. *Educational Psychology Review,* 23(1), 131–58.

Parker, S. K., Bindl, U. K., and Strauss, K. (2010). Making things happen: a model of proactive motivation. *Journal of Management,* 36(4), 827–56.

Petriglieri, G. and Petriglieri, J. L. (2010). Identity workspaces: the case of business schools. *Academy of Management Learning and Education,* 9(1), 44–60.

Pratt, M. G., Rockmann, K. W., and Kaufmann, J. B. (2006). Constructing professional identity: the role of work and identity learning cycles in the customization of identity among medical residents. *Academy of Management Journal,* 49(2), 235–62.

Ryan, R. M. and Deci, E. L. (2000). Self-determination theory and the facilitation of intrinsic motivation, social development, and well-being. *The American Psychologist*, 55(1), 68–78.

Schwartz, B. (2004). *The paradox of choice: why more is less*: New York: Harper Perennial.

Skinner, B. F. (1976). *About behaviorism*. New York: Vintage Books.

Snook, S., Nohria, N., and Khurana, R. (2012). *The handbook for teaching leadership: knowing, doing and being*. California: SAGE Publications.

Styles, R. and Atkins, P. W. B. (in preparation). Functional selfing coding and interview manual. Crawford School of Public Policy, Australian National University.

Sveningsson, S. and Alvesson, M. (2003). Managing managerial identities: organizational fragmentation, discourse and identity struggle. *Human Relations*, 56(10), 1163–93.

Thacher, D. and Rein, M. (2004). Managing value conflict in public policy. *Governance*, 17(4), 457–86.

Torneke, N. (2010). *Learning RFT*. Oakland, CA: New Harbinger Publications.

Williams, J. C. and Lynn, S. J. (2010). Acceptance: an historical and conceptual review. *Imagination, Cognition and Personality*, 30(1), 5.

7 | Improving decision making through mindfulness[1]

NATALIA KARELAIA AND JOCHEN REB

"Most men's awareness doesn't extend past their dinner plates."

Scott Westerfeld, *Leviathan*

Introduction

With perhaps a few exceptions per day, we are seldom fully aware of our thoughts, actions, emotions, and what is happening around us. Even when it comes to making decisions, an activity that is often quite conscious, deliberate, and intentional, people are typically not as aware as they could be. We argue that as a result, decision quality may suffer. Consequently, mindfulness, most often defined as the state of being openly attentive to and aware of what is taking place in the present, both internally and externally (e.g., Brown and Ryan 2003; Kabat-Zinn 1982; 1990), can help people make better decisions. Making judgments and decisions is a fundamental human activity in both personal and organizational contexts. Decisions hold the potential for great gains: marrying the right person, accepting a job that fits well, putting one's savings into the right investments, or choosing the appropriate strategy for an organization. Decisions also hold the potential for great loss, pain, and suffering. Wrong decisions can destroy people, families, and organizations. People are haunted by rumination, even depression, looking back with regret at some of the decisions they made. Organizations are also a place of great decision blunders, such as the "merger" between Daimler Benz and Chrysler, or Coca Cola's decision to introduce New Coke.

Decision research has generally painted a rather bleak picture of individual and organizational decision-making capabilities, compiling a long list of biases (i.e. systematic errors) and problems such as

[1] We are grateful to Paul W. B. Atkins, Max Bazerman, Andrew Hafenbrack, Robin Hogarth, and Tony Kong for their feedback and suggestions on the earlier versions of this chapter.

overconfidence, confirmation bias, or the sunk cost bias (Kahneman 2011). Arguably, errors are partly due to the daunting difficulty of decision making: the need to process large amounts of information with limited capacity and time, the need to be clear about one's values and objectives, and the need to make difficult trade-offs. We believe that if mindfulness helps even to a small extent to improve decision making, individuals and organizations stand to gain considerable accumulated benefits.

In this chapter, we explore various ways in which being mindful may affect our decisions. The questions we ask include: does mindfulness help us recognize decision opportunities? Does it influence how we frame decisions? Can it make us more decisive and reduce decision deferral and decision avoidance? Does it lead to more ethical decisions? Can it help us appreciate uncertainty while allowing us to make decisions in the face of it? Might it facilitate the resolution of trade-offs? Does mindfulness reduce or increase intuitive biases in information processing?

With research in this area being still in its nascent phase, our main objective in this chapter is to think through possible effects and mechanisms of mindfulness in decision making and outline directions for future studies. We postulate that the concept of mindfulness traverses many of the diverse phenomena studied in judgment and decision-making research. Although we invite readers to remain open-minded about possible adverse effects of mindfulness, we admit to believing that mindfulness holds great potential to improve human judgment and decision making in both personal and organizational contexts. Paradoxically, even though mindfulness is conceived as encompassing an attitude of non-judgment, we argue that it leads to better judgment – precisely by helping us to be less judgmental. Similarly, even though mindfulness entails an observing, witnessing stance that may be thought to imply passiveness, we explore the possibility that by reducing habitual, reactive behaviors, mindfulness may increase self-determination and thus ultimately be associated with less decision avoidance and more choiceful behavior.

We have organized this chapter by decision process stages. Broadly speaking, a decision-making process involves four stages: (1) framing the decision, (2) gathering and processing information, (3) coming to conclusions, and (4) learning from feedback (e.g. Russo and Schoemaker 2002). In what follows, we will think through the

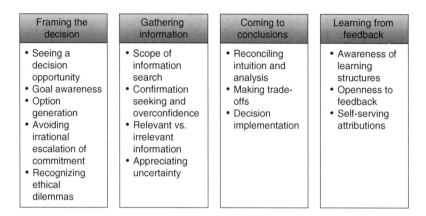

Framing the decision	Gathering information	Coming to conclusions	Learning from feedback
• Seeing a decision opportunity • Goal awareness • Option generation • Avoiding irrational escalation of commitment • Recognizing ethical dilemmas	• Scope of information search • Confirmation seeking and overconfidence • Relevant vs. irrelevant information • Appreciating uncertainty	• Reconciling intuition and analysis • Making trade-offs • Decision implementation	• Awareness of learning structures • Openness to feedback • Self-serving attributions

Figure 7.1 Decision-making stages and elements for which mindfulness may matter

different ways mindfulness may be helpful (or not) at each stage of the decision-making process. The elements of decision making that we consider at each stage are summarized in Figure 7.1.

During this journey, we will draw considerably on the metacognitive aspect of mindfulness whereby the emphasis is less on *what* is going on at the present moment but more on the individual's *awareness of*, or *noticing*, whatever is happening, both externally (i.e. in the environment) and internally (i.e. own thoughts, sensations, emotions). In other words, mindful decision making implies the ability to take a step back and to see oneself from a "balcony" – that is, the ability to maintain a certain distance from one's own thoughts and emotions and witness them impartially, without being fully absorbed by them (also referred to as *decentering* or *reperceiving*; Kabat-Zinn 1990; Shapiro *et al.* 2006; Teasdale *et al.* 2002).

Importantly, making every decision with conscious involvement such as when to breathe in and breathe out or when to lift a leg to make a step forward would not be an efficient use of one's limited mental resources (Bargh and Chartrand 1999). However, the importance of seeing oneself and the situation from the metaphorical "balcony" arguably rises dramatically with the importance and complexity of the decision to be made. Related evidence from a study conducted with nuclear power plant operators suggests that task complexity moderates the effect of mindfulness on task performance (Zhang *et al.* 2013). Dispositional mindfulness (as measured by the Freiburg

Mindfulness Inventory, Walach *et al.* 2006) was found to be associated with better individual performance in complex but not simple tasks. In the latter, mindfulness may delay task execution. Apart from personal "big" decisions such as deciding which degree or career to pursue, which country and city to live in, as well as partner- and family-related decisions, we believe that many public policy and managerial decisions, including strategic decisions, fall under the category of complex decisions involving high-magnitude and/or long-lasting broad consequences, and thus can potentially be improved through mindfulness.

Framing the decision

Decision framing is arguably the most important, foundational, aspect of decision making, yet it is often not given due attention by decision makers (Russo and Schoemaker 2002). If a decision is framed poorly, even good execution will typically not lead to good results. We discuss the following aspects of decision framing that may be influenced by mindfulness: noticing when a decision should or could be made and when not; clarifying objectives and generating options; avoiding irrational escalation of commitment and the sunk cost bias; and recognizing the ethical dimensions of decisions.

Realizing there is a decision to be made

Arguably, framing the problem starts with the realization that a decision exists. We posit that, to the extent that individuals and organizations are mindless, their judgments and choices are more habitual and reactive as opposed to proactive, and they are less likely to notice that there is a decision to be made. As a result, actors are likely to continue with the status quo, potentially missing important decision problems or opportunities. In contrast, mindfulness may enable actors to notice decision opportunities arise and actually *make a choice*, rather than just continuing with the status quo, or whatever they have been doing so far, which may not represent the best option going forward. Mindful decision makers are capable of recognizing their habitual reactions to certain "triggers" (e.g., conflict situation, angry customer) and by doing so, are less likely to act automatically according to pre-established behavioral scripts. Consequently, they are more likely to perceive more choice and sense more freedom and self-determination in choosing their actions. Indeed, practicing mindfulness increases a sense of *choicefulness* (Brown and Ryan 2003).

Knowing what you want and option generation

Decisions are often driven by the available options. For example, a headhunter may call a manager about a position, or a company is approached about an investment opportunity. Making choices between the option presented and the status quo exemplifies an option-driven approach to decision making. However, a more effective way to approach decisions is to start from understanding one's values and objectives, or goals, and from that clarity generate and consider options to achieve these objectives. Keeney (1994) argued that such a value-focused approach to decision making helps expand the set of options and leads to better decision outcomes, that is, outcomes that achieve one's fundamental objectives. We argue that because mindful individuals are more aware of their values, needs, and goals, they are less reactive to situational cues (Brown, Ryan, and Creswell 2007) and are more likely to approach situations as opportunities to fulfill their fundamental objectives. Moreover, recent evidence suggests that mindful individuals are more concerned with *internal* as opposed to *external* rewards such as an outward image they create of themselves (Ruedy and Schweitzer 2010). This implies that mindful individuals are more likely to focus on the objectives they value *themselves* as opposed to socially desirable or acceptable objectives, such as status or success, that may not lead to the satisfaction of fundamental objectives such as wellbeing.

As a consequence of these processes, less mindful decision makers may be more likely to experience *post-decision regret* (Festinger and Walster 1964), which occurs when people realize the course of action they have chosen brought them somewhere they do not feel comfortable or somewhere they do not really want to be. Because less mindful decision makers are less conscious of their internal objectives at the moment of making a decision, they may also be more likely to change their decisions frequently.

Mindfulness may also prevent premature and narrow problem definition. The "beginner's mind," associated with the open, non-judging aspect of mindfulness (Brown and Ryan 2003; Kabat-Zinn 1990), implies that the present moment is approached without pre-determined views about what to do, but instead with a curiosity that can lead to a deeper examination of the decision situation. This in turn can lead to reframing completely the decision to be made so that this specific decision is viewed as a path within a more complete picture of a series of interdependent decisions, all linked by a common thread or objective. In general, inasmuch as mindfulness is associated with creativity (see Chapter 8), it should lead to generating more ideas and more novel and higher quality options. As the quality of options in the choice set has a strong influence on decision outcomes, this indirect effect of mindfulness can be of substantial practical importance.

Overall, mindfulness is likely to increase the number and quality of options being considered and help generate options proactively rather than only passively reacting to given options. We also posit that more mindful decision makers are more focused on pursuing their fundamental objectives. On the other hand, mindfulness may hinder decision making if, as a consequence of a greater number of objectives considered, the individual is not capable of differentiating between less and more important objectives, and, as a consequence of a greater number of options considered, is not capable of choosing one. In such cases, mindfulness may increase vacillation between options and slow down decision making or, in extreme cases, lead to decision paralysis. (We will come back to this issue below when discussing how mindfulness may affect one's ability to make trade-offs.) On a related note, given that mindfulness implies heightened attention to the present, it is possible that mindfulness leads to giving priority to present rather than long-term objectives. Future studies should thus examine how mindfulness is linked to option generation, goal awareness, reliance on internal as opposed to externally defined goals and on present as opposed to long-term goals, post-decision regret, and decision reversals.

Prioritizing decisions

Mindfulness may also help decision makers differentiate between necessary and unnecessary decisions and thus allow a redirecting of the energy wasted on unnecessary, avoidable decisions to the necessary and important ones. In particular, sometimes decisions are made just because others (or the decision maker) expect the individual to "do something." In organizations, for example, newly hired managers are often expected to take action, to change something, when they start their mandate. Because mindfulness is linked to greater clarity and awareness of both the environment and one's own objectives, mindful decision makers will likely notice the social pressures to make a decision, but not necessarily act on them. As a consequence, more time will be dedicated to assessing the issues that do require action to ensure the achievement of organizational objectives.

Similarly, mindfulness may help individuals realize when they spend too much time on "micro decisions," that is the decisions that have little if any consequence for their fundamental objectives and wellbeing in general. Such understanding will in turn liberate attentional and cognitive resources for more important, consequential decisions as well as reduce anxiety associated with a sense of being overwhelmed by decisions to be made.

Reverting a failing course of action

While we have argued above that mindfulness should lead to greater consistency across one's decisions because of the heighted salience of one's values and goals, mindfulness may also introduce some apparent inconsistency in decision making. In particular, mindfulness may help individuals realize when to discontinue a formerly chosen course of action. The phenomenon of *irrational escalation of commitment* and the related *sunk cost bias* make individuals persist in a failing course of action, project, career, or relationship, not because a careful cost–benefit analysis suggests that it is the wise thing to do, but because they have already heavily invested in the course of action, emotionally, financially, or time-wise, and are unable to let go of the sunk costs (Arkes and Blumer 1985; Staw 1976).

Hafenbrack, Kinias, and Barsade (2013) have recently suggested that because mindfulness involves awareness of the *present* moment, mindful individuals are less likely to be fixated on sunk costs – incurred in the *past* – and less likely to experience anticipated *future* regret for giving up on the previously chosen course of action. Consequently, mindfulness should reduce the proneness to honor sunk costs. In support of this hypothesis, Hafenbrack and colleagues found that both dispositional (as measured by the Mindful Attention Awareness Scale (MAAS), Brown and Ryan 2003) and momentarily induced mindfulness (through a brief fifteen-minute breathing meditation exercise) was positively related to letting go of sunk costs. Further, the effect was mediated by a decreased focus on the past and future and consequently a decreased state negative affect.

We believe that yet another process may contribute to the effect of mindfulness on irrational escalation of commitment. Staw and Ross (1978) argued that self-image concerns enhance the resistance to see sunk costs as actually sunk. When new evidence suggests the previously made decision should be changed, an individual may experience *cognitive dissonance* (Festinger 1957) since revising a failing course of action implies recognizing that one was possibly wrong in the first place. To protect their self-image, less mindful individuals may be more likely to filter and interpret information in an overly optimistic manner to maintain the mistaken belief that the chosen course of action was indeed the right one. In contrast, mindful individuals are more likely to notice their personal "attachment" to past decisions and the uncomfortable feelings the criticism of these decisions generates. By reducing ego-involvement (Heppner *et al.* 2008; Lakey *et al.* 2008), mindfulness may diminish the sense of threat to self-esteem and help individuals tolerate these uncomfortable emotions or eliminate them altogether (Eifert and Heffner 2003). Consequently, mindful individuals will be able to recognize when a course of action has failed and avoid further escalation of commitment without construing the reversal as a personal failure. Future studies could examine the possible mediating role of self-image concerns in the effect of mindfulness on proactively reverting commitment to a failing course of action.

Recognizing ethical challenges

Another aspect of decision framing concerns whether the ethical aspects of a decision are being recognized. We suggest that mindfulness should help individuals recognize the ethical implications of the decisions they face, which might go unnoticed when decision makers act "on autopilot." The notion of *bounded ethicality* whereby people act unethically without being aware of it (Bazerman and Moore 2009; Chugh, Bazerman, and Banaji 2005) is consistent with the idea that heightened awareness is positively linked to ethicality. In support of this idea, research suggests a positive link between self-awareness and honesty (Bateson, Nettle, and Roberts 2006; Diener and Wallbom 1976; Haley and Fessler 2005). Preliminary evidence in mindfulness research is also suggestive of a positive link between mindfulness and ethicality. For example, Ruedy and Schweitzer (2010) showed that mindful individuals are more aware of their ethical principles, more concerned about preserving their integrity, and engage less in unethical behavior (in their study: cheating) than individuals scoring low on dispositional mindfulness (as measured by MAAS). Thus, more mindful decision makers may be less blinded by instrumental considerations such as financial consequences of a decision (see also Rest 1986) and more likely to act in accordance with their ethical/moral values.

An implication of the heightened ability to notice when one is about to do something that goes against one's personal values is that mindfulness might be closely linked to *authenticity*, defined as "the unobstructed operation of one's true, or core, self in one's daily enterprise" (Kernis and Goldman 2006, p. 294). Consistent with this suggestion, dispositional mindfulness (as measured by MAAS) has indeed been shown to correlate with dispositional authenticity (Lakey *et al.* 2008).

Nevertheless, it is not completely clear whether mindfulness is inherently connected to ethics. One can argue that mindfulness may facilitate antisocial decisions when these are aligned with one's antisocial values. However, preliminary evidence on both dispositional mindfulness (Beitel, Ferrer, and Cecero 2005) and mindfulness practice (Shapiro, Schwartz, and Bonner 1998) suggests that mindfulness enhances empathy and concern for others (Atkins 2013). The effect might be due to the reverse relationship between mindfulness and ego-concerns (Heppner *et al.* 2008; Lakey *et al.* 2008). A natural consequence of the enhanced empathy and concern for others is that mindful decision makers should be more likely to incorporate others' interests into their choices and thus make balanced (as opposed to self-centered) and comprehensive decisions aligned with a broad set of criteria. Further, recent evidence suggests that even brief mindfulness training improves working memory (Zeidan, Johnson, Diamond, David, and Goolkasian 2010). This may allow mindful decision makers to remain aware of multiple objectives, rather than focusing on a single selfish objective.

In line with these ideas, Brown and Kasser (2005) showed that dispositional mindfulness (as measured by MAAS) is positively linked to ecologically responsible behaviors in diet, transportation, and housing choices. Future studies should examine directly the

link between mindfulness, the extent to which individuals incorporate others' interests into their decisions, and the propensity to
notice ethical challenges and make ethical choices. The potential of
momentarily induced mindfulness and mindfulness training in this
domain is especially promising for uncovering ways of increasing
prosocial and ethical choices.

Gathering and processing information

At this second stage of decision making, information about relevant
options is being collected and processed. Two important aspects of this
stage are of particular relevance to mindfulness: the quantity and the
quality of information being collected and processed.

Scope of information search

Because mindfulness involves heightened attention (Kabat-Zinn, 1990)
and because attention is a limited cognitive resource (Hogarth, 1987;
2001; Simon, 1945), mindfulness may leave less attentional resources
for information search and therefore be associated with *less* extensive
information search. In turn, less extensive information search implies
higher chances that a relevant piece of evidence is overlooked and, as
a result, the quality of the final decision may suffer. At the same time,
research on decision heuristics, or cognitive shortcuts, shows that less
information does not necessarily mean that the quality of a judgment
or a decision is compromised and under certain circumstances, less
may actually be more (e.g., Gigerenzer and Goldstein 1996; Hogarth
and Karelaia 2007; Karelaia 2006). Moreover, an onerous information
search may increase negative effect during the process, make decision
makers rely more on external criteria to differentiate between what is
important and what is not, and as a result, reduce their satisfaction
with the final choice (Iyengar, Wells, and Schwartz 2006). Thus, while
mindfulness may be associated with less extensive information search,
the overall effect on decision quality is unclear.

Confirmation seeking and overconfidence

On the other side, mindfulness is likely to be positively linked to
the *quality* of information being used to make a decision. Because

mindfulness involves open-minded awareness and observation (Brown and Ryan 2003; Kabat-Zinn 1990), mindful individuals are likely to assess information neutrally rather than filter it through their "lenses," which may be biased due to past experiences, cognitive limitations, and/or motivational biases. In support of this idea, Kiken and Shook (2011) found that mindfulness reduces negativity bias, or the tendency to weigh negative information more heavily than positive information.

We posit that mindfulness is negatively associated with *confirmation seeking* whereby decision makers selectively use information that confirms their initial thoughts and preferences (Bruner, Goodnow, and Austin 1956; Klayman and Ha 1987). By the same token, it seems plausible that mindful decision makers are more likely to recognize the limits of their knowledge, acknowledge that they might be mistaken, and thus manifest less *overconfidence* in their judgments and predictions than the general population, which has been shown to be notoriously overconfident across a wide range of domains (e.g., Klayman *et al.* 1999; Moore and Healy 2008; Zacharakis and Shepherd 2001).

Being mindful implies shifting how one relates to one's thinking and experiencing into the direction of non-attachment and realizing that any thought and feeling, including the uncomfortable thought that one might be wrong, is non-permanent and transitional (Kabat-Zinn 1990). Consistent with this idea, mindfulness has been shown to reduce the fixation on protecting or enhancing self-esteem and to reduce ego-involvement (Heppner *et al.* 2008; Lakey *et al.* 2008). As a consequence, mindfulness should make it more likely that decision makers recognize and accept the possibility of being wrong. In turn, this should reduce the propensity to filter out information for the sake of maintaining a positive self-view at the cost of biasing judgment and lowering decision quality. In support of this idea, Lakey, Campbell, Brown, and Goodie (2007) showed that dispositional mindfulness (as measured by the MAAS) was negatively associated with overconfidence (as measured by individual calibration in a general knowledge task).

Further studies should provide additional evidence on the link between mindfulness and overconfidence in various domains as well as shed light on the mechanisms underlying such a link. It is important to note that positive illusions such as overconfidence can be functional in the sense that they promote action and task persistence (Taylor and

Brown 1988). Given that mindfulness may lead to a less overconfident self-view, future studies should examine whether this reduction in cognitive bias (e.g., in prediction) also leads to low confidence concerning action (e.g., when a decision is being implemented or when one tries to convince others (Anderson and Kilduff 2009; Russo and Shoemaker 1992).

Differentiating between relevant and irrelevant information

Mindfulness can also increase the quality of information used for making a decision by helping decision makers to separate relevant information from irrelevant. If relevant information is used, whatever heuristics decision makers employ will often lead to decision outcomes comparable with those made by a more sophisticated decision process (Hogarth and Karelaia 2007). A heightened ability to separate relevant information from irrelevant should also increase decision makers' ability to recognize when their judgment is blurred by stereotypes. For example, managers who have to select someone for promotion are often unaware how their implicit gender, age, or racial biases influence decisions (e.g., Banaji 2001; Rudman and Borgida 1995). They can also be blind to how ex-post rationalizations make the decision appear perfectly reasonable and justifiable and thereby reduce their sense of responsibility (Bandura 1999). Mindful managers, however, may be more likely to defer immediate judgment and be more conscious of how certain personal characteristics of the candidate such as gender, age, or race can bias assessment of candidates' performance, skill, and potential. Hodgins and Knee (2002) similarly proposed that individuals who are open to the present moment are less likely to show in-group biases and rely on stereotypic information when forming judgments. Exploring the link between dispositional and temporarily induced mindfulness and stereotyping – both implicit and explicit – seems to be a fruitful and important direction for further research.

The above discussion also suggests that despite its contemplative and nonjudgmental nature, mindfulness might lead to a more proactive, rather than passive, information search because mindful awareness should increase the likelihood that decision makers recognize when important information is missing and then actively search for this information.

Appreciating uncertainty

An important aspect of the knowledge-gathering stage is the appraisal of relevant uncertainties. A significant body of research shows that people often underestimate uncertainty associated with the outcomes of their decisions (Kahneman, Slovic, and Tversky 1982). On the one hand, through its focus on the present, mindfulness may reduce decision makers' ability to imagine how things can unfold in the future. Arguably, in some contexts, pessimistically playing out future scenarios (e.g., a lawyer or a manager thinking of everything that might go wrong) can improve decision making. On the other hand, it is also plausible that through its link with unbiased (or at least *less* biased) information processing (Brown *et al.* 2007; Kiken and Shook 2011) mindfulness may help decision makers become more aware of uncertainty surrounding them. In addition, we posit that mindfulness prevents individuals from being paralyzed in the face of uncertainty. High *intolerance of uncertainty* inhibits action leading consequently to decision delays or decision paralysis (Berenbaum, Bredemeier, and Thompson 2008; Birrell *et al.* 2011). Mindful awareness may help individuals recognize that their unease is caused by the perceived uncertainty associated with the decision and, further, observe their feelings with a sense of detachment, thereby reducing associated anxiety (Brown and Ryan 2003; Hofmann *et al.* 2010). These processes should result in making a (better) decision. Preliminary data we collected suggest that dispositional intolerance of uncertainty (Buhr and Dugas, 2002) is indeed negatively associated with dispositional mindfulness (MAAS), $r = -.35$, $p < .01$, $n = 78$. Further research is needed to better understand how mindfulness may help appraise uncertainty fully, deal with the negative affective states associated with it, and to act in the face of uncertainty.

High perceived uncertainty may also lead to excessive information search (Buhr and Dugas 2002; Tallis, Eysenck, and Mathews 1991) whereby individuals engage in data gathering beyond any reasonable level in an attempt to increase a sense of control or to avoid making a decision altogether. Mindfulness is likely to help decision makers recognize instances when they are involved in such unproductive data gathering and then channel their energy and time to more productive activities.

A related question is whether mindfulness may decrease *illusory pattern detection*. Whitson and Galinsky (2008) suggested that identification of illusory correlations in data is especially likely when significant randomness in the environment reduces a sense of control and increases the need for structure. In one of their experiments, participants were more likely to detect a false pattern in the information about a company in which it was possibile to invest when the market was described as volatile compared to when it was described as stable. It seems plausible that if mindfulness helps individuals to better tolerate uncertainty, mindful individuals should be less likely to detect false patterns and thus more likely to base their decisions on unbiased interpretations of data. On the other hand, since mindfulness implies giving extraordinary attention to the present, it could lead to seeing *more* connections between events, actions, thoughts, and emotions, and thus ultimately increase the propensity to see false patterns. Future studies will allow for a better understanding of the link between mindfulness and illusory pattern detection.

A more general related question is whether mindfulness might be linked to more risk seeking. On the one hand, it may – if it leads to greater recognition and acceptance of uncertainty as unavoidable. On the other hand, if mindfulness reduces defensive denial of uncertainty, it may lead instead to more prudent decision making. Recent evidence suggests that among frequent gamblers, people with higher dispositional mindfulness take less risk in an experimental gambling task (Lakey *et al.* 2007). Lakey and colleagues note, however, that risk taking in their study was not linked to any tangible consequence for participants. Future research is needed to better understand the effect of dispositional as well as temporarily induced mindfulness on the extent to which people are ready to embrace uncertainty across different domains, as well as the mechanisms behind such an effect.

Coming to conclusions

Reconciling intuition and analysis

At this stage of decision making, a conclusion is drawn as to which course of action to choose and then implement. Such conclusions can be the product of deliberate, logical analysis or can be intuitively reached through a less conscious process. While good judgment and decision making requires using both intuition and systematic analysis

(Hogarth 2001), we believe that mindfulness can be especially helpful when intuition suggests a course of action different from the one favored by analysis. In such situations, it may be desirable to examine closely the discrepancy between intuition and deliberation, rather than ignoring one or the other.

One's intuitive judgment may be misaligned with the analytical solution because something in the current situation reminds the decision maker of a similar experience or situation and thus triggers an implicit reaction, which the decision maker is (yet) unable to explain. When the decision to be made is in the domain in which the individual has extensive expertise, the intuition is likely to provide a valid – and fast – input to the decision. However, intuitive judgment may not be of high quality when such domain-specific expertise is lacking (Hogarth 2001). It seems plausible that mindfulness should help decision makers (1) be more aware of the instances when their intuition suggests a decision different from the solution emerging from the analytical appraisal of the situation and (2) evaluate whether this intuitive judgment is likely to be valid.

Making trade-offs

Choosing one course of action requires making trade-offs if none of the generated options dominates the other available options. Trade-offs make decision making especially challenging (Luce, Bettman, and Payne 1997). Struggling to make trade-offs may lead to indecision whereby decision makers reduce the negative affect associated with missing out on something in exchange for something else by postponing the decision or avoiding it altogether (Luce, 1998; Tversky and Shafir 1992). Decision deferral and avoidance are indeed widespread (Anderson 2003). Because mindfulness involves a nonjudgmental attitude and because making trade-offs requires making judgments with regard to attributes that characterize alternatives, one could argue that mindfulness should reduce the ability to make trade-offs. Similarly, as pointed out above, because mindfulness makes it more likely that the decision maker is aware of multiple objectives as opposed to a single goal, it may increase vacillation and doubt.

However, there are also reasons to expect the opposite. First, mindfulness is linked to emotional self-awareness, and being able to recognize one's emotions and see them as information helps in making trade-offs and is positively related to decisiveness (Damasio 1994; Dulewicz and Higgs 1999). Second, mindfulness is likely to help decision makers regulate emotions triggered by the conflict associated with making trade-offs: observing emotions as an ever-changing flow allows one to disassociate from them and thereby experience them with a greater ease, no matter how uncomfortable the emotions are (Eifert and Heffner 2003). Consequently, making a choice should become easier. Finally, as we have argued above, mindfulness should be associated with a heightened awareness of one's values and priorities. Value awareness can also help in making trade-offs by increasing the clarity regarding which attributes are important in a given situation (Anderson 2003).

An important trade-off dimension is intertemporal whereby immediate benefits and costs have to be traded off with future benefits and costs. Given its present orientation, mindfulness may lead to more discounting of future consequences, resulting in choices that favor the present over the future. On the other hand, as mindfulness is related to better emotional and behavioral self-regulation (Arch and Craske 2006; Brown *et al.* 2007; Goodall, Trejnowska, and Darling 2012; Lakey *et al.* 2007), it may also enable decision makers to forgo immediate gratification in exchange for higher future benefits. The evidence to date from delayed gratification research suggests that the ability to self-regulate in situations involving intertemporal trade-offs is developed in early childhood and is linked to superior coping competencies, academic achievement, and other positive outcomes later in life (Shoda, Mischel, and Peake 1990; cf. Kidda, Palmeria, and Aslina 2013). The potential role of mindfulness training in tuning one's ability to delay immediate gratification and make intertemporal choices clearly deserves scholars' attention.

Implementing decisions

Once a decision is made, it has to be implemented. We have argued above that being mindful helps decision makers factor their objectives into their decisions. As a consequence, mindful decision makers should be less likely to revert their choices and more likely to implement them. On the other side, because mindfulness implies taking an observing, witnessing, and possibly accepting stance, it may slow down or altogether prevent implementation through a more passive stance. However, it has also been argued that mindfulness should not be construed as inaction but as a process that precedes action. In particular, Salzberg (2011) suggested that an action is only possible when the current state is appraised and a need for change is recognized, and this is where mindfulness is especially helpful. While much remains to be done to understand how mindfulness is linked to decision implementation, recent research suggests that mindfulness may indeed help translate intentions into actions. For instance, Chatzisarantis and Hagger (2007) showed that dispositional mindfulness (MAAS) moderated the intention–behavior gap in a leisure-time physical activity context such that more mindful individuals were more likely to align their behavior with their intentions.

Learning from feedback

This last stage of decision making is arguably the most important for improving one's decision-making prowess in the long run and yet, paradoxically, it is often neglected by decision makers (Russo and Schoemaker 2002). Learning from past decisions, refining the decision-making process, and "educating intuition" (Hogarth 2001) is facilitated if the decision maker (1) has access to complete, quick, and accurate feedback on the outcomes of past decisions *and* (2) processes this feedback without bias.

Awareness of learning structures and openness to feedback

Because of heightened awareness, mindful individuals may be more likely to recognize when the *learning structure* of their decision environment (Hogarth 2001) is not conducive to learning. This is the case, for instance, when individuals have access to the feedback on the chosen course of action but are oblivious to the consequences of the foregone course(s) of action (e.g., the applicant hired versus the applicants not hired), or when the outcome is a sum of both individual skill and effort and other factors such as luck (e.g., successfully investing in the stock market). Being more aware of the limitations of available feedback, mindful individuals may be more likely to actively seek for missing feedback and correct for noise and other factors when interpreting feedback.

However, awareness of feedback limitations is not sufficient for effective learning. To learn from experience, individuals have to be open and receptive to whatever information they receive about their performance/outcomes, including negative information. We propose that mindfulness is related to more openness to feedback, especially negative. One reason behind high reactivity to positive and negative feedback is chronically high ego-involvement (Kernis 2003). When self-esteem is fragile and contingent on external reinforcement, any negative feedback or experience becomes potentially self-threatening. Because mindfulness is a state of open-mindedness and non-evaluative awareness, mindful individuals, as noted above, experience less ego-involvement and are better able to disengage from self-concerns (Brown *et al.* 2007; Heppner *et al.* 2008). Consequently, they are less likely to experience negative feedback as self-threatening and thus are more likely to be open to it (Heppner and Kernis 2007) and to see all facts as "friendly" (Rogers 1961, p. 25). These arguments imply that mindful individuals are more likely to accept both positive and negative feedback and proactively look for feedback on their decisions. As a consequence, they will be more likely to refine their judgment, improve their future decisions, and ultimately improve their intuition.

Self-serving attributions and learning

We further suggest that mindfulness is related to unbiased processing of feedback information. It is well documented that individuals often misinterpret outcome feedback. The *self-serving bias* (Miller and Ross 1975) in attributions of causality refers to the widespread tendency to attribute successes to internal factors such as skill and judgment while attributing failure to external factors such as "bad luck." One reason for the self-serving bias is the need to enhance personal self-worth (Shepperd, Malone, and Sweeny 2008), and the self-serving attributions of success and failure can be aggravated by ego-involvement (Miller 1976). Because mindfulness reduces ego-involvement, mindful individuals should be less likely to make self-protective biased causal attributions of their successes and failures. Hodgins and Knee (2002) made a similar argument by suggesting that openness to ongoing experience (which characterizes mindfulness) results in less cognitive defensiveness, including the self-serving bias. This reasoning implies that mindful individuals are less likely to develop unjustified overconfidence in their skill and decision-making ability after a series of past successes and are more likely to remain humble when facing new decision problems. Future studies should examine directly how mindfulness is related to feedback interpretation, the self-serving attribution bias, over-confidence, and learning in repeated decisions.

Conclusion

While few of us are fully mindful of what is happening in the present moment, the good news is that the potential for improvement is huge. Mindfulness does not only have a positive effect on health and wellbeing, but also, as we have discussed in this chapter, it is likely to improve one's ability to make high-quality judgments and decisions. The many avenues for future research discussed in this chapter have high potential for addressing a recent call for more studies on how to reduce biases in judgment and improve decision making (Milkman, Chugh, and Bazerman 2009).

We have proposed that mindfulness can help individuals at each stage of decision making (Russo and Schoemaker 2002). At the stage of *decision framing*, mindfulness is likely to increase one's awareness of the possibility (or the necessity) of making a decision and miti-gate the sunk cost bias. It may also increase goal awareness thereby enhancing decision consistency with one's objectives and reducing post-decision regret. Greater goal clarity will in turn facilitate option generation, which will be further enhanced by creativity that mind-fulness is likely to spark. Importantly, mindfulness is also likely to facilitate the recognition of ethical challenges and thereby reduce the instances of bounded ethicality (Chugh *et al.* 2005). Moreover, by increasing awareness of one's values and making it more likely that individuals consider how their decisions can affect others, mindfulness has the potential to increase the ethicality of decisions (e.g. Ruedy and Schweitzer 2010).

At the stage of *information gathering and processing*, mindful-ness may reduce the scope of information search and simultaneously increase the quality of information considered. In particular, mind-ful individuals are likely to be less prone to confirmation-seeking and overconfidence (e.g., Lakey *et al.* 2007), have a better ability to sep-arate relevant from irrelevant information, and rely less on stereo-types. Furthermore, we posit that mindful individuals are more likely to objectively assess uncertainty and productively work with it.

Mindfulness also has the potential to reduce illusory pattern detection, although more research is clearly needed to shed further light on these effects.

At the *coming to conclusions* stage, when the decision maker has to choose a course of action, mindfulness can help by improving one's ability to use both intuition and analysis to reach a decision, even when the two systems suggest different choices. Moreover, making trade-offs should be easier for more mindful decision makers, which will reduce decision deferral and decision avoidance. Mindfulness is also likely to facilitate decision implementation by reducing the intention–behavior gap (Chatzisarantis and Hagger 2007).

Finally, mindful decision makers are more likely to *learn from feedback* and, importantly, learn the right lessons. First, they are more likely to recognize when feedback is missing or noisy. Second, because they are more capable of disengaging from ego-concerns (Brown *et al.* 2007; Heppner *et al.* 2008), they are more open to both positive and negative feedback and less prone to misinterpret feedback by making self-serving attributions.

As we have discussed, mindfulness may be relevant to many diverse phenomena affecting human judgment and decision making. As our arguments make it clear, we believe that overall, mindfulness has great potential to improve the quality of judgment and decision making, both in personal and organizational contexts. However, one has to be cautious and consider potential adverse effects of mindfulness on judgment and decision making, as well as possible boundary conditions. For example, as noted above, although mindfulness is likely to increase the *quality* of information considered for making a decision, it may also reduce the *quantity* of information screened. In some circumstances, a limited information search may lead to overlooking important decision considerations and underestimating relevant uncertainties. While the "less-is-more" literature suggests that less information does not necessarily mean worse judgment (e.g., Gigerenzer and Goldstein 1996; Hogarth and Karelaia 2007), more studies are needed to understand whether mindfulness indeed reduces the quantity of information considered for a decision, and if so, whether the total *quantity* and *quality* effect of mindfulness is negative or positive.

Furthermore, because mindfulness is linked to observing and attending to details, it may slow down decision making. True, appraising one's objectives fully, considering a wide range of options, attending to all information including that contained in one's emotions takes time. We acknowledge that the trade-off between decision speed and decision quality is not easy to quantify. What should be valued more will largely depend on the context. However, we believe that although mindfulness may slow down the *decision making process*, it may also allow decision makers to "catch up" at the *decision implementation* stage. Because a decision made mindfully is more likely to reflect fundamental values and objectives, mindful decision makers will be less likely to oscillate between the chosen and forgone options and change their minds after the decision has been made. Moreover, because mindfulness increases the chances that others' goals are taken into consideration, relevant other parties are less likely to interfere with decision implementation. Furthermore, we have also argued that mindfulness may in fact be positively linked to decisiveness and help individuals to make faster decisions by, for example, increasing one's awareness and ability to deal with intuition/analysis conflicts as well as facilitating trade-offs between attributes that characterize alternatives. In any case, future studies should directly examine the link between mindfulness and the speed of decision making.

Much work remains to be done to better understand the effects of mindfulness on decision making, as well as the mediating processes, but the richness of the issues to be explored seem to warrant much future research in this domain. We encourage scholars to consider the effects of not only dispositional mindfulness but also of temporarily induced mindful states, mindfulness interventions, and regular, long-term mindfulness practice. We find it inspiring that mindfulness is not a fixed personality trait but an inherent human capacity that may be enhanced through practice. A significant body of research points to the effectiveness of mindfulness training (Brown *et al.* 2007). Furthermore, many studies quoted above have assessed the effects of either temporarily induced mindfulness or brief mindfulness training (e.g., Brown and Ryan 2003; Hafenbrack *et al.* 2013; Lakey *et al.* 2008; Zeidan *et al.* 2010). We hope many more studies will soon explore the potential of mindfulness training and interventions to improve judgment and decision making prowess.

References

Anderson, C. J. (2003). The psychology of doing nothing: forms of decision avoidance result from reason and emotion. *Psychological Bulletin*, 129(1), 139–66.

Anderson, C. and Kilduff, G. J. (2009). Why do dominant personalities attain influence in face-to-face groups? The competence-signaling effects of trait dominance. *Journal of Personality and Social Psychology*, 96(2), 491–503.

Arch, J. J. and Craske, M. G. (2006). Mechanisms of mindfulness: emotion regulation following a focused breathing induction. *Behaviour Research and Therapy*, 44(12), 1849–58.

Arkes, H. and Blumer, C. (1985). The psychology of sunk cost. *Organizational Behavior and Human Decision Processes*, 35, 124–40.

Atkins, P. W. B. (2013). Empathy, self-other differentiation and mindfulness. In K. Pavlovich and K. Krahnke (eds.), *Organizing through empathy*. New York: Routledge, pp. 49–70.

Banaji, M. R. (2001). Ordinary prejudice. *Psychological Science Agenda, American Psychological Association*, 14, 8–11.

Bandura, A. (1999). Moral disengagement in the perpetration of inhumanities. *Personality and Social Psychology Review*, 3(3), 193–209.

Bargh, J. A. and Chartrand, T. L. (1999). The unbearable automaticity of being. *American Psychologist*, 54, 462–79.

Bateson, M., Nettle, D., and Roberts, G. (2006). Cues of being watched enhance cooperation in a real world setting. *Biology Letters*, 2(3), 412–14.

Bazerman, M. and Moore, D. (2009). *Judgment in managerial decision making*. 7th edn. Hoboken, NJ: Wiley.

Beitel, M., Ferrer, E., and Cecero, J. J. (2005). Psychological mindedness and awareness of self and others. *Journal of Clinical Psychology*, 61(6), 739–50.

Berenbaum, H., Bredemeier, K., and Thompson, R. J. (2008). Intolerance of uncertainty: exploring its dimensionality and associations with need for cognitive closure, psychopathology, and personality. *Journal of Anxiety Disorders*, 22, 117–25.

Birrell, J., Meares, K., Wilkinson, A., and Freeston, M. (2011). Toward a definition of intolerance of uncertainty: a review of factor analytical studies of the intolerance of uncertainty scale. *Clinical Psychology Review*, 31, 1198–208.

Brown, K. W. and Kasser, T. (2005). Are psychological and ecological well-being compatible? The role of values, mindfulness, and lifestyle. *Social Indicators Research*, 74, 349–68.

Brown, K. W. and Ryan, R. M. (2003). The benefits of being present: mindfulness and its role in psychological well-being. *Journal of Personality and Social Psychology*, 84, 822–48.

Brown, K. W., Ryan, R. M., and Creswell, J. D. (2007). Mindfulness: theoretical foundations and evidence for its salutary effects. *Psychological Inquiry*, 18, 211–37.

Bruner, J. S., Goodnow, J. J., and Austin, G. A. (1956). *A study of thinking.* New York: Wiley.

Buhr, K. and Dugas, M. J. (2002). The intolerance of uncertainty scale: psychometric properties of the English version. *Behaviour Research and Therapy*, 40, 931–45.

Chatzisarantis, N. L. D. and Hagger, M. S. (2007). Mindfulness and the intention-behavior relationship within the theory of planned behavior. *Personality and Social Psychology Bulletin*, 33(5), 663–76.

Chugh, D., Bazerman, M., and Banaji, M. R. (2005). Bounded ethicality as a psychological barrier to recognizing conflicts of interest. In D. A. Moore, D. M. Cain, G. Loewenstein, and M. Bazerman (eds.), *Conflicts of interest*. Cambridge University Press, pp. 74–95.

Damasio, A. (1994). *Descartes' error: emotion, reason and the human brain.* New York: Putnam.

Diener, E. and Wallbom, M. (1976). Effects of self-awareness on antinormative behavior. *Journal of Research in Personality*, 10(1), 107–11.

Dulewicz, V. and Higgs, M. (1999). Can emotional intelligence be measured and developed? *Leadership and Organization Development Journal*, 20(5), 242–53.

Eifert, G. H. and Heffner, M. (2003). The effects of acceptance versus control contexts on avoidance of panic-related symptoms. *Journal of Behavior Therapy and Experimental Psychiatry*, 34(3/4), 293–312.

Festinger, L. (1957). *A theory of cognitive dissonance.* Stanford University Press.

Festinger, L. and Walster, E. (1964). Post-decision regret and decision reversal. In Festinger, L. (ed.), *Conflict, decision, and dissonance*. Stanford University Press, pp. 100–12.

Gigerenzer, G. and Goldstein, D. G. (1996). Reasoning the fast and frugal way: models of bounded rationality. *Psychological Review*, 103, 650–69.

Goodall, K., Trejnowska, A., and Darling, S. (2012). The relationship between dispositional mindfulness, attachment security and emotion regulation. *Personality and Individual Differences*, 52(5), 622–6.

Hafenbrack, A. C., Kinias, Z., and Barsade, S. (2014). Debiasing the mind through meditation: mindfulness and the sunk cost bias. *Psychological Science*, 25(2), 369–76.

Haley, K. J. and Fessler, D. M. T. (2005). Nobody's watching? Subtle cues affect generosity in an anonymous economic game. *Evolution and Human Behavior*, 26, 245–56.

Heppner, W. L. and Kernis, M. H. (2007). "Quiet ego" functioning: the complementary roles of mindfulness, authenticity, and secure high self-esteem. *Psychological Inquiry*, 18(4), 248–51.

Heppner, W. L., Kernis, M. H., Lakey, C. E., Goldman B. M., Davis, P. J., and Cascio, E. V. (2008). Mindfulness as a means of reducing aggressive behavior: dispositional and situational evidence. *Aggressive Behavior*, 34(5), 486–96.

Hodgins, H. S. and Knee, C. R. (2002). The integrating self and conscious experience. In E. L. Deci and R. M. Ryan (eds.) *Handbook of self-determination research*. Rochester, NY: University of Rochester Press, pp. 87–100.

Hofmann, S. G., Sawyer, A. T., Witt, A. A., and Oh, D. (2010). The effect of mindfulness-based therapy on anxiety and depression: a meta-analytic review. *Journal of Consulting and Clinical Psychology*, 78(2), 169–83.

Hogarth, R. M. (1987). *Judgement and choice: the psychology of decision*. 2nd edn. New York: Wiley.

(2001). *Educating intuition*. University of Chicago Press.

Hogarth, R. M. and Karelaia, N. (2007). Heuristic and linear models of judgment: matching rules and environments. *Psychological Review*, 114(3), 733–58.

Iyengar, S. S., Wells, R. E., and Schwartz, B. (2006). Doing better but feeling worse: looking for the "best" job undermines satisfaction. *Psychological Science*, 17, 143–50.

Kabat-Zinn, J. (1982). An out-patient program in behavioral medicine for chronic pain patients based on the practice of mindfulness meditation: theoretical considerations and preliminary results. *General Hospital Psychiatry*, 4(1), 33–47.

Kabat-Zinn, J. (1990). *Full catastrophe living: using the wisdom of your body and mind to face stress, pain, and illness*. New York: Delacorte.

Kahneman, D. (2011). *Thinking, fast and slow*. New York: Farrar, Strauss, Giroux.

Kahneman, D., Slovic, P., and Tversky, A. (1982). *Judgment under uncertainty: heuristics and biases*. New York: Cambridge University Press.

Karelaia, N. (2006). Thirst for confirmation in multi-attribute choice: does search for consistency impair decision performance? *Organizational Behavior and Human Decision Processes*, 100, 128–43.

Keeney, R. (1994). Creativity in decision making with value-focused thinking. *Sloan Management Review*, 35(4), 33–41.

Kernis, M. H. (2003). Toward a conceptualization of optimal self-esteem. *Psychological Inquiry*, 14(1), 1–26.

Kernis, M. H. and Goldman, B. M. (2006). A multicomponent conceptualization of authenticity: theory and research. In M. P. Zanna (ed.), *Advances in experimental social psychology*. San Diego: Elsevier Academic Press, pp. 284–357.

Kidda, C., Palmeria, H., and Aslina, R. N. (2013). Rational snacking: young children's decision-making on the marshmallow task is moderated by beliefs about environmental reliability. *Cognition*, 126(1), 109–14.

Kiken, L. G. and Shook, N. G. (2011). Looking up: mindfulness increases positive judgments and reduces negativity bias. *Social Psychological and Personality Science*, 2, 425–31.

Klayman, J. and Ha, Y-W. (1987). Confirmation, disconfirmation, and information in hypothesis testing. *Psychological Review*, 94(2), 211–28.

Klayman, J., Soll, J. B., González-Vallejo, C., and Barlas, S. (1999). Overconfidence: it depends on how, what, and whom you ask. *Organizational Behavior and Human Decision Processes*, 79(3), 216–47.

Lakey, C. E., Campbell, W. K., Brown, K. W., and Goodie, A. S. (2007). Dispositional mindfulness as a predictor of the severity of gambling outcomes. *Personality and Individual Differences*, 43(7), 1698–710.

Lakey, C. E., Kernis, M. H., Heppner, W. L., and Lance, C. E. (2008). Individual differences in authenticity and mindfulness as predictors of verbal defensiveness. *Journal of Research in Personality*, 42, 230–8.

Luce, M. F. (1998). Choosing to avoid: coping with negatively emotion-laden consumer decisions. *Journal of Consumer Research*, 24, 409–33.

Luce, M. F., Bettman, J. R., and Payne, J. W. (1997). Choice processing in emotionally difficult decisions. *Journal of Experimental Psychology: Learning, Memory, and Cognition*, 23, 384–405.

Milkman, K. L., Chugh, D., and Bazerman, M. (2009). How can decision making be improved? *Perspectives on Psychological Science*, 4(4), 379–83.

Miller, D. T. (1976). Ego involvement and attributions for success and failure. *Journal of Personality and Social Psychology*, 34(5), 901–6.

Miller, D. T. and Ross, M. (1975). Self-serving biases in the attribution of causality: fact or fiction? *Psychological Bulletin*, 82(2), 213–25.

Moore, D. A. and Healy, P. J. (2008). The trouble with overconfidence. *Psychological Review*, 115(2) 502–17.

Rest, J. (1986). *Moral development: advances in research and theory*. New York: Praeger.

Rogers, C. (1961). *On becoming a person: a therapist's view of psychotherapy*. New York: Houghton-Mifflin.

Rudman, L. A. and Borgida, E. (1995). The afterglow of construct accessibility: the behavioral consequences of priming men to view women as sexual objects. *Journal of Experimental Social Psychology*, 31, 493–517.

Ruedy, N. E. and Schweitzer, M. E. (2010). In the moment: the role of mindfulness in ethical decision making. *The Journal of Business Ethics*, 95, 73–87.

Russo, J. E. and Shoemaker, P. J. H. (1992). Managing overconfidence. *Sloan Management Review*, 33, 7–17.

Russo, J. E. and Schoemaker, P. J. H. (2002). *Winning decisions: how to make the right decision the first time.* New York: Doubleday.

Salzberg, S. (2011). *Real happiness: the power of meditation.* New York: Workman Publishing.

Shapiro, S. L., Carlson, L. E., Astin, J. A., and Freedman, B. (2006). Mechanisms of mindfulness. *Journal of Clinical Psychology*, 62, 373–86.

Shapiro, S. L., Schwartz, G. E., and Bonner, G. (1998). Effects of mindfulness-based stress reduction on medical and premedical students. *Journal of Behavioral Medicine*, 21, 581–99.

Shepperd, J., Malone, W., and Sweeny, K. (2008). Exploring causes of the self-serving bias. *Social and Personality Psychology Compass*, 2(2), 895–908.

Shoda, Y., Mischel, W., and Peake, P. K. (1990). Predicting adolescent cognitive and self-regulatory competencies from preschool delay of gratification: identifying diagnostic conditions. *Developmental Psychology*, 26(6), 978–86.

Simon, H. A. (1945). *Administrative behavior: a study of decision-making processes in administrative organization.* New York: Free Press.

Staw, B. M. (1976). Knee-deep in the big muddy: a study of escalating commitment to a chosen course of action. *Organizational Behavior and Human Performance*, 16, 27–44.

Staw, B. M. and Ross, J. (1978). Commitment to a policy decision: a multi-theoretical perspective. *Administrative Science Quarterly*, 23, 40–64.

Tallis, F., Eysenck, M., and Mathews, A. (1991). Elevated evidence requirements in worry. *Personality and Individual Differences*, 12, 21–7.

Taylor, S. E. and Brown, J. D. (1988). Illusion and well-being: a social psychological perspective on mental health. *Psychological Bulletin*, 103, 193–210.

Teasdale, J. D., Moore, R. G., Hayhurst, H., Pope, M., Williams, S., and Segal, Z. V. (2002). Metacognitive awareness and prevention of relapse in depression: empirical evidence. *Journal of Consulting and Clinical Psychology*, 70, 278–87.

Tversky, A. and Shafir, E. (1992). Choice under conflict: the dynamics of deferred decision. *Psychological Science*, 3, 358–61.

Walach, H., Buchheld, N., Buttenmüller, V., Kleinknecht, N., and Schmidt, S. (2006). Measuring mindfulness – the Freiburg Mindfulness Inventory (FMI). *Personality and Individual Differences*, 40(8), 1543–55.

Whitson, J. A. and Galinsky, A. D. (2008). Lacking control increases illusory pattern perception. *Science*, 322(5898), 115–17.

Zacharakis, A. L. and Shepherd, D. A. (2001). The nature of information and overconfidence on venture capitalists' decision making. *Journal of Business Venturing*, 16(4), 311–32.

Zeidan, F., Johnson, S. K., Diamond, B. J., David, Z., and Goolkasian, P. (2010). Mindfulness meditation improves cognition: evidence of brief mental training. *Consciousness and Cognition*, 19, 597–605.

Zhang, J., Ding, W., Li, Y., and Wu, C. (2013). Task complexity matters: the influence of trait mindfulness on task and safety performance of nuclear power plant operators. *Personality and Individual Differences*, 55, 433–9.

8 | Mindfulness and creativity in the workplace

RAVI S. KUDESIA

Introduction

In the spring of 2010, the technology and consulting organization IBM released a much-publicized opinion study of CEOs. Some 1,500 chief executives from 60 countries and 33 industries suggested that more than integrity, rigor, or even vision, creativity is the single most important leadership competency (Berman and Korsten 2010). Upon reflection, this finding is not entirely counterintuitive as creativity is a key driver of long-term organizational success (Florida, 2002). Far too often, top managers fall into routine and habitual ways of doing business that prevent them from adapting to changing conditions and recognizing new opportunities (Nystrom and Starbuck 1984). Firms such as Polaroid, whose management was wholly unprepared to adapt to the rise of digital photography, richly illustrate this point (Tripsas and Gavetti 2000). As business environments grow increasingly volatile and complex, managers who can navigate ambiguity and respond adaptively to change will be in ever-higher demand.

Yet, despite being of critical importance to firm success, academics and practitioners alike are uncertain how to best facilitate workplace creativity. Existing approaches largely seek to improve creativity either by hiring individuals perceived as particularly talented or by implementing policies and procedures that increase employees' motivation to think creatively. Mindfulness training may represent a third route to creativity. While typically conceptualized as a wellness intervention, mindfulness training was developed by Buddhist monastics to produce a state of mind that "differs profoundly" from "our usual mode of consciousness" (Bodhi 1984, p. 75). This state of mind speaks rather directly to the kind of cognitive flexibility and creative insight required in the modern workplace. As such, I suggest that mindfulness may provide a distinctive intrapsychic path to enhanced workplace creativity. In this chapter, I therefore outline an integrated perspective of creative cognition in light of mindfulness that I hope will be of benefit to academics and practitioners alike.

What is creativity?

Before we proceed, we must define creativity. Because the term carries so many meanings, the best way to tackle its definition is in regard to its constituent elements. A helpful heuristic is to distinguish between creative *products*, the *people* who originate them, the *places* that facilitate creativity, and the *process* by which it occurs (e.g. Rhodes 1961). In firms, these four Ps of creativity are related in a specific and noteworthy way. For example, creative products are distinguished by their novelty (i.e. distinctness from previous offerings) and usefulness (i.e. value to customers) (Barron 1969; Mumford 2003). Products originate from the interaction between people and place: firms seek to hire the right employees and design the right kind of workplace (see Woodman, Sawyer, and Griffin 1993). Creative people have a unique personality that is alert, non-conformist, flexible, intellectually curious, broad minded, self-confident, risk taking, attracted to complexity, and open to experiences (Barron and Harrington 1981; Martindale 1989; McCrae 1987). Creativity is greatest in those with positive, activating, and approach-oriented moods (Baas, De Dreu, and Nijstad 2008) and may require intelligence as a necessary but insufficient condition (Guilford 1967).

Creative workplaces are distinguished by their ability to generate intrinsic motivation, such that employees are motivated by the work itself instead of by external forces such as financial compensation or competitive pressure (Amabile 1998). As a result, employee creativity is higher given complex and meaningful jobs, supportive and non-controlling supervisors, developmental and nonjudgmental evaluation procedures, and office configurations that limit interruptions to work (Shalley, Zhou, and Oldham 2004). In firms, the creative process is ongoing and iterative. For example, past learning enables individuals and teams within firms to identify problems (i.e. *preparation*); these individuals and teams then attempt several solutions (i.e. *incubation*) until firm resources are marshaled behind a single plausible solution (i.e. *illumination*); consumers in the market then provide feedback about this solution through purchasing decisions (i.e. *verification*), which facilitates further learning and enables new creativity (Hurley and Hult 1998; Wallas 1926). Throughout this chapter, we will refer back to concepts related to the four Ps of creativity (i.e. product, person, place, process) as a helpful touchpoint to ground our conversations regarding mindfulness and creativity.

Creative cognition

While the above discussion can help us understand what creativity is, it does not explain the cognitive micro-processes that describe how creative insights actually emerge. Essentially, creative insight can come either from a shift in the way that the problem and solution are represented in the mind or in the way that knowledge structures informing possible solutions are organized. There are also certain modes of thinking that make these changes in representations and knowledge structures more likely. These cognitive micro-processes will be important to review before we delve into the potential role of mindfulness in enabling creativity.

Representing problems and solutions

There are three ways that changes in mental representations can lead to insight (Ohlsson 1992). *Elaboration* means adding information to a problem representation. For example, if asked to identify the link between "board" and "table," you may respond that a table is a wooden board. After elaborating the many meanings of "board," however, you may also realize that a company's board meets around a table. Insight came from adding new information to an initially incomplete representation. *Re-encoding* means rejecting part of the problem representation. For instance, suppose you were asked if it was legal for a man to marry his widow's sister. At first, you may consider this a legal question. However, if you rejected the legal interpretation and re-encoded the question, you may realize that a man with a widow is already dead and therefore cannot marry. Insight came from removing unhelpful information from the initial representation.

Constraint relaxation means changing assumptions about the solution representation. For example, if asked to help a company reduce the frequency with which their products break, you may think about better materials or stronger construction. Once in a mindfulness workshop, a participant responded by telling the company to make the product more beautiful. By relaxing the constraint that the solution must be product-oriented, he arrived at a relationship-oriented solution: users would better care for a product they found beautiful, reducing breakage. Insight came by relaxing constraints on the solution, thereby allowing for unprecedented strategies.

Organizing knowledge structures

However, even assuming that the problem and solution are properly represented, creativity still requires identifying and connecting the pieces of knowledge necessary to solve the problem. If the necessary connections already exist in the mind, one need only recall the solution, which makes the problem one of access to long-term memory. Creative problems, however, require individuals to re-organize their knowledge structures in some way before the solution emerges. This occurs through four processes of increasing complexity (Welling 2007).

Application entails applying an existing knowledge structure to an incrementally novel context. For example, a firm selling customer relationship management software to the insurance industry could apply the same process to sell its software to the banking industry. *Analogy* transfers an existing knowledge structure to an innovative context. In this case, the company could realize that software managing firm–customer relationships could also be used to manage firm–employee relationships. It could thus use the same software in a new way that helps send internal memos and manage paperwork with its employees. *Combination* integrates existing knowledge structures to form a new structure. The firm could thus combine client and employee communication concepts to produce a new combined software system. *Abstraction* creates a new superordinate concept that defines the relationship between lower order knowledge structures. For example, this new interface to manage both client and employee relationships could be seen as part of a new category: integrated workplace relationship solutions. Having this new concept helps make sense of the combination and facilitates the development of similar valuable insights.

Modes of thinking

While changing representations and organizing knowledge structures are important, how exactly do these processes occur? A key distinction made by Guilford (1959) identified convergent and divergent modes of thinking. In *convergent thinking*, individuals increasingly narrow their mental search processes until they arrive at a single correct answer. For example, if asked to identify the capital of California, your memory search would systematically narrow, perhaps from all cities, to cities in California, to the single capital city of Sacramento. In *divergent thinking*, however, mental processes are relatively unconstrained, and instead produce a variety of correct answers. For example, if asked to list as many cities in California as possible, you will notice that instead of directing your mind narrowly, you simply allow the bottom-up answers to emerge: San Francisco, Los Angeles, Sacramento, and so on. Creativity requires both of these processes: divergent thinking helps one elaborate representations and produce a variety of solutions, while convergent thinking helps one narrow representations and arrive at the best solution.

Creativity training

Given the importance of creativity, several training programs have been established and implemented in workplaces with some degree of success (see Puccio *et al.* 2010 and Scott, Leritz, and Mumford 2004). The earliest program, Creative Problem Solving, was developed by the advertiser Alex Osborn (1953), who is known for pioneering the concept of brainstorming. This process is similar to the typical creative process in that it entails gathering information, recognizing problems, generating solutions, and planning action. Its hallmark, however, is the way in which it alternates between divergent and convergent thinking in each step. Another well-known program is Synectics, which aims to "make the familiar strange and the strange familiar" (Gordon 1961). It challenges individuals to consider their creative problem by drawing upon various types of analogies that probe both related and fantastic solutions and contextualize the problem both personally and symbolically. The Six Thinking Hats program similarly utilizes techniques to help individuals shift perspectives (De Bono 1985). For example, it helps individuals alternate between information gathering, intuitive feeling, logical thinking, optimistic responses, and idea generation modes of problem solving.

The benefit of these aforementioned programs is that they essentially help structure the creative process in ways that mitigate common pitfalls. For example, the non-evaluative nature of brain-storming in the Creative Problem Solving approach helps avoid self-consciousness in divergent thinking, and the information gathering stage in the Six Thinking Hats program avoids the tendency to solve problems that have not yet been fully elaborated. These training programs thus offer benefits in that they provide heuristics to help individuals understand and participate in the creative process (Scott *et al.* 2004). Other means of facilitating creativity seek to maximize the interaction of people and place (i.e. individual differences and workplace conditions) (Woodman *et al.* 1993). This, however, leaves an important gap: instead of improving creativity by helping employees understand the process or by structuring the workplace, can firms improve creativity by strengthening employees' underlying cognitive abilities? The remainder of this chapter will address this question through mindfulness. It will paint a picture of what mindfulness is, where it came from, and why it might provide a unique intra-psychic method of improving creativity.

Buddhist psychology

Mindfulness is a fundamentally cross-cultural and pre-scientific construct as it emerged several millennia ago from the teachings and practices of Buddhist psychology. At first glance, this original context has little to say directly about creativity. It is significant that the Buddha and his successors "take care to explain their thought not as creation but as a retracing of forgotten eternal truth" and therefore they "compare their activity to the clearing of an overgrown ancient path in the jungle, not to the making of a new path" (Klostermaier 1991, p. 6). However, there is a deeper and more abiding relationship between Buddhist psychology and creativity that merits attention. In order to fully understand this link, we must briefly delve into the larger tradition of Buddhist psychology. Doing so will help ground our discussion moving forward.

Enlightenment and cognitive interpretations

The purpose of Buddhism is to attain *enlightenment* for the benefit of all sentient beings (for a review, see Kudesia and Nyima 2014). Enlightenment is a state of subjective experience that, unlike conventional experience, is firmly rooted in an understanding of reality *as it is* as opposed to some personally or socially constructed reality based on our personal history, language, ideologies, and desires. As such, Buddhism also suggests that those of us who are not yet enlightened misperceive reality. This misperception is evident in even simple statements such as "I saw the blue river." We can unpack this statement through the perspective of Buddhist psychology to better understand what enlightenment means and why it relates to creativity.

To begin with, there is no such thing as blue "out there" in the world. Colors do not reside in objects like rivers, but emerge from the interaction of reflective properties of objects, anatomical properties of our eyes, and electromagnetic radiation (Lakoff and Johnson 1999). Buddhism would then point out that beyond physics and physiology, language and culture also determine our experience of colors. For example, the exact same wavelength of light is classified by a Berinmo speaker from Papua New Guinea as green, while an English speaker would call it blue (Roberson, Davies, and Davidoff 2000). Thus, Buddhism would suggest that we do not *see* the river as blue, we *create* the river as blue through our biocultural interpretations. It is the same for the river. For example, in English, we have the words "river" and "stream." In French, "fleuve" and "rivière." The English words differ on the basis of size, as a river is larger than a stream. The French words differ on the basis of direction, as a fleuve flows to the sea while a rivière does not. As such, when an English speaker and French speaker look at the same flowing water, they actually create different mental images: one is determined by size, the other by direction (Culler 1986, pp. 33–4). So, according to Buddhism, the "blue river" is not something objective and independent of the viewer, but subjective and dependent on the viewer.

The Buddha once remarked that his entire teaching is encapsulated in the realization that subject and object are interdependent and co-created. We see the world based on our ideas of it, and our ideas define who we are and determine our place in the world. Subject and object are mutually created and mutually sustaining interpretations of reality. The purpose of meditation is to help us gradually drop these interpretations until we can view *what is* without imposing any top-down interpretive structures on reality. The metaphor given within Buddhism is that the enlightened mind is like a perfect mirror that reflects reality without any additions or subtractions. It sees the shapes, forms, and movements of the flowing water without externalizing and objectifying it and without feeling any need to interpret, analyze, or label it. Most of us, however, not only impose our interpretations on the world, but also mistake our interpretations for reality. This limits us in a number of ways. We often get entrenched in particular ways of viewing the world, assumptions about how people and situations are or should be, and wrong views of ourselves, our abilities, and our purpose in life.

What is mindfulness?

Mindfulness is the first stepping-stone to enlightenment: it creates the space in which we can start to gently unravel the tangled webs of our mistaken interpretations. The reason for our diversion into Buddhist psychology should now become apparent. It is impossible to exhibit creativity when one is firmly steeped in rigid and fixed views about objects, the world, and the self. In mindfulness, the habitual and conventional interpretations are held in abeyance, which allows one to pursue new and more adaptive ways of seeing the world. In some mindfulness training, this is called *beginner's mind* because it enables one to be "receptive to new possibilities" and not get "stuck in the rut" of expertise, "which often thinks it knows more than it does" (Kabat-Zinn 1990, p. 35). As suggested at this chapter's outset, I believe that mindfulness represents a state of mind that speaks rather directly to the kind of cognitive flexibility and creative insight required in the modern workplace. It builds unique cognitive abilities that enable creativity in individuals that otherwise would be trapped in conventional ways of interpreting their world. It is all the more promising because unlike other individual difference factors, it is directly trainable, which increases its promise as a possible workplace creativity intervention.

Remembering, focusing, and monitoring. Mindfulness is a complex and nuanced construct that has not yet been operationalized in a manner that both fully encompasses the original concept and enjoys broad consensus among researchers (Chiesa 2012). This is unsurprising as Buddhist psychology sees mindfulness as a state that is fundamentally inexpressible through language or statistics (Trungpa and Goleman 2005) and uses its Sanskrit term *smṛti* in a variety of ways that include remembering the past, focusing on a chosen stimulus, and monitoring mental activity (Lutz, Dunne, and Davidson 2007). To illustrate this diversity of uses, consider the context in which mindfulness originally arose. When the first Buddhist monks set the intention of attaining enlightenment, they could not simply sit and meditate all day. They had to engage in and organize a growing community of practitioners and undertake acts of service within their larger society. While acting, it is quite easy to lose track of one's higher intentions, especially when they are abstract like enlightenment. For this reason, the Buddha emphasized to monks the importance of *remembering* their intention of enlightenment, *focusing* on their actions in the present moment, and *monitoring* this activity in a particular way to ensure their actions are consistent with their intentions. This simultaneous combination of remembering, focusing, and monitoring constitutes mindfulness in its original context.

Although we all revert to our habitual ways of acting from time to time, it is mindfulness that helps us become aware of such transgressions and allows us to re-engage our intentions. Those who are low in mindfulness may only notice their transgressions after the fact. However, as mindfulness increases, individuals can monitor and adjust their behavior in real-time. This ensures that when one sets an intention, it is carried forward into one's actions. Mindfulness thus has the great value of making us self-aware and creating the space for us to shift out of our automatic, habitual, and mindless ways of thinking and acting. As mindfulness grew increasingly integrated into Western psychology, the importance of remembering and monitoring subsided and attending to the present moment was emphasized. What got lost in translation was that mindfulness is less about paying *attention* to whatever is *occurring* in the present and more about carrying forth one's *intentions* into whatever one is *doing* in the present (Kudesia and Nyima 2014). As such, mindfulness may be less akin to a state of attention and closer to a self-regulatory process. It is a particular way of remembering one's intentions while acting and adjusting one's attention accordingly. I suggest it is a particular way because it is certainly not the only way. You could put Post-It notes around the office reminding you to practice compassion, but that is certainly not mindfulness.

An operational definition. In an interesting and productive ongoing dialogue with a Buddhist monk, we jointly identified three components of mindfulness that are both consistent with its original meaning and tractable in research contexts (Kudesia and Nyima 2014). We define mindfulness as a state characterized by decreased discursive thought, heightened meta-awareness, and goal-based regulation of attention. By *discursive thought*, we refer to the tendency to put experience into words. In mindfulness, the present moment is experienced without the overlay of mental chatter. This helps us see things as they are, not as we imagine them to be in our linguistically constructed mental models. By *meta-awareness*, we refer to an increased state of detached self-observation. In mindfulness, one can more readily notice mental activity without getting caught up in it. It is akin to the difference between becoming angry and noticing that you are having angry thoughts and feelings; the latter shows greater psychological distance from mental experience and thus allows for greater regulation of it. By *goal-based regulation of attention*, we refer to the idea that higher order meta-cognitive faculties adjust attention so that it is focused only on goal-relevant aspects of the present moment and is broad enough to incorporate all relevant aspects. When mindful, individuals do not pay attention to the present in an indiscriminate way, but selectively attend to those aspects that are relevant to performing their intentions or goals. By defining mindfulness relative to these three components, we can understand the construct more fully and precisely.

Mindfulness and creativity

So far, we have reviewed creativity and mindfulness separately and explored their link in a general way. This section will highlight how mindfulness can impact creativity outcomes in two ways. It first reviews the existing empirical work and then delves into the underlying theoretical mechanisms, both direct and indirect.

Existing empirical studies

The extant literature is small, but supports links between mindfulness and creativity. For example, my colleagues and I have studied how mindfulness meditation impacts the process of incubation (Kudesia, Baer, and Elfenbein 2013). When individuals get stuck on a creative problem, they often take a break before approaching it once again. During this break period, the unconscious mind can either further activate past attempts or forget them. We hypothesized that allowing individuals' minds to wander during breaks will encourage further activation of their past attempts. Conversely, we hypothesized that having individuals meditate during the break would help them to forget their past attempts and approach the problem with fresh eyes. In meditation, the goal is to attend solely to the breath, so any arising thoughts related to past attempts would be goal-irrelevant and thus inhibited. Our results supported this hypothesis. For questions that required re-encoding of the initial representation (like the widow's sister question mentioned earlier), allowing subjects' minds to wander produced no improvement because it further activated their past attempts. However, when subjects meditated, they focused their attention on breathing in the present moment and thus inhibited all thoughts from the past. This helped them forget their past attempts and led to a nearly 40 percent improvement in the second attempt.

This finding is consistent with other work. For example, after meditating, subjects show improvement on never-before-seen problems that require re-encoding, but not on problems that are solved through straightforward logical processes (Ostafin and Kassman 2012). In another study, subjects who had practiced mindfulness meditation over eight weeks were faced with a task that required them to measure out various amounts of water using jugs of pre-specified capacities (Greenberg, Reiner, and Meiran 2012). When this paradigm was first created, subjects typically found a pattern of solving problems; once they had this solution representation, they fixated on it (Luchins 1942). As a result, when their initial representation no longer applied, they were unable to find the answer. However, Greenberg *et al.* (2012) found that those who underwent mindfulness training did not fixate on their initial solution representations and could flexibly adjust solutions in response to the demands of the situation. This led to greater rates of problem solving.

In another study, my colleagues and I looked at how mindfulness meditation impacts incubation in the divergent mode of thinking (Kudesia *et al.* 2013). We did so by asking subjects to think of as many unusual uses as they could for everyday objects like a brick. In line with our hypotheses, we found that when individuals' minds wander, they come up with new ideas that are further elaborations of their past attempts. As a result, their responses end up conceptually quite similar to each other: if they first saw the brick as a tool, they later produced a number of different ways it could be used as a tool (e.g. hammering, sanding, etc.). However, those who practiced mindfulness meditation in between attempts at divergent thinking questions thought more broadly: their new responses were less similar to their past attempts and conceptualized the brick in a variety of unique ways. For example, instead of listing a number of uses within a single category, their responses spanned categories by using the brick as, for instance, a tool, weapon, furniture, or art. Being mindful thus enables more flexible conceptualization and helps individuals let go of their past representations and solution strategies.

Direct theoretical mechanisms

The first component of mindfulness is decreased discursive thought, which means that mindful individuals do not process experience strictly through language. Instead of allowing their mind to chatter about and talk over the present moment, they engage with it more directly. This has been shown using function magnetic resonance imaging evidence in clinical settings. For example, individuals with social anxiety disorder have distorted self-views; mindfulness training benefits them by shifting them away from a mode of self-processing based on discursive thought to one based on experiencing the present moment experientially and without language (Goldin, Ramel, and Gross 2009). Mindfulness researchers suggest that when experience of the present is mediated by language, it is funneled through a particularly rigid, analytical, and evaluative mode of processing that diminishes cognitive flexibility (Hayes and Wilson 2003). Interestingly, creativity researchers have suggested the same: the language through which we interpret the world contains rigid assumptions that limit our ability to make "the creative leap" – language serves to "crystallize" thought, which is otherwise more "fluid" and flexible (Koestler 1964, p. 173). The way we talk about objects is derived from how we have experienced them in the past, which makes us unable to see them in new ways moving forward. Thus discursive thought not only crystallizes and makes thought rigid, but it does so in a way that is based on the past, and thus closes off new opportunities for the future.

This is directly in line with the original Buddhist focus on perceiving reality without fixed and narrow interpretations. By reducing the overlay of discursive thought and experiencing the present moment as it is, we can produce a space in which alternative ways of conceptualizing events appear. In another line of research, a colleague and I have found significant and strong associations between the ability to "step back" from discursive thought, described by mindfulness researchers as decentering or defusion, and cognitive flexibility (Kudesia and Parke 2014). For example, using self-report measures, we found that the decentering component of mindfulness was related to the ability to flexibly consider multiple alternative interpretations of life situations while the attention regulation component of mindfulness was not. In another study that explores how stepping back from discursive thought enables flexibility, we asked subjects to complete several word stems (e.g. PO_TA_). However, we first exposed them to an incorrect answer that seemed like it may work, but did not (i.e. POTATO). Although subjects were even informed that this was a "common, but incorrect response," many were nonetheless unable to step back from its priming effects and flexibly re-encode the problem. Again, we found that the decentering component of mindfulness, but not the attention component, predicted the ability to disengage from the negative prime and thereby arrive at the correct answer (e.g. PORTAL).

As such, the relationship between decreased discursive thought and increased cognitive flexibility is a potentially important one. Accordingly, a study by Schooler, Ohlsson, and Brooks (1993) found that subjects who verbalized their problem-solving strategies performed worse on creativity questions requiring shifts in problem representations, but performance was unimpaired for non-creative questions. Processing information and solving problems through discursive thought thus impairs creativity. As a result, mindfulness may benefit creativity because it shifts individuals out of the framework of discursive thought, allowing for more fluid and flexible modes of cognition.

The second component of mindfulness is heightened meta-awareness, the ability to observe the mind. An important aspect of meta-awareness is working memory, the system that holds information in the mind and enables the overriding of habitual behaviors. Working memory is known to enable creative modes of thinking (Lee and Therriault 2013) and is increased by mindfulness training (Jha, Stanley, and Baime 2010; Mrazek *et al.* 2013). Working memory helps divergent thinking by allowing individuals to generate and hold multiple ideas simultaneously and then select novel ideas over more conventional ideas. It helps convergent thinking by allowing individuals to override habitual problem and solution representations. As such, mindful individuals have greater mental space in which ideas can be held and manipulated. Thus, by increasing meta-awareness, mindfulness can improve creativity by increasing individuals' ability to utilize creative modes of thinking, more fully represent problems and solutions, and organize knowledge structures in new, complex, and creative ways.

The third component of mindfulness is attention regulation, the ability to modify the level of focus and breadth of attention to maximize goal-directed behavior. Mindful individuals can better engage in complex cognitive tasks by monitoring and regulating attention more efficiently (e.g. Brefczynski-Lewis *et al.* 2007; Kozasa *et al.* 2012). This can mean varying the level of focus and the breadth of attention when needed. These attention regulation abilities are being increasingly seen as important to creativity. One aspect that has been greatly emphasized is the ability to broaden attention and thereby incorporate greater amounts of data (Dewing and Battye, 1971; Kasof, 1997; Mendelsohn, 1976). In line with the concept of beginner's mind, creative individuals often exhibit decreased *latent inhibition*, which means they tend not to automatically exclude stimuli from attention that have been previously judged as being irrelevant (Dykes and McGhie 1976). Interestingly, decreased latent inhibition is a risk factor for psychosis and therefore may only serve as a benefit for creativity if individuals have sufficiently high intelligence to make sense of all the extra information they process (Carson, Peterson, and Higgins 2003).

Mindful individuals are also less likely to habituate and filter out stimuli simply because they correspond to past experience (Kasamatsu and Hirai 1966; Valentine and Sweet 1999). However, they also have greater abilities to regulate their attention processes, suggesting that the goal-directed attention regulation of mindfulness can maximize the positives of increased exposure to stimuli without engaging the negatives that lead to mental health issues. As such, mindful individuals may see improved creativity because they can selectively access greater information both externally, allowing them to take in more information from the world around them, and internally, allowing them greater access to take in their mental activity. For an overview of these paths, see Table 8.1.

Indirect theoretical mechanisms

In addition to its direct mechanisms, mindfulness may also increase creativity through a host of indirect mechanisms. For example,

Table 8.1 *Direct and indirect paths from mindfulness to creativity*

Mindfulness component	Mechanism	Explanation	Creativity outcome
Direct Paths			
Discursive cognition (-)	Cognitive flexibility	Reduced reliance on evaluative linguistic forms of processing	Beneficial for problems requiring shifts in mental representations or knowledge structures
Meta-awareness (+)	Working memory	Increased ability to hold multiple constraints and potential solutions in mind simultaneously	Beneficial for complex problems with many working parts or potential solutions
Attention regulation (+)	Access to information	Increased ability to broaden or narrow one's focus, thus controlling the flow of information	Beneficial for managing the creative process over time
Indirect paths			
Positive affect (+)	Category breadth	Broader categorization, thus increasing the number of possible connections of ideas	Beneficial for problems that require combination or abstraction processes
Task persistence (+)	Exploration behavior	More thorough and exhaustive exploration of the solution space	Beneficial for problems that persist over time and require external verification for each potential solution
Individual differences (+)	Personality change	Greater trait openness, acceptance, etc. enable creative cognition and its behavioral antecedents	Beneficial for seeking out creative problems, accessing diverse information, and thinking flexibly

mindfulness increases positive affect and reduces stress (Grossman *et al.* 2004). Positive affect refers to the subjective experience of pleasant feelings and increases creativity by broadening categorization, thereby creating new connections between ideas (Isen, Daubman, and Nowicki 1987). Likewise, as creativity is impaired by stress and negative affect (Shanteau and Dino 1993), the stress reduction benefits of mindfulness could translate to improved creativity as well. Mindfulness is also associated with greater task persistence in the face of failure (Evans, Baer, and Segerstrom 2009), which is an important contributor to creativity as well (Nijstad *et al.* 2010). With greater persistence comes a more thorough exploration of the conceptual space underlying a creative solution. Mindfulness is also associated with certain individual differences that are similar to the creative personality discussed earlier. Examples include being accepting and nonjudgmental, being willing to expose oneself to experiences, having insight into the nature of mental processes, and others (see Bergomi, Tschacher, and Kupper 2012). These traits could benefit creativity by increasing interest in open-ended problems, developing flexible ways of thinking, or prompting individuals to seek more diverse experiences (for similar arguments, see McCrae 1987). As such, mindfulness is related to creativity not only through its three components of diminished discursive cognition, heightened meta-awareness, and goal-directed regulation of attention, but also through additional indirect mechanisms.

Future research directions

While the empirical work and theoretical mechanisms I have outlined paint an initial picture of how mindfulness may relate to creativity, the potential body of future empirical work is large. One of the great benefits of mindfulness in theory testing is that meditation interventions can help manipulate potential mechanisms that cannot otherwise be measured. For example, my colleagues and I used mindfulness meditation and mind wandering to differentially impact two unconscious processes (i.e. activation of past attempts and forgetting of past attempts) that had not previously been tested side by side (Kudesia *et al.* 2013). Future work could also utilize findings relating mindfulness to flexibility in visual perception (e.g. Hodgins and Adair 2010) to explore how mindfulness may relate to spatial creativity problems to supplement existing work on verbal creativity problems. It could also move beyond individual levels of creativity to group processes and see whether the decreased sensitivity to social rejection embodied in mindfulness (e.g. Heppner *et al.* 2008) improves the creative process in group settings. Finally, work that brings mindfulness and creativity research outside the laboratory and into workplace field settings is important as well.

Workplace mindfulness and creativity training

In this section, we transition from theory to practice. Most of the extant workplace mindfulness training focuses on wellness and stress reduction. I suggest that this offers two limitations related to developing creativity in organizations. First, the individuals who self-select into wellness interventions are likely not the same as those who would self-select into creativity interventions. By conceptualizing mindfulness as a creativity intervention, new employees can get introduced to meditation practices. The second limitation is that without making certain benefits more explicit, individuals may not become aware of them. For example, if mindfulness is seen as a wellness intervention, creative ideas that emerge as a result may be misattributed to other causes. Furthermore, individuals may not realize that these practices can apply to problem solving contexts and thus may have the tools but not the knowledge to fully apply them. While a full mapping of a workplace mindfulness and creativity training program is beyond the scope of this chapter, I have listed two key principles below that deserve practitioner attention.

Applied process knowledge

One of the most efficacious aspects of extant creativity interventions is that they deliver a great deal of knowledge about how the creative process works and thereby encourage individuals to alternate between divergent and convergent thinking and engage in sequential stages of gathering information, recognizing problems, generating solutions, and planning action. Any mindfulness creativity training should incorporate this valuable knowledge regarding the creative process. However, this process knowledge can be made more applied when integrated with mindfulness practices. For example, meditative practices vary along the continuum between focusing attention on particular stimuli and broadening attention to openly monitor all arising stimuli. These techniques can be useful at different stages in the process to greater effect. For example, broadening attention will be more helpful in recognizing problems and generating solutions, while narrowing attention may be more helpful for verifying solutions and planning action. Likewise, means of inhibiting discursive cognition will be especially helpful in cases that require combination and abstraction rather than application and analogy. Furthermore, it is possible to develop meditative techniques specific for creativity that simultaneously activate important concepts while inhibiting common and conventional associations. As such, workplace mindfulness and creativity training should go beyond simply outlining the creative process, but instead tailor mindfulness practices to each stage of the process. Thus, applied process knowledge is the first guideline for such training.

Creative self-efficacy

Another important aspect of workplace mindfulness and creativity training is instilling the belief that one is capable of creative behavior. This is known as *creative self-efficacy*, and is an important predictor of creativity in the workplace (Tierney and Farmer 2002). It is quite possible that by highlighting the relationship between mindfulness and creativity and by providing specific techniques to facilitate creative cognition, employees would have greater creative self-efficacy. If this was paired with the understanding that creativity can be developed and is not some inherent and immutable property of people, training could increase the tendency of individuals to think creatively and to apply mindfulness to their creative projects.

Conclusion

In this chapter, I sought to make the link between workplace creativity and mindfulness more explicit. To do so, I first reviewed the creativity construct by highlighting the creative product, person, place, and process, examining its underlying cognitive mechanisms, and reviewing common means of training. I then overviewed Buddhist psychology to contextualize mindfulness as a process that reduces the rigidity of how we interpret our environment before defining mindfulness as a state characterized by decreased discursive thought, heightened meta-awareness, and goal-directed attention regulation. After doing so, I reviewed the extant empirical literature and highlighted the theoretical mechanisms by which mindfulness can impact creativity, both direct and indirect. I then suggested future areas for research before providing some basic guidelines for workplace mindfulness and creativity training. It is my hope that this chapter can serve as a basis for a fruitful program of research and practice that pairs mindfulness and creativity.

References

Amabile, T. M. (1998). How to kill creativity. *Harvard Business Review*, Sept–Oct, 77–87.

Baas, M., De Dreu, C. K., and Nijstad, B. A. (2008). A meta-analysis of 25 years of mood-creativity research: hedonic tone, activation, or regulatory focus? *Psychological Bulletin*, 134(6), 779–806.

Barron, F. (1969). *Creative person and creative process*. New York: Holt, Rinehart, and Winston.

Barron, F. and Harrington, D. M. (1981). Creativity, intelligence, and personality. *Annual Review of Psychology*, 32(1), 439–76.

Bergomi, C., Tschacher, W., and Kupper, Z. (2012). The assessment of mindfulness with self-report measures: existing scales and open issues. *Mindfulness*, 4, 191–202.

Berman, S. and Korsten, P. (2010). *Capitalising on complexity: insights from the global chief executive officer (CEO) study*. Portsmouth, UK: IBM Institute for Business Value.

Bodhi, B. (1984). *The noble eightfold path: way to the end of suffering*. Onalaska, WA: Pariyatti.

Brefczynski-Lewis J. A., Lutz, A., Schaefer, H. S., Levinson, D. B., and Davidson, R. J. (2007). Neural correlates of attentional expertise in long-term meditation practitioners. *Proceedings of the National Academy of Sciences*, 104(27), 11483–8.

Carson, S. H., Peterson, J. B., and Higgins, D. M. (2003). Decreased latent inhibition is associated with increased creative achievement in high-functioning individuals. *Journal of Personality and Social Psychology*, 85(3), 499–506.

Chiesa, A. (2012). The difficulty of defining mindfulness: current thought and critical issues. *Mindfulness*, 4(3), 255–68.

Culler, J. D. (1986). *Ferdinand de Saussure*. Ithaca, NY: Cornell University Press.

De Bono, E. (1985). *Six thinking hats*. New York: Little Brown and Company.

Dewing, K. and Battye, G. (1971). Attentional deployment and non-verbal fluency. *Journal of Personality and Social Psychology*, 17(2), 214–18.

Dykes, M. and McGhie, A. (1976). A comparative study of attentional strategies in schizophrenics and highly creative normal subjects. *British Journal of Psychiatry*, 128, 50–6.

Evans, D. R., Baer, R. A., and Segerstrom, S. G. (2009). The effects of mindfulness and self-consciousness on persistence. *Personality and Individual Differences*, 47(4): 379–82.

Florida, R. (2002). *The rise of the creative class*. North Melbourne: Pluto Press.

Goldin, P., Ramel, W., and Gross, J. (2009). Mindfulness meditation training and self-referential processing in social anxiety disorder: behavioral and neural effects. *Journal of Cognitive Psychotherapy*, 23(3), 242–57.

Gordon, W. J. (1961). *Synectics: the development of creative capacity*. New York: Harper and Row.

Greenberg, J., Reiner, K., and Meiran, N. (2012). "Mind the trap": mindfulness practice reduces cognitive rigidity. *PLoS ONE*, 7(5), e36206.

Grossman, P., Niemann, L., Schmidt, S., and Walach, H. (2004). Mindfulness-based stress reduction and health benefits: a meta-analysis. *Journal of Psychosomatic Research*, 57(1), 35–43.

Guilford, J. P. (1959). Three faces of intellect. *American psychologist*, 14(8), 469–79.

(1967). *The nature of human intelligence*. New York: McGraw-Hill.

Hayes, S. C. and Wilson, K. G. (2003). Mindfulness: method and process. *Clinical Psychology: Science and Practice*, 10(2), 161–5.

Heppner, W. L., Kernis, M. H., Lakey, C. E., Campbell, W. K., Goldman, B. M., Davis, P. J., and Cascio, E. V. (2008). Mindfulness as a means of reducing aggressive behavior: dispositional and situational evidence. *Aggressive Behavior*, 34(5), 486–96.

Hodgins, H. S. and Adair, K. C. (2010). Attentional processes and meditation. *Consciousness and Cognition*, 19(4), 872–8.

Hurley R. F. and Hult, G. T. M. (1998). Innovation, market orientation, and organisational learning: an integration and empirical examination. *Journal of Marketing*, 62(3), 42–54.

Isen, A. M., Daubman, K. A., and Nowicki, G. P. (1987). Positive affect facilitates creative problem solving. *Journal of Personality and Social Psychology*, 52(6), 1122–31.

Jha, A. P., Stanley, E. A., and Baime, M. J. (2010). What does mindfulness training strengthen? Working memory capacity as a functional marker of training success. In Baer, R. (ed.), *Assessing mindfulness and acceptance: illuminating the processes of change*. New York: New Harbinger Publications, pp. 207–25.

Kabat-Zinn, J. (1990). *Full catastrophe living: using the wisdom of your body and mind to face stress, pain and illness*. New York: Delacorte.

Kasamatsu, A. and Hirai, T. (1966). An electroencephalographic study on the Zen meditation (Zazen). *Folia Psychiatrica et Neurologica Japonica*, 20(4), 315–36.

Kasof, J. (1997). Creativity and breadth of attention. *Creativity Research Journal*, 10(4), 303–15.

Klostermaier, K. (1991). The nature of Buddhism. *Asian Philosophy: An International Journal of the Philosophical Traditions of the East*, 1(1), 29–37.

Koestler, A. (1964). *The act of creation*. London: Hutchinson and Co.

Kozasa, E. H., Sato, J. R., Lacerda, S. S., Barreiros, M. A. M., Radvany, J., Russell, T. A., Sanches, L. G., Mello, L. E. A. M., and Amaro, E. (2012). Meditation training increases brain efficiency in an attention task. *NeuroImage*, 59(1), 745–9.

Kudesia, R. S. and Nyima, T. (2014). Mindfulness contextualized: a review and integration of Buddhist and neuropsychological approaches to cognition. *Mindfulness*, doi: 10.1007/s12671-014-0337-8.

Kudesia, R. S. and Parke, M. R. (2014). The flexible mind: the role of mindfulness in cognitive adaptation. Paper presented at the Academy of Management Annual Meeting, Philadelphia, PA.

Kudesia, R. S., Baer, M., and Elfenbein, H. A. (2013). Letting go: How mindfulness meditation impacts creativity and decision making. Paper presented at the Academy of Management Annual Meeting, Orlando, FL.

Lakoff, G. and Johnson, M. (1999). *Philosophy in the flesh: the embodied mind and its challenge to Western thought*. New York: Basic Books.

Lee, C. S. and Therriault, D. J. (2013). The cognitive underpinnings of creative thought: a latent variable analysis exploring the roles of intelligence and working memory in three creative thinking processes. *Intelligence*, 41(5), 306–20.

Luchins, A. S. (1942). Mechanization in problem solving. *Psychological Monographs*, 54(6), 1–95.

Lutz, A., Dunne, J. D., and Davidson, R. J. (2007). Meditation and the neuroscience of consciousness. In P. Zelazo, M. Moscovitch, and E. Thompson (eds.), *Cambridge handbook of consciousness*. New York: Cambridge University Press, pp. 480–551.

Martindale, C. (1989). Personality, situation, and creativity. In J. A. Glover, R. R. Ronning, and C. R. Reynolds (eds.), *Handbook of creativity*. New York: Plenum Press, pp. 211–32.

McCrae, R. R. (1987). Creativity, divergent thinking, and openness to experience. *Journal of Personality and Social Psychology*, 52(6), 1258–65.

Mendelsohn, G. A. (1976). Associative and attentional processes in creative performance. *Journal of Personality*, 44(2), 341–69.

Mrazek, M. D., Franklin, M. S., Phillips, D. T., Baird, B., and Schooler, J. W. (2013). Mindfulness training improves working memory capacity and GRE performance while reducing mind wandering. *Psychological Science*, 24(5), 776–81.

Mumford, M. D. (2003). Where have we been, where are we going? Taking stock in creativity research. *Creativity Research Journal*, 15, 107–20.

Nijstad, B. A., De Dreu, C. K., Rietzschel, E. F., and Baas, M. (2010). The dual pathway to creativity model: creative ideation as a function of flexibility and persistence. *European Review of Social Psychology*, 21(1), 34–77.

Nystrom P. C. and Starbuck, W. H. (1984). To avoid organizational crises, unlearn. *Organizational Dynamics*, 12(4), 53–65.

Ohlsson, S. (1992). Information-processing explanations of insight and related phenomena. In M. T. Keane and K. J. Gilhooly (eds.), *Advances in the psychology of thinking*. London: Harvester Wheatsheaf, pp. 1–44.

Osborn, A. F. (1953). *Applied imagination: principles and procedures of creative problem-solving*. New York: Scribner's Sons.

Ostafin, B. D. and Kassman, K. T. (2012). Stepping out of history: mindfulness improves insight problem solving. *Consciousness and Cognition*, 21(2), 1031–6.

Puccio, G. J., Cabra, J. F., Fox, J. M., and Cahen, H. (2010). Creativity on demand: historical approaches and future trends. *Artificial Intelligence for Engineering Design, Analysis and Manufacturing*, 24(2), 153–9.

Rhodes, M. (1961). An analysis of creativity. *Phi Delta Kappan*, 42, 305–10.

Roberson, D., Davies, I., and Davidoff, J. (2000). Color categories are not universal: replications and new evidence from a stone-age culture. *Journal of Experimental Psychology: General*, 129(3), 369–98.

Schooler, J. W., Ohlsson, S., and Brooks, K. (1993). Thoughts beyond words: when language overshadows insight. *Journal of Experimental Psychology: General*, 122(2), 166–83.

Scott, G., Leritz, L. E., and Mumford, M. D. (2004). The effectiveness of creativity training: a quantitative review. *Creativity Research Journal*, 16(4), 361–88.

Shalley, C. E., Zhou, J., and Oldham, G. R. (2004). The effects of personal and contextual characteristics on creativity: where should we go from here? *Journal of Management*, 30(6), 933–58.

Shanteau, J. and Dino, G. A., (1993). Environmental stressor effects on creativity and decision making. In O. Svenson and A. J. Maule (eds.), *Time pressure and stress in human judgment and decision making*. New York: Plenum Press,pp. 293–308.

Tierney, P. and Farmer, S. M. (2002). Creative self-efficacy: its potential antecedents and relationship to creative performance. *Academy of Management Journal*, 45(6), 1137–48.

Tripsas, M. and Gavetti, G. (2000). Capabilities, cognition, and inertia: evidence from digital imaging. *Strategic Management Journal*, 21(10–11), 1147–61.

Trungpa, C. and Goleman, D. (2005). *The sanity we are born with: a Buddhist approach to psychology.* Boston, MA: Shambhala.

Valentine, E. R. and Sweet, P. L. G. (1999). Meditation and attention: a comparison of the effects of concentrative and mindfulness meditation on sustained attention. *Mental Health, Religion and Culture*, 2(1), 59–70.

Wallas, G. (1926). *The art of thought.* New York: Harcourt Brace.

Welling, H. (2007). Four mental operations in creative cognition: the importance of abstraction. *Creativity Research Journal*, 19(2–3), 163–77.

Woodman, R. W., Sawyer, J. E., and Griffin, R. W. (1993). Toward a theory of organizational creativity. *Academy of Management Review*, 18(2), 293–321.

9 How being mindful impacts individuals' work-family balance, conflict, and enrichment: a review of existing evidence, mechanisms and future directions

TAMMY D. ALLEN AND E. LAYNE PADDOCK

Introduction

Growing exponentially over the past several decades, the topic of work and family has fueled a large body of scholarship (see Allen 2012 for a review). Interest in work and family is expansive. The struggle to balance work and family is one that resonates with many adults. It is a topic of concern to organizations (Society for Human Resource Management Workplace Forecast 2008) and to societies across the globe (Poelmans, Greenhaus, and Las Heras Maestro 2013). Indeed, work-family issues have captured the attention of the public at large, frequently appearing as a focal topic in the popular press with titles such as "Why Women Still Can't Have It All" (Slaughter 2012) and "Men Want Work-Family Balance, and Policy Should Help Them Achieve It" (Covert 2013).

To date, the majority of work-family scholarship has focused on situational factors that help or inhibit individuals' abilities to manage multiple role responsibilities. This focus has resulted in a considerable body of work that has demonstrated links between stressors and demands emanating from the work and the family domains with constructs such as work-family conflict (Michel, Kotrba, Mitchelson, Clark, and Baltes 2011). Much of the attention aimed at reducing work-family conflict has centered on organizational practices such as flexible work arrangements and dependent care supports, despite findings that such practices have limited effectiveness in terms of alleviating work-family conflict (Allen *et al.* 2013; Butts, Casper, and Yang 2013). Work-family intervention research has focused on training supervisors to be more family-supportive (e.g., Hammer *et al.* 2011) or on flexible work practices (e.g., Perlow and Kelly 2014). Such approaches are based on the notion that experiences such as work-family conflict are primarily provoked by the situation.

There is also a growing body of research that demonstrates that personality variables are associated with work-family experiences, which suggests that individual differences beyond demographic variables also contribute to work-family experiences (Allen *et al.* 2012). Other individual difference approaches that have been applied to the study of work-family include the selection, optimization, and compensation model (Baltes and Heydens-Gahir 2003). This model is based on individuals' use of problem-focused coping strategies such as selecting goals and priorities, optimizing those goals and priorities, and compensating for losses in energy and resources (Baltes, Zhdanova, and Clark 2011). Relative to research on situational stressors and organizational policies, individual cognitive and behavioral strategies have received less attention in the work-family literature. In the current chapter we add to the individual approach by suggesting ways in which mindfulness may play a role in the work-family interface.

Mindfulness has been described as the ability to be present in the moment through attention and awareness (Brown, Ryan, and Creswell 2007). It requires an attitude of non-judging, non-striving, and patience (Kabat-Zinn 1990). Mindfulness is thought to enhance self-regulation in that a more mindful person allows sensory input and simply notices it rather than comparing, evaluating, or ruminating about it (Brown *et al.* 2007). Multiple streams of mindfulness research exist. One focus is on mindfulness-based training as a therapeutic intervention, often incorporating meditation (e.g., Kabat-Zinn 1990). Another focus is on trait-like mindfulness as an individual difference (e.g., Brown and Ryan 2003). Both types of studies show that a variety of positive outcomes are associated with mindfulness such as improvements in stress, depression, anxiety, sleep quality, physical health symptoms, and interpersonal relationship quality (see Brown *et al.* 2007 and Glomb *et al.* 2011 for reviews). Functional magnetic resonance imaging studies help explain the mechanisms through which mindfulness results in such positive outcomes; mindfulness-based training alters brain processes in a way that reflects more consistent attentional focus, enhanced sensory processing, and reflective awareness of sensory experience (e.g., Kilpatrick *et al.* 2011).

In the current chapter we review the literature on mindfulness that has implications for how individuals manage their work and family roles. Because the two critical components to mindfulness are (1) self-regulation of attention and (2) the adoption of an orientation toward one's experiences in the present moment, it has the potential to help individuals manage multiple role responsibilities. Further, a consideration of mindfulness-based concepts introduces the possible development of training tools that can be used to enhance work-family experiences. In our review, we include research investigating work-family variables as well as research with implications for work-family research. We delineate four pathways by which we believe mindfulness may relate to work-family experiences. The chapter closes with further suggestions for future research.

A review of relevant work-family literature

Current approaches to work-family research

Research on the work-family interface continues to grow at a rapid pace. Having long differentiated the domain-based roles of individuals into those that relate to work and those that do not, this literature now also distinguishes types of non-work roles (e.g., volunteer) including family roles (e.g., parent, spouse). For purposes of parsimony, we focus on the latter in this chapter, although much of our summary should also relate to the broader category of non-work roles.

As noted by Gutek, Searle, and Klepa (1991), the spillover between domains is bidirectional, such that work impacts family and family impacts work. One of the longest-studied paradigms of the work-family literature is that examining negative interdependencies between work and family roles. Studied under the rubric of work-family conflict (Greenhaus and Beutell 1985), we now have a large literature base identifying the causes, correlates, and outcomes associated with work-family conflict. More recently, positive interdependencies between these domains became a focus as theories concerning constructs such as work-family enrichment have been developed and tested (e.g., Greenhaus and Powell 2006). Another variable of interest within the work-family literature is work-family balance (Greenhaus and Allen 2011). Whereas work-family conflict and enrichment serve as linking mechanism constructs between work and family roles, work-family balance takes a holistic, inter-domain focus. Specifically, work-family balance reflects an overall inter-role assessment of compatibility between work and family roles.

Historically, the majority of work-family research has been based on correlational, between-person investigations, studying the variation among people (e.g., women versus men). However, recent research includes the use of alternative designs such as diary or daily event methodologies (Paddock *et al.*, in progress; Rothbard and Wilk 2011; Shockley and Allen 2013) and quasi-experimental designs (e.g., Hammer *et al.* 2011). Daily methods allow for assessment within-people across work-family domains and highlight that a moderate amount of the variance in work-family concepts, including conflict and enrichment, occur within and between individuals. Quasi-experimental designs allow for the assessment of work-family interventions and are used to help clarify when and which work-family interventions are likely to be especially effective.

Defining work-family constructs

The concept of how conditions or experiences in one domain (e.g. work) negatively impact conditions or experiences in another domain (e.g. family) is termed *work-family conflict* (Greenhaus and Beutell 1985). More specifically, work-family conflict is defined as "a form of interrole conflict in which the role pressures from the work and family domains are mutually incompatible in some respect" (p. 77). It can be time, strain, or behavior-based conflict. Time-based conflict results when time spent in one domain (e.g. home with young children) hinders the performance of responsibilities in the other domain (at work). Strain-based conflict occurs when demands including psychological pressures from one role (e.g. low autonomy work) make it difficult to engage in the other role (with family). Finally, behavior-based conflict results when behaviors required in one domain (e.g. objectivity at work) are carried into and conflict with the other domain (e.g. caring for others at home). The direction of the conflict is also commonly distinguished. Specifically, work interference with family (WIF) and family interference with work (FIW) are delineated as two related, but distinct variables.

A large body of research has investigated the predictors and outcomes associated with work-family conflict. For example, work-related factors such as job stressors and job demands are positively associated with WIF while family-related factors such as family stressors and family demands are associated with FIW (e.g. Byron 2005). Dispositional variables such as negative affect have also been identified as predictors of both directions of work-family conflict (Allen *et al.* 2012). Both WIF and FIW have been associated with a wide variety of work-related (e.g. lower job satisfaction), family-related (e.g. lower family satisfaction), and health-related (e.g. higher depression) outcomes (Greenhaus, Allen, and Spector 2006).

Largely within the last decade, researchers have also assessed the positive impact resources within one domain (e.g. work) can have on a second domain (e.g. family), termed *work-family enrichment* (Greenhaus and Powell 2006). Like work-family conflict, work-family enrichment is a linking mechanism between domains. It builds on the perspective that individuals may benefit from holding multiple roles in different domains, and suggests two pathways – instrumental and affective – by which resources generated in one domain can benefit another domain. Resources included in Greenhaus and Powell's enrichment model consist of skills and perspectives, psychological and physical resources, social capital resources, flexibility, and material resources. Work-family enrichment shares many of the same predictors and outcomes associated with work-conflict, but with generally opposite relationships (Allen 2012). For example, greater work-family enrichment has been associated with higher job satisfaction and higher family satisfaction (e.g. Carlson *et al.* 2006).

A recent work-family concept is work-family balance. *Work-family balance* is defined as people's overall appraisal of their effectiveness and satisfaction with work and family life (Greenhaus and Allen 2011). Theoretically, role balance includes approaching all roles held and associated people with attentiveness and with care (Marks and MacDermid 1996). Balance is a relatively new concept to the work-family literature. Empirical evidence to date shows that longer work hours are associated with less perceived balance (Valcour 2007) and that greater time spent engaged in quality time with children is positively associated with perceived balance (Milkie, Kendig, Nomaguchi, and Denny 2010). With regard to outcomes, greater balance has been positively associated with greater satisfaction, organizational commitment, family satisfaction, family performance, and family functioning (Carlson, Grzywacz, and Zivnuska 2009).

Review of existing research connecting mindfulness and work-family

To date only a handful of studies have investigated linkages between work-family variables and mindfulness. These studies are reviewed below.

Mindfulness and work-family balance. Allen and Kiburz (2012) is the first study of which we are aware that linked trait mindfulness and a work-family construct. The authors examined the relationship between trait mindfulness and work-family balance among a sample of working parents. Drawing on self-regulation theory, Allen and Kiburz suggested that the present moment awareness associated with mindfulness should enable individuals to immerse themselves with care and attentiveness while engaged in family and work roles, ultimately resulting in individuals feeling more effective and satisfied in these roles. As hypothesized, they found that those higher on trait mindfulness also reported greater work-family balance. They also reported that the relationship was mediated by sleep quality and by vitality.

Mindfulness and work-family conflict. Kiburz and Allen (2012) examined the link between trait mindfulness and each direction of work-family conflict in married employees with at least one child at home. Trait mindfulness explained significant unique variance in both WIF and FIW beyond known antecedents (number of children, work hours, and Big 5 personality variables) and contemplative practices (exercise frequency and yoga practice).

Building on these initial favorable cross-sectional results, Kiburz and Allen (2014) developed a mindfulness-based intervention (MBI) and tested its effectiveness in increasing trait mindfulness and decreasing work-family conflict. Training consisted of a one-hour workshop followed by thirteen days of behavioral self-monitoring (BSM). The workshop included an introduction to the concept of mindfulness, an opportunity to practice mindfulness through three exercises (sitting with the breath, body scan, and walking meditation), and tips for applying mindfulness into everyday life. At the end of the workshop, participants set goals for increasing their own mindfulness-based behaviors (i.e. *dismiss thoughts and bring mind back to present*).

The training was effective in increasing mindfulness. Participants also reported a decrease in WIF pre- and post-training, but not in FIW. Participants who returned the BSM diaries had significantly higher knowledge of mindfulness and an increase in trait mindfulness at post-training in comparison with those who did not return the BSM diaries. BSM participants also had significantly lower post-intervention FIW than non-BSM participants.

Mindfulness and work-family enrichment. We are not aware of research to date that has examined mindfulness and positive inter-dependencies between work and family roles. However, there is some indirect evidence to suggest that such spillover may occur. In a three-person study, mothers who worked as caregivers within group homes for individuals with profound disabilities received mindfulness training (Singh *et al.* 2010). The training was pro-vided to enhance their work with individuals with disabilities. The research showed that following mindfulness training, noncompli-ant behaviors of their own children decreased. The authors suggest this illustrates a transfer of training effect in that providing mind-fulness training to employees responsible for the care of others at work transfers to the family domain through the interactions of the employees with their own children. Said in enrichment terms, these mothers were able to use the resource of mindful behavior learned at work with their children at home, obtaining benefit from this resource at home.

Other mindfulness research with work-family implications. While the research investigating mindfulness and work-family variables is sparse, there is a growing body of research demonstrating that mind-fulness is associated with work-related wellbeing (e.g. Hulsheger *et al.* 2013; Leroy *et al.* 2013). This is relevant in that work-family con-flict has long been linked with the stressor-strain literature (Greenhaus *et al.* 2006). Moreover, mindfulness training has been shown to be an effective tool for helping individuals cope with stress. For example, Roeser *et al.* (2013) examined the effects of mindfulness training on elementary and secondary school teachers from Canada and the United States. Outcomes investigated were occupational stress, absences from work, symptoms of anxiety and depression, and occupational burn-out. They also assessed physiological indicators such as salivary corti-sol, blood pressure, and resting heart rate. Teachers who completed the mindfulness training reported feeling less stressed, anxious, depressed, exhausted, and burned out due to their jobs than those who did not complete the training. In addition, those who completed the training demonstrated greater focused attention and working memory capacity.

No differences were found with regard to physiological measures of stress.

Summary. Research demonstrating links between work-family experiences and mindfulness constructs (i.e., trait-like mindfulness or MBIs) is in its infancy. Initial studies that directly link these constructs, as well as research that indirectly speaks to these links, underscore the merit of further investigation of the mechanisms that potentially underlie these relationships. In the following section we describe four mechanisms that we believe may help explain linkages between work-family constructs and mindfulness.

Theory and mechanisms that underlie the link between mindfulness and work-family experiences

The central mechanism thought to be responsible for the beneficial effects of mindfulness is the improved self-regulation of thoughts, behaviors, psychological reactions, and emotions (Desrosiers *et al.* 2013; Glomb *et al.* 2011). In this section we elaborate on four specific pathways.

Attention and the minimization of distractions

Attention is a key aspect of mindfulness. Mindfulness is "intentionally paying attention to present-moment experience (physical sensations, perceptions, affective states, thoughts and imagery) in a nonjudgmental way, thereby cultivating a stable and nonreactive awareness" (Carmody *et al.* 2008, p. 394). Attention research concerns how voluntary control and subjective experience arise from and regulate behavior (Posner and Rothbart 2007). The capacity to sustain attention is important to various aspects of life. Attention requires focus and concentration. It essentially requires withdrawal from some things in order to deal with others. Self-regulation of attention enables a person to be more aware of their present situation so that they are more quickly able to recognize any discrepancies from a standard. Dane (2011) explains that mindfulness is unique from other states of attention because it includes a wide field of attention and a focus on the present moment.

The opposite of attention is distraction. The promulgation of new technologies has given rise to what has been referred to as a societal attention deficient disorder (Jackson 2009). Writers have opined that the Internet is demolishing our capacity for deep, sustained, and perceptive attention (Carr 2011; Jackson 2009). Texting during family dinners or reading work emails while attending a child's soccer game are frequent occurrences in everyday family life. Cultivating a mindful awareness can be a valuable self-regulatory behavior that facilitates greater attentional control (Carmody *et al.* 2008), which can impact work-family perceptions in several ways.

First, bringing full attentiveness to work and family roles while in the roles helps reduce the perceived problem of role management, helping to facilitate effective personal resource allocation (Marks and MacDermid 1996). Thus, more mindful individuals should be more effective in both roles and report overall appraisals of work-family balance that are higher than less mindful individuals. Second, full attentiveness provides the opportunity to increase the sense of connection with others that is an essential component of overall psychological wellbeing (Baumeister and Leary 1995). Greater connection should help foster greater role satisfaction, heightening work-family balance perceptions. Further, connection is itself a resource within each domain, and as a component of the enrichment process (i.e., elements of both social capital and psychological resources) it may help in another domain, heightening work-family enrichment perceptions. Third, the self-regulatory skills enhanced by mindfulness should enable individuals to maintain focus in a given domain, particularly when demands in the other domain are high. This should result in greater effectiveness across both domains, and thus higher perceptions of work-family balance. Similarly, individuals who are able to maintain focus should feel less strain-based conflict between domains, reducing work-family conflict. Finally, self-regulatory skills are themselves a resource and to the extent that these are deepened in one or both domains, they should help increase work-family enrichment.

Emotion regulation

Another pathway by which mindfulness may relate to work-family experiences is emotion regulation. Emotion regulation has been defined as the process by which individuals modify their emotional experiences, expressions, and physiology and the situations that elicit the emotions in an effort to produce appropriate responses to the demands imposed by the environment (Aldao 2013). Emotion regulation processes include those that require significant effort (e.g., remaining calm while accompanying an injured child to the hospital) as well as those that are nearly automatic (e.g., laughing at a friend's funny joke). The process model of emotion regulation distinguishes between antecedent-focused processes (those that occur prior to appraisals generating a full-blown emotional response) and response-focused strategies (those that occur after emotional responses are generated) (Gross 1998; Webb, Miles, and Sheeran 2012).

Mindfulness has been referred to as an antecedent-focused form of emotion regulation as it changes the person's relationship to his or her emotions rather than the nature of the emotions themselves (Teper, Segal, and Inzlicht 2013). Recent meta-analytic work reveals that such cognitive change emotional regulation strategies are more effective than other strategies such as response modulation (e.g., attempting to control the experience of emotion) (Webb *et al.* 2012). In addition, trait mindfulness has been associated with reduced use of maladaptive emotion regulation strategies such as rumination (e.g. Desrosiers *et al.* 2013). Rumination is defined as "the process of thinking perseveratively about one's feelings and problems rather than in terms of the specific content of thoughts" (Nolen-Hoeksema, Wisco, and Lyubormirsky 2008, p. 400).

Effective emotion regulation is important to consider in the context of work-family in that mood states and traits have been consistently associated with work-family conflict (Allen *et al.* 2012; Judge, Ilies, and Scott 2006) and with work-family enrichment (Carlson *et al.* 2011; Paddock *et al.*, in progress; Wayne, Musisca, and Fleeson 2004). As Teper and colleagues explain (2013), mindful individuals still experience initial affective reactions. However, more mindful individuals experience fewer of the negative consequences of the long-term activation of affect. Based on emotion regulation more mindful individuals should experience more satisfaction with work and family roles (a primary component of work-family balance) and less negative affect or emotion over durations (associated with work-family conflict). In fact, mindfulness heightens the experience of visceral, short-term affect (Williams 2010). To the extent that the affective pathway of work-family enrichment involves experienced transient positive affect rather than founded positive emotions, mindful individuals who are better at emotion regulation should have greater experiences of enrichment.

In addition, improved emotional self-regulation may also help facilitate effective work and family boundary management (Allen, Cho, and Meier 2014). To achieve a desired boundary between work and family, individuals may have to regulate emotions that they experience, such as suppressing negative emotions from work or expressing positive emotions to family members. Ineffective emotion management may result in emotional dissonance; Sonnentag, Kuttler, and Fritz (2010) reported that emotional dissonance at work resulted from the necessity to display positive emotions when they were not felt, and this was negatively associated with psychological detachment from work. Mindfulness may better enable individuals to detach from negative events in one role while present in another (e.g., stop ruminating about a disagreement with a co-worker while helping a child with homework), a skill that should lessen the emotional dissonance experienced in each domain. Less dissonance should relate positively to work-family balance, and less dissonance may take the form of less strain-based conflict. Further, given mindful individuals' ability to be in the moment and focus on the positive affect they are experiencing, they may be better able to utilize the affective pathway of work-family enrichment, resulting in higher levels of enrichment.

Optimization of resource allocation

Mindfulness may help optimize resource allocation, resulting in improved work-family experiences. Time and energy have been referred to as the two most critical personal resources required for meeting work and family demands (Valcour 2007). Individuals simultaneously managing work and family roles are faced with a variety of choices on any given day with regard to how they expend their time and energy resources; they must make decisions with regard to where, when, and how they expend their personal resources across various tasks within and across life domains.

For example, consider the typical faculty member. Time may be allocated to designing a new research study, answering email, meeting with a student, preparing for a lecture, reviewing a colleague's grant application, attending a dissertation proposal meeting, and meeting with a curriculum review committee, all within one day. Non-work time may be allocated to grocery shopping, meal preparation and cleaning, picking up children from school, driving children to and from afterschool activities, miscellaneous childcare (e.g., helping with homework, bathing), miscellaneous household chores (e.g., laundry, paying bills), exercise, leisure, and sleep. Daily life requires performing multiple tasks simultaneously or in rapid alternation. For example, a parent may be cooking dinner and answering a child's question about homework. Switching from one task to another requires use of mental executive control processes (Rubinstein, Meyer, and Evans 2001). Executive control includes two distinct processes that involve the frontal lobes of the brain. One is goal shifting (deciding to do this versus that), and the second is rule activation (turning off the rules for that and turning on the rules for this). Switching from one task to another takes time. The time costs increase along with the complexity of the tasks. The awareness that is inherent in mindfulness should facilitate individuals' determinations of when it is best to engage in what task and enable them to do so with an attentiveness that promotes more effective completion of tasks. Effective resource allocation should make individuals more effective at both work and family roles, increasing work-life balance. Further, given the time savings associated with more accurately and effectively managing tasks in either role, more mindful individuals should experience less time-based work-family conflict. As it relates to work-family enrichment, optimizing use of energy and time within the work or family domain allows for greater flexibility in completing tasks. Recall that flexibility, defined as "the discretion to determine the timing, pace, and location at which role requirements are met" (Greenhaus and Powell 2006, p. 80), is itself a resource identified in the work-family enrichment model. Thus, more mindful individuals should also report greater work-family enrichment perceptions as the flexibility experienced at work (family) results in more time or energy that can be accessed within the family (workplace).

Time perception

Mindfulness impacts the way individuals perceive time, including the time perspective they take. Time perspective refers to an individual's typical way of relating to the psychological concepts of past, present, and future (Boniwell and Zimbardo 2004). Time perception is important in that it plays a fundamental role in the selection and pursuit of social goals, motivation, and behavior (Cartensen 2006).

Although objectively time is a fixed resource, the subjective perception of time availability can be shifted (Rudd, in progress, manuscript a). Kramer, Weger, and Sharma (2013) focused on changes in state mindfulness and compared reports of time duration across participants who engaged in a ten-minute mindfulness meditation versus participants who listened to a ten-minute audio excerpt of *The Hobbit*. Afterwards both groups were asked to classify the duration of a stimulus. Those in the meditation condition classified the duration of the stimulus activity as longer than those in the audiobook condition. Similarly Rudd (in progress, manuscript a) compared the perceptions of time pressure of participants assigned to a future-focused condition and those assigned to a present-focused condition, finding that heightened present-focus during an event (watching a nature video) expanded participants' ensuing perceptions of current time availability. Other research has shown that thinking about the present moment slows down the perceived passage of time. Participants instructed to take long and slow breaths versus short and quick breaths perceived their day to be longer and felt that there was more time available to get things done (Rudd, in progress, manuscript b).

Related research shows a direct link between trait mindfulness and reports of time affluence (Kasser and Sheldon 2009; LaJeunesse and Rodriguez 2012). Time affluence is the feeling that one has sufficient time to pursue activities that are personally meaningful, to reflect, and to engage in leisure (Ben-Shahar 2007). Those who report high degrees of time affluence, report the ability to perform tasks at leisure and to deeply reflect on life's experiences.

Research on time perception is important to consider in the context of work-family experiences. Time scarcity has long been associated with multiple role engagement (Goode 1960) and much has been written about the "time famine" associated with modern life (e.g. O'Brien 2012; Perlow 1999). Central to the experience of work-family conflict is the feeling of insufficient time to effectively perform work and family responsibilities, thus we expect mindfulness relates to less work-family conflict through the reduction of perceived time scarcity.

The perception of time scarcity has downstream consequences in that time scarcity creates a mindset that leads individuals to engage in behaviors that help manage scarcity in the short term, but may not be beneficial for the long term. That is, time scarcity changes how individuals allocate attention. Because scarcity elicits engagement in the problem at hand, it can result in the attentional neglect of other situations (Shah, Mullainathan, and Shafir 2012). This may result in a focus on the work or family role with the most immediate demands, resulting in the neglect of other roles. For example, a working parent with a project deadline may stay at work late to respond to this immediate demand, canceling plans to go to a movie with the family. The accumulation of these attention allocation decisions may result in a decrement of relationship satisfaction among family members as well as a lack of work-family balance.

Further, the time scarcity associated with lower mindfulness should relate positively to work-family conflict, and especially time-based conflict, as individuals perceive insufficient time to complete tasks in both domains. Finally, because they are focused on the task at hand these same individuals may take a narrower perspective and thus be less able to assess which resources from one domain will benefit the other domain.

For reasons reviewed in our discussion of attention, shifting individuals time perceptions to encourage them to stay in the present moment may allow individuals to derive more from work and home domains, resulting in heightened perception of work-family balance. Work-family conflict may be mitigated given that perceptions of time affluence provide individuals a chance for recovery from strain. Finally, work-family enrichment and the transfer of resources that it includes should be facilitated as individuals are able to reflect deeply on each domain, likely coming to a better understanding of how to function in that domain as well as what resources may be transferable across domains.

Additional suggestions for future research

In the previous section we posed four pathways by which mindfulness may be linked to work-family constructs: attention and minimizing distractions, emotion regulation, optimization of resource allocation, and time perception. Research investigating these pathways is important to further our understanding of how mindfulness may be beneficial to individuals managing multiple role responsibilities. In the following section we further draw from the mindfulness and work-family literatures to offer several directions for future research that go beyond these specific mechanisms identified. As discussed in this review, research linking mindfulness and work-family is in a nascent stage, leaving the door open for many new lines of research.

Consideration of multiple construct dimensions

Mindfulness has been conceptualized in multiple ways. Most workplace mindfulness research to date has been based on the dispositional, single dimension approach as assessed by the Mindful Attention Awareness Scale (Brown and Ryan 2003). However, mindfulness has also been conceptualized as multidimensional, with subscales that include observing, describing, acting with awareness, nonjudging of inner experience, and nonreactivity to inner experience (Baer, Smith, and Allen 2004; Baer *et al.* 2008). These facets are correlated modestly and have demonstrated discriminant validity (Baer *et al.* 2008; Emanuel *et al.* 2010). For example, research has shown that mindfulness facets do not operate homogeneously with regard to outcomes such as depression and anxiety (Desrosiers *et al.* 2013).

Work-family constructs are also multidimensional. As described previously, work-family conflict includes dimensions such as time, strain, and behavior. Constructs reflecting the positive side of the work-family interface (e.g., work-family enrichment) also include multiple dimensions such as development (e.g., skills, knowledge, behaviors), affect (e.g., positive emotional state or attitude), and capital (e.g., security, confidence) as different resources that can be transferred from one domain to another (Carlson *et al.* 2006).

Taking a more granular approach may yield new insights into the beneficial links between mindfulness and work-family experiences. It could be speculated that the ability to distance oneself from everyday thoughts and worries (e.g., nonjudgment and nonreactivity to inner experiences) would be more likely to prevent strain-based work-family conflict than would the observation of the present moment aspect of mindfulness. In contrast, acting with awareness may enable individuals to identify and develop solutions for time-based conflicts more so than labeling emotions and cognitions. With regard to work-family enrichment, distancing oneself from everyday thoughts and worries may better allow for use of the affective pathway while acting with awareness and being attentive to role-partners may enable the development and transfer of skills.

Mindfulness and family-supportive supervision

Thus far, we have primarily considered mindfulness as a tool that individuals can cultivate to improve their own multiple role management. However, work-family experiences do not occur in a vacuum. Others within an individual's social system also contribute to the ease or difficulty by which individuals are able to juggle work and family roles (Kossek *et al.* 2011). Research has shown that supervisor behaviors in particular are associated with work-family experiences. Family-supportive supervision is defined as behaviors displayed by supervisors that are supportive of employees' family roles (Hammer *et al.* 2009). A considerable body of research has demonstrated that greater family-supportive supervision is associated with less work-family conflict (e.g., Allen 2001; Lapierre and Allen 2006) and that supervisors can be trained to be more family-supportive (Hammer *et al.* 2009).

Brown *et al.* (2007, p. 225) suggested that mindfulness may "promote interaction styles that support healthy relationship functioning and enhance overall relationship quality." Thus, mindfulness training may be useful as a component of family-supportive supervisor training. Indeed, in a study investigating leader mindfulness Reb, Narayanan, and Chaturvedi (2014) found that greater leader trait mindfulness was associated with employees who reported more work-life balance. More mindful supervisors may respond to employee requests for accommodations that enable them to manage multiple role responsibilities with greater creativity and attentiveness. This is important in that informal accommodations have been shown to relate to less work-family conflict (Behson 2005).

Methodological advancements

Consideration of methodological issues is needed to advance mindfulness-based work-family research. As discussed earlier, one aspect of mindfulness that we believe is powerful for improving work-family experiences is attention within role. The ability to remain attentive to others and in the present moment is a hallmark of mindfulness. The former of these especially can best, and possibly only, be captured through reports provided by others. For example, spouses can provide reports of the extent that the partner is attentive in the family domain, while supervisors can provide reports of attention and engagement in the work domain. Such data could be particularly useful in investigating the effectiveness of MBIs.

Investigating episodes of work-family conflict in addition to the common between-subjects levels approach may also be useful (Maertz and Boyar 2011; Shockley and Allen 2013; Shockley and Allen, in press), especially because results based on episodes differ from those based on levels. For example, Shockley and Allen (in press) found no differences in the frequency that WIF episodes versus FIW episodes were reported by participants, whereas between-subjects levels assessment of work-family conflict consistently finds higher reported levels of WIF than FIW. Conflicts between work and family typically transpire at specific times and require in-the-moment behavioral decisions (e.g., agreeing to stay late at work to make a deadline, thus missing a child's baseball game). Given that mindfulness has been shown to improve decision making (e.g., by reducing the sunk cost bias, Hafenbrack, Kinias, and Barsade 2014), it may also help individuals make decisions that involve competing work and family demands with clarity (Shockley and Allen, in press). Assessment of work-family enrichment episodes may yield similarly interesting findings, and may better highlight the role of decision making in resource allocation between domains.

Another avenue for future research is to supplement survey data with data collected through other methodologies. Wearable technology tools such as mobile neurophysiological monitoring devices and sociometric badges have the potential to illuminate the processes by which mindfulness is beneficial.

Evidence shows mindfulness meditation training to alter neural activity (Berkovich-Ohana, Glicksohn, and Goldstein 2012). Brain functioning can be characterized by three fundamental electrophysiological concepts: (a) characteristics of the electrical signal in terms of frequency and amplitude, (b) spatial location of the sources of brain electrical activity, and (c) pattern of connectivity across the brain (neural network dynamics). For example, relaxed and inattentive states are associated with greater amplitude and lower frequency brain wave patterns, while excited, working or attentive states are associated with lower amplitude and greater frequency (Hannah *et al.* 2013). Recent advances in mobile neurophysiological monitoring devices capture real-time electroencephalography (EEG) data that provide information on neurological processes. Such devices permit the practical application of quantitative EEG in studying interactions as they occur. This methodology could be used to compare the neurophysiological patterns that occur when responding to a work-family conflict or enrichment as moderated by trait mindfulness.

Sociometric badges are wearable sensing devices that collect data on face-to-face communication interaction in real time (Waber 2013). The device is able to record multiple types of information such as the physical proximity to others, location in the environment, motions (e.g., posture, running), and communication patterns (e.g., volume of speech, speaking speed, turn taking). Sociometric devices could be used to examine work-family phenomena such as those that involve interactions between employees and supervisors negotiating the use of flexible work arrangements. Based on the research concerning mindfulness and leadership noted above, one might expect these negotiations to be more successful with leaders higher rather than lower in trait mindfulness. Sociometric devices may also provide support for mindfulness-based training, as those who receive such training may engage more in these interactions. Such beneficial interactions with others likely produce patterns (e.g., in proximity to others and communication patterns) that differ from less mindful interactions.

Role transitions

The cultivation of mindfulness may be particularly beneficial to the process of transitioning across work and family roles (Allen, Cho, and Meier 2014). Because role crossing is an effortful process that involves self-regulation, the present moment awareness component of mindfulness may better enable individuals to psychologically detach from one role and smoothly enter into another, possibly relating positively to work-family balance and negatively to work-family conflict. Effectively transitioning across roles may be particularly challenging when self-regulatory resources are depleted. As an example, consider the employee whose last interaction while at work was with an angry customer who upon returning home is greeted with the news that his child failed an exam at school. The employee may still be preoccupied with emotions associated with the customer interaction while simultaneously experiencing emotional responses of anger, disappointment, and/or worry activated by the news of the failed exam.

The effortful suppression of negative emotions while dealing with the angry customer at work would require the employee to draw upon self-regulatory resources. Such self-regulation draws on finite resources and impacts subsequent performance of behaviors necessitating self-regulation (Baumeister, Vohs, and Tice 2007). To effectively transition to the family role this individual must put aside thoughts of the angry customer (i.e., leave the work role) and engage with family members with regard to the failed exam (i.e., enter the family role). An individual higher in mindfulness and better able to regulate emotion is better able to make this transition.

Less favorable effects of mindfulness

Consistent with the larger literature on mindfulness as reviewed, the relationships we propose between mindfulness and work-family experiences take a decidedly positive perspective. However, it seems possible that mindfulness may also have some negative consequences, and identifying these also deserves research attention.

One way in which mindfulness may have potential negative ramifications is that completely investing a present role may encourage individuals to view their underlying identities as being in conflict and manage them as such. Individuals' identities (e.g., employee, parent) are evident in, and sometimes even synonymous with, the roles they hold in work and family domains. By focusing entirely on the present role, individuals may be less likely to integrate the identities that make up these roles. Individuals manage their identities in multiple ways, including a focus on one identity to the exclusion of others (as discussed in the previous paragraph) to an integration of identities into a compatible whole (Roccas and Brewer 2002). Individuals who view their own identities – their values, attitudes, and expectations– as more compatible are high in identity integration (Cheng, Sanchez-Burks, and Lee 2008). In contrast, individuals low in identity integration view roles as less compatible, suppress one identity while the other is activated, and alter their behaviors between contexts. Individuals high in identity integration are able to access resources from both domains simultaneously and thus show higher levels of creativity (Cheng *et al.* 2008) and have more diverse social networks (Mok, Morris, Benet-Martinez, and Karakitapoglu-Aygun 2007) than individuals low in identity integration. With regard to work-family experiences this is important in that higher identity integration may result in greater transference of resources across domains, resulting in greater work-family enrichment.

Multivariate models are needed to better understand the potential interplay between both the positive and the negative links between mindfulness and work-family experiences. For example, it may be that the detrimental effects of a negative relationship between mindfulness and identity can be compensated by other benefits of mindfulness. This is an empirical question, and as with the other ideas for future research discussed here, further research is required to identify how this aspect of work-family and mindfulness relates.

Conclusion

In addition to better understanding the role that trait mindfulness plays in individuals' work-family experiences, the cultivation of mindfulness practice through training may be one tool that can help regulate affect and promote healthy work-family connections. In this chapter we review the literature that links mindfulness with work-family constructs, identify four potential mechanisms that may help explain this link, and suggest future directions for research. We hope these ideas inspire additional research on this timely topic.

References

Aldao, A. (2013). The future of emotion regulation research: capturing context. *Perspectives on Psychological Science*, 8, 155–72.

Allen, T. D. (2001). Family-supportive work environments: the role of organizational perceptions. *Journal of Vocational Behavior*, 58, 414–35.

Allen, T. D. (2012). The work-family interface. In S. W. J. Kozlowski (ed). *The Oxford handbook of organizational psychology*. New York: Oxford University Press, pp. 1163–98.

Allen, T. D., Cho, E., and Meier, L. (2014). Work-family boundary dynamics. *Annual Review of Organizational Psychology and Organizational Behavior*, 1, 99–121.

Allen, T. D., Johnson, R. C., Kiburz, K., and Shockley, K. M. (2013). Work-family conflict and flexible work arrangements: deconstructing flexibility. *Personnel Psychology*, 66, 345–76.

Allen, T. D., Johnson, R. C., Saboe, K., Cho, E., Dumani, S., and Evans, S. (2012). Dispositional variables and work-family conflict: a meta-analysis. *Journal of Vocational Behavior*, 80, 17–26.

Allen, T. D. and Kiburz, K. M. (2012). Trait mindfulness and work-family balance among working parents: the mediating effects of vitality and sleep quality. *Journal of Vocational Behavior*, 80, 372–9.

Baer, R. A., Smith, G. T., and Allen, K. B. (2004). Assessment of mindfulness by self-report: the Kentucky Inventory of Mindfulness Skills. *Assessment*, 11, 191–206.

Baer, R. A., Smith, G. T., Lykins, E., Button, D., Krietemeyer, J., Sauer, S., Walsh, E., Duggan, D., and Williams, J. M. (2008). Construct validity of the Five Facet Mindfulness Questionnaire in meditating and nonmeditating samples. *Assessment*, 15, 329–42.

Baltes, B. B. and Heydens-Gahir, H. (2003). Reduction of work–family conflict through the use of selection, optimization, and compensation behaviors. *Journal of Applied Psychology*, 88, 1005–18.

Baltes, B. B., Zhdanova, L. S., and Clark, M. A. (2011). Examining the relationships between personality, coping strategies, and work-family conflict. *Journal of Business and Psychology*, 26, 517–30.

Baumeister R. F. and Leary, M. R. (1995). The need to belong: desire for interpersonal attachments as a fundamental human emotion. *Psychological Bulletin*, 117, 497–529.

Baumeister, R. F., Vohs, K. D., and Tice, D. M. (2007). The strength model of self-control. *Current Directions in Psychological Science*, 16, 351–5.

Behson, S. J. (2005). The relative contribution of formal and informal organizational work-family support. *Journal of Vocational Behavior*, 66, 487–500.

Ben-Shahar, T. (2007). *Happier: learn the secrets to daily joy and lasting fulfillment*. New York: McGraw-Hill Professional.

Berkovich-Ohana, A., Glicksohn, J., and Goldstein, A. (2012). Mindfulness-induced changes in gamma band activity – implications for the default node network, self-reference and attention. *Clinical Neurophysiology*, 123(4), 700–10.

Boniwell, I. and Zimbardo, P. G. (2004). Balancing one's time perspective in pursuit of optimal functioning. In P. A. Linley and S. Joseph (eds.), *Positive psychology in practice*. Hoboken, NJ: Wiley.

Brown, K. W. and Ryan, R. M. (2003). The benefits of being present: mindfulness and its role in psychological well-being. *Journal of Personality and Social Psychology*, 84(4), 822–48.

Brown, K. W., Ryan, R. M., and Creswell, J. D. (2007). Mindfulness: theoretical foundations and evidence for its salutary effects. *Psychological Inquiry*, 18(4), 211–37.

Butts, M. M., Casper, W. J., and Yang, T. S. (2013). How important are work-family support policies? A meta-analytic investigation of their effects on employee outcomes. *Journal of Applied Psychology*, 98, 1–25.

Byron, K. (2005). A meta-analytic review of work-family conflict and its antecedents. *Journal of Vocational Behavior*, 62, 169–98.

Carlson, D. S., Grzywacz, J., and Zivnuska, S. (2009). Work-family balance: is balance more than conflict and enrichment? *Human Relations*, 20, 1–28.

Carlson, D. S., Kacmar, K. M., Wayne, J. H., and Grzywacz, J. G. (2006). Measuring the positive side of the work–family interface: development and validation of a work–family enrichment scale. *Journal of Vocational Behavior*, 68, 131–64

Carlson, D., Kacmar, K. M., Zivnuska, S., Ferguson, M., and Whitten, W. (2011). Work-family enrichment and job performance: a constructive replication of affective events theory. *Journal of Occupational Health Psychology*, 16, 297–312.

Carmody, J., Reed, G., Kristeller, J., and Merriam, P. (2008). Mindfulness, spirituality, and health-related symptoms. *Journal of Psychosomatic Research*, 64, 393–403.

Carr, N. (2011). *The shallows: what the internet is doing to our brains.* New York: W. W. Norton and Company.

Cartensen, L. L. (2006). The influence of a sense of time on human development. *Science*, 312, 1913–15.

Cheng, C.-Y., Sanchez-Burks, J., and Lee, F. (2008). Connecting the dots within: creative performance and identity integration. *Psychological Science*, 19, 1178–84.

Covert, B. (2013). Men want work-family balance, and policy should help them achieve it. *The Nation*, July 8, retrieved from www.thenation .com/blog/175158/men-want-work-family-balance-and-policy-should-help-them-achieve-it#.

Dane, E. (2011). Paying attention to mindfulness and its effects on task performance in the workplace. *Journal of Management*, 37, 997–1018.

Desrosiers, A., Vine, V., Klemanski, D. H., and Nolen-Hoeksema, S. (2013). Mindfulness and emotion regulation in depression and anxiety: common and distinct mechanisms of action. *Depression and Anxiety*, 30, 654–61.

Emanuel, A. S., Updegraff, J. A., Kalmbach, D. A., and Ciesla, J. A. (2010). The role of mindfulness facets in affective forecasting. *Personality and Individual Differences*, 49, 815–18.

Glomb, T. M., Duffy, M. K., Bono, J. E., and Yang, T. (2011). Mindfulness at work. In J. Martocchio, H. Liao, and A. Joshi (eds). *Research in personnel and human resource management*, vol. 30. Bingley: Emerald Group Publishing Limited, pp. 115–57.

Goode, W. J. (1960). A theory of role strain. *American Sociological Review*, 25, 483–96.

Greenhaus, J. H. and Allen, T. D. (2011). Work-family balance: a review and extension of the literature. In L. Tetrick and J. C. Quick (eds.),

Handbook of occupational health psychology. 2nd edn. Washington, DC: American Psychological Association, pp. 165–83.

Greenhaus, J. H., Allen, T. D., and Spector, P. E. (2006). Health consequences of work-family conflict: the dark side of the work-family interface. In P. L. Perrewe and D. C. Ganster (eds.), *Research in occupational stress and well being*, vol. 5. Oxford: JAI Press/Elsevier, pp. 61–99.

Greenhaus, J. H. and Beutell, N. (1985). Sources and conflict between work and family roles. *Academy of Management Review*, 10, 76–88.

Greenhaus, J. H. and Powell, G. N. (2006). When work and family are allies: a theory of work-family enrichment. *Academy of Management Review*, 31, 72–92.

Gross, J. J. (1998). Antecedent- and response-focused emotion regulation: divergent consequences for experience, expression, and physiology. *Journal of Personality and Social Psychology*, 74, 224–37.

Gutek, B. A., Searle, S., and Klepa, L. (1991). Rational versus gender role explanations for work family conflict. *Journal of Applied Psychology*, 7, 560–8.

Hafenbrack, A. C., Kinias, Z., and Barsade, S. G. (2014). Debiasing the mind through meditation: mindfulness and the sunk-cost bias. *Psychological Science*, 25, 369–76.

Hammer, L. B., Kossek, E. E., Anger, W. K., Bodner, T., and Zimmerman, K. L. (2011). Clarifying work-family intervention processes: the role of work-family conflict and family-supportive supervisor behavior. *Journal of Applied Psychology*, 96, 134–50.

Hammer, L. B., Kossek, E. E., Yragui, N. L., Bodner, T. E., and Hanson, G. C. (2009). Development and validation of a multidimensional measure of family supportive supervisor behaviors (FSSB). *Journal of Management*, 35, 837–56.

Hannah, S. T., Balthazard, P. A., Waldman, D. A., Jennings, P. L., and Thatcher, R. W. (2013). The psychological and neurological bases of leader self-complexity and effects on adaptive decision-making. *Journal of Applied Psychology*, 98, 393–411.

Hulsheger, U. R., Alberts, H. J. E. M., Feinholdt, A., and Lang, J. W. B. (2013). Benefits of mindfulness at work: the role of mindfulness in emotion regulation, emotional exhaustion, and job satisfaction. *Journal of Applied Psychology*, 98, 310–25.

Jackson, M. (2009). *Distracted: the erosion of attention and the coming dark age*. Amherst, NY: Prometheus Books.

Judge, T. A., Ilies, R., and Scott, B. A. (2006). Work-family conflict and emotions: effects at work and at home. *Personnel Psychology*, 59, 779–814.

Kabat-Zinn, J. (1990). *Full catastrophe living: using the wisdom of your body and mind to face stress, pain, and illness*. New York: Dell Publishing.

Kasser, T. and Sheldon, K. M. (2009). Time affluence as a path toward personal happiness and ethical business practice: empirical evidence from four studies. *Journal of Business Ethics*, 84, 243–55.

Kiburz, K. M. and Allen, T. D. (2012). Dispositional mindfulness as a unique predictor of work-family conflict. Paper presented at the 27th Annual Conference of the Society for Industrial and Organizational Psychology, April 2012, San Diego, CA.

Kiburz, K. M., and Allen, T. D. (2014). Examining the effects of a mindfulness-based work-family intervention. In J. G. Randall and M. Beier (Co-chairs), in Mind Wandering and Mindfulness: Self-regulation at Work. Symposium presented at the 29th Annual Conference of the Society for Industrial and Organizational Psychology, May 2014, Honolulu, HI.

Kilpatrick, L. A., Suyenobu, B. Y., Smith, S. R., Bueller, J. A., Goodman, T., Creswell, J. D., Tillisch, K., Mayer, E. A., and Naliboff, B. D. (2011). Impact of mindfulness-based stress reduction training on intrinsic brain connectivity. *NeuroImage*, 56, 290–8.

Kossek, E. E., Pichler, S., Bodner, T., and Hammer, L. B. (2011). Workplace social support and work–family conflict: a meta-analysis clarifying the influence of general and work–family specific supervisor and organizational support. *Personnel Psychology*, 64(2), 289–313.

Kramer, R. S., Weger, U. W., and Sharma, D. (2013). The effects of mindfulness meditation on time perception. *Conscious Cognition*, 22, 246–852.

LaJeunesse, S. and Rodriguez, D. A. (2012). Mindfulness, time affluence, and journey-based affect: exploring relationships. *Transportation Research Part F*, 196–205.

Lapierre, L. M. and Allen, T. D. (2006). Work-supportive family, family-supportive supervision, use of organizational benefits, and problem-focused coping: implications for work-family conflict and employee well-being. *Journal of Occupational Health Psychology*, 11, 169–81.

Leroy, H., Anseel, F., Dimitrova, N. G., and Sels, L. (2013). Mindfulness, authentic functioning, and work engagement: a growth modeling approach. *Journal of Vocational Behavior*, 82, 238–47.

Maertz, C.P. and Boyar, S.L. (2011). Work-family conflict, enrichment, and balance under "levels" and "episodes" approaches. *Journal of Management*, 37(1), 68–98.

Marks, S. R. and MacDermid, S. M. (1996). Multiple roles and the self: a theory of role balance. *Journal of Marriage and the Family*, 58, 417–32.

Michel, J. S., Kotrba, L. M., Mitchelson, J. K., Clark, M. A., and Baltes, B. B. (2011). Antecedents of work-family conflict: a meta-analytic review. *Journal of Organizational Behavior*, 32, 689–725.

Milkie, M., Kendig, S., Nomaguchi, K., and Denny, K. (2010). Time with children, children's well-being, and work-family balance among employed parents. *Journal of Marriage and Family*, 72, 1329–43.

Mok, A., Morris, M. W., Benet-Martinez, V., and Karakitapoglu-Aygun, Z. (2007). Embracing American culture: structures of social identity and social networks among first-generation biculturals. *Journal of Cross-Cultural Psychology*, 38, 629–35.

Nolen-Hoeksema, S., Wisco, B. E., and Lyubomirsky, S. (2008). Rethinking rumination. *Perspectives on Psychological Science*, 3, 400–24.

O'Brien, K. (2012). How to make time expand. *Boston Globe*, September 9. Retrieved from www.bostonglobe.com/ideas/2012/09/08/how-make-time-expand/26nkSfyQPEetCXXoFeZEZM/story.html.

Paddock, E. L., Smith, C. V., Bagger, J., and Webster, G. D. (manuscript in preparation). Extraversion impacts work-family enrichment via multiple pathways: a multilevel diary study.

Perlow, L. A. (1999). The time famine: toward a sociology of work time. *Administrative Science Quarterly*, 44, 57–81.

Perlow, L. A. and Kelly, E. (2014). Toward a model of work redesign for better work and better life. *Work and Occupations*, 41(1), 111–34.

Poelmans, S. E. A., Greenhaus, J. H., and Las Heras Maestro, M. (2013). *Expanding the boundaries of work-family research: a vision for the future*. Basingstoke: Palgrave Macmillan.

Posner, M. I. and Rothbart, M. K. (2007). Research on attention networks as a model of the integration of psychological science. *Annual Review of Psychology*, 58, 1–23.

Reb, J., Narayanan, J., and Chaturvedi, S. (2014). Leading mindfully: two studies on the influence of supervisor trait mindfulness on employee well-being and performance. *Mindfulness*, 5, 36–45.

Roccas, S. and Brewer, M. B. (2002). Social identity complexity. *Personality and Social Psychology Review*, 6, 88–106.

Roeser, R. W., Schonert-Reichl, K. A., Jha, A., Cullen, M., Wallace, L., Wilensky, R., Oberle, E., Thomson, K., Taylor, C., and Harrison, J. (2013). Mindfulness training and reductions in teacher stress and burnout: results from two randomized, waitlist-control field trials. *Journal of Educational Psychology*, 105, 787–804.

Rothbard, N. P. and Wilk, S. L. (2011). Waking up on the right or wrong side of the bed: start-of-workday mood, work events, employee affect, and performance. *Academy of Management Journal*, 54, 959–80.

Rubinstein, J. S., Meyer, D. E., and Evans, J. E. (2001). Executive control of cognitive processes in task switching. *Journal of Experimental Psychology*, 27, 763–97.

Rudd, M. (manuscript in preparation a). The power of being present: how momentary temporal focus influences perceived time affluence.

(manuscript in preparation b). Expand your breath, expand your time: Boosting perceived time affluence through slow controlled breathing.

Shah, A. K., Mullainathan, S., and Shafir, E. (2012). Some consequences of having too little. *Science*, 338, 682–5.

Shockley, K. M. and Allen, T. D. (2013). Episodic work-family conflict, cardiovascular indicators, and social support: an experience sampling approach. *Journal of Occupational Health Psychology*, 18, 262–75.

(in press). Deciding between work and family: an episodic approach. *Personnel Psychology*.

Singh, N. N., Lancioni, G. E., Winton, A. S. W., Singh, J., Singh, A. N., Adkins, A. D., and Wahler, R. G. (2010). Training in mindful caregiving transfers to parent-child interactions. *Journal of Child Family Studies*, 19, 167–74.

Slaughter, A. (2012). Why women still can't have it all. *The Atlantic*, July/August. Retrieved from www.theatlantic.com/magazine/archive/2012/07/why-women-still-cant-have-it-all/309020/.

Society for Human Resource Management (2008). *Workplace Forecast*. Alexandria, VA: Society for Human Resource Management.

Sonnentag, S., Kuttler, I., and Fritz, C. (2010). Job stressors, emotional exhaustion, and need for recovery: a multi-source study on the benefits of psychological detachment. *Journal of Vocational Behavior*, 76, 355–65.

Teper, R., Segal, Z. V., and Inzlicht, M. (2013). Inside the mindful mind: how mindfulness enhances emotion regulation through improvements in executive control. *Current Directions in Psychological Science*, 22, 449–54.

Valcour, M. (2007). Work-based resources moderators of the relationship between work hours and satisfaction with work-family balance. *Journal of Applied Psychology*, 92, 1512–23.

Waber, B. (2013). *People analytics*. Upper Saddle River, NJ: FT Press.

Wayne, J. H., Musisca N., and Fleeson, W. (2004). Considering the role of personality in the work-family experience: relationships of the big five to work-family conflict and facilitation. *Journal of Vocational Behavior*, 64, 108–30.

Webb, T. L., Miles, E., and Sheeran, P. (2012). Dealing with feeling: a meta-analysis of the effectiveness of strategies derived from the process model of emotion regulation. *Psychological Bulletin*, 138, 775–808.

Williams, J. M. (2010). Mindfulness and psychological process. *Emotion*, 10, 1–7.

10 | *Building and maintaining better leadership relationships through mindfulness*

RICHARD E. BOYATZIS

Introduction

As his wife drove up to the train station, Dimitrios picked up his atta-ché and opened the car door. They were chatting about something seemingly unimportant as the 7:10 train arrived into the station. They kissed good bye and yet he sat there, with the car door open but not moving. The train blew its whistle and his wife said, "You're going to miss the train." His shoulders slumped, he still sat there. The train began to leave the station and she said, "What's wrong?" "There is another train at 7:20," he explained. Then added, "I just don't want to go to work." She asked, "Why?" He then said an odd thing, "I don't like it there." While this exchange could have happened in hundreds, if not thousands of homes that day about people not wanting to go to work for a wide variety of reasons, Dimitrios' wife's response clarified that most of the reasons others might have had were not his: "But you're the boss. You are the CEO. If you don't like what it's like in the company, change it!" So he smiled and said, "Yeah, sure." And then kissed her again and begrudgingly walked through the station to the train platform.

It did not make sense to him. The company was doing well. It had grown under his leadership from about sixteen people to over one hundred. It was a well-respected consulting company sought after by many organizations around the world. Dimitrios was not aware that the changes had happened inside him, not the company. The "thing" he did not like was how he was feeling, but he did not know why and had misdiagnosed it.

This happens to almost everyone at some point in their life. For some, it happens like a bad habit which you cannot shake. You change slowly and do not notice until the signs are too obvious to ignore. We adjust to little things and ignore them as warning signs of something important shifting inside us. It is like gaining weight for males, you add a few pounds and most men do not notice. Actually, most do not notice until it requires a change in size of clothes! But by then, the likelihood of acknowledging the real causes has become masked and elusive.

Dimitrios was mindless about himself – caught up in behavioral routines and had slipped into mindlessness about his internal states. He was still focused on staying in touch with his clients' moods and desires, and those of his staff. But he had become a stone wall to himself. He had even taught a variation of what was later called mindfulness in therapy programs and in training programs to executives and professionals. But that was ten years earlier.

The state of mind called mindfulness is one of being awake, aware, and tuned into yourself, others around you in your family, others around you at work and in life, and the natural environment (Boyatzis and McKee 2005). The label emerged from Buddhist philosophy and later psychology, in particular the work of Ellen Langer and, of course, the key work of Jon Kabat-Zinn (Kabat-Zinn 1990; Langer 1989; 1997). Its earliest forms were found in meditation, martial arts, yoga, and many practices more associated with the Orient or Far East than Western cultures. But it had its roots in ancient Greek philosophy as well as Chinese philosophy (Boyatzis 2007).

So what happened to Dimitrios and how did someone who had taught mindfulness years earlier lose it? Before examining what mindfulness is and how to develop it, we should first examine why so few people seem to demonstrate or experience it and why it is so critical to effective leadership.

Being mindless about mindfulness

There are four major factors that derail someone from the natural process of tuning in and being mindful within yourself, toward others, and the environment (Boyatzis and McKee 2005). In leadership roles, with the burden of responsibility and power stress, a normal person is seduced into levels of chronic, annoying stress that compromise their ability to be an effective leader, to build and maintain the relationships needed. They are: (1) the ravages of chronic stress; (2) life and career stages and cycles; (3) antagonistic neural networks; and (4) living and working around mindless others. Of course, there are more factors that might affect people this way, such as the tragic loss of a loved one, a major natural disaster, or being the victim of an act of terrorism. But in this chapter, we will focus on the typical factors, the ones most likely to affect the most people in leadership and professions.

The ravages of chronic stress

Anyone in professional, managerial or executive roles is likely to be suffering from an overload of chronic, annoying stress. This is not the "tear your hair out" response to an acute problem which would be labeled acute stress, such as a product recall or losing several major clients all at once, but the response to someone cutting you off in traffic, your cell phone dropping a call, or someone missing a meeting. There are four events or conditions that invoke this reaction in our body: being uncertain of something; doing something that is important to us; feeling that people are watching or evaluating you; and uniquely human, the mere anticipation of any of these conditions (Segerstrom and Miller 2004). When in positions of responsibility, most of our day is spent in tasks that have one or more of these conditions.

This results in an overload of stress, or "strain," which results in your body's sympathetic nervous system being overworked (Sapolsky 2004). The result is cognitive, emotional, and perceptual impairment (Boyatzis, Smith and Blaize 2006).

When we encounter this somewhat normal but harmful degree of strain, we retreat into defensive postures and habits in dealing with life (Sapolsky 2004). As we close our perceptual fields of vision, literally and figuratively, we close ourselves from new ideas and even self-awareness (Goleman, 2013). The slip into dissonance is a human, defensive response, which then provokes more of the conditions that create even more stress. It has been observed that we typically lose mindfulness about our bodies first (or it might be said that males lose this one first), then with our families and closest loved ones, then with co-workers, and then eventually the natural environment (Boyatzis and McKee 2005). Although the sequence may vary by person and gender, one leads to other forms of mindlessness. The end result is Dimitrios, the CEO of a company, sitting in a car and not wanting to go to work.

By this point, Dimitrios had been CEO of the company for about eleven years. He had the burden of two of his partners' homes mortgaged to guarantee the bank loan that was needed to buy them back from a corporate parent. The company was growing quickly, so fast that receivables lagged the actual work, for which the staff expected to be paid promptly. During the years of 18–22 percent interest on cash flow loans, this was crippling. When the company was smaller, he could spend a third of his time managing, a third working with clients and a third on research. As the company grew, they sold to be part of a larger group of consulting companies, he became Chief Operating Officer of another market research consulting company, and was in a role of potentially buying and selling consulting companies for their corporate parents.

He had loved it once, but the power stress had taken its toll. He was heavier than he had ever been. At times, he drank too much. Because of the travel and preoccupation, he and his wife barely had Saturday evenings together. Dimitrios even found the dinner parties they would host with friends were drawing less and less laughter – danger signs for him and his wife. He found himself not sharing things that he used to have in common with his wife and son. He was occasionally surprised at conflicts emerging at work – when in the past he could sense or see dynamics emerging months or a year in advance. He was out of touch!

Some people discuss mindfulness as if it is synonymous with "presence." I believe, however, that presence is not mindfulness, but one of a number of paths to it. I have known people who are present, and in wallowing in their moment, they ignore others and their responsibilities to others and the natural environment. So being present does not absolve a leader of his or her responsibilities, but it can enhance their path in the perpetual need to return to mindfulness.

Life and career stages and cycles

Not all of this dynamic may be attributable to chronic stress as discussed above. Some of it might come as a result of what Levinson (Levinson *et al.* 1978) called a "mid-life crisis." As Sheehy (1995) popularized the idea, it was recognized that all of us go through a form of existential dilemma. This appears to occur about every seven to ten years throughout our lives. When it occurs, we feel lost and search for relief. If a person is relatively mindless to this typical human event, he or she may act out and do things to feel better that provoke more emotional crises, like having an extra-marital affair. The lack of appropriate awareness and labeling may come from not knowing how to interpret or label these feelings, or an even more basic process of not noticing that something has changed inside.

Here too, Dimitrios was approaching forty and had been running the company for almost eleven years. He felt that he had "been there, done that" with almost every challenge that emerged at work. There was a time when a support staff crisis about recognition or career prospects would bring him into high gear. Or the junior consultants worrying about their futures as the more senior staff seemed to have been there for years and were still relatively young. When each of these periodic quakes would hit, the first time he involved everyone in discussing and addressing the issue. Now that it was the third cycle for many of these, he was listening to others pour their hearts out, but thinking "Oh yeah, the first time we handled it this way. The second time we did it that way." He was not as tuned into other people and their emotions as he should have been. He was recycling previous interpretations and not even aware that, as a result, he was discounting their importance and devaluing the emotional input from others.

Inappropriate acting out of such mid-life transitions or crises can be costly to the leader but also to the organization. Dysfunctional sexual encounters, taking up surprisingly expensive hobbies, seeking "fun" that is far more risky than appropriate will distract the leader. If they expose him or her to criticism, they distract many within the organization. If the leader is elected, they distract the public and press from the agenda and policy work that needs to be done in governing. I noticed after decades of consulting that most of the time when a top leader was championing a strategic acquisition or merger that did not make business sense to an informed outsider, the champion was often someone within five years of being forty, or fifty, or sixty. Their quest to "grow" the business may have been acting out a mid-life crisis and not an insightful strategic opportunity.

Dimitrios was ready for a life and career change. He wanted to go back to doing research and fantasized that a full-time academic career would be perfect. Of course, he ignored the politics of academia, the shift in values involved, and likely loss of a sense of team work. But the yearning for something different was filling his thoughts. He felt that it was not fun anymore – the music was gone! Every leader has these experiences. And yet, few teach and prepare leaders to notice them. Surprisingly few coaches use this framework to help someone consider alternatives. Therapists might. Those coaching or counseling leaders within an organization might be so caught up in the performance rhetoric or consumed by progress on measurable goals and metrics that they fail to help the leader know what is happening. How few tell the Emperor that he has no clothes? How many fewer tell the leader in an organization that he or she is having a mid-life crisis and needs help instead of acting it out? These internal sensations, if not properly noticed and labeled, will create feelings and events that provoke more stress, adding, or more accurately, multiplying the escalation of stress and its ravages as described earlier in this chapter.

Antagonistic neural networks

I took a break from writing this paper and went downstairs to make some tea. I mentioned to my wife that I was writing a paper on mindfulness. Her response was, "Why is that not surprising? When will you read it and apply it to yourself?" This was not a rare moment but a typical one that occurs when I am writing research papers or worse when writing a book. She knows I become emotionally unavailable and have a difficult time even noticing that it is snowing outside. The cause is a zone I enter when writing.

When writing, I focus and activate a neural network called the task positive network (TPN). This network allows us to focus, solve problems, make decisions, and analyze things (Jack, Dawson, Begany, Leckie, Barry, Ciccia, and Snyder 2013).

Another neural network, the default mode network (DMN), which is sometimes called the task negative network, allows us to be open to new ideas, scan the environment, to be open to people and social encounters, emotions and moral concerns (Buckner, Andrews-Hanna, and Schacter 2008). This network allows us to tune into people and things happening around us – to be mindful of things outside ourselves. Decety and Batson (2007) report research that shows this as the network that allows for a genuine form of empathy, or tuning into others as opposed to components of the prefrontal cortex and TPN within it that are more self-referential. Unfortunately, these networks suppress each other. So when focused on writing or something analytic, we tune out others around us and the environment (Jack *et al.* 2013). As my wife reflected in her comments during my break from writing, I was significantly in the TPN at the time and, therefore, likely to be relatively mindless.

For Dimitrios, dealing with company financials, planning, client problems, and an occasional research project was putting him into repeated TPN activation. It presented a challenge to him at the time, with increasing responsibility and growth of the company. As someone who had always been a fountain of new ideas and alternatives, he was becoming less open to new ideas. His DMN was not active a sufficient amount of time each day for relief or even seeing the emotional issues of those closest to him.

Leaders can become so preoccupied with budgets and metrics that they lose the ability to switch fluidly between these crucial neural networks. On the other hand, they might have been someone who was attracted to a field that focuses on analytics, such as finance, and they have that disposition reinforced through a Master's degree or other repeated training in it (and valuing it more than other activities). How often have you heard some refer to social and emotional abilities as "soft skills," when in fact, lacking these can cause more derailment of executive careers than financial analytics (McCall, Lombardo, and Morrison 1988).

To this point, we have examined three of the four major factors: chronic stress, life and career changes, and neural antagonistic networks. All of these are inside the person. All of these factors for leaders in their positions of visibility and responsibility will function to increase mindlessness, like movement toward entropy in a closed system. But the fourth factor can hurt or help – the role of others and the quality of one's relationships.

Leadership can spread mindlessness or mindfulness

Leaders are people in positions of authority, whether formal or informal (Yukl 2006). The leadership process occurs through relationships – it is difficult to be a leader without followers (Riggio, Chaleff, and Lipman-Blumen 2008). This basic aspect of leadership means that leaders are highly infectious, or contagious, to others regarding their relative degree of mindfulness or mindlessness (Dasborough, Ashkanasy, Tee, and Tse 2009). An untested idea would be to see if leaders who are more mindful are less vulnerable to these infections.

Emotional contagion spreads mindlessness and mindfulness

In organizations, people focus on the leader or observe the leader with more intensity than others (McClelland 1975). The leader spreads his or her mood through a neural process involving several networks, the mirror neuron network (Cattaneo and Rizolatti 2009; Iacoboni 2009) and aspects of the DMN. Although the mirror neuron network allows a person to mimic the actions of others, it is the social aspects of the DMN that enable a person to tune into and pick up the mood and feelings of others (Buckner *et al.* 2008; Decety and Batson 2007).

We are hard wired to tune into others, so the social awareness aspect of mindfulness is one of the most natural human processes unless something interferes. This is called emotional contagion (Hatfield, Cacioppo, and Rapson 1994). The neural mechanism explains how the contagion spreads. It is amplified by people watching each other and the development of social norms.

Although there are people with neurological challenges that make it difficult to activate these social networks (i.e., those with autism or milder forms formerly called Asberger's Syndrome (Baron-Cohen 2008)), blocking these networks in the receiver either involves over-emphasis of the TPN or chronic stress. Except in these instances, the leader's degree of mindfulness or lack thereof spreads to others around him or her through these social and mirror neuron networks.

Given the heavy load of chronic power stress related to their responsibility and the substantial number of people observing them (remember, this is one of the stimulants of human stress), we can hypothesize that leaders are more likely to slip into mindlessness than those in positions with fewer sources of power stress or those factors that arouse the human stress response. Although we are focusing on leaders, the same can be said of those in positions of responsibility like doctors, nurses, teachers and professors, clerics, and other "helpers." But for leaders of many organizations, and those in analytic fields, when the heavy demands of analytic tasks also fall on them, leaders will further withdraw their attention from people and the environment. Because people are holistic beings, it is likely that when a leader is less mindful toward others at work, he or she will also be less mindful toward the people at home.

In one function magnetic resonance imaging (fMRI) study, we asked executives (average age 49.5) to remember key moments they had with resonant leaders and key moments with dissonant leaders in their past (Boyatzis *et al.* 2012). Weeks later, when they were strapped into an fMRI, we then reminded them of those moments with audio recordings and asked some questions about how they felt about the leader and his or her style and impact. The regions of the brain that were statistically significantly activated showed that specific memories of resonant leaders activated parts of the mirror neuron networks and DMN. Memories of dissonant leaders suppressed these areas and activated those associated with stress and the TPN. This study showed us that not only do leaders with different relationships invoke different neural networks, but the emotional contagion created by leaders lasts for years.

Research has also shown that this emotional contagion can, if reinforced, become a part of the organization's culture, norms, and values (Dasborough *et al.* 2009; Barsade and Gibson 2007). Then it becomes a part of the socialization of new members into the organization and the norms are perpetuated. This would apply to norms of nastiness, indifference to others, or mindfulness and attentiveness to others.

Dimitrios' slide into mindlessness did seem to have an effect on the climate in the consulting company. People were focused on their clients, their projects, and showed little extra effort for others, unless they were personal friends. There were increasing conflicts among account managers and product managers about territorial issues. This was most evident in the major disruptions caused by several spin-offs, consultants leaving and setting up their own companies and competing with this company.

The return path to mindfulness

If the forces moving a leader toward mindlessness are so prevalent, the metamorphosis to mindfulness must be intentional. Beyond that, the maintenance of such a state must also be intentional. Inattention, or being mindless about mindfulness, will result in the slips discussed earlier. Effort, focus, and intention are needed to flip the state. Goleman (2013) explains that there are many kinds of focus needed to be effective, enjoy life, and be a good person. You need to be focused on yourself and self-aware. You need to be empathic toward others. You need to focus on the natural environment and the larger systems dynamics surrounding your piece of the world. He calls these different forms of mindfulness. They are different forms of focusing one's attention and being attentive.

Vision and positive emotional attractors

Based on research on what produces sustained, desired change, intentional change theory provides some insight as to how such change can be achieved (Boyatzis 2008). The two drivers of sustained, desired change, according to intentional change theory, are a person's personal vision and the resonant relationships that help that person see or find their personal vision, move toward it, and maintain the desired changes. In other words, a person's vision becomes the purpose driving the intentional change process, and thereby invoking mindfulness, or increasing degrees of mindfulness.

The realization or articulation of a person's dream, their personal vision, will help them to enter the parasympathetic nervous system, which is the body's antidote to stress and the sympathetic nervous system (Boyatzis and Akrivou 2006). Discussing one's personal vision for thirty minutes resulted in neural activations in aspects of the DMN, which in turn, help a person to be open to new ideas and people (Jack, Boyatzis, Khawaja, Passarelli, and Leckie 2013). But even in this fMRI study, Jack and colleagues showed that it was talking to someone in a resonant relationship that invoked the neural activation sought. A mere thirty minutes talking to someone about things that one should do activated brain regions that were antagonistic to the DMN (Jack, Boyatzis, Khawaja, Passarelli, and Leckie 2013).

In a series of studies of different approaches to coaching, it has been shown that coaching with compassion (to the positive emotional attractor, or PEA, (Boyatzis 2013)) accounted for the results mentioned above. Coaching with compassion is an interaction that invokes primarily the PEA in the person being coached (and the coach) often through discussion of their dreams and vision, values, gratitude, and mindfulness. This is coaching a person toward their own desired state or future. But coaching for compliance, trying to change someone in a direction you or the family or the company want, appears to invoke the negative emotional attractor (NEA) and the corresponding neural networks and hormonal systems that result in a defensive and stress response – the person closes down to new ideas and others. Khawaja (2010) showed that a more PEA than NEA relationship

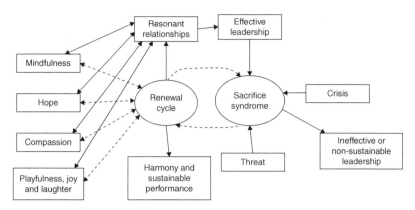

Figure 10.1 The cycles of resonance, stress, and renewal
Source: Adapted from © Richard E. Boyatzis and Annie McKee, 2005. Playfulness was added in 2009. Boyatzis and McKee (2005). For a more technical explanation of the stress and renewal dynamics, read also Boyatzis, Smith, and Blaize (2006).

with one's physician resulted in more treatment adherence for Type II diabetics. Howard (2006) showed that a PEA approach to coaching mid-career dentists resulted in more positive affect and excitement about their future than spending time with someone coaching them to address their weaknesses. Dyck (2009) showed that third-year medical students received much better evaluations from standardized patients (who complete an evaluation of each medical student) and their supervising physician faculty when they showed more PEA behavior in the fifteen-minute attempts to diagnose mystery maladies.

Coaching with compassion, or coaching others in the PEA experience, invokes the parasympathetic nervous system and renewal (Boyatzis, Smith, and Blaize, 2006; Boyatzis, Smith, and Beveridge, 2013). This means building more positive, resonant relationships with others. It means focusing on the other person and their dreams, values and concerns, not yours. Boyatzis, Smith, and Blaize (2006) contend that leaders would become more sustainable themselves and experience more renewal from coaching or motivating others this way. Boyatzis and McKee (2005) contend that this process not only achieves more resonant relationships but also prepares the person, whether the leader or the other person around the leader, to be more mindful, as shown in Figure 10.1.

Focusing on the other person helps this process (Goleman 2013). By moving from concerns about yourself to the other person, you shift into a different form of empathy (Decety and Michalska 2010). This form activates parts of the DMN and invokes the more open, renewing processes explained earlier. And it helps you to build or maintain better relationships.

A review of medical research shows that there are a variety of activities that can invoke mindfulness such as meditation, yoga, tai chi, prayer to a loving God, moderate exercise, massage, and such.However, some of these activities, such as meditation in highly experienced meditators (i.e. those regularly meditating ten years or more), may invoke other neural networks and not the DMN.

At the organizational level, Bennis and Nanus (1985) claimed that one of the indicators of an effective leader is that he or she manages attention through vision. They use a vision of the organization to drive people to focus on purpose and the future. By reminding everyone about the purpose of the organization, the executive or manager is calling on others to be mindful of why they exist, their collective sense of purpose. This is modeling mindfulness *and* using emotional contagion to spread it to others.

To be more effective, leaders should help people in any organization remember why they are doing what they do, their purpose or vision. The vision should evolve and be readjusted through conversation to keep it active and relevant. It is a way to invoke the shared values of those in the organization. Sometimes, leaders do this by telling stories, at other times they ask others in the meeting to share stories of when a client or patient was helped.

Returning to Dimitrios, it was a series of soul-searching activities and long discussions with his wife, close friends, and mentors that led him to the conclusion that he needed a major change in his life. Since his company conducted these types of program, he decided to use the company's own technology on himself. He and his wife built a new personal vision of the long-term future. He was excited about doing research, developing graduate students in a wide variety of ways, and learning new ideas, which doctoral students will generate in their search for truth and justice. He decided it was time to return to academia, but this time as a full-time faculty member. He had refused an earlier offer at one university, but decided to reconsider it. He was worried about protecting the company and the people who worked there. So he began to plan, a year and a half ahead of when he might leave, ways to create what he called a firewall around the company and its systems. Oddly, he was probably more in tune with the staff and his colleagues than earlier because he had decided to leave. He felt free and hopeful about both his own future and that of the people at the company.

With his wife and close friends, his issues came into clear focus. Many consequences of such a big career and life move were discussed. Little by little, a clear plan emerged. Within two months of the move to a new career and city, he began to practice some of the mindfulness techniques such as meditating that he had done many years earlier. He spent time with a new intern and began to lose weight, exercise, and change his diet. It worked! How do I know? Because this was my story. And if there is a possibility of self-delusion, check with my wife. I had her read this chapter carefully and change anything that was not how she remembered it (I have at times not remembered things as accurately as she did).

Resonant relationships are key to effective leadership

The return to mindfulness or, retaining some degree of humility as one is never truly as mindful as one would like, at least a relative return to it, only seems to occur when one is able to build or rebuild a set of resonant relationships in one's life and work system (Boyatzis and McKee 2005). For me, it was rebuilding a resonance with my wife, returning to a state in which each of us felt in tune with each other. Building these resonant relationships with the people I interact with daily at the university such as faculty colleagues, administrators, doctoral and master's students, I was then able to engage in new, positive working relationships with former colleagues at other universities, consulting companies, and in the government.

As I said earlier in this chapter and exhaustively in earlier publications, the path to creating or maintaining resonant relationships is through mindfulness, hope, compassion, and playfulness. Once one person in a relationship begins to invoke any of these experiences, through the process of emotional contagion, the other person is infected and moves into that state – unless something is blocking or inhibiting them, such their own fear, negativity, or defensiveness (Boyatzis and McKee 2005; Boyatzis, Smith, and Beveridge 2013). These resonant relationships helped to reinforce a new, more gratifying and centering level of mindfulness. They allowed for more hope, compassion, and playfulness. Not every relationship became resonant, nor was I always able to maintain the degree of mindfulness I desired. But resonance became possible. Of course, it is a perpetual battle to stay intentional and focused, to stay mindful. All of the distractions and factors discussed earlier are still operating around each one of us at full power. But having returned to a state of mindfulness once, it makes it easier to do again, and again and again. It is through practice that a person learns techniques to change their own mood and activate corresponding neural networks and endocrine secretions.

Conclusion

Effective leaders are mindful on many levels. They are tuned into what is going on inside their hearts, minds, and bodies. They build resonant relationships with others in which people experience mutual mindfulness, tuning into each other on a regular basis. They are tuned into the larger environment of their community, industry, and the natural environment. While these people sound like superhuman beings, the humbling realization is that it is still relatively rare for someone to be able to maintain mindfulness at all these levels. There are major forces at play which drive leaders into mindlessness. Chronic stress pushes us into dissonant relationships and disengagement. We defend ourselves and inadvertently threaten our relationships to others and the environment. If that was not enough (and often it is sufficient to render most leaders mindless most of the time), periodic life and career transitions (i.e., crises) distract us and speed up the slide. Lastly, the antagonistic neural networks of analytics versus openness to others and new ideas make it increasingly difficult to remain mindful, even if we achieve some modicum of that desired state.

Research has helped us understand these derailers. Future research should help us understand how it happens and point to ways to create antidotes or stress inoculation. Practitioners already suggest that mindful practices can do just this. More experimentation can help us understand how to make these practices more accessible for most leaders.

Any progress on being more mindful will help people to be better leaders and may lead us into more mindful dyads, teams and organizations.

References

Baron-Cohen, S. (2008). *Autism and asperger syndrome: the facts.* London: Oxford University Press.

Barsade, S. G. and Gibson, D. E. (2007). Why does affect matter in organizations? *Academy of Management Perspectives*, 21, 36–59.

Bennis, W. and Nanus, B. (1985). *Leaders: strategies for taking charge.* New York: HarperRow.

Boyatzis, R.E. (2007). Interpersonal aesthetics: emotional and social intelligence competencies are wisdom in practice. In E. Kessler and J. Bailey (eds.). *Handbook of organizational wisdom.* Thousand Oaks, CA: Sage Publications, pp. 223–42.

Boyatzis, R. E. (2008). Leadership development from a complexity perspective. *Consulting Psychology Journal*, 60(4), 298–313.

Boyatzis, R. E. (2013). When pulling to the negative emotional attractor is too much or not enough to inspire and sustain outstanding leadership. In R. J. Burke and C. L. Cooper (eds.). *The fulfilling workplace: the organization's role in achieving individual and organizational health.* Burlington, VT: Ashgate Publishing. pp. 139–50.

Boyatzis, R. E. and Akrivou, K. (2006). The ideal self as a driver of change. *Journal of Management Development*, 25(7), 624–42.

Boyatzis, R. E. and McKee, A. (2005). *Resonant leadership: renewing yourself and connecting with others through mindfulness, hope, and compassion.* Boston, MA: Harvard Business School Press.

Boyatzis, R. E., Passarelli, A. M., Koenig, K., Lowe, M., Mathew, B., Stoller, J. K., and Phillips, M. (2012). Examination of the neural substrates activated in memories of experiences with resonant and dissonant leaders. *The Leadership Quarterly*, 23(2), 259–72.

Boyatzis, R.E., Smith, M., and Beveridge, A. (2013). Coaching with compassion: inspiring health, well-being and development in organizations. *Journal of Applied Behavioral Science*, 49(2), 153–78.

Boyatzis, R.E., Smith, M., and Blaize, N. (2006). Developing sustainable leaders through coaching and compassion. *Academy of Management Journal on Learning and Education*, 5(1), 8–24.

Buckner, R. L., Andrews-Hanna, J. R., and Schacter, D. L. (2008). The brain's default network. *Annals of the New York Academy of Sciences*, 1124(1), 1–38.

Cattaneo, L. and Rizzolatti, G. (2009). The mirror neuron system. *Archives of Neurology*, 66, 557–60.

Dasborough, M., Ashkanasy, N, Tee, E., and Tse, H. (2009). What goes around comes around: how meso-level negative emotional contagion can ultimately determine organizational attitudes toward leaders. *The Leadership Quarterly*, 20(4), 571–85.

Decety, J. and Batson, C. D. (2007). Social neuroscience approaches to inter-personal sensitivity. *Social Neuroscience*, 2, 151–7.

Decety, J. and Michalska, K. J. (2010). Neurodevelopmental changes in the circuits underlying empathy and sympathy from childhood to adult-hood. *Developmental Science*, 13(6), 886–99.

Dyck, L. (2009). Resonance and dissonance in professional helping rela-tionships at the dyadic level: Determine the influence of positive and negative emotional attractors on effective physician-patient com-munication. Doctoral Dissertation, Case Western Reserve University, Cleveland, OH.

Goleman, D. (2013). *Focus: the hidden driver of excellence*. New York: Harper Collins.

Hatfield, E., Cacioppo, J., and Rapson, R. (1994). *Emotional contagion*. New York: Cambridge University Press.

Howard, A. (2006). Positive and negative emotional attractors and inten-tional change. *Journal of Management Development*, 25(7), 657–70.

Iacoboni, M. (2009). Imitation, empathy, and mirror neurons. *Annual Review of Psychology*, 60, 653–70.

Jack, A., Boyatzis, R. E., Khawaja, M., Passarelli, A. M., and Leckie, R. (2013). Visioning in the brain: an fMRI study of inspirational coaching and mentoring. *Social Neuroscience*, 8(4), 369–84.

Jack, A. I., Dawson, A. J., Begany, K. L., Leckie, R. L., Barry, K. P., Ciccia, A. H., and Snyder, A. Z. (2013). fMRI reveals reciprocal inhibition between social and physical cognitive domains. *NeuroImage*, 66, 385–401.

Kabat-Zinn, J. (1990). *Full catastrophe living: using the wisdom of your body and mind to face stress, pain, and illness*. New York: Dell Publishing.

Khawaja, M. (2010). The mediating role of positive and negative emotional attractors between psychosocial correlates of doctor-patient relation-ship and treatment of Type II diabetes. Doctoral Dissertation, Case Western Reserve University; Cleveland, OH.

Langer, E. J. (1989). *Mindfulness*. Cambridge, MA: Perseus Publishing.

Langer, E. J. (1997). *The power of mindful learning*. Cambridge, MA: Perseus Books.

Levinson, D. J., Darrow, C. N., Klein, E. B., Levinson, M. H., and McKee, B. (1978). *The seasons of a man's life*. New York: Knopf.

McCall, M., Lombardo, M., and Morrison, A. (1988). *Lessons from experi-ence*. New York: Free Press.

McClelland, D. C. (1975). *Power: the inner experience*. New York: Irvington.

Riggio, R. E., Chaleff, I., and Lipman-Blumen, J. (eds.) (2008). *The art of followership: how great followers create great leaders and organiza-tions*. San Francisco, CA: Jossey-Bass.

Sapolsky, R. M. (2004). *Why zebras don't get ulcers*. 3rd edn. New York: Harper Collins.

Segerstrom, S. C. and Miller, G. E. (2004). Psychological stress and the human immune system: a meta-analytic study of 30 years of inquiry. *Psychological Bulletin*, 130(4), 601–30.

Sheehy, G. (1995). *New passages: mapping your life across time*. New York: Ballantine.

Yukl, G. (2006). *Leadership in organizations*. 6th edn. Upper Saddle River, NJ: Prentice-Hall.

11 | Leading with mindfulness: exploring the relation of mindfulness with leadership behaviors, styles, and development

JOCHEN REB, SAMANTHA SIM,
KRAIVIN CHINTAKANANDA AND
DEVASHEESH P. BHAVE

Introduction

A recent *Forbes* article stated that "Mindfulness is hot right now – Hollywood hot, Davos hot, Main Street hot … For business leaders, encouraging mindfulness is more than just being tuned in; it's a strategy to improve person and company-wide performance and productivity" (Bruce 2014). Leadership is a perennially trendy topic, and its fusion with mindfulness creates a combination of potential über-trendiness. But is this hype justified? Our endeavour in this chapter is to elaborate on the connections between mindfulness and leadership. A related goal is to take a critical look: generally both mindfulness and leadership are viewed in a positive light. Although "leadership" evokes ideas of strengths and charisma, transformation, and achievement. Yet at the same time, a "dark side" of leadership and leaders also surfaces in the form of leader arrogance, hubris, cronyism, abusive supervision, and outright dictatorships.

Perhaps even more so than with leadership, mindfulness appears to be seen as almost universally positive. Indeed, a large number of studies have found beneficial effects of mindfulness for, among others, individual health, psychological wellbeing, and functioning (Chiesa and Serretti 2010; Eberth and Sedlmeier 2012). Also, as shown in the various chapters of this book and other work, a strong case can be made that mindfulness and mindfulness practice have substantial potential to improve the quality and outcomes of work life (see also Glomb *et al.* 2011). Finally, empirical research on the effects of leader mindfulness provides evidence of beneficial consequences for employees including

256

increases in employee job performance, job satisfaction, and need satisfaction, and reductions in emotional exhaustion (Reb, Narayanan, and Chaturvedi 2014).

Although we are in broad agreement with claims regarding the benefits of mindfulness in general and for leadership in particular, at the same time, one can wonder whether there are any downsides to leaders being mindful. For example, might a more "present" (i.e., mindful) leader be perceived as more charismatic, and could this person take advantage of their charismatic appearance in order to pursue their own political agenda at the expense of others' and organizational goals?

In this chapter we explore such questions about the "bright" and also the potentially "dark" sides of mindfulness for leaders. In addition to the theoretical importance of such questions, they are also relevant when considering the design of mindfulness training for leadership and possibly other areas such as employee wellbeing. We believe that being open to the complexities of mindfulness in leadership, rather than painting a perhaps unrealistically positive picture, will increase the chances of mindfulness surviving beyond the current buzz as a valid construct and training intervention that has implications for leadership research and practice.

In elaborating on the connections between leadership and mindfulness, we adopt an illustrative approach where we trot down paths that appear particularly interesting and have potential for major impact for research and practice. Such an approach, understandably, misses out on other worthy points of interest and convergence across these two areas, and represents an opportunity for future exploration.

Connecting mindfulness and leadership: three important distinctions

To examine the connections between mindfulness and leadership, we make three important distinctions. First, we distinguish between several dimensions of mindfulness, such as presence, intention, and witnessing awareness. This allows us to explore whether mindfulness, when understood and practiced in certain limited or "minimalistic" ways, will not lead to an unfolding of its full potential. In fact, we will argue that it may then even support "darker" aspects of leadership, making leaders more effective in achieving unwholesome goals. In so doing, we echo some of the concerns about "McMindfulness" (Purser and Loy 2013). This is the sense that popularized versions of mindfulness and mindfulness practice do not faithfully present, or even entirely misrepresent, the essence of mindfulness as understood in contemplative traditions. In such traditions mindfulness practice holds a special, perhaps even sacred, space as a path to liberation and enlightenment. In contrast, "McMindfulness" stands for a limited, perhaps shallow practice of mindfulness that we believe may not provide the full benefits of a more holistic, genuine approach, and may even lead to several negative consequences, as elaborated further in this chapter.

Second, we make a distinction between the *construct* of mindfulness and mindfulness as a *practice*. As a construct, mindfulness can be seen as a mental state, skill, or trait. As a practice, mindfulness involves certain formal and informal practices that have the purpose of inducing a state of mindfulness, improving mindfulness skills, or increasing trait-level mindfulness. We believe that this distinction is helpful for several reasons. First, factors other than mindfulness practice might affect state, skill, or trait levels of mindfulness. These factors could include genetics, personal development, and the work environment. For example, Reb, Narayanan, and Ho (2015) found that employees who faced more constraints on the job were less mindful and those who felt more supported were more mindful, providing empirical evidence for the influence of the work environment. Second, mindfulness practice may not always achieve its intended effects of increasing mindfulness for different reasons. For example, people may not practice consistently enough for effects to occur, or they may practice in ways that the training fails to transfer into their (work) lives, or they may practice with attitudes such as perfectionism that may increase tension and anxiety, rather than reduce it. Third, mindfulness practice may have effects apart from increasing mindfulness (e.g., reducing stress or increasing confidence) and/or effects that are not captured by current mindfulness scales, such as the setting of intentions and the persistence in implementing these intentions. For all these reasons, it makes sense to distinguish between mindfulness and mindfulness practice.

Third, we make a distinction between intrapersonal (i.e., within the mindful/mindless individual) and interpersonal (i.e., beyond the individual and in relation to others and/or the organization) effects of mindfulness. Most existing research on mindfulness has focused on intrapersonal effects such as how mindfulness is related to stress, anxiety, or performance within the *same* person. Particularly given that our interest is in leadership, which is to a large extent an interpersonal phenomenon (Uhl-Bien 2006), it is crucial to move beyond the intrapersonal effects of mindfulness to study the interpersonal, organizational, or even societal effects. In this chapter, we focus specifically on the interpersonal effects of leaders' mindfulness.

We are not trying to offer the one "true" definition of mindfulness. Rather than trying to resolve definitional issues of mindfulness, we treat mindfulness as an umbrella term, and then examine the potential role and consequences of the different dimensions of mindfulness for leadership. This approach has limitations; for instance we only draw on dimensions of mindfulness discussed in the modern scientific literature on mindfulness but neglect the contemplative literature.

Building on these three distinctions (dimensions of mindfulness, mindfulness as a construct versus mindfulness as a practice, and the intrapersonal versus interpersonal effects of mindfulness), in the next sections we first outline relationships between the dimensions of mindfulness to leadership behaviors; second, we explore how mindfulness may be related to three specific leadership styles (authentic, charismatic, and servant); third, we outline the relationship between mindfulness and leadership development.

Exploring the relations between dimensions of mindfulness and leadership behaviors

Present-moment attention

Perhaps the dimension most widely associated with mindfulness in the general public is present-moment attention. Attention to the present moment also features in most academic definitions of mindfulness (e.g., Bishop *et al.* 2004; Brown and Ryan 2003; Kabat-Zinn 2003). Colloquially, this is often expressed as being "fully in the here and now." Present-moment attention can be contrasted with states in which attention seems to be away from the present moment, such as absent-mindedness, daydreaming, worrying about the future, or ruminating about the past. Present-moment attention can be considered a self-regulatory skill of attention regulation.

At the *intra*-individual level, a variety of benefits are associated with being fully in the here-and-now. For example, increasing present-moment attention can counteract tendencies towards rumination and thereby avoiding the negative mental health outcomes associated with rumination (Brown and Ryan 2003). Being more in the present moment could be associated with intra-individual benefits related to leader functioning, such as a reduction in multitasking, which tends to reduce efficiency and effectiveness, and improved performance (Beal *et al.* 2005; Dalal, Bhave, and Fiset 2014).

The benefits of present-moment attention are derived to a large extent from avoiding unhealthy and ineffective aspects of paying attention to the past or the future. These include rumination, worries, and anxiety. However, not all occupation with past and future are necessarily unhealthy and some may actually be rather functional. It seems possible that a strong present-moment orientation may prevent a leader from engaging in functional past- and future-oriented activities. In particular, we suggest that a strong present-moment orientation may result in too little future-oriented planning as well as past-oriented learning and reflection. While this may be beneficial for the leader's wellbeing, at least in the shorter run, at the intra-individual level, it may not be ideal from an organizational or even an individual's longer-term learning perspective. In other words, in such situations, a trade-off might exist between individual and organizational, and shorter-term and longer-term goals. Ultimately, a leader needs to find a balance between past, present, and future orientation. What proponents of mindfulness have alerted us to is that for many of us, the imbalance exists in being too little in the present. However, it would probably be a mistake to go to the opposite extreme and be entirely in the present.

Another possible downside of present-moment attention is a resulting depletion in self-regulatory resources. To the extent that focusing attention on the present moment requires effortful self-regulation of attention (as compared to, for example, mind wandering), it would consume limited mental resources that could then not be used for other tasks. In contrast, working on "auto pilot" or using routine behaviors, rather than mindfully, on certain tasks could save mental resources for times when they are needed (Dalal *et al.* 2014; Levinthal and Rerup 2006).

As for *inter*-individual effects, present-moment attention may also have positive consequences. Kahn (1992) proposes that a supervisor's psychological presence at work, defined as being attentive, connected, integrated, and focused, could increase employee work engagement. Thus, when leaders pay attention and are aware of the people around them, it signals interest and respect for employees. By receiving a leader's full attention, an employee may feel more acknowledged and appreciated. When followers perceive leader interest, it could possibly increase self-esteem of followers and legitimize follower concerns, which, in turn, increase follower commitment or engagement in leaders' goals. Leaders high in presence and awareness dimensions of mindfulness are likely to be influential over their followers; this presence could be natural (i.e. trait mindfulness), or cultivated (i.e., developed through mindfulness training, or utilizing a mindfulness exercise moments before meeting their audience). Contrast such "present" leaders with those who are distracted (e.g., writing emails or checking SMS) while conversing with their subordinates: "present" leaders will have higher quality relationships that may also contribute to employee wellbeing and performance (Reb *et al.* 2014).

However, present-moment attention and respect are two distinct constructs. Crossing the two variables results in four possible combinations: present leaders who respect their employees (and are perceived as such), present leaders who do not respect (but are incorrectly perceived to, because of their presence), leaders who are not present and respect (but are not perceived to because of their lack of presence), and finally leaders who are not present with their employees and do not respect them (and are perceived as such).

As such, while leader presence (which can easily be observed by employees), may be *interpreted* by an employee as a signal of respect (which is less easily observed directly), and the employee may indeed feel respected (i.e., perceive interpersonal fairness) the leader may or may not actually respect the employee. Cunning leaders may thus use their ability to be present to create the impression of respecting and caring for their subordinates. Subordinates may, as a result, have a more favorable attitude toward the leader and may also feel a certain obligation or compulsion to reciprocate the perceived respect, for example, by acting in the leader's interest (through higher performance). In this way, a leader may use presence for selfish, political, or antisocial goals (i.e., unwholesome goals). Conversely, leaders who lack the ability to be present with their employees due to poor attention regulation, but who truly respect and care for their employees may not be perceived as such to the extent that employees use leader presence as an accessible cue to make judgments about leaders not having directly observable respect (Brunswik 1952).

In summary, we posit that present-moment attention can enable leaders to better communicate their genuine care and respect to their subordinates; and while we do believe that, overall, present-moment attention and care and respect go together and are positively correlated, this relation is not a necessary one and sometimes leaders may use their ability to be present with others to give an impression of care and respect that may not accurately reflect their true attitudes. Empirical research could examine the prevalence of such instrumental use of presence, as well as employees' ability to notice such instances.

Another benefit to leader present-moment attention suggested by Reb *et al.* (2014) is that it might help leaders to better understand their employees (e.g., their situation, needs, aspirations) and, as a result, be more supportive. This is because being fully present would allow a leader to notice factors about the employee that an absent-minded (or distracted) leader would not (e.g., signs of stress) (Atkins and Parker 2012). Further, research has shown that attentive listeners have the power to shape a narrative in face-to-face communication via their nonverbal participation (Bavelas, Coates and Johnson 2000). Attentive listening elicits more emotion-laden and information-rich narration and leaders who attend while listening may better understand what their employees are trying to communicate than leaders who are distracted. Thus, present-moment attention can have positive inter-individual effects to the extent that leaders use this improved understanding to better support their employees in achieving goals, such as performing well on their assigned work tasks or helping their co-workers.

However, an improved understanding may also be exploited by a leader for unwholesome purposes. For example, becoming aware that an employee is under great pressure to not lose their job due to financial obligations, a leader might more easily push an employee to engage in unethical actions. Thus, again, this suggests that leaders' goals are important factors to consider in combination with leaders' present-moment attention in better understanding the resulting consequences for followers.

Intentionality

Intentionality is another aspect that is considered by some scholars as essential to mindfulness. For example, Shapiro and Carlson (2009) define mindfulness as "the awareness that arises through intentionally attending in an open, caring, and nonjudgmental way" (p. 4); Kabat-Zinn (2003) also refers to mindfulness as paying attention to the present moment on purpose (i.e., with intention).

In the practice of mindfulness, intention is important at least partly because it is thought to facilitate an important element of the practice: keeping in mind, or remembering, the intention to keep one's attention focused on a particular stimulus such as the breath, as well as remembering to return one's attention to the breath when it has wandered away.

It is easy to see how keeping one's intentions in mind can be beneficial far beyond meditation practice. Good intentions, such as eating more healthily or abstemiously, for example, are easily "crowded out" as the mind is occupied with various information processing activities, such as worrying about problems. However, without holding one's intentions in mind, it is easy to make the wrong choices, in the sense of choices that are inconsistent with one's intentions (e.g., snacking mindlessly).

Similarly, leaders who might get easily overwhelmed by the myriad demands on their attention might find it valuable to learn how to hold onto their intentions. Effective leadership can be viewed as the ability to attain organizational goals through influencing others. Given that the organization presents a dynamic environment with multiple stakeholders, there are potentially many issues that could redirect attention from organizational goals. While some of these issues legitimately deserve attention and require action, it may often be more important for the leader to maintain attentional focus on the goal at hand. In addition, the complexity of the organization means that enacting organizational change, one of the prime tasks of leaders, requires both persistence in the face of obstacles and time. For leaders who need to adhere to intentions (e.g., enacting certain behaviors to change corporate culture, or motivating employees), the ability to bring attention back to their intention may be hugely valuable. Thus, mindfulness, in the form of being focused, and refocusing, on purpose and goals, seems fundamental to effective leadership.

So far we have focused on the process of remembering intentions. However, the content of intentions is also important. When the content of intention is "wholesome" (e.g., prosocial), mindfulness, in the sense of the ability to remember intentions moment-to-moment, would be beneficial as it aids the implementation of these intentions.

↳ Remember to be intension

However, when intentions are unwholesome (e.g., antisocial), *mindlessness* arguably would be more desirable from a societal perspective, as it makes the implementation of such intentions less likely (it may be worth noting that less likely does not mean impossible, as intentions and goals can also be pursued without conscious awareness). Thus, as with mindfulness as present-moment awareness, mindfulness as the ability to remember one's intentions could be understood as a self-regulatory skill and resource that is best viewed together with the leader's values, goals, and intentions to better understand its consequences and whether they are desirable not only for the individual but also for the organization.

Attitude of self-compassion

Another important dimension referred to in particular in mindfulness-based interventions (MBIs) such as mindfulness-based stress reduction (MBSR) and mindfulness-based cognitive therapy (MBCT; Segal, Williams, and Teasdale, 2013) is self-compassion. As mentioned above, in mindfulness meditation, the mind often wanders away from the object of attention (e.g., the breath). It is the function of intention to return attention to the breath. However, practitioners are typically instructed to do so in a gentle, kind way, showing self-compassion. One reason for this is to counterbalance any tendencies to criticize oneself for being so poor at performing a seemingly easy task such as observing one's breath. Such criticism would only lead the practitioner further away from letting attention rest on the process of breathing, and, as such, is counterproductive.

Thus self-compassion can be crucial in helping the practitioner to bring back, over and over again, a wandering mind without getting frustrated, de-motivated, angry, or caught up in conceptual self-criticism. If leaders can transfer this attitude toward failure into their work context, developing self-compassion may allow leaders to persist in the face of repeated failures, without criticising themselves too harshly or giving up prematurely because of frustration. Moreover, the transfer from self-compassion to compassion for others may naturally occur, and as leaders experience the value of being compassionate towards themselves they may become more compassionate towards their colleagues and subordinates.

However, in a more shallow ("McMindfulness") approach, self-compassion in mindfulness practice could be viewed from an instrumental perspective as a means to an end: as an emotion applied with the purpose of being more mindful (in the sense of returning attention to the intended object of attention). As such, one can wonder if the kind of self-compassion in mindfulness practice is different from self-compassion (and perhaps compassion) espoused and practiced in contemplative traditions through techniques such as loving-kindness meditation (LKM). This is a contemplative, emotion-focused practice in which one directs positive feelings of loving-kindness toward the self and real or imagined others using attention, visualization, and emotion. It is designed to promote feelings of warmth, caring, and kindness toward the self and others (Salzberg 1995). Thus, in LKM feelings such as (self-)compassion are the purpose, or end of the practice, not a means to attain personal goals.

From this perspective, an empirical question is whether leaders who have applied self-compassion as a means to an end in their mindfulness practice may also attempt to "act compassionately" in an *interpersonal* context. For instance, emotional labor research has highlighted that employees modify their expressions (surface acting) when interacting with co-workers (Kim, Bhave and Glomb 2013). Along similar lines, leaders may engage in faking expressions of compassion in order to to gain subordinates' goodwill and obligation rather than from a genuine sense of concern for their colleagues. Such an instrumental approach to compassion may be problematic. First, it may serve "unwholesome" ends. Second, in general, regulating emotional expressions will also be detrimental to leaders' wellbeing (Grandey, Diefendorff, and Rupp 2013). An alternative to regulating expressions is to regulate feelings – deep acting, aligning with the objectives of LKM – generating feelings of compassion. It is plausible, then, that through deep acting leaders may experience and exhibit "true" compassion that helps them to focus on the fulfillment of other-oriented goals. Furthermore, emotional labor research reveals that deep acting, in general, is also related to superior wellbeing (Grandey *et al.* 2013). In sum, it stands to reason that through the genuine practice of self-compassion, even if from an instrumental motivation at first, actual self-compassion and compassion for others are experienced and developed through MBIs. Hopefully, future research will be able to shed more light on this matter.

Witnessing awareness

Witnessing awareness is another important dimension of mindfulness and mindfulness practice. This dimension has been referred to by various names including cognitive defusion, non-reactivity, non-judgment, decentering, reperceiving, metacognition, witnessing, or simply awareness. In essence, it refers to the awareness of, or witnessing of an experience (where the experience is often a thought or an emotion). For example, rather than "only" breathing and paying attention to breathing, mindfulness also involves an awareness that one is breathing. The direct consequence of this witnessing of experience is a certain dis-identification with the experience. In other words, the experience is recognized as separate from the self, the self and the experience are "defused" and thus the experience exerts less control over behavior.

This dimension of mindfulness has been emphasized particularly in clinical approaches such as acceptance and commitment therapy (ACT; Fletcher and Hayes 2005) and MBCT (Segal *et al.* 2013) because of its potential to address mental health problems such as (relapses of) depression. Arguably, many mental health problems are partly due to a fusion of self with experiences, to the point at which individuals identify too closely with negative thoughts, emotions, and the affect they experience. This fusion can severely bias and limit individuals' awareness of what kind of choices and actions are available to them. For example, a person may be having the thought "I am no good at anything. I am a useless person." Taking a witnessing stance to this thought allows a person to create some distance and recognize the thought as a thought, rather than "the truth." Thus, while not necessarily changing the content of experiences such as thoughts and emotions, witnessing awareness changes one's relation to these experiences.

This change in perspective is considered by many to be crucial for the mental health benefits of mindfulness. However, we would argue that the benefits extend beyond clinical populations and wellbeing-related consequences. First, defusion may lead to a clearer, less biased, less restrictive view of the environment and the self, as the person de-identifies with what is going on inside and out. This may provide substantial benefits for making more informed choices. Second, the reduced identification may lead to less ego involvement and ego defensiveness of the leader, which could result in actions that are targeted more at organizational goals rather than protecting or advancing the leader's ego. Third, being able to "just notice" things without jumping to premature judgments and conclusions may be very valuable in interpersonal interactions with employees. In essence, a witnessing stance may allow leaders to create a sense of (safe) space for employees to articulate their ideas, concerns, and feedback. As a result, relationships with employees may improve as may employee productivity.

In addition to these potential benefits, we can speculate that taking a stance of witnessing awareness may carry some less desirable consequences from an organization's perspective. We present two such possible consequences: perceived leader apathy and reduced organizational commitment. First, followers may perceive a leader's stance of witnessing awareness as a sign that their leader is apathetic or indifferent. It has been argued that successful managers are those who influence employee behaviour by embracing emotion and being evocative (Ashforth and Humphrey 1995; Brief and Weiss 2002). However, witnessing awareness calls for a disidentification of the self from emotional experience. This may create the impression of being detached and unemotional. Emotions in general fulfil social functions, such as signaling beliefs and intentions and coordinating group goals (Keltner and Haidt, 1999). Thus, leaders who appear to be unemotional may be less effective in influencing followers. Without intending to do so, the leader practicing witnessing awareness may be viewed as apathetic and their passion for work may be called into question. On the other side, it could also be that witnessing awareness enables leaders to express (or not express) emotions more consistently with their intentions. Thus, rather than making leaders unemotional, it could be that such leaders become better able to express emotions that are motivating and engaging. Future empirical research will hopefully shed light on this issue.

Drawing on the burnout literature, one could speculate that in some cases, witnessing awareness may have similar effects on organizational commitment as distancing. Maslach, Schaufeli, and Leiter (2001) suggest that when people are burnt out, they distance themselves emotionally and cognitively from their work as a way to cope. Although distancing is a reaction to negative work experiences and these negative work experiences bring about reduced commitment, part of the reduced commitment is a result of work featuring weakly in an employee's identity. Similarly, witnessing awareness provides psychological distance between the self and experience such that identity is not strongly founded on work. Thus, witnessing awareness may lead to reduced organizational commitment as identification with the organization is reduced.

Clarity

Clarity is sometimes claimed as a dimension of mindfulness, or at least a proximal effect. We again argue that clarity may not necessarily lead to "better" leader behaviors. Clarity is likely a resource that helps leaders implement their goals: the clearer the goal, the more likely they are to be implemented. However, seeing one's goal more clearly may not necessarily affect the goal itself. One possibility is that clarity does indeed help a leader become aware when lower-level goals conflict with more deeply held goals, values, and beliefs (e.g., not to use other people as a means to an end). However, another possibility is that such clarity may not lead to conflict, as these goals may not conflict with deeply held higher-order goals and beliefs (e.g. employees' welfare depending on a company's survival). For instance, a firm's leader may come to a clear decision that laying off employees is the best approach to minimize the firm's payroll and takes action with less hesitation. Due to their clarity, the leader may decide to overlook other possible approaches that are less certain to be successful, and will thus cause psychological pain and financial difficulty to the laid-off employees.

In addition, if a person is deeply convinced of something (e.g., that certain people are inferior), gaining more clarity on this belief may lead to more harmful behaviors (e.g., discrimination). For instance, a leader may gain clarity on the belief that young workers are more skilful and comfortable adapting to the firm's new technology. Thus, during a crisis, the leader may act on this clearer belief and overlook older employees' loyalty and years of contributions to the firm. In this sense, less clarity on unwholesome goals could be preferable from a societal perspective. Thus, to give an example, a leader who is clear that his or her goal is to become the "number one" executive or company may be more likely to resort to extreme and unethical means to achieve this goal.

Of course, we would expect that a genuine, holistic mindfulness practice would help most if not all practitioners to connect with a deeper purpose, to feel more connected to others and the environment and, by realizing the causes of suffering and happiness, become more strongly committed to wholesome values; and that only in the case of a shallow practice of mindfulness, or perhaps for beginner practitioners, the above-mentioned possibility becomes more likely.

Mindfulness practice

We have already discussed several aspects of mindfulness particularly related to the practice of mindfulness, such as intention. However, we argue that over and above these aspects, mindfulness as a practice may have further effects on leaders. Many MBIs demand a daily formal practice, such as a sitting meditation. The expected duration of practice varies depending on the MBI, but can be substantial (e.g., forty minutes). Perhaps more important than the duration of each session, managing to establish and maintain a regular formal practice might bring several benefits.

Most obviously, such practice should increase the practitioner's ability to be mindful during practice and throughout the day and at work. In addition, such training might increase self-regulatory capacity – a crucial resource for leaders (Tsui and Ashford 1994). Further, increased self-efficacy may result from the experience of being able to sit quietly, despite all the difficulties, as well as from a perceived progress and sense of control over one's mind and impulses.

Beyond such concrete benefits, a formal practice of mindfulness may allow leaders to attain a sense of balance between doing and being. Leaders are expected to be active, to "do things," and their workdays are full of activities. Mindfulness practice provides a welcome and perhaps much-needed opportunity to switch from a doing mode to a being mode. This may allow leaders to recharge their energies – a phenomenon aligned with the conservation of resources (Hobfoll 1989). It may also provide them with a more balanced approach to decision making and action stemming from a fuller appreciation of life in its different modalities.

Whereas all of the above suggest beneficial effects of mindfulness practice, especially at the intra-individual level, we can think of at least two potential negative effects. First, to the extent that leaders do not live up to self- or trainer-set expectations of formal practice and progress in practice, this may add to their frustration and stress, and thus have negative effects on their wellbeing as well as their ability to perform.

Second, at the inter-individual level, having a regular practice of mindfulness may lead to a sense of separation from those who do not, or perhaps even worse, a sense of superiority. Social identification theory (Ashforth and Mael 1989; Tajfel and Turner 1979) suggests that individuals who practice mindfulness may socially categorize according to their practice and distinguish themselves from others who do not practice mindfulness. Along with this categorization, an enhancement of the in-group status happens organically as a function of implicit self-image concerns. In addition, being only introduced to the mainstream relatively recently as well as being generally positively received, mindfulness enjoys vogue status. In turn, the perceived distinctiveness and prestige of the group may fuel the salience of the non-practicing out-group. In other words, leaders who formally practice mindfulness as part of an MBI may consider themselves to be part of a special group of people, superior to others. The resulting superiority could potentially have negative effects on their relationships with "non-practitioners". Interestingly, it could also be that such an effect could at least partly be driven not by leaders' feelings of superiority, but by employees believing, counterfactually, that their leaders may consider themselves superior as a result of engaging in some form of "spiritual" practice, even if leaders do not think of themselves as superior. The distinction of an in-group of mindfulness practitioners from an outcome of non-practitioners may potentially also result in some form of (sub-conscious) bias such that leaders favour employees who are part of the in-group. Clearly, at this point, the above considerations are highly speculative and empirical research is needed to bring more clarity to the more indirect effects of formal mindfulness practice.

Mindfulness as resource versus mindfulness as value

Overall, much of the above discussion can be summarized by making a distinction between goals/values and resources. Our analysis suggests that mindfulness and mindfulness practice can often be viewed as leading to an increase in resources available to pursue a leader's goals and values. These resources include self-regulatory skills and capacities related to the self-regulation of attention, emotions, and behaviors, to energy, clarity, self-compassion, and mental balance. Thus, one could argue that mindfulness makes people more resourceful (ACT takes a related view differentiating mindfulness and acceptance processes, from values-infused commitment and behavioral activation processes, see e.g., Hayes 2004). This view is consistent with some empirical research. For example, Chatzisarantis and Hagger (2007) found that the more mindful someone was, the more likely this person was to implement intentions to exercise more.

However, in order to evaluate whether the effect of mindfulness in leadership is beneficial a consideration of leader values and goals is also required, and perhaps even more important than a consideration of resources. The reason is that resources are the means to achieve certain ends. Thus, a lack of resources such as mindfulness might be considered a problem only when leaders pursue wholesome goals, but might be considered at least socially desirable when leaders pursue unwholesome goals that are antisocial or selfish at the expense of others. To give a perhaps dramatic example, mindfulness may make it more likely that a sniper hits a target.

While the positive effect of mindfulness on resources seems fairly clear to us, evidence for positive effects of mindfulness on goals and values appears less clear. One possible way in which mindfulness may influence values and goals is through witnessing awareness. Specifically, by reducing ego involvement, leaders' goals and efforts oriented towards ego advancement and protection might be reduced. Similarly, Atkins and Parker (2012) have argued that mindfulness can increase prosocial values and actions by reducing defensiveness in emotionally difficult situations through the processes of self-affirmation (Sherman and Cohen 2006) and self-transcendence (Crocker, Niiya, and Mischkowski 2008). Another possible pathway may be that by developing an attitude of self-compassion and extending this attitude towards others, leaders' goals and values may shift towards accepting and helping others.

Overall, from the perspective of mindfulness as a resource one can propose that mindfulness can serve both "wholesome" and "unwholesome" goals (these and other concerns have prompted cautions about "McMindfulness"). This is perhaps different from prevailing voices that suggest only positive effects of mindfulness and mindfulness practice and do not make a distinction between mindfulness and "right mindfulness" (mindfulness within a certain ethical framework).

However, we believe that, perhaps particularly because of this contradiction, this presents an interesting area for future research.

Mindfulness and leadership styles

The leadership literature discusses a plethora of leader styles (transactional versus transformational leadership, task versus relationship oriented leadership, etc.). Rather than trying to identify linkages between mindfulness and all leadership styles, we adopt a selective approach. In particular, we consider three leadership styles – authentic, charismatic, and servant – that are widely considered in contemporary conceptualizations of leadership and that have an inherent link to mindfulness, and whose effectiveness can be regulated by mindfulness. We also take this opportunity to further clarify goal quality (wholesome versus unwholesome goals) by contrasting the dimensions of mindfulness with the different leadership styles.

Authentic leadership

One leadership style that seems closely related to mindfulness is authentic leadership. Luthans and Avolio (2003) define authentic leadership as a multi-level and multi-dimensional construct. Specifically, they view authentic leadership as a process drawing from both the personal resources of the leader (i.e., confidence, optimism, hope, and resilience) and the organizational context (i.e., an open organizational climate and trigger events or challenges), which results in greater self-awareness and self-regulated positive behaviors on the part of both leaders and followers.

Research in authentic leadership suggests that leaders' self-awareness, unbiased processing, and clarity behaviors and relational authenticity foster and strengthen exchange relationships between the leader and followers (Avolio and Gardner 2005). The findings suggest that authentic leaders have a strong influence on follower enactment of leaders' goals. For example, authentic leadership has been shown to relate positively to follower identification (Wong, Spence Laschinger, and Cummings 2010), and strengthened trust in leadership (Wong and Cummings 2009).

Given how authentic leadership has been defined, its relationship to mindfulness is straightforward. First, awareness is a key ingredient to both leading authentically and to being mindful. One difference is that awareness is considered a cause or enabler of authentic leadership in that literature, whereas in the mindfulness literature, awareness is a dimension of mindfulness. Thus, the relation between mindfulness and authentic leadership can be considered one of cause and effect.

This leads us to another important difference: whereas the literature on authentic leadership is relatively mute on how leaders can develop awareness, research on mindfulness focuses substantially on practices that increase awareness. In this sense, mindfulness practice can be considered as an avenue to develop authentic leader behavior. As we detail below, mindfulness, either as a skill, trait, or a cultivated practice, may facilitate authentic leadership.

The dimensions of present-moment attention and witnessing awareness should facilitate leader self-awareness; a leader who is paying attention to his internal states will be self-aware, providing the building blocks for clarity and self-disclosure in authentic relationships. Further, another important process by which authentic leadership influences follower outcomes is through providing developmental feedback and support for followers' self-determination. In doing so, leaders themselves have to adopt a learning goal orientation grounded in unbiased processing (Ilies, Morgeson, and Nahrgang 2005). To this end, the nonjudging aspects of mindfulness may also facilitate authentic leadership.

Interestingly, authenticity is not explicitly advocated in MBIs such as MBSR. This brings us to another potential difference between mindfulness and authentic leadership (in addition to one being the cause, the other the effect). Specifically, the literature on authentic leadership largely endorses this leadership style as desirable and exhorts leaders to be authentic. In contrast, MBIs tend to emphasize observing, witnessing, and being nonjudgmental. Thus, leaders would be encouraged to become more aware and observe their typical (and untypical) leadership behaviors in an open, non-judging way. By doing so in a patient, non-striving, and self-compassionate way, over time, insight will emerge into ways in which one's behaviors may or may not be appropriate, providing an impetus to explore and experiment with other behaviors. Notice the difference of doing so as compared to starting from the premise that leading authentically is good. In a way, leading mindfully allows for great flexibility to deploy different leader behaviors based on the needs of the specific situation (consistent with contingency approaches to leadership).

Charismatic leadership

The literature on charismatic leadership proposes that followers' attribution of charismatic qualities to a leader, as jointly determined by leaders' behavior, expertise, and dimensions of the situation, can greatly influence followers (Conger 1989; Conger and Kanungo 1998). Charismatic leadership is characterized by the leaders' appearance of being extraordinary and visionary and by followers' personal identification (Conger 1989; Shamir, House, and Arthur 1993), social identification (Conger, Kanungo, and Menon 2000) and internalization of new values and attitudes (Conger 1989). In addition, charismatic leadership is characterized by emotion contagion, charismatic leaders being perceived as having higher emotional expressiveness (Bono and Ilies 2006) and employing emotional appeals to values.

We see at least two ways in which a leader's mindfulness might be related to how charismatic that leader is perceived to be. First, the ability to be fully in the "here and now" with another person may contribute to a leader's charisma. Leaders' presence could be perceived as extraordinary. It could also lead to personal and social identification as presence allows leaders to quickly create a connection with others and as employees respond positively to the full attention given to them. Indeed, it seems that many political leaders have developed the ability to connect with and leave a positive impression on others through presence. This clearly seems to be a use of mindfulness, in the sense of present-moment attention, as a resource. Whether this resource is being put to wholesome ends, or simply used as a means to whatever ends the leader may pursue is an entirely different question.

Second, given emotional contagion is an important process of charismatic leadership, the increased ability of mindful leaders to regulate their emotions could also be used in the service of charismatic leadership. We highlighted in the previous section that one aspect of mindful practice relates to non-evaluation of inner experiences (i.e., defusion). The result is a certain level of detachment, as identification with experiences such as emotions is reduced. Thus, a deliberate use of mindful practice may allow a leader to reduce negative emotions, and maintain positive emotions. Specifically, being more mindful may allow leaders to regulate emotion, such as down-regulating negative affect and up-regulating positive affect in order to give an impression of enthusiasm and confidence that charismatic leaders are often perceived as portraying. Drawing from research in emotional labor (Bhave and Glomb, in press; Grandey, Kern, and Frone 2007), leaders can be expected to manage emotional displays to internal audiences, such as subordinates, peers, and superiors (Gardner and Avolio 1998), and to influence these audiences to follow them in pursuit of desired goals. Thus, mindfulness may help align leader emotional response with followers' expectations of a charismatic leader.

In line with our distinction between wholesome and unwholesome goals, there has also been a distinction between positive and negative charismatics within the charismatic leadership literature. On the one hand, positive charismatics focus on a socialized power orientation, with the emphasis on followership toward ideology rather than the leader. On the other hand, negative charismatics focus on a personalized power orientation, with the emphasis of followership toward themselves rather than to the guiding ideology (House and Howell 1992; Musser 1987). Thus, negative charismatics may possibly hide behind a concerted effort at regulating emotion through mindfulness, for example, masking anger at a small misstep and create impressions of magnanimity and temperance.

Overall, while we can see that certain dimensions of mindfulness may allow leaders to be perceived as more charismatic, we also see important differences. Perhaps most importantly, while mindfulness may be used in the service of charismatic leadership, most mindfulness practitioners will probably not pursue a goal of being perceived as charismatic. Relatedly, the intention of most MBIs is to help improve emotion regulation skills for the purpose of wellbeing (e.g., managing stress, reducing negative affect). Further, the witnessing awareness aspect of mindfulness may lead to lower perceptions of charisma in that a mindful leader may experience and display less intense emotions.

Servant leadership

In 1970, Greenleaf coined the term "servant leadership". His essay served as an introduction to an idea of leaders who lead by serving and fostering the development of followers, who put their own interests behind those of others, and, subsequently, gain trust and develop long-term relationships with their followers. The concept of servant leadership received great interest, as it challenged the then conventional notions of what it took to be an effective leader.

Recently, the concept of servant leadership has re-emerged and attracted wide attention from both organizational researchers and practitioners. Liden and colleagues (2008) identified eight dimensions of servant leadership: emotional healing, creating value for the community, conceptual skills, empowering, helping subordinates grow and succeed, putting subordinates first, behaving ethically, and servanthood. Essentially, servant leadership places a strong emphasis on leaders' selfless behaviors and motivation to serve others (Van Dierendonck and Nuijten 2011; Liden et al. 2008).

Based on this conceptualization, it appears that being a servant leader would require a considerable level of awareness of self, others, and of relations between self and others. For example, leaders would have to be aware of their own needs and employees' needs, as well as how they can support their employees. Such awareness should be facilitated by both state mindfulness and mindfulness practice.

Perhaps even more importantly, servant leadership requires a certain detachment and transcendence of the immediate pursuit of personal needs to prioritize those of others. While we do not believe that mindfulness and mindfulness practice necessarily lead to such an attitude, it seems that they could be very helpful for those wanting to be servant leaders. In particular, the ability to defuse and detach from self-serving thought and emotional processes as well as the insights gained from observing the consequences of one's actions without judging may be essential in learning, over time, to replace self-serving behaviors with those serving others.

On the other hand, by emphasizing the self, several aspects of mindfulness practice may be potential obstacles to developing servant leadership. These include the self-focused nature of many mindfulness practices, such as observing one's breath, the focus on compassion toward the self while practicing, as well as most broadly the fact that most participants in MBIs likely participate for self-related reasons, such as enjoying better health for themselves (rather than other-related reasons which may be more common for practitioners of, for example, LKM). Nevertheless, it could be that an attitude of other-orientation and compassion for others develops through mindfulness practice even without an explicit intention toward this effect. Clearly, research is needed to learn more about these matters.

Mindfulness and leadership development

Having selectively explored some relationships between mindfulness and leadership behaviors and styles, we now turn to an even higher level of abstraction: leadership development. One way to view leadership development is as a process of moving from one leadership style to another, more "developed" one, as in Kegan's (1982) theory of constructive development of the self, which has subsequently been applied to leadership development (e.g. Kuhnert and Lewis 1987). Thus, in this section, we suggest how mindfulness may affect the developmental process of leadership, focusing specifically on how the witnessing awareness quality of mindfulness could play an important role in facilitating constructive development.

There are many constructive development theories that have been used to explain leadership development. Examples of other well-known theories are Loevinger's stages of ego development (Loevinger, 1976) and Lawrence Kohlberg's stages of moral development (Kohlberg, 1971). However, Kegan's theory perhaps demonstrates particularly well how the witnessing awareness quality of mindfulness can help to facilitate self-awareness and subsequent leadership improvement. In addition, the theory can be applied to various important leadership styles in the management literature, such as the transactional and transformational styles of leadership.

According to Kegan's theory of constructive development people evolve through five developmental stages (impulsive, imperial, interpersonal, institutional, and inter-individual balance) as a result of life experiences, life crises, or trigger events. In each subsequent stage, individuals become able to view more and more of their experiences (thoughts, emotions, desires) as separate from their self (in the language of the theory, what was considered a subject, and part of the self, becomes an object). When this happens, individuals can think more objectively about these experiences and as a result can make more reasoned choices. The group of experiences individuals learn to treat more objectively as they progress through the five stages are: reflexes, immediate needs and feelings, personal objectives and goals, interpersonal ties and reciprocal obligations, and finally individual values and standards.

The theory of constructive development has been used as a framework to understand leadership development. For example, Kuhnert and Lewis (1987) suggested that the differences between transactional and transformational styles of leadership can be understood as differences in development stages, involving progression from the second to the fourth stage of development. Initially, transactional leaders, at the second stage of development, construct their reality around personal goals and agendas, and tend to assume that others are also driven by similar motives. At this point, leaders are incapable of perceiving their interpersonal ties and mutual obligations with their followers, and tend to evaluate their followers in terms of adherence to their personal goals and agendas.

In the third stage, leaders can now perceive personal objectives and goals as objects (i.e., distinct from the self) and thus begin to think about their objectives and goals with critical distance, coordinate their agendas with those of their followers, and make sacrifices to maintain their relationships with their followers. As leaders start to become transformational they begin to inspire their followers to consider the value of their work from other perspectives beyond external rewards such as financial compensation. In the fourth stage, interpersonal ties become objects and leaders' values and standards, from the perspective of which leaders create meaning and make decisions. At this stage, leaders espouse values of fairness, trustworthiness, and self-sacrifice to inspire their followers.

Along similar lines, Phipps (2010) argued that it is impossible for leaders to become servant leaders until at least the third stage where leaders are able to perceive individual objectives and goals as objects. During the fourth stage, while still constrained by personal values and standards, leaders are able to think critically and meaningfully about their interpersonal ties and reciprocal obligations with their followers. As leaders progress into the fifth stage, they become capable of serving others without enforcing their values and standards onto themselves and others.

From this perspective, an evolving self is thus central to leadership development and the different stages are associated with different leadership styles. There seems to be a clear connection between the theory of constructive development and mindfulness. Specifically, as described previously, an important aspect of mindfulness is witnessing awareness, or the ability to observe experiences nonjudgmentally and with detachment. Such experiences could be anything, from internal feelings, thoughts, or values, to external interactions. Thus, witnessing awareness may allow leaders to re-perceive experiences that were in the subject domain of identification as being in the object domain, where they are perceived as distinct from the self.

For instance, it could be that as leaders move to higher stages of development, they manage to bring witnessing awareness to experiences with which it is more and more difficult not to identify. Thus, for example, as leaders are able to bring witnessing awareness to their personal objectives and goals, the insights and new perspectives gained allow them to move onto the next stage, where now the challenge becomes to apply the same kind of awareness to interpersonal ties and reciprocal obligations.

Overall, it seems that by facilitating the shifting of experiences from identification ("subject") to some detachment ("object"), mindfulness, in the form of witnessing awareness, provides a way of constructive development that can allow leaders to progress through different stages of leadership styles. One interesting difference between a mindfulness-based approach and many leadership development approaches seems to be in the basis of development. Whereas in much leader development theories development is hypothesized to be caused by life experiences, crises, triggers or "leadership moments," mindfulness-based approaches emphasize regular, disciplined, formal, and informal mindfulness practices. Thus, the latter place much more emphasis on intentional activities under the control of the leader (e.g., sitting daily for a breath meditation), as compared to external events such as triggers. We feel that this is one advantage of mindfulness-based approaches and hope that future research will explore the potential of MBIs for leadership development.

Conclusions

The predictions resulting from our analyses and speculations in the preceding sections will need to be tested empirically in order to truly gain more insights into the relation between mindfulness and leadership behaviors, styles, development, and outcomes. One interesting aspect of following this path would be that this research would move away from largely looking at main effects and treating mindfulness as the sole independent variable. Instead, in many designs, mindfulness would have to be looked at as a moderating variable and interactive effects would have to be investigated. In particular, as we suggested repeatedly, mindfulness can often be considered as a (self-regulatory) resource and this resource, we argue, is likely to interact with values and goals to influence behaviors. This view is consistent with the study by Chatzisarantis and Hagger (2007) of mindfulness as moderator that facilitates the implementation of intention.

A potential challenge in such research will be to examine MBIs as moderators, as moderating variables are more commonly measured (even when independent variables are manipulated). However, while perhaps less common, we see no inherent problem with such an approach. For example, in a study leaders' goals, values, and/or intentions could be measured (or manipulated, e.g., via priming) while participants are randomly assigned to mindfulness practice and control conditions in order to examine the potential moderating role of mindfulness.

In closing, we believe that mindfulness and mindfulness practice have tremendous potential for not only understanding processes of leadership and leadership development, but also improving leadership in practice. However, our analysis suggests that to achieve that potential, mindfulness may need to be accompanied by the "right" goals and values, that is, ethical and organizationally and societally valued goals. In the presence of unwholesome goals we suggest that mindfulness may actually contribute to negative consequences. The reason, as we pointed out, is that we view several dimensions of mindfulness largely as a (self-regulatory) resource that can be directed towards wholesome or unwholesome purposes. We are hopeful that in most cases, leaders have ethical values and goals, and this mindfulness can support them in achieving these goals and as a result be a force for good.

An alternative possibility is that the development of formal and informal practice of mindfulness and the development of values, ethics, other-orientation, and compassion go hand in hand with each other. Moreover, we also suggest that the mindfulness dimensions of witnessing awareness, or defusion, or re-perceiving, hold particular promise in going beyond being a resource to changing the fundamental way in which leaders relate to themselves, others, and the external environment. As such, this aspect of mindfulness seems to have particular potential for leadership development and may deserve particular emphasis in MBIs for leadership development.

References

Ashforth, B. E. and Humphrey, R. H. (1995). Emotion in the workplace: a reappraisal. *Human Relations*, 48(2), 97–125.

Ashforth, B. E. and Mael, F. (1989). Social identity theory and the organization. *Academy of Management Review*, 14(1), 20–39.

Atkins, P. W. B. and Parker, S. K. (2012). Understanding individual compassion in organizations: the role of appraisals and psychological flexibility. *Academy of Management Review*, 37(4), 524–46.

Avolio, B. J. and Gardner, W. L. (2005). Authentic leadership development: getting to the root of positive forms of leadership. *The Leadership Quarterly*, 16(3), 315–38.

Bavelas, J. B., Coates, L., and Johnson, T. (2000). Listeners as co-narrators. *Journal of Personality and Social Psychology*, 79(6), 941.

Beal, D. J., Weiss, H. M., Barros, E., and MacDermid, S. M. (2005). An episodic process model of affective influences on performance. *Journal of Applied Psychology*, 90, 1054–68.

Bhave, D. P. and Glomb, T. M. (in press). The role of occupational emotional labor requirements on the surface acting – job satisfaction relationship. *Journal of Management*.

Bishop, S. R., Lau, M., Shapiro, S., Carlson, L., Anderson, N. D., Carmody, J. ... and Devins, G. (2004). Mindfulness: a proposed operational definition. *Clinical Psychology: Science and Practice*, 11, 230–41.

Bono, J. E. and Ilies, R. (2006). Charisma, positive emotions and mood contagion. *The Leadership Quarterly*, 17(4), 317–34.

Brief, A. P. and Weiss, H. M. (2002). Organizational behavior: affect in the workplace. *Annual Review of Psychology*, 53(1), 279–307.

Brown, K. W. and Ryan, R. M. (2003). The benefits of being present: mindfulness and its role in psychological well-being. *Journal of Personality and Social Psychology*, 84(4), 822–48.

Bruce, J. (2014). Become a mindful leader: slow down to move faster. Retrieved from www.forbes.com.

Brunswik, E. (1952). *The conceptual framework of psychology*. University of Chicago Press.

Chatzisarantis, N. L. and Hagger, M. S. (2007). Mindfulness and the intention-behavior relationship within the theory of planned behavior. *Personality and Social Psychology Bulletin*, 33(5), 663–76.

Chiesa, A. and Serretti, A. (2010). A systematic review of neurobiological and clinical features of mindfulness meditations. *Psychological Medicine: A Journal of Research in Psychiatry and the Allied Sciences*, 40, 1239–52.

Conger, J. A. (1989). *The charismatic leader: behind the mystique of exceptional leadership*. San Francisco, CA: Jossey-Bass.

Conger, J. A. and Kanungo, R. N. (1998). *Charismatic leadership in organizations*. Thousand Oaks, CA: Sage.

Conger, J. A., Kanungo, R. N., and Menon, S. T. (2000). Charismatic leadership and follower effects. *Journal of Organizational Behavior*, 21(7), 747–67.

Crocker, J., Niiya, Y., and Mischkowski, D. (2008). Why does writing about important values reduce defensiveness? Self-affirmation and the role of positive other-directed feelings. *Psychological Science*, 19, 740–7.

Dalal, R.S., Bhave, D. P., and Fiset, J. (2014). Within-person variability in job performance: an integrative review and research agenda. *Journal of Management*, 40, 1396–436.

Eberth, J. and Sedlmeier, P. (2012). The effects of mindfulness meditation: a meta-analysis. *Mindfulness*, 3(3), 174–89.

Fletcher, L. and Hayes, S. C. (2005). Relational frame theory, acceptance and commitment therapy, and a functional analytic definition of mindfulness. *Journal of Rational-Emotive and Cognitive-Behavior Therapy*, 23(4), 315–36.

Gardner, W. L. and Avolio, B. J. (1998). The charismatic relationship: a dramaturgical perspective. *Academy of Management Review*, 23(1), 32–58.

Glomb, T. M., Duffy, M. K., Bono, J. E., and Yang, T. (2011). Mindfulness at work. *Research in Personnel and Human Resources Management*, 30, 115–57.

Grandey, A. A., Diefendorff, J. M., and Rupp, D. E. (2013). Bringing emotional labor into focus: a review and integration of three research lenses. In A. A. Grandey, J. M. Diefendorff, and D. E. Rupp (eds.), *Emotional labor in the 21st century: diverse perspectives on emotion regulation at work*. New York: Psychology Press/Routledge, pp. 3–27.

Grandey, A. A., Kern, J. H., and Frone, M. R. (2007). Verbal abuse from outsiders versus insiders: comparing frequency, impact on emotional exhaustion, and the role of emotional labor. *Journal of Occupational Health Psychology*, 12(1), 63.

Greenleaf, R. K. (1970). *The leader as servant*. Indianapolis, IN: Greenleaf Center.

Hayes, S. C. (2004). Acceptance and commitment therapy and the new behavior therapies: Mindfulness, acceptance, and relationship. In S. C. Hayes, V. M. Follette, and M. M. Linehan (eds.). *Mindfulness* and acceptance: *expanding the cognitive-behavioral tradition.* New York: Guilford Press, pp. 1–29.

Hobfoll, S. E. (1989). Conservation of resources: a new attempt at conceptualizing stress. *American Psychologist*, 44(3), 513–24.

House, R. J. and Howell, J. M. (1992). Personality and charismatic leadership. *The Leadership Quarterly*, 3(2), 81–108.

Ilies, R., Morgeson, F. P., and Nahrgang, J. D. (2005). Authentic leadership and eudaemonic well-being: understanding leader–follower outcomes. *The Leadership Quarterly*, 16(3), 373–94.

Kabat-Zinn, J. (2003). Mindfulness-based interventions in context: past, present, and future. *Clinical Psychology: Science and Practice*, 10, 144–56.

Kahn, W. A. (1992). To be fully there: psychological presence at work. *Human Relations*, 45(4), 321–49.

Kegan, R. (1982). *Evolving self: problem and process in human development.* Cambridge, MA: Harvard University Press.

Keltner, D. and Haidt, J. (1999). Social functions of emotions at four levels of analysis. *Cognition and Emotion*, 13(5), 505–21.

Kim, E., Bhave, D. P., and Glomb, T. M. (2013). Emotion regulation in work groups: the role of demographic diversity and relational work context. *Personnel Psychology*, 66, 613–44.

Kohlberg, L. (1971). *From is to ought: how to commit the naturalistic fallacy and get away with it in the study of moral development.* New York: Academic Press.

Kuhnert, K. W. and Lewis, P. (1987). Transactional and transformational leadership: a constructive/developmental analysis. *Academy of Management Review*, 12(4), 648–57.

Levinthal, D. and Rerup, C. (2006). Crossing an apparent chasm: bridging mindful and less-mindful perspectives on organizational learning. *Organization Science*, 17(4), 502–13.

Liden, R. C., Wayne, S. J., Zhao, H., and Henderson, D. (2008). Servant leadership: development of a multidimensional measure and multi-level assessment. *The Leadership Quarterly*, 19(2), 161–77.

Loevinger, J. (1976). *Ego development.* San Francisco: CA: Jossey-Bass.

Luthans, F. and Avolio, B. J. (2003). Authentic leadership: a positive developmental approach. In K. S. Cameron, J. E. Dutton, and R. E. Quinn (eds.), *Positive organizational scholarship.* San Francisco, CA: Barrett-Koehler, pp. 241–61.

Maslach, C., Schaufeli, W. B., and Leiter, M. P. (2001). Job burnout. *Annual Review of Psychology*, 52(1), 397–422.

Musser, S. J. (1987). *The determination of positive and negative charismatic leadership.* Grantham, PA: Messiah College.

Phipps, K. A. (2010). Servant leadership and constructive development theory. *Journal of Leadership Education*, 9(2), 151–70.

Purser, R. and Loy, D. (2013). Beyond McMindfulness. *Huffington Post*, January. Retrieved from www.huffingtonpost.com.

Reb, J., Narayanan, J., and Chaturvedi, S. (2014). Leading mindfully: two studies on the influence of supervisor trait mindfulness on employee well-being and performance. *Mindfulness*, 5(1), 36–45.

Reb, J., Narayanan, J., and Ho, Z. W. (2015). Mindfulness at work: antecedents and consequences of employee awareness and absent-mindedness. *Mindfulness*, 6(1), 111–22.

Salzberg, S. (1995). *Loving-kindness: the revolutionary art of happiness*. Boston, MA: Shambala Publications.

Segal, Z. V., Willaims, J. M. G., and Teasdale, J. D. (2013). *Mindfulness-based cognitive therapy for depression*. New York and London: The Guilford Press.

Shamir, B., House, R. J., and Arthur, M. B. (1993). The motivational effects of charismatic leadership: a self-concept based theory. *Organization Science*, 4(4), 577–94.

Shapiro, S. L. and Carlson, L. E. (2009). *The art and science of mindfulness: integrating mindfulness into psychology and the helping professions*. Washington, DC: American Psychological Association Publications.

Sherman, D. K. and Cohen, G. L. (2006). The psychology of self-defense: self-affirmation theory. *Advances in Experimental Social Psychology*, 38, 183–242.

Tajfel, H. and Turner, J. C. (1979). An integrative theory of intergroup conflict. The social psychology of intergroup relations. In W. G. Austin and S. Worchel (eds.), *The social psychology of intergroup relations*. Monterey, CA: Brooks-Cole, pp. 33–47.

Tsui, A. S. and Ashford, S. J. (1994). Adaptive self-regulation: a process view of managerial effectiveness. *Journal of Management*, 20(1), 93–121.

Uhl-Bien, M. (2006). Relational leadership theory: exploring the social processes of leadership and organizing. *The Leadership Quarterly*, 17(6), 654–76.

Van Dierendonck, D. and Nuijten, I. (2011). The servant leadership survey: development and validation of a multidimensional measure. *Journal of Business and Psychology*, 26(3), 249–67.

Wong, C. A. and Cummings, G. G. (2009). The influence of authentic leadership behaviours on trust and work outcomes in healthcare staff. *Journal of Leadership Studies*, 3(2), 6–23.

Wong, C. A., Spence Laschinger, H. K., and Cummings, G. G. (2010). Authentic leadership and nurses' voice behaviour and perceptions of care quality. *Journal of Nursing Management*, 18(8), 889–900.

12 Mindfulness in interpersonal negotiations: delineating the concept of mindfulness and proposing a mindful, relational self-regulation (MRSR) model[1]

DEJUN TONY KONG

Introduction

People frequently negotiate with others. Employees negotiate salary with their employers, vendors negotiate supply chain contracts with suppliers, and couples negotiate vacation plans. However, many negotiators are not effective in negotiating and only achieve suboptimal outcomes. Many negotiation scholars claim that negotiation ineffectiveness is caused by negotiators' cognitive limitations and biases, which are inherent flaws of humans (Bazerman *et al.* 2000; Malhotra and Bazerman 2008; Thompson, Neale, and Sinaceur 2004). Recently, negotiation scholars have started paying attention to mindfulness (e.g., Brach 2008; Riskin 2010), claiming that mindfulness can increase negotiators' attention and awareness and thus facilitate negotiation effectiveness. Reb and Narayanan (2014), for example, provided the first empirical evidence that mindfulness facilitated negotiators' distributive performance, that is, mindfulness allowed them to achieve a larger share of the bargaining zone.

Although some view negotiations as purely economic transactions, in fact, all negotiations are relational in nature. Negotiation scholars start adopting a relational view on negotiations (Bendersky and McGinn 2010; Gelfand *et al.* 2006; McGinn 2006; McGinn and Keros 2002). According to this view, negotiation ineffectiveness is not a result of cognitive limitations and biases, but rather is caused by a deteriorating relationship between negotiators (McGinn and Keros

---

[1] I wish to thank Natalia Karelaia, Shirli Kopelman, and Jochen Reb for their comments and suggestions on this chapter.

285

2002). In order to achieve negotiation effectiveness, negotiators need to co-create the meaning of their exchange and build/maintain their relationship (McGinn 2006; McGinn and Keros 2002). However, evidence on the effect of mindfulness on relational negotiation outcomes (e.g., relational satisfaction; Curhan *et al.* 2008) is extremely sparse and there is a lack of strong theoretical models that can guide empirical investigation. Adopting a humanistic psychological perspective, Kopelman, Avi-Yonah, and Varghese (2012) provided the first such model, suggesting that mindfulness enables negotiators to approach negotiations holistically by co-creating narratives. Although it seems challenging to empirically test Kopelman *et al.*'s (2012) model, their model emphasizes the importance of relationships in the context of negotiations.

In this chapter, I will provide an alternative theoretical model – a mindful, relational self-regulation (MRSR) model. It differs from Kopelman and colleagues' model in that it treats mindfulness as a moderator for negotiators' relational self-regulation. That is, mindfulness is viewed as a factor that changes how individuals manage their relationships in negotiation settings. As mentioned earlier, mindfulness is a relatively novel concept in negotiation research and some negotiation scholars may question the value of studying it. This chapter, which delineates the nature of mindfulness and proposes an MRSR model, explains why mindfulness is important to negotiation effectiveness and provides guides to future empirical investigations on negotiator mindfulness. In doing so, this chapter also provides implications for negotiation practice.

I organize the chapter as follows. First, considering the confusion negotiation scholars may have regarding the definition of mindfulness, I briefly describe the concept of mindfulness and its distinction from four nomologically-related concepts – absorption, flow, emotional intelligence (EI), and intuition (also see other chapters of this book). Second, I propose a mindful, relational self-regulation (MRSR) model of interpersonal negotiations, delineating the moderator role that mindfulness plays in the system of negotiators' relational self-regulation. Finally, I discuss the implications of the proposed model and provide suggestions for future research on mindfulness in negotiations.

The concept of mindfulness

According to the conceptualization of Brown and Ryan (2003) and Brown, Ryan, and Creswell (2007), mindful individuals are attentive to and aware of their feelings, thoughts, and motives as well as their external environment. Yet they take in information by simply noticing without judgment. Second, mindfulness facilitates intentional and controllable behavioral regulation and goal attainment. Third, mindfulness entails stability or continuity of attention and awareness. Mindful individuals recognize their current thoughts and emotions rooted in their past experience or anticipated future. Finally, mindfulness facilitates integrated functioning given that it disengages individuals from egocentric biases in interpreting reality or impulses (Brown *et al.* 2007; Chatzisarantis and Hagger 2007).

Given that the concept of mindfulness is relatively novel in negotiation research and a plethora of concepts capture individual differences or psychological processes in self-regulation, it is important to differentiate mindfulness from nomologically related concepts such as absorption, flow, EI, and intuition. First, absorption is a state of being deeply attentive to and engrossed with a particular experience (Agarwal and Karahanna 2000; Rothbard 2001). It directs attention to the present moment like mindfulness, but unlike mindfulness, it narrows the focus of attention (Dane 2011). When individuals have high absorption, they devote all their attentional resources to fully engaging in the present experience (Tellegen and Atkinson 1974). Brown and Ryan (2003) found that mindfulness and absorption were negatively correlated ($r = -.15$).

Second, flow refers to high engagement in an optimally challenging activity (Csikszentmihalyi 1990; Nakamura and Csikszentmihalyi 2009). Individuals in a state of flow tend to have intense and focused concentration on the present experience, merge their awareness and action, experience intrinsic motivation, and have a strong sense of control, but they lose reflective self-consciousness and distort temporal experience (Dane 2011; Nakamura and Csikszentmihalyi 2009; Quinn, 2005). Unlike mindful individuals, those in a state of flow are unlikely to notice the external environment peripherally related to the activity at hand (Csikszentmihalyi 1990).

Third, EI is defined as "the capacity to reason about emotions, and of emotions to enhance thinking" (Mayer, Salovey, and Caruso 2004, p. 197; see also Mayer, Roberts, and Barsade 2008). Mindfulness is highly associated with emotion regulation (Brown and Ryan 2003; Chambers, Gullone, and Allen 2009; Schutte and Malouff 2011). However, unlike mindfulness, EI entails an implicit motivation of regulating one's own and others' emotions. Mindfulness facilitates the development of emotion regulation through awareness and attention to inner feelings and external environment, but there is no clear evidence suggesting that mindfulness is also associated with abilities to perceive emotions and use emotions for cognition.

Finally, intuition entails effortless, autonomous processing rather than effortful, controlled processing (Evans 2008; Osman 2004; Sloman 2002; Smith and DeCoster 2000). Mindfulness is not intuition because the former entails nonjudgmental, bare attention and awareness whereas the latter entails subconscious judgment or reasoning (Evans 2008; Khatri and Ng, 2000; Smith and DeCoster 2000).

Having clarified the relations between mindfulness and nomologically related constructs, I now propose an MRSR model.

An MRSR model of interpersonal negotiations

Dane (2011) argued that due to its wide external and internal attention breadth, mindfulness facilitates task performance when the task environment is dynamic. Negotiations are complex and dynamic decision-making processes; as a way to deal with the complexity and dynamism of negotiations, negotiators often engage in improvisation, defined as "the degree to which the composition and execution of an action converge in time" (Moorman and Miner 1998, p. 698). McGinn and Keros (2002) found that negotiators tend to quickly coordinate their shared logic of negotiation exchange and engage in improvisation, in the forms of trust testing, process clarification, and emotional punctuation, according to the implicit rules through their exchange. This seems consistent with Kopelman et al.'s (2012) claim regarding the role mindfulness plays in the narrative or meaning-creating process of negotiations. McGinn and Keros's (2002) findings emphasized the importance of the negotiator relationship. Mindfulness is likely to play a key role in the relational exchange aspect of negotiations. Accordingly, I focus on this key role of mindfulness and propose an MRSR model of interpersonal negotiations (see Figure 12.1).

The proposed MRSR model rests on Gelfand *et al.*'s (2006) relational negotiation theory, Brett, Northcraft, and Pinkley's (1999) interlocking self-regulation model, and Ajzen's (1991) theory of planned behavior. First, Gelfand *et al.*'s theory delineates the dynamic processes entailing relational motivation, relational cognition, relational emotions, relational (self-regulation) behaviors, and

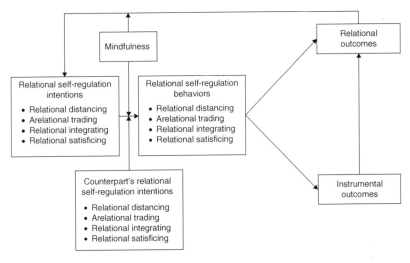

Figure 12.1 A mindful, relational self-regulation (MRSR) model of interpersonal negotiations

relational outcomes. According to their theory, different relational self-regulation behaviors determine different relational outcomes as well as instrumental outcomes (e.g., material or economic outcomes). However, their model is a static one without considering the feedback loop from relational outcomes to the determinants of relational self-regulation behaviors.

Second, Brett *et al.*'s (1999) model suggests that negotiators engage in internal self-regulation (as well as external interpersonal regulation) to reduce the detected discrepancy between their desired goals and current goal attainment progress. This model provides a dynamic view of the negotiation process, suggesting that negotiators have ongoing monitoring of their goal attainment and reduce detected discrepancy between their desired goals and the current states until the end of negotiations. Brett *et al.*'s model can be used to explain negotiators' relational self-regulation dynamics. For example, if one is dissatisfied with relational outcomes, he or she may downwardly adjust his or her intentions to build or maintain a relationship with his or her counterpart. This adjustment process is ongoing till the end of the negotiation.

Finally, Ajzen's (1991) theory of planned behavior differentiates between two important factors in self-regulatory systems: behavioral intentions and actual behaviors. Behavioral intentions, a function of attitude toward the behaviors, subjective norms, and perceived behavioral control, indicate individuals' readiness to engage in specific behaviors and are assumed to be the most proximate determinant of actual behaviors (Ajzen 2002). In addition to its main effect on behavioral intentions, perceived behavioral control was also found to strengthen the intention–behavior association (Armitage and Conner 2001).

Negotiation scholars have categorized negotiation outcomes into two forms: relational outcomes (e.g., relational satisfaction; Curhan *et al.* 2008) and instrumental outcomes (e.g., economic gains; Thompson 1990). The proposed MRSR model does not assume that negotiators have specific instrumental motives (e.g., increasing economic gains); instead, it assumes that negotiators' instrumental motives are influenced by relational self-regulation intentions. If a negotiator intends to build or maintain a relationship with his or her counterpart, he or she is likely to have a low level of self-serving instrumental motivation. Negotiators are assumed to have motivation to build or maintain a relationship with their counterpart to varying degrees and reduce the discrepancy between their desired relational goals and the current state of their relationship with their counterpart. This assumption is consistent with Baumeister and Leary's (1995) claim that the desire for interpersonal relationships is a fundamental human motivation. In the MRSR model, relational outcomes are considered the central consequences of relational self-regulation behaviors whereas instrumental outcomes are the peripheral consequences.

Four types of relational self-regulation behaviors on a continuum

Gelfand *et al.* (2006) proposed four types of relational regulation behaviors: relational distancing, arelational trading, relational integrating, and relational satisficing. These behaviors can be ordered based on the degree to which they facilitate relationship building and maintenance. Relational distancing has a negative effect on relationship building/maintenance; arelational trading has no or a modest, negative effect on relationship building/maintenance; relational integrating has a moderate, positive effect on relationship building/ maintenance; and relational satisficing has a strong, positive effect on relationship building/maintenance. For the sake of parsimony, I place these four types of relational self-regulation behaviors on a continuum, with a higher score more likely to represent relational satisficing and a lower score more likely to represent relational distancing.

First, relational distancing occurs when two negotiators have incongruent relational goals. Consequently, the negotiator who has a stronger relational goal and greater effort to cultivate the relationship feels distressed or angry, causing relational withdrawal or aggression. In either way, the negotiator relationship deteriorates and instrumental outcomes decrease (largely due to decreased value creation). Second, arelational trading occurs when both negotiators have low relational goals, that is, neither negotiator strives for a strong relationship. Instead, they deem negotiations as economic or material transactions and focus on the economic or material aspect of their interactions. Therefore, negotiators who engage in arelational trading usually have low relational outcomes and low instrumental outcomes (largely due to decreased value creation) as well. Third, relational integrating occurs when both negotiators have moderate relational goals. Although both negotiators are motivated to cultivate their relationship with one another, they do not lose sight of their instrumental outcomes. Therefore, relational integrating mixes cooperation and competition, typically leading to both high relational outcomes and high instrumental outcomes (due to increased value creation). Finally, relational satisficing occurs when both negotiators have strong relational goals. For example, couples are more likely to have stronger relational goals than strangers in negotiations, that is, couples are more likely to strive for relationship maintenance than strangers. In order to achieve their relational goals, couples are more likely to accommodate each other's needs (i.e., relational satisficing) than strangers (Fry, Firestone, and Williams 1983). Although relational satisficing brings about high relational outcomes, it usually reduces instrumental outcomes (largely due to reduced value creation).

Mindfulness as a moderator for the intention–behavior association in relational self-regulation

Negotiators' relational self-regulation intentions are likely to drive their relational self-regulation behaviors, according to the theory of planned behavior. Mindfulness is likely to moderate this intention–behavior association. Awareness helps individuals monitor their internal experiences and external factors and attention helps individuals focus their awareness on limited experiences (Chatzisarantis and Hagger 2007; Westen 1999). Chatzisarantis and Hagger argued that mindfulness can strengthen the intention–behavior association because it strengthens individuals' ability to control their cognition and emotions that are counter to ongoing intentions and reduce the rigidity of their behaviors. Mindfulness is also likely to increase perceived behavioral control (Brown *et al.* 2007). Chatzisarantis and Hagger (2007) demonstrated that mindfulness strengthened the intention–behavior association by heightening individuals' awareness and attention to situational cues and internal experiences in the contexts of physical exercises and indeed found that mindfulness acted as a moderator, strengthening the relation between intentions to exercise and actual exercise behavior. Likewise, mindfulness is likely to strengthen the intention–behavior association in relational self-regulation by heightening individuals' awareness and attention to situational cues and inner feelings about relationships as well as perceived control over their relational self-regulation.

Proposition 1: Mindfulness strengthens the association between relational self-regulation intentions and behaviors.

In addition, negotiators' own relational self-regulation intentions, their counterpart's relational self-regulation intentions, and mindfulness may have a three-way interactive effect on negotiators' own relational self-regulation behaviors. According to trust congruence theory, when one negotiator is more trusting than the other, behaviors are more likely to be self-serving than cooperative, but when negotiators trust one another at the same level, they are more likely to be cooperative than self-serving (Kong, Dirks, and Ferrin 2014; Tomlinson, Dineen, and Lewicki 2009). As relational self-regulation intentions are closely related to other relational psychological states such as trust (Gelfand *et al.* 2006), it is likely that the (in)congruence of relational self-regulation intentions between negotiators will enhance (reduce) a negotiator's relational self-regulation behaviors. In other words, negotiators' own and their counterparts' relational self-regulation intentions are likely to have a positive interactive effect on negotiators' relational self-regulation behaviors. Mindfulness may moderate this interactive effect in that mindfulness increases negotiators' attention and sensitivity to their counterparts' intentions and strengthens the joint influence of their own and the counterparts' relational self-regulation intentions on their own relational self-regulation behaviors.

Proposition 2: Mindfulness strengthens the interactive effect of negotiators' own and their counterparts' relational self-regulation intentions on negotiators' relational self-regulation behaviors.

Mindfulness as a moderator for the association between relational outcomes and relational self-regulation intentions

According to Brett *et al.*'s (1999) interlocking self-regulation model, negotiators monitor their internal experience and engage in self-regulation to reduce the internal discrepancy between their desired and current states. Relational outcomes are likely to provide feedback to individuals regarding the current state of their relationship with their counterpart. If relational outcomes are dissatisfactory, negotiators are likely to lower their motivation to build or maintain a relationship with their counterpart and thus change their relational self-regulation intentions (e.g., from relational satisficing to relational distancing). However, if relational outcomes are satisfactory, negotiators are likely to keep or even increase their relational motivation and thus maintain or increase their relational self-regulation intentions (e.g., from relational distancing to relational satisficing).

Mindfulness is likely to alter the association between relational outcomes and relational self-regulation intentions through two processes. First, the detected discrepancy between the desired relational goals and current relational outcomes can provoke negative emotions such as disappointment, distress, and anxiety. These negative emotions signal the need to increase self-control such that individuals can direct their behaviors away from undesirable situations. Therefore, in order to escape undesirable situations and repair their negative emotions (George and Zhou, 2002; Hülsheger, Alberts, Feinholdt, and Lang, 2013), negotiators are likely to decrease their relational self-regulation intentions so as to reduce their further disappointment, distress, and anxiety regarding their negative relationship with their counterpart. In contrast, the congruence between the desired relational goals and current relational outcomes generates positive emotions such as satisfaction, happiness, and gratitude, which signal the positive nature of their relationship with their counterpart and the reduced need for self-control. As negotiators are motivated to maintain their positive emotions, they are also likely to maintain their relational self-regulation intentions (cf. Isen and Simmonds 1978). Mindfulness increases positive emotions and decreases negative emotions (Brown and Ryan 2003; Chambers *et al.* 2009; Glomb *et al.* 2011; Hofmann, Sawyer, Witt, and Oh 2010; Kong 2012). Therefore, it is likely to reduce the negative emotional consequence of the detected discrepancy between the desired relational goals and current relational outcomes and maintain the positive emotional consequence of the detected congruence between the desired relational goals and current relational outcomes, thus attenuating the relationship between relational outcomes and relational self-regulation intentions.

Second, mindfulness may also change the way negotiators interpret their relational outcomes. Specifically, mindfulness disengages them from egocentric interpretations (Brown *et al.* 2007; Davidson 2010) of relational outcomes, which is particularly likely to occur when relational outcomes are unsatisfactory and egocentric biases are triggered (e.g., egocentric fairness bias; Thompson and Loewenstein 1992). For instance, when negotiators are unhappy with the quality of their relationship with their counterpart, they may perceive their counterpart as being unfair to them, even though it is not true. Mindfulness helps negotiators "step outside" their cognitive operations that may fuel egocentric interpretations of relational outcomes (Brown *et al.* 2007, p. 227), thus attenuating the association between relational outcomes and relational self-regulation intentions.

Proposition 3: Mindfulness attenuates the association between relational outcomes and relational self-regulation intentions.

The main effect of mindfulness on relational self-regulation behaviors?

Kopelman *et al.*'s (2012) model and Reb and Narayanan's (2014) research findings in the context of distributive negotiations seem to suggest that mindfulness has some major effects on negotiation behaviors and outcomes. Since mindfulness can facilitate perceived behavioral control and perceived behavioral control facilitates actual behaviors (Armitage and Conner 2001), is mindfulness likely, then, to have a positive main effect on relational self-regulation behaviors? I argue that mindfulness is more likely to play a moderator role than a (main-effect) determinant role. The nature of the negotiation context determines negotiators' relational self-regulation intentions. That is, negotiators are likely to have stronger intentions of relational self-regulation when the negotiation context is integrative or variable-sum (i.e., negotiators can create value by integrating their differences in preferences and beliefs), but weaker when the negotiation context is distributive or zero-sum.

The moderating effect of mindfulness on the intention–behavior association in relational self-regulation can also be understood from the perspective of empathy. Mindfulness promotes empathy (Brown *et al.* 2007), but empathy can moderate the effect of social motives on interpersonal cooperation or competition. According to reactive egoism theory, when situations are perceived competitive or distributive in nature, empathy actually strengthens the effect of self-serving motivation on interpersonal competition (relational distancing/aggression) (Epley, Caruso, and Bazerman 2006). Thus, in competitive/distributive negotiations, mindfulness, as a moderator, facilitates the relationship between weak intentions of relational self-regulation and a low level of relational self-regulation behaviors, thus promoting distributive behaviors and performance (Reb and Narayanan 2014), whereas in cooperative/integrative negotiations, mindfulness, as a moderator, facilitates the relationship between strong intentions of relational self-regulation and a high level of relational self-regulation behaviors, thus promoting integrative behaviors and joint performance.

Theoretical implications and suggestions for future research

Mindfulness is a new but promising concept in negotiation research. Like EI, there are different conceptualizations of mindfulness. In this chapter, I adopted Brown and Ryan's (2003) conceptualization of mindfulness (also see Brown *et al.* 2007). Although there are rumors regarding the death of EI in organizational behavior (Ashkanasy and Daus 2005), EI has been one of the most important concepts for leadership and negotiation training (Ashkanasy and Dasborough 2003; Boyatzis, Stubbs, and Taylor 2002; Walter, Cole, and Humphrey

2011). Likewise, mindfulness is a promising concept for negotiation theory and practice, despite the debate and confusion regarding its conceptualization and measurement. Although mindfulness training has not been widely included in negotiation programs in business schools, its importance has been noted by legal scholars who teach negotiation, mediation, and other forms of dispute resolution (Kuttner 2010; Riskin 2004).

In this chapter, I briefly described the concept of mindfulness by differentiating it from four nomologically related concepts – absorption, flow, EI, and intuition. Following that, I proposed an MRSR model of interpersonal negotiations. Unlike Kopelman *et al.*'s (2012) humanistic holistic model, which treats mindfulness as an input for negotiation behaviors and outcomes, I conceptualized mindfulness as a moderator that alters negotiators' relational self-regulation processes.

Theories and models developed in the 1980s and 1990s such as the dual concern model (Pruitt and Rubin 1986), social motive theory (De Dreu, Weingart, and Kwon 2000; Van Lange, De Bruin, Otten, and Joireman 1997), and behavioral decision theory (Bazerman *et al.* 2000; Malhotra and Bazerman 2008; Thompson *et al.* 2004) have dominated the negotiation literature. These theories largely conceptualize negotiations as closed systems without dynamic feedback loops and focus on a single-person view without considering the counterpart. Brett *et al.* (1999) proposed that negotiators' self-regulation is a dynamic process: negotiators monitor their inner experience and adjust it according to the perceived discrepancy between their desired and current states of goal attainment. Gelfand *et al.* (2006) shifted from a single-person view and focused on the interactive dynamics of negotiators' relational psychological states and their resultant relational self-regulation behaviors. The MRSR model proposed in this chapter, integrating Brett *et al.*'s (1999) dynamic self-regulation model, Gelfand *et al.*'s (2006) interactive view on relationships between negotiators, and Ajzen's (1991) theory of planned behavior, delineates the moderating effects of mindfulness on the association between relational self-regulation intentions and behaviors, the interactive effect of negotiators' own and counterparts' relational self-regulation intentions on their relational self-regulation behaviors, and the association between relational outcomes and relational self-regulation intentions. The model assumes that negotiators' MRSR is a dynamic and intentional process, thereby making negotiations open systems (Bendersky and McGinn 2010) in which relational self-regulation intentions, behaviors, and outcomes influence one another in a dynamic way.

Methodological issues

In order to establish a promising research program that focuses on mindfulness in negotiations, there are several methodological issues that deserve attention. Mindfulness can be treated as either a trait or a psychological state. Both dispositional and situationally triggered mindfulness should moderate negotiators' relational self-regulation as the MRSR model suggested. However, this claim requires empirical examination. If negotiation scholars operationalize mindfulness as a trait and conceptualize mindfulness as attention and awareness, I recommend that they use Brown and Ryan's (2003) mindful attention awareness scale (MAAS). This scale has been well validated and widely used for empirical research. If negotiation scholars conceptualize that mindfulness entails more than attention and awareness, they may consider Baer, Smith, Hopkins, Krietemeyer, and Toney's (2006) Five Facet Mindfulness Questionnaire (FFMQ). However, previous research has identified some psychometric problems of FFMQ. For example, the observing facet of FFMQ was unexpectedly positively correlated with absent-mindedness, thought suppression, psychopathological categories, and mental disorders, and in a hierarchical factor-analytic model, this facet did not load onto the second-order latent factor of mindfulness (Baer *et al.* 2006; Bergomi, Tschacher, and Kupper 2013).

Those who are interested in experimentally manipulating mindfulness can adopt several methods such as the raisin-eating task (Reb and Narayanan 2014), the mindful attention exercise (Reb and Narayanan 2014), and Zen music listening (Kong 2012). By using loving-kindness meditation (LKM) to direct individuals' compassion and wishes for others' wellbeing, Hutcherson, Seppala, and Gross (2008) found that LKM for just a few minutes could increase individuals' implicit and explicit positive attitudes toward strangers. As LKM generates loving and kindness and thus promotes relational self-regulation intentions, it is likely to capture the interaction of mindfulness and relational self-regulation intentions in the MRSR model rather than mindfulness alone. Mindfulness is characterized by nonattachment and nonjudgment (Brown *et al.* 2007) and strengthens the intention–behavior association due to its attention and awareness components (Chatzisarantis and Hagger 2007), whereas LKM generates the sense of interpersonal attachment (Hutcherson *et al.* 2008) as well as attention and awareness.

Additionally, although this has not yet been a trend for negotiation research for many reasons, researchers may consider employing neuro-imaging to examine mindfulness when the condition permits. This method can decidedly reduce social desirability bias, common method bias, and common source bias inherent in self-report measures. The mechanisms of mindfulness are associated with various brain areas. Attention regulation is associated with the anterior cingulated cortex; body awareness is associated with the insula, temporo-parietal junction; emotion regulation (reappraisal) is associated with the (dorsal) prefrontal cortex (PFC); emotion regulation (exposure, extinction, and reconsolidation) is associated with the ventro-medial PFC, hippocampus, and amygdala; and change in perspective on the self is associated with the medial PFC, posterior cingulated cortex, insula, and temporo-parietal junction (see Hölzel *et al.* 2011 for a review). Negotiation scholars can investigate which brain areas are activated when mindful negotiators regulate their relationship with their counterpart. The anterior cingulated cortex and the insula, temporo-parietal junction, which are associated with attention and awareness, are likely to be activated when mindful negotiators are implementing their relational self-regulation intentions. The (dorsal) PFC and ventro-medial PFC, hippocampus, amygdala, medial PFC, posterior cingulated cortex, insula, and temporo-parietal junction are likely to be activated when mindful negotiators are interpreting their relational outcomes and adjusting their relational self-regulation intentions.

Some suggested directions for future research

There are plenty of opportunities to examine the role of mindfulness in negotiations. First, the very limited empirical research has focused on distributive or competitive negotiations (Kong 2012; Reb and Narayanan 2014). Kong used a negotiation simulation with contingency contracting and uncertain payoff structures in lieu of payoff structures with certainty, creating an uncertain and anxiety-provoking negotiation environment. Therefore, mindfulness could change negotiation behaviors by reducing negotiators' anxiety. The nature of the negotiation in his study was competitive. Consistent with the model proposed in this chapter (specifically, mindfulness strengthening the association between relational self-regulation intentions and behaviors), Kong (2012) found that mindfulness induced by Zen music, in comparison to anxiety induced by a music segment from *the Rite of Spring*, facilitated negotiators' distributive behaviors and choice of making a contingency agreement to resolve disagreement and haggling. Future research should examine the moderator role of mindfulness for negotiators' relational self-regulation in highly integrative or cooperative negotiation. According to the proposed MRSR model, mindful negotiators who intend to build or maintain a relationship with their counterpart are likely to engage in relational satisficing instead of relational distancing, but this is likely to change over time when their counterpart does not share the same relational self-regulation intentions.

Second, the MRSR model proposed that mindfulness should strengthen the interactive effect of both negotiators' relational self-regulation intentions on one negotiator's relational self-regulation behaviors. Kong *et al.*'s (2014) meta-analytic evidence suggests that reciprocated trust increases cooperation and decreases competition in negotiations. As proposed in this chapter, it is likely that congruent relational self-regulation intentions increase cooperation and decrease competition in negotiations. This is an interesting research topic deserving empirical investigations in the future.

Conclusion

In this chapter, I briefly described the concept of mindfulness, proposed an MRSR model of interpersonal negotiations for future empirical investigations, and discussed the theoretical implications and directions for future research. As mindfulness is a relatively novel concept in negotiation research, it is poorly understood how it operates in negotiation settings. The proposed MRSR model is just a modest step toward a better understanding of this issue and serves as a springboard for future research.

References

Agarwal, R. and Karahanna, E. (2000). Time flies when you're having fun: cognitive absorption and beliefs about information usage. *MIS Quarterly*, 24, 665–94.

Ajzen, I. (1991). The theory of planned behavior. *Organizational Behavior and Human Decision Processes*, 50, 179–211.

(2002). Perceived behavioral control, self-efficacy, locus of control, and theory of planned behavior. *Journal of Applied Social Psychology*, 32, 665–83.

Armitage, C. J. and Conner, M. (2001). Efficacy of the theory of planned behaviour: a meta-analytic review. *British Journal of Social Psychology*, 40, 471–99.

Ashkanasy, N. M. and Dasborough, M. T. (2003). Emotional awareness and emotional intelligence in leadership teaching. *Journal of Education for Business*, 79, 18–22.

Ashkanasy, N. M. and Daus, C. S. (2005). Rumors of the death of emotional intelligence in organizational behavior are vastly exaggerated. *Journal of Organizational Behavior*, 26, 441–52.

Baer, R. A., Smith, G. T., Hopkins, T., Krietemeyer, J., and Toney, L. (2006). Using self-report assessment methods to explore facets of mindfulness. *Assessment*, 13, 27–45.

Baumeister, R. F. and Leary, M. R. (1995). The need to belong: desire for interpersonal attachments as a fundamental human motivation. *Psychological Bulletin*, 117, 497–529.

Bazerman, M. H., Curhan, J. R., Moore, D. A., and Valley, K. L. (2000). Negotiation. *Annual Review of Psychology*, 51, 279–314.

Bendersky, C. and McGinn, K. L. (2010). Open to negotiation: phenomenological assumptions and knowledge dissemination. *Organization Science*, 21, 781–97.

Bergomi, C., Tschacher, W., and Kupper, Z. (2013). The assessment of mindfulness with self-report measures: existing scales and open issues. *Mindfulness*, 4, 191–202.

Boyatzis, R. E., Stubbs, E. C., and Taylor, S. N. (2002). Learning cognitive and emotional intelligence competencies through Graduate Management Education. *Academy of Management Learning and Education*, 1, 150–62.

Brach, D. (2008). A logic for the magic of mindful negotiation. *Negotiation Journal*, 24, 25–44.

Brett, J. F., Northcraft, G. B., and Pinkley, R. L. (1999). Stairways to heaven: an interlocking self-regulation model of negotiation. *Academy of Management Review*, 24, 435–51.

Brown, K. W. and Ryan, R. (2003). The benefits of being present: mindfulness and its role in psychological well being. *Journal of Personality and Social Psychology*, 84, 822–48.

Brown, K. W., Ryan, R. M., and Creswell, J. D. (2007). Mindfulness: theoretical foundations and evidence for its salutary effects. *Psychological Inquiry*, 18, 211–37.

Chambers, R., Gullone, E., and Allen, N. B. (2009). Mindful emotion regulation: an integrative review. *Clinical Psychology Review*, 29, 560–72.

Chatzisarantis, N. L. D. and Hagger, M. S. (2007). Mindfulness and the intention-behavior relationship within the theory of planned behavior. *Personality and Social Psychology Bulletin*, 33, 663–76.

Csikszentmihalyi, M. (1990). *Flow: the psychology of optimal experience.* New York: Harper and Row.

Curhan, J. R., Neale, M. A., Ross, L., and Rosencranz-Engelmann, J. (2008). Relational accommodation in negotiation: effects of egalitarianism and gender on economic efficiency and relational capital. *Organizational Behavior and Human Decision Processes*, 107, 192–205.

Dane, E. (2011). Paying attention to mindfulness and its effects on task performance in the workplace. *Journal of Management*, 37, 997–1018.

Davidson, R. J. (2010). Empirical explorations of mindfulness: conceptual and methodological conundrums. *Emotion*, 10, 8–11.

De Dreu, C. K. W., Weingart, L. R., and Kwon, S. (2000). Influence of social motives on integrative negotiation: a meta-analytic review and test of two theories. *Journal of Personality and Social Psychology*, 78, 889–905.

Epley, N., Caruso, E. M., and Bazerman, M. H. (2006). When perspective taking increases taking: reactive egoism in social interaction. *Journal of Personality and Social Psychology*, 91, 872–89.

Evans, J. S. B. T. (2008). Dual-processing accounts of reasoning, judgment, and social cognition. *Annual Review of Psychology*, 59, 255–78.

Fry, W. R., Firestone, I. J., and Williams, D. L. (1983). Negotiation process and outcome of stranger dyads and dating couples: do lovers lose? *Basic and Applied Social Psychology*, 4, 1–16.

Gelfand, M. J., Major, V. S., Raver, J. L., Nishii, L. H., and O'Brien, K. (2006). Negotiating relationally: the dynamics of the relational self in negotiations. *Academy of Management Review*, 31, 427–51.

George, J. M. and Zhou, J. (2002). Understanding when bad moods foster creativity and good ones don't: the role of context and clarity of feelings. *Journal of Applied Psychology*, 87, 687–97.

Glomb, T. M., Duffy, M. K., Bono, J. E., and Yang, T. (2011). Mindfulness at work. *Research in Personnel and Human Resources Management*, 30, 115–57.

Hofmann, S. G., Sawyer, A. T., Witt, A. A., and Oh, D. (2010). The effect of mindfulness-based therapy on anxiety and depression: a meta-analytic review. *Journal of Counseling and Clinical Psychology*, 78, 169–83.

Hölzel, B. K., Lazar, S. W., Gard, T., Schuman-Olivier, Z., Vago, D. R., and Ott, U. (2011). How does mindfulness meditation work? Proposing mechanisms of action from a conceptual and neural perspective. *Perspectives on Psychological Science*, 6, 537–59.

Hülsheger, U. R., Alberts, H. J. E. M., Feinholdt, A., and Lang, J. W. B. (2013). Benefits of mindfulness at work: the role of mindfulness in emotion regulation, emotional exhaustion, and job satisfaction. *Journal of Applied Psychology*, 98, 310–25.

Hutcherson, C. A., Seppala, E. M., and Gross, J. J. (2008). Loving-kindness meditation increases social connectedness. *Emotion*, 8, 720–4.

Isen, A. M. and Simmonds, S. (1978). The effect of feeling good on a helping task that is incompatible with good mood. *Social Psychology Quarterly*, 41, 345–9.

Khatri, N. and Ng, H. A. (2000). The role of intuition in strategic decision making. *Human Relations*, 53, 57–86.

Kong, D. (2012). Negotiation, emotions, and contingent contracting decisions. Ph.D. Dissertation, Olin Business School, Washington University in St. Louis.

Kong, D. T., Dirks, K. T., and Ferrin, D. L. (2014). Interpersonal trust within negotiations: meta-analytic evidence, critical contingencies, and directions for future research. *Academy of Management Journal*, 57, 1235–55.

Kopelman, S., Avi-Yonah, O., and Varghese, A. K. (2012). The mindful negotiator: Strategic emotion management and well-being. In K. S. Cameron and G. M. Spreitzer (eds.), *The Oxford handbook of positive organizational scholarship*. New York: Oxford University Press, pp. 591–600.

Kuttner, R. (2010). From adversity to relationality: a Buddhist-oriented relational view of integrative negotiation and mediation. *Ohio State Journal of Dispute Resolution*, 25, 931–74.

Malhotra, D. and Bazerman, M. H. (2008). Psychological influence in negotiation: an introduction long overdue. *Journal of Management*, 34, 509–31.

Mayer, J. D., Roberts, R. D., and Barsade, S. G. (2008). Human abilities: emotional intelligence. *Annual Review of Psychology*, 59, 507–36.

Mayer, J. D., Salovey, P., and Caruso, D. R. (2004). Emotional intelligence: theory, findings, and implications. *Psychological Inquiry*, 15, 197–215.

McGinn, K. (2006). Relationships and negotiations in context. In L. Thompson (ed.), *Negotiation theory and research*. Madison, CT: Psychological Press, pp. 129–33.

McGinn, K. L. and Keros, A. T. (2002). Improvisation and the logic of exchange in socially embedded transactions. *Administrative Science Quarterly*, 47, 442–73.

Moorman, C. and Miner, A. S. (1998). Organizational improvisation and organizational memory. *Academy of Management Review*, 23, 698–723.

Nakamura, J. and Csikszentmihalyi, M. (2009). Flow theory and research. In C. R. Snyder and S. J. Lopez (eds.), *Oxford handbook of positive psychology.* 2nd edn. Oxford University Press, pp. 195–206.

Osman, M. (2004). An evaluation of dual-process theories of reasoning. *Psychonomic Bulletin and Review*, 11, 988–1010.

Pruitt, D. G. and Rubin, J. Z. (1986). *Social conflict: escalation, stalemate, and settlement.* New York: Random House.

Quinn, R. W. (2005). Flow in knowledge work: high performance experience in the design of national security technology. *Administrative Science Quarterly*, 50, 610–41.

Reb, J. and Narayanan, J. (2014). The influence of mindful attention on value claiming in distributive negotiations: evidence from four laboratory experiments. *Mindfulness*, 5(6), 756–66.

Riskin, L. L. (2004). Mindfulness: foundational training for dispute resolution. *Journal of Legal Education*, 54, 79–90.

Riskin, L. L. (2010). Annual Saltman Lecture. Further beyond reason: emotions, the core concerns, and mindfulness in negotiation. *Nevada Law Journal*, 10, 289–337.

Rothbard, N. P. (2001). Enriching or depleting: the dynamics of engagement in work and family roles. *Administrative Science Quarterly*, 46, 655–84.

Schutte, N. S. and Malouff, J. M. (2011). Emotional intelligence mediates the relationship between mindfulness and subjective well-being. *Personality and Individual Differences*, 50, 1116–19.

Sloman, S. A. (2002). Two systems of reasoning. In T. Gilovich, D. Griffin, and D. Kahnaman (eds.), *Heuristics and biases: the psychology of intuitive judgment.* Cambridge University Press, pp. 379–98.

Smith, E. R. and DeCoster, J. (2000). Dual-process models in social and cognitive psychology: conceptual integration and links to underlying memory systems. *Personality and Social Psychology Review*, 4, 108–31.

Tellegen, A. and Atkinson, G. (1974). Openness to absorbing and self-altering experiences ("absorption"), a trait related to hypnotic susceptibility. *Journal of Abnormal Psychology*, 83, 268–77.

Thompson, L. (1990). Negotiation behavior and outcomes: empirical evidence and theoretical issues. *Psychological Bulletin*, 108, 515–32.

Thompson, L. and Loewenstein, G. (1992). Egocentric interpretations of fairness and interpersonal conflict. *Organizational Behavior and Human Decision Processes*, 51, 176–97.

Thompson, L., Neale, M., and Sinaceur, M. (2004). The evolution of cognition and biases in negotiation research: an examination of cognition, social perception, motivation, and emotion. In M. J. Gelfand and J. M.

Brett (eds.), *The handbook of negotiation and culture*. San Francisco, CA: Stanford University Press, pp.7–44.

Tomlinson, E. C., Dineen, B. R., and Lewicki, R. J. (2009). Trust congruence among integrative negotiators as a predictor of joint-behavioral outcomes. *International Journal of Conflict Management*, 20, 173–87.

Van Lange, P. A. M., De Bruin, E. M. N., Otten, W., and Joireman, J. A. (1997). Development of prosocial, individualistic, and competitive orientations: theory and preliminary evidence. *Journal of Personality and Social Psychology*, 73, 733–46.

Walter, F., Cole, M. S., and Humphrey, R. H. (2011). Emotional intelligence: sine qua non of leadership or folderol? *Academy of Management Perspectives*, 25, 45–59.

Westen, D. (1999). *Psychology: mind, brain, and culture*. 2nd edn.. New York: John Wiley.

13 Drawing the line: sketching out the role of visual templates in individual mindfulness and mindful organizing

CHRISTIAN GÄRTNER AND
CHRISTIAN HUBER

Introduction

During the last decade, a recommendation for organizations that operate in fast-moving and constantly changing (business) environments
has become popular: 'Good management of the unexpected is *mindful
management*' (Weick and Sutcliffe 2007, p. 17). In exploring the role
of mindfulness in organizations and management, research has studied both individual (e.g., Dane 2011) and collective mindfulness (e.g.,
Ray, Baker, and Plowman 2011). Further, most research has focused
on the beneficial outcomes of individual or collective mindfulness
(e.g., Weick, Sutcliffe, and Obstfeld 1999). In the present chapter we
aim to both shed some light on the linkages between mindfulness at
the individual and collective levels as well as examine mindfulness as
a mediating process.

Vogus and Sutcliffe (2012) note a difference between 'mindful organizing' and 'mindful organization': the latter is characterized by enduring organizational features while the former is about the more fluid
and fragile bottom-up processes of organizing. Building on this distinction, we argue that a focus on organizational members' practices
to re-accomplish mindfulness – the bottom-up processes – is crucial
in understanding the mechanisms that link individual and collective
forms of mindfulness (Gärtner 2011; Vogus and Sutcliffe 2012).

Moreover, we argue that exploring the role of tools is crucial for
improving our understanding of this linkage. Tools are 'mediating
artefacts' (Miettinen and Virkkunen 2005) that organizational members draw upon while engaging in processes of organizing. Tools are
artefacts (i.e. human-made non-human objects) that bridge time,
space, and people. They enable individual actors as well as collectives

to draw upon them more or less regularly. Nevertheless, tools are more fluid than structural properties. In order to explore the role of tools in inducing or inhibiting mindfulness, we draw on visual templates as a specific kind of tool. We focus on visual templates because they have been identified as important tools for organizing within contemporary organizations (Meyer *et al.* 2013).

The main contribution of this chapter is thus to outline the connection between mindfulness and tools: by the example of visual templates, we discuss the impact of tools on mindfulness along the distinction proposed by the literature, i.e. we 'draw a line' between individual mindfulness and collective processes of mindful organizing. Thereby, we do not only focus on outcomes but also explain how tools can induce or inhibit individual mindfulness and mindful organizing. Finally, we also contribute to the growing body of literature that explores the role of visualizations in organizations.

The remainder of this chapter is structured as follows. The next section presents a brief review of different conceptualizations of mindfulness. Here, we outline the necessary background information that we will draw upon in our analysis of the role of visualizations as the antecedent of mindfulness. We start by discussing the cognitive approach to mindfulness as propagated by Langer. This is followed by a discussion of mindful organizing, which builds on Langer's insights. Afterwards, we summarize some key themes and open questions. We define visual templates as gestalt-like graphical elements and discuss their impact along the distinction proposed in our literature review, i.e. we 'draw a line' between the individual level and mindful organizing. We conclude the chapter by outlining possibilities for future research.

Outlining the concepts of mindfulness and mindful organizing

Mindfulness has become an important concept in organization studies. However, together with its popularity, the number of different conceptualizations has risen and made mindfulness a quite heterogeneous and elusive construct. In order to provide a basis for our discussion of the role of tools, we will first outline the main characteristics that define mindfulness and then review the different views on mindfulness in the context of work and organization studies.

Defining mindfulness

The roots of mindfulness lie within Eastern philosophy and Buddhism, but the concept has been further elaborated in medicine, medical psychology, and social psychology. Most of the other chapters of this volume draw on Kabat-Zinn's (1990) approach to mindfulness. In contrast, we focus on the concept of mindfulness as being about the way people interpret external and internal stimuli and react with a focus on drawing new distinctions (Langer 1989).[1] Langer's (1989) psychological perspective argues that mindfulness includes the active refinement of existing categories, openness to new information created out of the continuous streams of events, and a more nuanced appreciation of contexts by applying more than one perspective. More recently, she summarized it concisely: mindfulness is 'the process of drawing novel distinctions' (Langer and Moldoveanu 2000, p. 1).

The notion of mindfulness was introduced to organization studies by Sims and Gioia (1986), who contrasted automatic and non-automatic information processing. In a similar vein, Louis and Sutton (1991) offered the metaphor of 'switching cognitive gears', i.e., changing from routine-based to attentive thinking and action. Mindfulness became more popular in organizational scholarship when Weick and colleagues introduced it to the context of high-reliability organizations, i.e., organizations that must ensure near-error free operations in order to prevent catastrophes and to survive (Weick *et al.* 1999; Weick and Sutcliffe 2006; 2007). Adopting Langer's definition, they describe mindfulness as the 'capability to induce a rich awareness of discriminatory detail and a capacity for action' (Weick *et al.* 1999, p. 88). In contrast, mindlessness is characterized by fewer cognitive processes, acting on 'automatic pilot', precluding attention to new information, relying on past categories, and fixating on a single perspective (Langer 1989; Weick *et al.* 1999).

Although this brief introduction might create the impression that there is a common basis for understanding mindfulness, there are many other approaches to mindfulness (for extensive reviews see Brown, Ryan, and Creswell 2007; Sternberg 2000). If we focus on

[1] We focus on Langer's account because notable organization scholars – in particular Weick and colleagues – draw on her work. An exception is the paper by Weick and Putnam (2006) where they refer to Eastern philosophy and Buddhist thinking.

Table 13.1 Notions of *mindfulness*

	Medicine and clinical psychology	(Social) psychology/Langer tradition	Workplace mindfulness	Mindful organizing
Ontological level	individual	individual	individual	collective processes
Occasion	everyday life, in particular stress situations, e.g. in clinical settings	everyday life	(dynamic) workplace settings	unexpected events, anomalies, constant change
Functional mode	■ meta-awareness skill: sustained attention and awareness of internal stimuli (thoughts, emotions) in which sensations are acknowledged without elaborative processing ■ informs explicit knowledge, tacit know-how and values	■ creative cognitive process: construction of new categories while attending to external stimuli (opposite of 'being on automatic pilot') ■ elaborative processing by reframing cognitive structures to more accurately reflect reality	■ cognitive style or skill (seldom: trait) that allows decoupling interpretations from automatic mental processes and observe as well as possibly change them	■ *early studies*: treating experience with ambivalence, simultaneity of knowing and doubting ■ *recently*: cognitive style or knowledge context of sensemaking, i.e. for the construction of new categories and meanings
Characteristics, qualities	curiosity, openness, and acceptance, non-judgmental	■ continuous creation of new categories ■ open to surprise and new information (sensitive to context) ■ awareness of more than one perspective	■ maintaining wide breadth of attention ■ scrutiny and continuous refinement of existing expectations and judgments ■ appreciation of context	■ reluctance to simplify interpretations ■ sensitivity to operations ■ commitment to resilience ■ deference to expertise ■ preoccupation with failure

Outcomes	■ reduction in the use of repressive coping style ■ recognize bias and increase in dispositional openness to new experiences ■ emotional distress is experienced as less unpleasant and threatening	■ increase in openness to new experiences and flexibility ■ increase in creativity ■ increased wellbeing	■ improved coping with stress and affect regulation ■ increased wellbeing, less frustration ■ faster recovery from negative events ■ less biased decision making ■ increase in task performance	■ refined and vast repertoire of situational discriminators ■ enriched action repertoire ■ improved safety, organizational resilience and foresight ■ nearly error-free performance (high-reliability organizations)
Means to achieve mindfulness	■ meditation (focus on inner experiences e.g. thoughts, emotions) ■ observation ■ mentor–learner relationships ■ discussion of critical incidents	■ seminars and training courses with exercises on thinking patterns, categorization processes, learning styles, etc. ■ interventions are based on active and goal-oriented cognitive tasks	■ experience and practising (on-the-job training) ■ seminars and training courses ■ selection and incentivizing of mindful organizational members	■ check-lists for small wins (e.g. STICC briefing protocol) ■ HR policies ■ development of organization culture (trust, honesty and mutual respect)

the most crucial differences, we see four major streams in the literature that vary with regard to the ontological level (where mindfulness takes place), occasion (when mindfulness takes place), functional
mode (how mindfulness takes place), characteristics (what the qualities of mindfulness are), outcomes (what mindfulness brings about),
and means (how mindfulness can be achieved). In order to provide a
clear structure, we will organize the discussion around the ontological
level while providing an overview of the different characteristics of
each notion in Table 13.1. Due to space limitations, we cannot discuss
every feature in detail, thus while we describe the difference between
individual mindfulness and mindful organizing the table provides an
overview of the complexities of different notions of mindfulness.

Individual mindfulness

The accounts that locate mindfulness on the individual level dominate
philosophy, in particular Buddhist thought, and medicine, as well as
clinical and social psychology. Mindfulness is here defined as a state of
consciousness in which people focus attention on what is happening
here and now while adjusting the focus and content of awareness in
order to accurately reflect on reality (Kabat-Zinn 1990). Medical and
clinical psychological studies show that training techniques improve
the capacity to create more mindful states and have positive effects
(Baer 2003). For example, meditation practices or mindfulness-based
stress reduction (Kabat-Zinn 1990) yield positive outcomes such as a
reduction of stress, frustration, anxiety, and depression, while interpersonal relationship quality is improved, because mindful people show
less resistance, defensive or aggressive behaviour (Brown and Ryan
2003; Epstein 1999).

Since these outcomes are relevant to work in organizations, management and organization scholars have become increasingly interested
in mindfulness. Recently, this stream has been labelled 'workplace
mindfulness' (Dane and Brummel, 2014; see also Glomb *et al.* 2011).
This view also adheres to the individual perspective that defines
mindfulness as a cognitive state. The functional mode of mindfulness means that mindful people are able to decouple their interpretations from automatic mental processes, such as habits or intuitions
that are often biased or inaccurate, observe and possibly change them
(Dane 2011; Rerup 2005). In other words, mindfulness enables the

context-sensitive refinement of existing expectations and judgments (Dane 2011).

Cognitive accounts of mindfulness are often interested in the way agents cope with new and ill-defined situations because this is vital for work in modern organizations. Mindful people do not fall back into old habits when facing changes and are not constrained by already known concepts, but are flexible when it comes to interpreting and coping with changed situations (Langer 1997). It has been argued that mindful people are more likely to enact new ways of behaviour, reduce commitment to previous decisions and action patterns and react in a more composed way to breakdowns and (unexpected) changes (Glomb *et al.* 2011).

In addition to this focus on cognitive mechanisms and outcomes of mindfulness, organizational scholars have also stressed that workplace mindfulness promotes processes of physiological and emotional regulation (Hülsheger *et al.* 2013). Related research has been conducted in the field of positive organizational scholarship. These studies find that becoming more mindful of one's thoughts and emotional response patterns is a potential source for altering them and choosing more efficacious, optimistic, and resilient ways of dealing with change (e.g. Avey, Wernsing, and Luthans 2008; Gärtner 2013). In particular, research interest in the impact of mindfulness on (psychological and physical) wellbeing is increasing (Reb, Narayanan, and Chaturvedi 2014; for a review see Hülsheger *et al.* 2013).

Besides these commonalities, the various accounts differ with regard to their emphasis on judgment/non-judgmental awareness and the importance they put on cognitive processes of drawing novel distinction. Accordingly, the perspectives also vary in the means they suggest to achieve mindfulness. Whereas medical and philosophical accounts focus on meditation-based practices, (social) psychological approaches suggest interventions that are based on active and goal-oriented cognitive tasks and training programmes. For example, Langer (1997) describes exercises on thinking patterns (outcome focused versus process focused), categorization processes and communication styles. In one of the exercises, participants are encouraged to reflect on the extent to which they use a language of contingencies and possibilities. Langer (1997) recommends using the subjunctive mode and context-related statements instead of the indicative mode because the former encourages considering different perspectives and thereby fosters mindfulness.

In organization and workplace studies about mindfulness, we can see an amalgam of suggestions that are known from medical and psychological approaches: meditation practices and training that build on programmes such as mindfulness-based stress reduction (Sadler-Smith and Shefy 2007), but also seminars and interventions whose effectiveness is hardly backed by scientific evaluation (see Glomb *et al.* 2011). Beyond that, there are only rather unspecific recommendations to select, train and incentivize mindful employees (Dane and Brummel 2014).

Mindful organizing

There is no single characterization of mindful organizing. However, the most popular one is the seminal paper of Weick and colleagues on how mindfulness underpins the operating processes of high reliability organizations. Weick and colleagues (1999) adopt Langer's definition of mindfulness. However, they describe mindfulness as a collective capacity – instead of an individual's state of consciousness or cognitive style – that is constituted by specific processes of organizing. Since Weick's ontology has been and still is that organizational phenomena emerge out of interactions and alongside processes, mindful organizing as a collective capability comprises five processes: (1) preoccupation with failure, (2) reluctance to simplify interpretations, (3) sensitivity to operations, (4) commitment to resilience, and (5) underspecification of structures[2] (Weick *et al.* 1999). The line of argument that connects these five processes is the following: preoccupation with failure (1) means that weak and mixed signals or deviations from what is routinely expected can be noticed before they amplify to serious errors or catastrophes. In order to address such unexpected changes or an uncertain course of events it is necessary that their distinctiveness and current details have to be retained rather than lost in a few taken-for-granted categories (2). If people want to notice such nuances they must remain aware of and establish an integrated 'big picture' of the interrelated work in organizations (3). In addition, they must be

---

[2] In later versions 'underspecification of structure' has been replaced by 'deference to expertise' (Weick and Sutcliffe 2006; 2007). We can only speculate why this was done but probably because the original term reminded readers of structural features such as the allocation of roles and responsibilities which counteracted the idea of focusing on processes.

able to see how ongoing events may unfold and be able to locate pathways to recovery (4). Eventually, organizing for mindfulness means allowing decision-making authority to migrate along with problems (5), i.e. problems and decisions 'circle' in an organization in search of a person who has the sought expertise (Weick *et al.* 1999).

It is argued that the main outcomes of mindful organizing relate to the enhancement of an organization's reliability and resilience in the face of uncertainty by enriching its action repertoire (Weick *et al.* 1999). The quality and scope of the action repertoire is related to the quality of concepts, such that better concepts sweep in more interconnected details so that people know more fully what is happening (Weick and Putnam 2006). Collectives that have established the processes of mindful organizing are able to continuously scrutinize and refine expectations based on newer experiences and can draw on a more nuanced appreciation of context as well as ways to deal with it (Weick and Sutcliffe 2007). Due to this capacity of introducing new concepts to existing ones, mindful organizing is like constantly 'putting some new wine into old bottles' (Gärtner 2011). There is a growing body of research that theorizes about other benefits of mindful organizing. In particular, the five principles stabilize organizational attention and allow a focusing on discriminatory details that otherwise get lumped into categories (Weick and Sutcliffe 2006), improve an organization's ability to cope with complexity (Eisenberg 2006) and engage in a flexible range of behaviours (Levinthal and Rerup 2006), disrupt bandwagons (e.g., adopting management fads; Fiol and O'Connor 2003), improve innovation (Vogus and Welbourne 2003[3]), and reduce the likelihood and severity of organizational accidents (Weick *et al.* 1999). Put briefly, mindful collectives – just like mindful individuals – are able to spot unexpected changes in the making, counteract pitfalls that are built into expectations and remain focused on a bundle of tasks even in the face of breakdowns or changes (Weick and Sutcliffe 2006; 2007).

The means to achieve mindful organizing are, first of all, to implement the five processes. In order to support their continuous enactment, some scholars have analysed antecedents and facilitating (or inhibiting) structures. It is then argued that specific structures or policies

---

[3] Vogus and Welbourne's study is the only one with quantitative empirical data. The other studies rely on case illustrations, anecdotal evidence, or theorizing.

on a supra-individual level ensure that individuals act and think in a more mindful way . For example, Vogus and Welbourne (2003) have examined how certain HR policies impact the establishment of the five processes of mindful organizing.[4] They argue that the use of skilled temporary employees creates divergent ideas and a reluctance to simplify interpretations, that positive employee relations create a climate that facilitates intensive ongoing communication and sensitivity to operations, and that an emphasis on training advances recovery skills and resilience. Other scholars find that information technology can promote mindfulness by engaging organizations in more extensive search processes and by fuelling organizational innovations with a repertoire of routines (Butler and Gray 2006, Valorinta 2009). In addition to these structural antecedents, Weick and colleagues emphasize the importance of a culture that favours trust, honesty, and mutual respect for establishing mindful organizing (Vogus, Sutcliffe, and Weick 2010; Weick and Roberts 1993; Weick and Sutcliffe 2007).

While there is considerable research about long-term and supra-individual mechanisms such as policies, structures, and cultures, organizational scholars have only described a few concrete methods that employees can draw upon for facilitating mindful organizing. So far, the majority of available methods aim at auditing how well an organization has already implemented the five principles. For example, a nine-item-questionnaire is presented that assesses how strong a firm's mindful organizing practices are (Weick and Sutcliffe 2007, p. 103). A more elaborate survey with validated items for measuring the five processes of mindful organizing is presented by Vogus and Sutcliffe (2007). In addition to these questionnaires for assessing the status quo, Weick and Sutcliffe (2007, p. 156) suggest a method for structuring meetings called STICC, which is used by the US Forest Service to give direction to firefighters. STICC is an acronym for situation, task, intent, concern, calibrate. They argue that the major benefit of this briefing protocol is that it asks people to watch out for small events, failures, anomalies or anything else that would change the situation and require recalibration. Arguably, this method does not only prepare firefighters to

---

[4] Actually, Vogus and Welbourne (2003) are referring to HR 'practices' not 'policies'. However, in order to clearly differentiate that they are not dealing with what is actually done, but with what is *supposed* to be done because of prescribed rules, we use the term policies.

sense an unexpected course of events but also prevents communication failures in healthcare contexts and ambiguous organizational settings in general (Weick 2002).

The role of tools: a research desideratum

Prior empirical research on mindful organizing has focused on groups at one hierarchical level rather than on organizations as a whole (Vogus and Sutcliffe 2012). This raises the question of what the specifics of 'organization/organizing' are. Following Weick's philosophy, there is no point in focusing on nouns (organization); the social and organized world is constituted by processes of organizing, thus we should focus on verbs (see Weick 2001). We acknowledge and build on this view. However, we argue that some processes of organizing show characteristics that most other 'social' processes (e.g., dancing, having dinner with the family) do not display. In fact, the implications drawn from Weick's writings direct scholars to a form of ad hoc structuring in face-to-face situations rather than thinking about the role of organizational features such as rules, tools, or IT-based procedures that structure what people should do. The only truly enduring phenomenon that is studied and for which recommendations have been provided is culture.

Although the discussion of the processes of organizing, HR policies, or culture is valuable from a high-level perspective, it hardly sheds light on how mindful organizing is facilitated (or inhibited) in the daily practice of what organizational members really do. Culture, goal, or incentive systems and managerial role models are somewhat distant and their impact on the ongoing organizational practices is mediated by several factors (e.g. task structure/complexity, time pressure, standard operating procedures, or guidelines). In a similar vein, Vogus and Sutcliffe (2012, pp. 730, 733) have stressed that scholars need to explore the role of routines, guidelines, tools and templates if they want to understand mindful organizing. We address this research desideratum by enquiring into the impact of visual templates on mindfulness and mindful organizing.

Visualizations and mindful organizing

In this section we discuss the impact of visual templates on mindfulness and mindful organizing in order to add to the scarce literature scrutinizing the role of mediating artefacts for inducing and/or inhibiting mindfulness. We focus on visual templates and visualizations because they have been identified as important tools for organizing within contemporary organizations (Meyer *et al.* 2013). Although previous research has stressed their relevance for managing risks (e.g. Eppler and Aeschimann, 2009; Jordan, Jørgensen, and Mitterhofer, 2013) and coping with complexity (e.g., Lurie and Mason 2007; Yates 1985), uncertainty and (strategic) change (Eppler and Platts 2009; Ewenstein and Whyte 2009), they have not yet been linked to mindfulness. We argue that visual templates affect both individual and collective forms of mindfulness. Consequently, the rest of this section starts by outlining our understanding of visual templates. We then proceed to discuss how these visual templates induce or inhibit individual mindfulness and mindful organizing.

Outlining the functions of visual templates

Visualizations have a long tradition as aids for management. In the early twentieth century, DuPont used graphs for achieving mainly two goals: analysis and communication (Yates 1985). Since then, visualizations have become institutionalized in several forms and presentation technologies of which PowerPoint is only the most well-known medium. The use of PowerPoint and visual templates has been conceived as one of the most popular organizational genres, i.e., socially recognized types of communicative actions that over time become organizing structures through being routinely enacted by organizational members to realize particular social purposes in recurrent situations (Yates and Orlikowski 2007).

We conceive of visual templates as gestalt-like graphical elements that are either digitally available (e.g., via PowerPoint slide decks) or printed in field manuals and books. In fact, visualizations come in many forms, ranging from mandalas to safety posters and messages (at construction sites) or emergency maps. In the following, for the sake of brevity, we focus mainly on visual templates. In principle, however, a vast array of visualizations can be scrutinized for their influence on mindfulness. Visual templates are often composed of simple elements such as lines, arrows, dots, squares, bars and circles that are arranged to form a gestalt, for example a portfolio, roadmap, phased timeline, cause-and-effect or influence diagram. Although the range of subjects and business issues that visual templates represent or aim to solve is quite broad, Yates and Orlikowski (2007) have observed that different companies use the same or at least very similar visual templates. Amongst the most popular ones are Gantt charts, portfolios, process maps or roadmaps, and cause-and-effect diagrams (Eppler and Pfister 2012; Sibbet 2013). In particular, knowledge-intensive organizations (e.g. consultancies, or law or accounting firms) produce such templates on PowerPoint slides and hand them out to new employees on their first day in the company.

In everyday life, visual information is used to interpret experience and build understanding. Visualizations operate in a rather immediate and vivid mode, using 'the power of the visual' (Meyer *et al.* 2013, p. 499) to shape sensemaking processes on a pre-reflective level. Building on this feature of visualizations, we argue that visual templates afford[5] certain cognition and action because they shape what agents think when they see them and act upon the meaning they perceive in them. Tversky (2005) has summarized some empirical evidence about what visuals afford: charts with bars or stacks afford containing entities (because we are used to seeing something within the bar or the stack); groups of graphical elements (squares, circles, etc.) prompt thinking and acting in terms of similarity; and rankings prompt thinking and acting in dimensions or continua. In contrast to texts or numbers that verbalize arguments or causes and effects, thereby accommodating sequential processing of information, visualizations show them spatially (Meyer *et al.* 2013; Tversky, 2005; 2011). In sum, visual templates shape attention and sensemaking processes which is why the analysis of their beneficial as well as non-beneficial effects on mindfulness is of specific interest for us.

Visual templates and individual mindfulness

In this section, a discussion of prior literature allows us to identify some facets by which visual templates might induce or inhibit individual-level mindfulness. We present three facets inducing mindfulness and four facets inhibiting mindfulness and put them in relation to the characteristics of individual mindfulness identified by Langer

---

[5] We build on Gibson's (1986) notion of affordances which is used to denote that the non-human environment furnishes, demands, or invites certain sensemaking activities whereas others are less supposable.

(i.e., continuous creation of new categories, openness to new information, implicit awareness of more than one perspective).

Inducing individual mindfulness. First, it has been argued that mindful behaviour rests on an existing repertoire of action because the availability of such routines allows actors 'to respond rapidly to stimuli and to engage in a wide set of possible actions' (Levinthal and Rerup 2006, p. 505). Mindfulness depends on routines because they provide the raw material for recombination *and* relieve the mind from attending to too many objects (Levinthal and Rerup, 2006). It has been frequently argued that visualizations are means of documenting knowledge and that visual templates serve organizational learning because they codify prior experiences, thereby synthesizing information about 'best practices' or at least information about what worked out well (Cacciatori 2008; Eppler and Burkhard 2007). Based on the assumption that visual templates embody previous experiences and exhaustive evaluations that integrate different perspectives about the represented subject, we argue that they assist organizational members to consider a variety of categories and to be aware of more than one perspective because these are already incorporated within the template. Thus, having a set of commonly accepted visual templates readily at hand allows actors to know more fully what is happening and potentially speeds up sensemaking processes or reactions to changes. This is particularly relevant in times of crisis.

Second, although visual templates are common and similar within and between organizations, this does not mean that there are no differences in their usage. Rather, the responses to what the templates afford are bound to agents' abilities (see Costall 1995; Gibson 1986), thus multiple or divergent enactments of visual templates are the norm. In particular, organizational members who already display a high degree of mindfulness can use visual templates to maintain a wide breadth of attention (see Dane 2011). Moreover, visual templates may enable less mindful users to appreciate the context because re-fitting a routine according to the specifics (anomalies, small deviations, etc.) of the situation at hand is an effortful accomplishment that stimulates attention and awareness. Thus, the process of enactment continuously re-creates the perspective on visual templates, which means that new categories are created, especially when visualizations are continuously re-interpreted and treated as flexible and amenable tools. For example, think of emergency escape plans in public buildings such as hospitals, schools, or hotels. Generally, we are all familiar with their gestalt, their lines and colour schemes, the visualization of staircases and so on (especially when facing them). This visualization enables people to find their way out in case of an emergency, say a fire. For escaping, we do not need to know the building in advance; we only need to be familiar with the general gestalt of an emergency escape plan.

Third, research that explores visual templates as epistemic artefacts emphasizes that visual representations support the development and refinement of knowledge. The very fact that visual representations are incomplete evokes actors to search for information in order to make them complete (Ewenstein and Whyte 2009). Obviously, visual templates display a similar lack of completeness because they must be filled and populated. Moreover, related work on boundary objects shows that visualizations, drawings, sketches, and so on enable shared understanding between different organizational groups (Nicolini, Mengis, and Swan 2012). A recurrent line of argument is that visualizations offer a way to build a shared understanding between members of different organizational units or professional groups because visualizations allow others' perspectives to be adopted. While negotiating a common understanding, visualizations also help in stimulating new ideas and innovative solutions (Eppler and Platts, 2009; Henderson 1991). Building on these findings, we argue that visual templates offer a knowledge context that enables organizational members to create new categories, to be open to others' point of view and thus consider more than one perspective. As a consequence, they are valuable tools for facilitating individual mindfulness. While these facets of visual templates may induce individual mindfulness, there are others which may well inhibit individual mindfulness.

Inhibiting individual mindfulness. First, and quite generally, psychological research indicates that the human mind is prone to wander away from the present and take hold of any number of objects including memories of the past or thoughts about the future (Smallwood, McSpadden, and Schooler 2007). Since visual templates prompt a certain cognition while making others less likely, they induce the mind to wander along a certain pathway. This is quite clearly at odds with the call for being aware of more than one perspective.

Second, and more problematic regarding the aspect of continuously differentiating and creating new categories, the repertoire of available visual templates seems to be rather narrow. For example, Eppler and

Pfister (2012) outline thirty-five visual representations that are presented as being able to solve issues ranging from analysis and (strategic) planning to meeting moderation and sales negotiations. Yates and Orlikowski (2007) also report that the companies they investigated only used a few visual templates. However, regarding the multitude of business-related problems and the specifics of each analysis, planning or meeting situation, the provided visualizations may not be fine-grained enough to capture the many existing details. Reducing the variety of specifics by consolidation is the opposite of creating new categories and being aware of more than one perspective. Rather, anything outside these visual templates and routines of using them is effectively rendered unthinkable. For example, drawing a visualization which refrains from using the usual templates composed of arrows, circles, and rectangles is likely to be judged as weird or useless. Lines do connect, bars do contain entities, just as similarity is indicated via grouping or spatial proximity. Actors who violate this routinized usage of visual templates risk the breakdown of collective sensemaking. Thereby, the cognitive content is directly shaped by visual templates. For example, there is a broad discussion about how PowerPoint slides and the visual templates provided by PowerPoint might impact cognitive processes and subsequent action. Several scholars have argued that this visual genre affords simplification and over-generalization (Tufte 2003). Without replicating the different lines of argument (for discussions see Meyer *et al.* 2013), we hold that visual templates, as one example of the plethora of visualizations occurring in processes of organizing, increase the possibility that organizational members consolidate and simplify rather than think and act mindfully.

Third, visual templates and routines of using them are rarely reflected upon. Rather, what visual templates afford taps into a pre-reflective, habitual knowledge about what 'we' use the template 'for' (see Costall 1995; Yates and Orlikowski 2007). Whereas textbooks and field manuals provide more or less detailed recommendations about when and how to use the templates, most employees learn about when and how to use visual templates by imitating others and through socialization processes. What individuals use a template for becomes a socially stabilized and institutionalized practice (Yates and Orlikowski 2007). Rather than consciously acquiring knowledge about situations, benefits, and possible concerns of usage, organizational members rely on learned habits. By definition, acting on automatic pilot by adhering to such socially internalized patterns of thinking and acting contradicts the notion of mindfulness, which rests on an openness to surprises and new information. When dealing with innovation or newness, agents pre-reflectively perceive of a visual template as a means conducive to addressing the problem at hand.

Visual templates and mindful organizing

Mindful organizing is characterized by the five processes of organizing specified by Weick and colleagues. Thus, our discussion of the facilitating or inhibiting impact of visualizations is structured along these processes.

Inducing mindful organizing. First, Weick and colleagues explained that a reluctance to simplify interpretations, sensitivity to operations and commitment to resilience are related. The reluctance to simplify interpretations includes taking deliberate steps to question assumptions and retain the distinctiveness and details of what is happening. If people want to notice and retain their awareness of such nuances, they must create an integrated 'big picture' of the distributed but related tasks at work and how ongoing events may unfold in order to think about pathways to recovery.

Considering a popular visual template, we can see how its distribution and socially stabilized usage facilitates these processes. The various cause-and-effect diagrams (e.g., ishikawa, trees, and flowcharts) afford what Carroll and Rudolph (2006) term 'root cause analysis'. This is first of all a means to deliberately seek complex interpretations that consider inputs and outputs of interconnected work processes. Since these templates provide specific techniques for mapping causal relationships between events as well as noting and accounting for time delays, they (literally) create a big picture that not only draws possible pathways of interaction but also allows a group to see and discuss points of leverage for system change that might be invisible otherwise.

Second, visual templates – just like many other artificial objects – depersonalize organizational processes. It is a crucial feature of mediating artefacts such as tools and templates that the topic (problem, error, solution etc.) rather than the person is at the focus of attention (Nicolini *et al.* 2012). Moreover, visual templates not only downplay the emphasis on a single actor but also enable a group to contribute to the discussion and solution of an issue according to their expertise: Since templates have to be filled by various specialists (which is why such artificial objects cross boundaries), we can say that the authority to solve a problem migrates to the people with the most expertise in the problem at hand.

Third, the already-mentioned incompleteness of visual templates prompts groups to operate in a chronic wariness of the possibility that new information about events, problems, or solutions might appear and jeopardize what groups thought they knew. Thus, although not necessarily focused on failures, the lack of completeness fosters a pre-occupation with the simultaneity of knowing and doubting, or, in other words, it fosters an attitude of wisdom and treats experience with ambivalence. These mediating artefacts remind groups of people constantly that they should never fully trust or rely on their experiences. Thereby, they provide a structural element of mindful organizing that transcends face-to-face situations.

Opposing this positive potential, some aspects of visual templates could potentially inhibit mindful organizing. We present four possible mindfulness-inhibiting features of visual templates.

Inhibiting mindful organizing. First, Weick and Sutcliffe (2006) stress that routines and mindfulness are distinct because they cannot occur simultaneously. They suggest that routines go along with a single distinction and simple interpretations, whereas mindful organizing is associated with multiple distinctions and a variety of interpretations. In other words, mindful organizing is about seeing the limits of a category and the act of categorizing itself (Weick and Putnam 2006; Weick and Sutcliffe 2006). In contrast, routines are presented as repeated activity which can be conducted in a 'simple-minded' way. A specific feature of visual templates increases the possibility that details get lost: they provide actors with a set of cognitive categories by presenting graphical elements as self-containing entities. Using visual entities gives the impression that the representation of an issue is encompassing and composed of mutually exclusive categories. Visual templates might also describe a course of action that then becomes routine in the sense that the prescribed course is enacted without reflecting on possible other routes. Thus, organizational members are prompted to simplify their interpretations as well as think and act along preconfigured routes. Consequently, cognition and decision making are distributed between human actors and non-human artefacts. However, mindful organizing is based upon the migration of decision-making authority to problems not visual templates. Similarly, deference to human experts is at least partially replaced by reliance on such mediating artefacts.

Second, and echoing a point already discussed concerning individual mindfulness, the available repertoire of different visual templates is rather narrow. This is directly at odds with Weick and Sutcliffe's caution over simplification. Given the limited number of available sketches (Eppler and Pfister 2012), in contrast to the endless multiplicity of organizational problems, it is hard not to imagine routines lending themselves to simplifications. Drawing a weird and daringly new graph is likely to inhibit the key benefit of visualization for organizing: that they simplify and are easy to understand. This accessibility is, however, especially common on the collective level, since they are used to coordinate action at a distance. Think of a schedule on display in a factory. Its coordinating potential is due to its readily interpretable form. Situational complexity is deliberately ignored. Moreover, it shifts the attention away from operations to representations of operations that cannot entail the same level of detail as the actual practices do. Organizational members' sensitivity to what is going on is at least partially distracted because they attend to a visual with less discriminatory details. Another process of mindful organizing potentially hampered by the narrow repertoire of available visual templates is the commitment to resilience. Acting with a focus on maintaining vital organizational functions is likely to require a broad range of alternatives or a broad action repertoire and significant 'out-of-the-box thinking'. This is, again, directly at odds with a stable and small set of available templates.

Third, challenging the sensitivity to operations, visual templates, as outlined before, prompt actors to neglect other means of sensemaking. Proponents of mindful organizing stress the importance of constantly enacting the context and develop a fine-tuned understanding of local differences (Vogus and Sutcliffe 2012) and thereby foster deference to expertise that rests on the primacy of local knowledge over universal and context-free approaches. Visual templates, on the other hand, afford users to use them and prioritize them over other means of sensemaking and thereby limit actors' abilities to adopt their means of sensemaking flexibly to the local context. To put it another way: rather than putting the emphasis on experts at the front-line who know the local context, the attention is on the centrally distributed visual templates, thereby replacing individual expertise with codified and universal knowledge that is embodied in such mediating artefacts.

Fourth, recurring use of visual templates tempts actors to fall into habitual behaviour and bury much of their potential to anticipate unexpected information. Such behaviour challenges the reluctance to simplify because automatically referring to the same templates (probably due to learned habits) in order to represent a business issue means simplifying the modality or 'knowledge context' of generating information and interpretations. Doing something a certain way because it has always been done this way is a ubiquitous pitfall for mindful organizing. Repeatedly drawing on the same visual templates is likely to make it easier for actors to fall into this trap. Habitual behaviour is also a hallmark of the expectation of future success based on past experiences, which Weick and Sutcliff (2007) challenge when they call for a preoccupation with failure.

In sum, visual templates play an ambiguous role in mindful organizing. While there are some inducing features, there are substantial reasons for being wary of their potential to inhibit mindfulness. Rerup (2005) has argued that there is an optimum of being mindful when organizing depends on several factors. Further research will need to determine such an optimal point for individual contexts and situations. This chapter has been a first step for such work by examining the potential effects, and the directionality of these effects, of visual templates for individual mindfulness and mindful organizing on the collective level. We will now conclude and discuss areas for future research that could help to deepen our understanding of different forms of mindfulness and the role of visualizations, or tools, respectively.

Conclusion

Mindfulness has become an important concept in work and organization studies because it helps to explain the micro-foundations of several aspects of organizations (e.g., wellbeing, stress, task performance, reliability, readiness for change, dynamic capabilities). Building on our review of different approaches to mindfulness, we examined the inducing and inhibiting effects of visual templates on mindfulness and mindful organizing. To date, we know little about the tools that organizational members draw upon in their everyday practices to re-accomplish mindfulness. By exploring visual templates as one example of such mediating artefacts, we aim to address this research gap in the extant literature. Moreover, while there is apt literature on the beneficial consequences of mindfulness, there is comparatively little research about antecedents or mediating artefacts and their impact on mindfulness. By discussing the ambivalent way in which visual templates affect mindfulness, we extend Rerup's (2005) finding that there is an inverted u-shaped relation between mindfulness and (organizational) outcomes. However, several questions for future research appear along our line of discussion (other research areas have been described by Vogus and Sutcliffe 2012).

First, there are many and ambiguous definitions of mindfulness, both between and within the perspectives we identified. Therefore, there is still a need for clarification. Neither the notion of mindfulness nor the five processes are defined unequivocally in organization studies. For example, there is some ambiguity around the notion of having a 'big picture'. Weick and Sutcliffe (2007, p. 32) define mindfulness as 'a rich awareness of discriminatory detail' and move on to explain their definition: 'Mindful people have the "big picture", but it is a big picture of the moment' (Weick and Sutcliffe 2007, p. 32). One might be puzzled how having a big picture *and* seeing discriminatory details might work. Moreover, the term 'having a big picture' is frequently used to explain sensitivity to operations (e.g., Vogus and Sutcliffe 2012, pp. 723, 725; Weick *et al.* 1999, p. 93), but how can it both define mindful *people* and be *part* of what constitutes the *collective* phenomenon? Being clear about definitions, explanations, and metaphors is only the first step, which brings us to the next area for future research.

Second, there is a need for multi-level conceptions and analyses. The issue of mindfulness in organizations involves, like most management problems, multilevel phenomena, but management and organization research on mindfulness has either used a single level of analysis or did not clearly delineate the differences and relations between the levels. There are some general issues that have to be considered when conducting multilevel research (see Salvato and Rerup 2011). Few studies to date have dealt with the connection between individual and collective forms of mindfulness. Extant literature draws on empirical examples that are related to small groups and localized expertise, but argues that this approach is suitable and mirrors mindfulness on a collective of a somewhat centralized level.[6] In their comprehensive literature review, Vogus and Sutcliffe (2012, p. 726) propose that middle managers act as facilitators to 'bridge the gap' from decentralized, local mindful organizing by individuals and more or less small groups to the more centralized, organizational level. We agree with this approach, but we have also aimed to extend this person-centric view on what happens in organizations. Rather than allocating the work of connecting different levels to a certain group of people, we have argued that non-human factors such as tools are involved in mindful organizing. Tools play a crucial role in connecting people and structuring their actions over time and space. Thus, they must not be neglected when theorizing on the relation between the multiple levels that are at work in organizations.

Third, this chapter has focused on a very specific kind of tool, namely visual templates. It is obvious that other tools are also used in organizations. Thus, our work presents only a first step in determining the potential effects of tools on mindfulness. Although we have set a possible pathway to conduct such an analysis, more systematic and encompassing theorizing is necessary. For example, one short-coming of our work is quite evident: arguing that visual templates have ambivalent effects on mindfulness raises the question of boundary conditions specifying when visual templates induce mindfulness and when they inhibit mindfulness. One boundary condition could be whether the templates are fixed (e.g. printed on paper) or can be changed more or less easily (e.g. when they are distributed as electronic documents such as PowerPoint slides). Other boundary conditions concern the work context (e.g., high-reliability organizations versus knowledge-intensive organizations versus industrial firms etc.) which is likely to impact the degree of diffusion and acceptance of using tools/visual templates. This, in turn, can serve as an indicator for the degree of socialization, i.e., the extent to which organizational members routinely draw on a specific set of tools/visual templates. In addition to more elaborated theorizing, empirical research is needed to examine these issues. There is still a long way to go until we have robust data on hypotheses concerning the optimum of the hypothesized inverted u-shaped relation between mindfulness and (organizational) performance.

---

[6] For a summary of these criticisms see Vollmer (2013, Chapter 4.5).

Fourth, the findings of this paper are a first step towards fully understanding the power and influence of visualization on cognition and processes of organizing. For practitioners it will be crucial to reflect on which visual templates, or tools in general, affect their daily work routines, which induce or inhibit mindfulness, and how to design tools that induce mindfulness. The scarce literature that deals with how to design tools often draws on a vital principle of engineering design: ease-of-use. Well-designed products or systems are those that are easy to use because they engender user trust, confidence and conform to users' preferred perspectives and expectations (Butler and Gray 2006; Hartson 2003). However, from a mindfulness perspective, tools and templates should rather *not* tap into preferred and routinized courses of action, but stimulate actors to reflect or even leave them puzzled, so that they stop and think about what is happening. Thus, it might be worthwhile to use templates that afford thinking in feedback loops, circles, and systems dynamics (for examples see Senge 1996). Since these templates and tools are attuned to complex problems, their interrelatedness and dynamics, as well as to the creation of a 'big picture', they should afford the refinement of existing categories, a nuanced appreciation of contexts and perspectives, a reluctance to simplify interpretations, and sensitivity to operations. At least, they should be a remedy to what Weick famously diagnosed as a managerial disease: 'Most managers get into trouble because they forget to think in circles. I mean this literally' (Weick 1979, p. 86).

References

Avey, J. B., Wernsing, T. S., and Luthans, F. (2008). Can positive employees help positive organizational change? Impact of psychological capital and emotions on relevant attitudes and behaviours. *Journal of Applied Behavioral Science*, 44(1), 48–70.

Baer, R. A. (2003). Mindfulness training as a clinical intervention: a conceptual and empirical review. *Clinical Psychology: Science and Practice*, 10(2), 125–43.

Brown, K. W. and Ryan, R. M. (2003). The benefits of being present: mindfulness and its role in psychological well-being. *Journal of Personality and Social Psychology*, 84(4), 822–48.

Brown, K. W., Ryan, R. M., and Creswell, J. D. (2007). Mindfulness: theoretical foundations and evidence for its salutary effects. *Psychological*

Inquiry: An International Journal for the Advancement of Psychological Theory, 18(4), 211–37.

Butler, B. S. and Gray, P. H. (2006). Reliability, mindfulness, and information systems. *MIS Quarterly*, 30(2), 211–24.

Cacciatori, E. (2008). Memory objects in project environments: storing, retrieving and adapting learning in project-based firms. *Research Policy*, 37(9), 1591–601.

Carroll, J. S. and Rudolph, J. W. (2006). Design of high reliability organizations in health care. *Quality and Safety in Health Care*, 15 (suppl. 1), i4–i9.

Costall, A. (1995). Socializing affordances. *Theory and Psychology*, 5(4), 467–81.

Dane, E. (2011). Paying attention to mindfulness and its effects on task performance in the workplace. *Journal of Management*, 37(4), 997–1018.

Dane, E. and Brummel, B. J. (2014). Examining workplace mindfulness and its relations to job performance and turnover intention. *Human Relations*, 67(1), 105–28.

Eisenberg, E. M. (2006). Karl Weick and the aesthetics of contingency. *Organization Studies*, 27(11), 1693–707.

Eppler, M. J. and Aeschimann, M. (2009). A systematic framework for risk visualization in risk management and communication. *Risk Management*, 11(2), 67–89.

Eppler, M. J. and Burkhard, R. A. (2007). Visual representations in knowledge management: framework and cases. *Journal of Knowledge Management*, 11(4), 112–22.

Eppler, M. J. and Pfister, R. A. (2012). *Sketching at work: 35 starke Visualisierungs-Tools für Manager, Berater, Verkäufer, Trainer und Moderatoren*. Stuttgart: Schäffer-Poeschel.

Eppler, M. J. and Platts, K. (2009). Visual strategizing: the systematic use of visualization in the strategic planning process. *Long Range Planning*, 42(1), 42–74.

Epstein, R. M. (1999). Mindful practice. *The Journal of the American Medical Association*, 282(9), 833–9.

Ewenstein, B. and Whyte, J. (2009). Knowledge practices in design: the role of visual representations as 'epistemic objects'. *Organization Studies*, 30(1), 7–30.

Fiol, M. C. and O'Connor, E. J. (2003). Waking up! Mindfulness in the face of bandwagons. *Academy of Management Review*, 28(1), 54–70.

Gärtner, C. (2011). Putting new wine into old bottles: mindfulness as a micro-foundation of dynamic capabilities. *Management Decision*, 49(2), 253–69.

Gärtner, C. (2013). Enhancing readiness for change by organizing for mindfulness. *Journal of Change Management*, 13(1), 52–68.

Gibson, J. J. (1986). *An ecological approach to visual perception*. Hillsdale, MI: Erlbaum.

Glomb, T. M., Duffy, M. K., Bono, J. E., and Yang, T. (2011). Mindfulness at work. In: A. Joshi, H. Liao, and J. J. Martocchio (eds.), *Research in personnel and human resources management 30*. Bingley: Emerald, pp. 115–57.

Hartson, R. H. (2003). Cognitive, physical, sensory, and functional affordances in interaction design. *Behaviour and Information Technology*, 22(5), 315–38.

Henderson, K. (1991). Flexible sketches and inflexible databases: visual communication, conscription devices, and boundary objects in design engineering. *Science, Technology, and Human Values*, 16(4), 448–73.

Hülsheger U. R., Alberts, H. J. E. M., Feinholdt, A., and Lang, J. W. B. (2013). Benefits of mindfulness at work: the role of mindfulness in emotion regulation, emotional exhaustion, and job satisfaction. *Journal of Applied Psychology*, 98(2), 310–25.

Jordan, S., Jørgensen, L., and Mitterhofer, H. (2013). Performing risk and the project: risk maps as mediating instruments. *Management Accounting Research*, 24(2), 156–74.

Kabat-Zinn, J. (1990). *Full catastrophe living: using the wisdom of your body and mind to face stress, pain, and illness*. New York: Delacorte.

Langer, E. J. (1989). *Mindfulness*. Cambridge: Perseus Publishing.

(1997). *The power of mindful learning*. Reading, MA: Addison-Wesley.

Langer, E. J. and Moldoveanu, M. (2000). The construct of mindfulness. *Journal of Social Issues*, 56(1), 1–9.

Levinthal, D. and Rerup, C. (2006). Crossing an apparent chasm: bridging mindful and less-mindful perspectives on organizational learning. *Organization Science*, 17(4), 502–13.

Louis, M. R. and Sutton, R. I. (1991). Switching cognitive gears: from habits of mind to active thinking. *Human Relations*, 44(1), 55–76.

Lurie, N. H. and Mason, C. H. (2007). Visual representation: implications for decision making. *Journal of Marketing*, 71(1), 160–77.

Meyer, R. E., Höllerer, M. A., Jancsary, D., and van Leeuwen, T. (2013). The visual dimension in organizing, organization, and organization research. *The Academy of Management Annals*, 7(1), 487–553.

Miettinen, R. and Virkkunen, J. (2005). Epistemic objects, artefacts and organizational change. *Organization*, 12(3), 437–56.

Nicolini, D., Mengis, J., and Swan, J. (2012). Understanding the role of objects in cross-disciplinary collaboration. *Organization Science*, 23(3), 612–29.

Ray, J. L., Baker, L. T., and Plowman, D. A. (2011). Organizational mindfulness in business schools. *Academy of Management Learning and Education*, 10(2), 188–203.

Reb, J., Narayanan, J., and Chaturvedi, S. (2014). Leading mindfully: two studies on the influence of supervisor trait mindfulness on employee well-being and performance. *Mindfulness*, 5(1), 36–45.

Rerup, C. (2005). Learning from past experience: footnotes on mindfulness and habitual entrepreneurship. *Scandinavian Journal of Management*, 21(4), 451–72.

Sadler-Smith, E. and Shefy, E. (2007). Developing intuitive awareness in management education. *Academy of Management Learning and Education*, 6, 186–205.

Salvato, C. and Rerup, C. (2011). Beyond collective entities: multilevel research on organizational routines and capabilities. *Journal of Management*, 37(2), 468–90.

Senge, P. (1996): *The fifth discipline fieldbook: strategies and tools for building a learning organization*. 3rd edn. London: Nicholas Brealey Publishing.

Sibbet, D. (2013). *Visual leaders: new tools for visioning, management, and organizational change*. Hoboken, NJ: John Wiley and Sons.

Sims, H. P. and Gioia, D. A. (1986). *The thinking organization*. San Francisco, CA: Jossey-Bass.

Smallwood, J., McSpadden, M., and Schooler, J. W. (2007). The lights are on but no one's home: meta-awareness and the decoupling of attention when the mind wanders. *Psychonomic Bulletin and Review*, 14, 527–33.

Sternberg, R. J. (2000). Images of mindfulness. *Journal of Social Issues*, 56(1), 11–26.

Tufte, E. R. (2003): *The cognitive style of PowerPoint*. Cheshire: Graphics Press.

Tversky, B. (2005). Visuospatial reasoning. In K. J. Holyoak and Morrison, R. J. (eds.), *The Cambridge handbook of thinking and reasoning*. Cambridge University Press, pp. 209–40.

Tversky, B. (2011). Visualizing thought. *Topics in Cognitive Science*, 3(3), 499–535.

Valorinta, M. (2009). Information technology and mindfulness in organizations. *Industrial and Corporate Change*, 18(5), 963–97.

Vogus, T. J. and Sutcliffe, K. M. (2007). The safety organizing scale: development and validation of a behavioral measure of safety culture in hospital nursing units. *Medical Care*, 45 (1), 46–54.

Vogus, T. J. and Sutcliffe, K. M. (2012). Organizational mindfulness and mindful organizing: a reconciliation and path forward. *Academy of Management Learning and Education*, 11(4), 722–35.

Vogus, T. J. and Welbourne, T. M. (2003). Structuring for high reliability: HR practices and mindful processes in reliability-seeking organizations. *Journal of Organizational Behavior*, 24, 877–903.

Vogus, T. J., Sutcliffe, K. M., and Weick, K. E. (2010). Doing no harm: enabling, enacting, and elaborating a culture of safety in health care. *The Academy of Management Perspectives*, 24(4), 60–77.

Vollmer, H. (2013). *The sociology of disruption, disaster and social change: punctuated cooperation*. Cambridge University Press.

Weick, K. E. (1979). *The social psychology of organizing*. 2nd edn. New York: McGraw-Hill.

Weick, K. E. (2001). *Making sense of the organization*. Malden: Blackwell.

Weick, K. E. (2002). Puzzles in organizational learning: an exercise in disciplined imagination. *British Journal of Management*, 13(S2), S7–S15.

Weick, K. E. and Putnam, T. (2006). Organizing for mindfulness. Eastern wisdom and Western knowledge. *Journal of Management Inquiry*, 15(3), 275–87.

Weick, K. E. and Roberts, K. H. (1993). Collective mind in organizations: heedful interrelating on flight decks. *Administrative Science Quarterly*, 38, 357–81.

Weick, K. E. and Sutcliffe, K. M. (2006). Mindfulness and the quality of organizational attention. *Organization Science*, 17(4), 514–24.

(2007). *Managing the unexpected: resilient performance in an age of uncertainty*. San Francisco, CA: Jossey-Bass.

Weick, K. E., Sutcliffe, K. M., and Obstfeld, D. (1999). Organizing for high reliability: processes of collective mindfulness. *Research in Organizational Behavior*, 21, 81–123.

Yates, J. (1985). Graphs as a managerial tool: a case study of Du Pont's use of graphs in the early twentieth century. *Journal of Business Communication*, 22(1), 5–33.

Yates, J. and Orlikowski, W. (2007). The PowerPoint presentation and its corollaries: How genres shape communicative action in organizations. In Zachry, M. and Thralls, C. (eds.), *Communicative practices in workplaces and the professions: cultural perspectives on the regulation of discourse and organizations*. Amityville, NY: Baywood Publishing, pp. 67–92.

PART III

Applications

14 | Awakening at work: introducing mindfulness into organizations

MIRABAI BUSH

Introduction

In this chapter, I discuss implementing mindfulness into organizations, with emphasis on Monsanto and Google as examples. I summarize research by the Center for Contemplative Mind in Society conducted from 2000 to 2004 and published in 2004 on early attempts at forming contemplative organizations. I discuss not only the benefits for individuals and organizations but also how each organizational culture requires different framing and language. I also discuss concerns from the dharma community that introducing mindfulness encourages organizations, especially corporations, to continue unwholesome practices by helping employees be more content with their work. This chapter proposes that mindfulness and related practices can lead to insight and then to wisdom and compassion, encouraging new forms of inquiry and creativity, potentially taking organizations and their leaders from good to great and from great to wise and compassionate. The chapter suggests that future research is needed to explore and document the transformative impact of mindfulness training on both the individual and the organization.

History

The exploration of the integration of mindfulness practices into corporate settings described in this chapter began when the Center for Contemplative Mind in Society – which I co-founded with two foundation presidents, Charles Halpern (Nathan Cummings Foundation) and Robert Lehman (Fetzer Institute) – carried out a search for organizations that were using these practices. I had first studied mindfulness in 1970 with the Burmese teacher S. N. Goenka, a pioneer in the introduction of secular mindfulness, in Bodh Gaya, where the Buddha had been enlightened, and then studied with Tibetan teachers including Kalu Rinpoche, Gelek Rinpoche, and Tsoknyi Rinpoche. I had also taught mindfulness at retreat centers across the United States and had introduced the practice to the sixty-five employees of Illuminations, Inc., a company I co-founded in Cambridge, Massachusetts in 1978. So I was enthusiastic about introducing mindfulness to mainstream organizations.

In 2004, the Center published *A Powerful Silence: The Role of Meditation and Other Contemplative Practices in American Life and Work* (Duerr 2004), a report that summarized the findings of the Center's qualitative research project called The Contemplative Net, conducted by the Center from 2001 to 2004 and funded by the Ford Foundation and Fetzer Institute. The study defined contemplative practices as practices that quiet the mind in order to cultivate a personal capacity for deep concentration and insight; this definition included mindfulness, which is often defined as the awareness that arises by paying attention on purpose in the present moment non-judgmentally. This project was, to our knowledge, the first systematic effort to map the use of contemplative practices across diverse secular settings including business, healthcare, education, law, social change, and prisons. In-depth interviews were conducted with eighty-four professionals who incorporated contemplative practices into their work. The data was then analyzed for recurring patterns and themes.

The report confirmed the growing use of contemplative practice in secular settings and found that it was a phenomenon worthy of further study. Findings included:

1. The use of contemplative practices in professional settings was on the rise.
   At the time *A Powerful Silence* was written, at least 135 companies, nonprofit organizations, and government agencies offered their employees classes in some form of meditation and/or yoga. The number of hospitals and medical clinics that provided

mindfulness-based stress reduction training for patients had increased from 80 in 1993 to 250 in 2003.

2. Individuals who regularly meditate or have other contemplative practices reported a difference in the quality of their work experiences and personal relationships.

    In addition to well-documented stress reduction benefits, interviewees described how contemplative practices helped to increase self-awareness and served as a vehicle for forgiveness and reconciliation. They reported a renewed sense of commitment to their work, improved workplace communication, and an increased ability to deal with organizational challenges. In addition, they spoke of how these practices enhanced their personal relationships with family, friends, co-workers, and significant others.

    ↑ Emotional Intelligence

3. The emergence of a new organizational paradigm: the contemplative organization. Thirty-eight of the 84 interviewees (32 percent), many of them in leadership and/or managerial positions, described bringing contemplative practices into their workplace with the intention of creating a more reflective environment. Analysis of these interviews revealed a new organizational paradigm, one that uses contemplative awareness as an organizing principle for the workplace. In these companies and organizations, meditation and other practices are not simply add-on benefits but are incorporated into the structure of daily work and decision-making processes.

Contemplative organizations share the following characteristics:

*   Embodying values: the organization models, as best it can, the values it wishes to see in society. The mission, vision, and strategic plan emphasize the importance of the organization's core values.
*   Moving between cycles of action and reflection: the organization explicitly honors the belief that there is a time to work and a time to step back, rest, and learn from the past in order to plan for the future.
*   Balancing process with product: the way in which an organization works toward its goals is equally as, and sometimes more important than, the achievement of the goal.
*   Having an organizational structure that reflects a contemplative philosophy.

At a contemplative organization, these efforts to bring more reflection into the workplace are not segregated from the core of the organization's work, but are seen as integral to it. During the survey, Peter Senge, founder of the Society for Organizational Learning, told us: "One of the problems we have in business is that people want to programatize things. That itself is a source of a lot of limitation because programs come and go." Rather, he suggested, organizations could benefit by an ongoing exploration of the question, "What does it mean to create a climate in which people are working where reflection, deep conversation, and becoming more and more open is basically how we work together?"

In the *Powerful Silence* survey, the Center heard interesting and profound reports of the benefits of contemplative practices in the workplace. Some examples are:

- an ability to be present with difficulty (one's own and that of others) without withdrawing, repressing, or ignoring it;
- renewing commitment to work and remembering original motivations. For example, at a mindfulness retreat for leaders of national environmental organizations, participants realized that they had been wasting precious time and energy competing with each other for resources. This realization helped them re-commit to working more cooperatively toward their shared goal of a sustainable planet;
- improved relationships with others: interpersonal intelligence and the ability to understand another point of view. After a mindfulness retreat, lawyers reported greater understanding of their clients and also their opposing counsels and clients. Environmentalists reported that they were more effective in getting the Clean Air Act passed by working together collaboratively;
- greater emotional intelligence: the ability to monitor one's own and others' feelings and emotions, to discriminate among them, and to use this information to guide one's thinking and actions. Google engineers reported being able to work better in teams and being more understanding of cultural differences after learning mindfulness and compassion practices;
- appreciation for the role of non-action (not inaction), for listening before leaping;
- a deeper understanding of anger and the cultivation of more sustainable sources of energy, like compassion and loving-kindness. Many people worry that if they give up acting from anger they will

*[handwritten margin notes: "*Commit to work", "*Improve interrelational skills", "*A.E.I."]*

be ineffective, even though they know it leads to burnout. Learning
to manage anger and tapping into deeper, more positive sources of
inspiration sustains energy for the long term;
- improved listening skills;
- an ability to move gracefully with change, based on an understanding of the nature of impermanence;
- an ability to live *in* the moment, rather than *for* the moment, reducing greed and self-centered behavior;
- enhanced creativity and problem-solving skills;
- appreciation of the interconnection of all life, which values all of
  nature as well as human life.

✱ Ability to go w/ flow

(This list leaves aside the physical benefits of contemplative practices,
such as stress reduction, pain management, reduced blood pressure,
and better sleep patterns, all of which are related to the capacities
listed above.)

Since *A Powerful Silence* was published, the use and integration of
these practices has continued to grow. From 2005 to 2010, a number
of polls, surveys, and research projects have explored the role of religion and spirituality (including contemplative practices) in American
life. Viewed collectively, the data from these studies indicates that
the use of meditation and other contemplative practices continues to
increase (Duerr 2011). The Pew Religious Landscape Survey (2007),
for example, found that almost four in ten adults (39 percent) say
they meditate at least once a week, compared with three-quarters of
Americans who say they pray at least once a week.

Businesses of all kinds, including General Mills, Hoffman LaRoche,
Green Mountain Coffee Roasters, Hearst Publications, and American
Express, have now explored the uses and benefits of mindfulness.
Hochman (2013) writes in *The New York Times*: "Like yoga, the
word [mindfulness] reaches the height of trendiness, on the tongues of
TV stars, executives and even techies."

Transforming traditional contemplative practices for organizations

The Center for Contemplative Mind in Society was itself an early laboratory for mindful work practices. The staff of ten to twelve people, aged
twenty-two to sixty, had a range of spiritual affiliations and practices

and was diverse also in ethnicity, class, gender, and race. We were challenged to find practices and language that would work for all.

As a full staff, through experimentation and discussion, we developed a program that included:

- beginning meetings with silence or mindfulness practice;
- use of reflective dialogue and the mindfulness bell in meetings;
- permission to take "contemplative breaks" during the day;
- creation of special space in the office for yoga, meditation, and/or quiet;
- use of contemplative group techniques such as appreciative inquiry and council circle to conduct strategic planning for the organization;
- use of mindful office practices, such as mindful emailing and mindful conference calls;
- scheduling regular contemplative staff retreats as a source of unity and inspiration – everyone had an opportunity to design and lead one of these retreats;
- publication of the *Activist's Ally*, a handbook for developing contemplative nonprofit organizations.

Establishing these as best practices at the Center was relatively easy, since they aligned with the Center's mission: to integrate contemplative practice and awareness into contemporary life in order to create a more just, compassionate, and sustainable society. But even there, we encountered challenges. From them, we established some basic guidelines for implementing the contemplative program:

1. Not everyone knows the value of mindfulness. We introduced practices by first giving some history of how the forms we were using evolved from spiritual and religious traditions and then reviewing the current research showing the physiological, psychological, and cognitive benefits of the practices.
2. Leadership and presence are important. A leader who appreciates the potential of such programs and practices needs to restate their purpose regularly; others who have experienced benefit can add their support. Participants at the Center would sometimes wonder why they should be doing this when they have so much work waiting for them at their desks, why we used space for a meditation room when it could be used for more offices, why we gave time to employees to do an annual retreat but not for them to extend

their vacations. The value of mindfulness and other practices has to be revisited regularly and related clearly to the goals of the organization.

3. All practices have to be optional. For example, since this was a Center-wide program, if an employee did not want to learn mindfulness because sitting in silence brought up disturbing emotions or because it seemed contradictory to religious beliefs ("silence creates space for the devil to enter") or because they just didn't think it had value, that employee could participate in a contemplative retreat day by taking a silent walk, writing in a journal, or reading, but they had to attend.

4. Sharing leadership of the practices. Everyone was encouraged to take a turn leading a short mindfulness practice with a script if necessary, and to offer other optional practices to the group from their own traditions. We explored tai chi, chi gong, yoga, making prayer flags, drumming, mindful eating, a tea ceremony, and a Day of the Dead ritual.

5. Processing is helpful. We discussed our personal experience with the practices using mindful listening in pairs or small groups, and we encouraged regular feedback, sometimes anonymous, with methods such as Survey Monkey.

6. Connecting the practices to the organization's goals. Not everyone figured out the connection between practice and their day-to-day work, so we worked to align our values and practices with the purpose and mission of the organization and translate them into guidelines for working together in relationships. During the survey that led to *A Powerful Silence*, one discussion led to a list of values for the project. An example of how we expressed one of these values follows:

High-quality qualitative research with honesty and integrity. We believe that high-caliber research will lend credibility and legitimacy to contemplative approaches, thus benefiting our research participants.

We value the act of research itself as an opportunity to practice contemplative principles: being aware of our own assumptions and biases, openness to "not knowing," valuing questions as much as answers, a willingness to be surprised. We believe in being participants as well as observers in this process of research. We will explore the core questions of our project within our team and the organization as well as in other organizations: What does it mean to work with a contemplative approach? What is the actual experience of working in a contemplative organization? In what ways do we (and do we not) live up to those principles? We will have to keep each other honest in our research efforts and be aware of our own attachments to ego and outcome.

7.   You can't practice mindfulness without humility and humor.

Corporate examples

Monsanto: entering unknown territory

The Center began its exploration of the integration of contemplative practices into corporate settings in 1996, when we worked with Monsanto to develop the first program of in-depth mindfulness meditation within a large corporation in the United States.

We had been invited into Monsanto by their new CEO, Robert (Bob) Shapiro, who began his tenure by launching what they called a "cultural revolution" to change what had been a chemical company to one of the first life-science companies. They had studied the population projections for the twenty-first century and saw that there would likely be a food shortage on the planet causing mass migrations and starvation. To respond to that, Bob proposed genetically engineering seeds to increase yields. It was a radically different role for Monsanto, and Bob recognized that his key people would need to think creatively and be resilient as they explored this new technology. He talked to them about new ways of thinking. He imagined a new relationship with both technology and agriculture. He encouraged a free flow of ideas and imagination: "Think about things you haven't been thinking about. Take risks. Don't be afraid to make mistakes: mistakes are an integral part of any process of creation. Be leaders and encourage everyone around you to be leaders. To be leaders, people need freedom to choose, ability to take risks, and technique or competence. Trust is essential."

Bob had read Jon Kabat-Zinn and he knew something about Zen, how it can open up the mind to fresh ways of seeing, and he asked his old friend Charlie Halpern, the Center's chairperson, whether the Center could teach meditation to his top executives.

We chose mindfulness as the core practice for the workplace because of its four qualities: not forgetting or losing what is in the mind in the present moment; directly facing what is arising; remembering what is skillful, refined, and beneficial; and its close association with wisdom. This understanding of mindfulness gave the participants a sense of its potential to transform the way they lived their lives as well as how they performed at work.

In 1996, very few people had tried teaching mindfulness in secular settings except in the field of health and healing, and there was no model for business. The meditation teachers I asked only knew how to teach practice in a retreat setting, which is what we planned to do, but they did not know how to frame or adapt it for business executives. I asked friends who knew more than I did about corporate business for their advice. Walter Link, founder of Social Ventures Network Europe and a member of Businesses for Social Responsibility (BSR), knew Bob through BSR. He said it was important that the retreat should create the right environment. It should not be held in a Buddhist retreat center. We should avoid the word "spiritual" and find language that makes sense in business. "They understand stress and stress reduction, dealing with time, being in the moment, conflict, resistance to things they don't want to do." He was helpful, and it was going to be a quick, deep study of a whole subculture I hadn't glimpsed since I worked on weather satellites for RCA in the sixties, the only woman among ex-fighter pilots and engineers. Much time had passed since then.

Framed terms that made sense to the organization

I needed to know more, so I called Peter Buckley, former CEO of Esprit Europe. He said he had never been very corporate, more "a hippie entrepreneur who just happened to make it." He talked about a retreat he had attended for environmental leaders. Many had never meditated, but thought that "no matter how strange and flaky it might seem, other leaders were doing it so it must be OK. After five days, many wanted to leave; they thought it was a big waste of time. But by the end, they all thought it was beneficial." Try to get a teacher with a sense of humor, he advised, someone who is "a real regular guy, funny, self-deprecating, watches basketball." I was beginning to get a bit of a feel for this, even though when I asked Mitch Kapor, the founder of Lotus, about Monsanto, he said they should just blow it up and start over.

I knew that the Monsanto executives would be coming because their CEO had asked them, not because they were yearning to learn mindfulness, an obscure concept at the time. And I also knew that without the right motivation, it is very hard to appreciate the practice.

So I visited the St. Louis headquarters and spent time with each participant. I asked them a number of questions, including whether they had spent any time in silence, since much of the retreat would be silent. Silence is often, at the beginning, the hardest element of a meditation retreat, even though at the end of the retreat it is often the part most cherished. It has an outer and inner dimension. On the outside, you don't speak, and you refrain from disturbing the silence around you – you tread lightly, don't use words, and don't use body language or notes to replace speech. On the inside, you quiet the mind by letting go of "noisy" or unnecessary thoughts. I imagined that in a Midwestern corporation, some people would have gone to a Catholic retreat or spent time alone camping or walking in the woods. I wanted to connect those experiences to what they would do at the retreat.

I asked the executive in an office next to a larger-than-life sculpture of a cow on Monsanto-manufactured bovine growth hormone, "Have you spent any time in silence?" He paused and thought about it. "Well, yes," he said. "When I read the newspaper." Well, I thought, not quite what I had in mind, but, remember, start where people are. I learned that day that the Monsanto executives were all polite, overworked, and stressed enough that even a bizarre opportunity like sitting on a cushion and not talking to other people for three days sounded like a break. They were all going to do it. Stress is still the door to mindfulness for many business people.

We designed a three-day silent retreat, in which they learned deep relaxation, mindful sitting and walking, insight meditation, and loving-kindness for all living things. We held it at Seasons, the Fetzer Institute's retreat/conference center in Kalamazoo, Michigan, a serene space created on principles of sacred hospitality, "a place where we come together in dialogue to create that which we cannot do alone." It was not religious and not created for business meetings, but this would be the first silent retreat held there.

We tried to avoid Sanskrit and Pali terms and used direct, honest language to help them see these practices as not esoteric, not religious, but simply ancient methods for understanding the mind and experiencing change and interconnection by carefully watching the processes of their minds and bodies. We talked about the importance of creating a safe space of "non-harming" for each other.

We talked about seeing interrelationships rather than linear chains. We explained that deep practice frees you from the tyranny of linear cause and effect and leads to an understanding of the mystery of how things actually happen – how any act can change the direction or quality or outcome in a profound way.

Some were resistant to the silence, and others kept striving for some tangible result. They found the idea of the goalless goal, the way that striving impedes awakening, very difficult to appreciate. They wanted to be told that if you do this practice then certain things would happen in a certain sequence. Not if you do this practice to make certain things happen, they are less likely to happen. It was subtle.

Bob said it was the hardest thing he had ever done. "Really?" I said. "What about managing 30,000 employees?" "No," he said, "this is harder." We later discovered that presenting mindfulness as not easy and a formidable challenge motivated upper management, and emphasizing that it is simple and anyone can do it motivated middle management. By the retreat's end, most of the seventeen participants had taken up the challenge and turned their potent left-brain focus inward, into the moment. They had learned a lot in a short time.

After the initial retreat, in partnership with volunteers from the retreat, we built a program called Mindfulness at Monsanto. It included off-site retreats, on-site mindfulness, and meditation rooms. Monsanto encouraged employees to attend retreats, with literature that spoke of

mindfulness as a tool that will allow you to purposefully *respond* rather than just *react* to change. When practiced regularly, mindfulness provides a variety of personal and organizational benefits, which include increased adaptability, non-judgmental listening, enhanced clarity and creativity, and greater integration of your personal and professional life.

We established important guidelines:

- The exploration of mindfulness is completely voluntary and is not part of any corporate-wide program. Although the benefits of mindfulness deepen with practice, determining how far to pursue the opportunity is entirely up to the individual – one step at a time.
- Just as each person is different, it is expected that each person's experience with mindfulness will be different.
- While some religions have incorporated mindfulness in their practices, it's also been taught in other settings. At Monsanto, there's no

link whatsoever between mindfulness and any religion; the primary focus is self-development.

At a time when many at Monsanto were worried that another company would acquire the corporation and that they could lose their jobs, we focused a retreat on dealing with change. The invitation read:

Monsanto exists in a world of constant challenge and change. Its long-term direction is set as much as it can be within a future that is fundamentally unknowable. Helping Monsanto travel the path from what it is to what it can become requires creativity, focus, caring, working closely with others, authenticity, excellence, adaptability, learning and much more. It places great demands on personal and professional lives. It has the potential to be exhilarating and fulfilling. Handling its demands also has the potential to be discouraging, or even devastating. It may require new abilities and sources of strength. For some, the practice of mindfulness is a place where these abilities and strengths can be found.

While we were helping Monsanto learn about resilience in the face of change, the unforeseen consequences of bioengineered seeds were making headlines. Monsanto was not being celebrated as a company contributing to environmental sustainability and food security but as the home of "terminator technology," the creator of "superweeds," and a threat to the survival of monarch butterflies. Bob's dream of feeding the world for the twenty-first century looked less and less likely, and finally he stepped down as CEO. His successor immediately eliminated the mindfulness program, which he associated with Bob. We knew we had made a difference for many people there – I still hear from people who first learned mindfulness in that program – but we had put huge effort into building a program that was designed to grow, and it was gone in a moment.

While honoring the nature of impermanence, I felt discouraged about starting over in another corporation. As if to make sure I got the message, a small mindfulness program that we did for the staff of *Marie Claire*, a Hearst magazine in New York, was also eliminated when the publisher changed. And then, in 2007, along came an invitation from Google, where the corporate policy encouraged diverse ways of understanding, and I took the risk.

Google: searching inside

Chade-Meng Tan (widely known as Meng) was among the earliest engineers to be hired at Google. He and his team worked on ways to improve the quality of the site's search results and also played a key role in the launch of mobile search. He helped Google become indispensible to people around the world, providing free information for everyone who seeks it. When Google allowed engineers to spend 20 percent of their time pursuing their passion, Meng decided to spend his time on a cause dear to his heart: bringing meditation into Google.

He saw that mindfulness-based stress reduction, the program originally developed by Jon Kabat-Zinn, was being used in other organizations, so he found a local teacher in Mountain View, California, and offered MBSR at Google Headquarters as a free course for anyone who wanted to sign up. But no one did. He was mystified. Employees were already doing yoga, getting massages, and coming to the small introductions to meditation that Meng led. Why didn't they sign up for a free course in mindfulness-based stress reduction? No one knew. Then a friend told Meng that I had been helping diverse professionals discover the power of contemplation and that I might be able to help. He also liked that I thought that there are many other important benefits of mindfulness in addition to stress reduction. Meng was really interested in benefits that would lead to world peace – he is convinced that it will happen if people cultivate the conditions for inner peace within themselves.

So I flew to Silicon Valley, and together we studied why MBSR did not appeal to Googlers. The first thing I noticed was the diversity: an unscientific study in their renowned cafeteria/restaurant indicated that the Google staff were about one-third Chinese (and Chinese Americans), one-third Indian (and Indian Americans), and one-third a mix of everybody else. A majority was male. They were young (twenties and thirties), very smart, very competitive (graduating top of their classes at Stanford, MIT, etc.), and had spent most of their lives in front of screens. They had expertise, and some had considerable experience. They were brilliant at writing algorithms but they were not so good at working in teams. We realized that what most Googlers needed was better emotional intelligence (EI, self-awareness and awareness of others), and I realized that we could offer the same practices, beginning with mindfulness, but focus on the way in which they cultivate these capacities. We could use mindfulness to train a quality of clear and stable attention and then direct this attention to emotion so we can see it with high vividness and resolution.

Daniel Goleman had written in *Working with Emotional Intelligence* (1998) that EI skills are synergistic with cognitive ones; top performers have both. "The more complex the job, the more emotional intelligence matters – if only because a deficiency of these skills can hinder the use of technical expertise or intellect a person may have." But not everyone at Google knew this. They were so successful at so many things that it was hard to appreciate that they could still go from good to great (or from great to awesome). I asked Dan to give a Google Talk to the staff to get them thinking. Although he was no longer giving talks in corporations, he agreed to come to Google because he liked the idea of offering mindfulness practices as a method for developing emotional competencies. He gave a compelling talk and ended by saying that mindfulness and the related practices of loving kindness and compassion were a direct route to EI. In 4 hours, 100 Googlers signed up.

Meng and I, with the help of Norman Fischer, former abbot of the San Francisco Zen Center, set about creating the first draft of what became Search Inside Yourself: Mindfulness-Based Emotional Intelligence (SIY). We linked each of the EI competencies to a meditative practice:

- self-awareness (knowing one's internal states, preferences, resources, and intuitions): mindful sitting, standing, walking, journaling, body scan and scan for emotion;
- self-regulation (managing one's internal states, impulses, and resources): mindful sitting, awareness of emotions, working with anger, letting go, writing about feelings;
- motivation (emotional tendencies that guide or facilitate reaching goals): journaling and mindful listening on values;
- empathy (awareness of others' feelings, needs, and concerns) and compassion (awareness of others' suffering, with the desire to relieve it): *tong len* (giving and receiving practice), Just Like Me, loving kindness;
- social skills (adeptness at inducing desirable responses in others): mindful listening and speaking from the heart, mindful emailing.

Over time, we refined and expanded the curriculum. Philippe Goldin, a neuroscience researcher at Stanford, joined the team and introduced the relevant research on the effects of meditation, including the work of Richard Davidson at the University of Wisconsin, Sara Lazar at Harvard, and his own work on social anxiety. This was important for Googlers, most of whom were engineers and scientists and are proud that their work is data-driven, scientifically based.

Meng described the course in an interview with Wharton (Knowledge@wharton 2012):

Three steps are involved in developing emotional intelligence in the SIY framework. The first is to train attention in a way that allows you to make your mind calm and clear on demand. At any time, whatever is happening to you – whether you're under stress, you're being shouted at, or anything else – you have the skill to bring the mind to a place that's calm and clear. If you can do that, it lays the foundation for emotional intelligence. Step two is creating self-mastery. Once your mind is calm and clear, you can create a quality of self-knowledge or self-awareness that improves over time and it evolves into self-mastery. You know about yourself enough that you can master your emotions. The third step is to develop good mental habits. For example, there is the mental habit of kindness, of looking at every human being you encounter and thinking to yourself, "I want this person to be happy." Once that becomes a habit, you don't have to think about it, it just comes naturally. Then everything in your work life changes because people want to associate with you and they like you. It operates on the subconscious level. Those are the skills that SIY is designed to develop.

After each time SIY was taught, participants filled out a self-report evaluation, which was a combination of qualitative and quantitative responses: respond from 1–5 (from "don't agree" to "strongly agree") on statements such as "I would recommend this training to others" and "I'll be able to apply what I learned here to my work." The average score was never below 4, and by 2012, it was at 4.9. That's what Googlers aim for!

Although there was an occasional comment like "I was upset by how often the instructors made claims by confusing correlation with causation," which was then deconstructed with care, most of the feedback was extremely positive:

I was contemplating quitting and not wanting to be in my current job. I now find myself actually enjoying my work.

My communication skills improved a lot. I found myself making better decisions faster and sticking with them more often.

I became more focused during work. I am more attentive when I listen to people. I am more relaxed. I find myself stopping circular/obsessive thought patterns, which normally distract me. Overall, I really feel this was life changing.

The way I respond to situations under pressure has changed. I am able to stop and think before I respond (instead of react). I am also more sensitive to other people's needs.

I haven't seen the instructors walk on water yet. Maybe they reserve that for advanced students only?;-)

We talked from the beginning about measuring the results of SIY in other ways as well: physiological measures, computer-based tests of attention, and function magnetic resonance imaging studies. To date, no one has done this research, but it is a promising area for the future.

More than 1,000 employees at Google offices in Mountain View, San Francisco, New York City, London, Zurich, Beijing, and other cities have completed SIY. Meng then decided to open-source the SIY program by making its principles and components available to companies everywhere. He has written a book, *Search Inside Yourself: The Unexpected Path to Achieving Success, Happiness (and World Peace)* (Tan, 2012), which has been on bestseller lists all over the world.

Further research and reflection

The need for research

More research is needed both to demonstrate the value of mindfulness in the workplace and to respond to the critiques of Buddhist teachers and others who fear that in the workplace mindfulness is doing more harm than good. It is not an easy task. I remember that executives at Monsanto kept asking for measures to improve results, and in 1997 I didn't have anything to give them. I wasn't trained in either quantitative or qualitative research, much less neuroscience, and I knew that there were so many factors affecting each person's readiness for change and awakening that it would be a nearly impossible task. And during a loving kindness retreat at the Insight

Meditation Society, I remembered that kindness, compassion, equanimity, and sympathetic joy, cultivated through meditation, are called the Immeasurables.

But now we are in a new time. There are hundreds of studies on mindfulness, some more rigorous than others. For many corporate managers who want to try a mindfulness program for their staff, the existing research is convincing enough. But I would like to see more qualitative in-depth and longitudinal studies of how these practices change people over time and how those internal changes affect their behaviors at work and in the rest of their lives. It takes an in-depth study to see the effects of mindfulness on complex behaviors such as leadership and in community development.

I've been working with Fetzer Institute for years now to look at how mindfulness and other contemplative practices contribute to building a sense of community within the organization: how they help employees identify shared values and understand the common vision at Fetzer. All sixty-five employees, from groundskeepers to the president, meet every Wednesday morning to practice mindfulness together and learn mindful listening, facilitation, communication, meeting process, and other methods for building a more mindful organization. We have not documented it yet, but we are experiencing a strong sense of common purpose, increased enthusiasm and energy for the work, and frequent humor and joy.

Implications of the instrumental use of mindfulness

The most common resistance to teaching mindfulness in organizations and corporations for stress reduction or EI is that we are reducing it to a technique or instrument that is used to increase productivity of goods that might be better not produced in the first place; that it is not being taught in a way that will lead to inquiry into the ethics of the corporation but rather either as a soporific that will make employees more relaxed and mindlessly accepting of unjust working conditions; or as a technique to enhance attention only (without inquiry) to increase efficiency. These critics hold that teaching mindfulness as a means to an end is counter to its nature. They fear that it is being sold as a commodity. They are concerned that mindfulness is being reduced to a practice that ignores its potential, understood in Buddhism as a method of great transformative power that can lead to full awakening. In the *Satipaṭṭhāna Sutta*, the great teaching on mindfulness, the Buddha says: "This is the direct path for the purification of beings, for the surmounting of sorrow and lamentation, for the disappearance of pain and grief, for the attainment of the true way, for the realization of nibbana [liberation]" (Goldstein 2013, p. 425).

My experience is that decision makers in organizations often do invite mindfulness programs into the workplace because they hope mindfulness will reduce stress, improve productivity, decrease absenteeism, and increase creativity. No doubt some at Google and in other tech businesses see mindfulness as another utility widget for staying ahead. And often these results do occur. But other things happen too, especially when a skilled teacher grounded in the foundations of mindfulness leads the practice. Once a person is given a way to explore the inner life, there is no predicting what he or she will find. After a session at Google, one young engineer said: "Cool. I just defragged my hard-drive!" But another said: "I saw that all of life was interconnected, not just by the Internet but by something more mysterious."

When asked about business leaders practicing mindfulness, Thich Nhat Hanh said that as long as they practice "true" mindfulness, it doesn't matter if "the original intention is triggered by wanting to be more effective at work or make bigger profits ... the practice will fundamentally change their perspective on life as it naturally opens hearts to greater compassion and develops the desire to end the suffering of others." (Confino, 2014).

Mindfulness as a secular practice

Do we have to omit the "spiritual element" in offering mindfulness practice in the workplace? I would say, not if "spiritual" means that aspect of life that relates to spirit – to the values and meaning by which people live, to the interconnection of all life. I started doing this work to encourage people to experience the initial benefits of practice. But even with this minimal guidance, I often saw people experience a sense of calm and quiet clarity and stability, which can increase insight and kindness and compassion toward others. Do I think that sustained guided practice over time with a good teacher is more likely to lead toward a deeper awakening? Yes, I do. But this is a doorway – an experienced teacher giving simple instructions to begin to shift the way we think about work and act toward each other in our organizations. These are entrenched institutions, even those that try to be cutting edge, and our relation to them and each other is often inherited and unconscious. These practices help us see through our automatic behaviors and ask ourselves how we can align our work with our deepest values.

Reflections on factors that turn the mind away from worldly concerns and toward the essential questions of life, which establish the motivation behind one's practice, can be woven into an introduction to practice. It is possible to talk about one's fortunate human existence by leading a short reflection on being grateful that we can be here today to take this time to practice together. And the teachings of impermanence and karma naturally arise in discussions of thoughts rising and passing away and of the clear glimpses of cause and effect that meditation provides: I skipped breakfast to get to this meditation session on time, so now I am hungry. The limitations of the material world also arise in conversation. Many people I have taught, for example, begin to question why they are working so much to buy material goods and experiences that rarely satisfy their deep yearning for wholeness.

The importance of a skillful teacher

To date, not enough research has been done on how mindfulness in the workplace is actually transforming participants. My experience is that, when taught by skillful teachers who appreciate the potential of mindfulness, students begin to open their minds to its power to change their lives. As Joseph Goldstein says in his brilliant new book, *Mindfulness: A Practical Guide to Awakening* (2013, p. xv), "When we open any one door of the Dharma, it leads to all the rest." But my experience is limited and circumstantial, and we have not yet determined the right extent and nature of training for a skillful teacher in the corporate setting, although Spirit Rock Meditation Center, the Center for Mindfulness at the University of Massachusetts, UCLA's Mindful Awareness Research Center, and the Search Inside Yourself Leadership Institute are exploring that now.

The role of ethics

Traditionally, *sila*, or Buddhist training in morals and ethics, preceded training in mindfulness. Monks had to explore the practical implications of non-harming before learning the focus that mindfulness cultivates, since that focus can be used for wholesome or non-wholesome purposes. The Dalai Lama points to this in relation to Western education – through scientific method and critical thinking we have developed immense knowledge but without compassion and wisdom we can use it with negative results (examples include the atomic bomb, chemical weapons, the skewed distribution of resources causing starvation). But in a secular setting, how do we introduce moral and ethical principles without seeming to proselytize? At Monsanto, we talked about "nonharming" as a guide for behavior during the retreat. At Google, we talk more freely about kindness, compassion, and even love. And although the golden rule is nearly universal in religious contexts, it is still a delicate but critical area for discussion in corporations and a fruitful area for research.

I have been asked whether working with people who appear to be so off the grid in terms of contemplative values required a lot of faith on my part. But it is mysterious to me who in these retreats and programs suddenly has an *Ah-ha!* experience, the kind that changes the way they work and the way they live. I really trust the process of the dharma unfolding, of the truth emerging, and I think that our work is to create environments in which that is more likely to happen. If there is to be a shift in the direction that global society is moving, we need the power of spirit, of truth, of creativity, of insight. I think it is the only way that things can change.

Organizational change

The other subject ripe for research is whether a more mindful workforce will change the underlying nature of the corporation or the way it acts in the world. As my friend and fellow Seva Foundation co-founder Wavy Gravy says to himself in the morning while looking in the mirror, "It's all done with people." The corporation is a legal structure, based on return for investors, and that basic nature is unlikely to change until we develop a new economic system. But it is people who make the decisions, create the products, and determine the profit margin.

As a Monsanto scientist once said to me, people decide whether to "create products that kill or those that support life." People at Google decide whether to change their China policy when Tibet activists are harassed; litigators at the Federal Trade Commission, for whom I ran a mindfulness program, decide whether to search their networks to find more lawyers of color to hire rather than just waiting for resumés. And if alternative economic systems will serve us all more equitably and sustain the planet longer, it will be people who develop them, often people who have worked in and been unhappy with corporations.

Conclusion

An enlightened workforce doesn't happen all at once. But as more awakened employees become committed to principles of right livelihood through mindfulness and compassion practice, they may change corporations in important ways. They could:

- bear witness to the operation and what the company is producing, whether goods or information;
- apply standards of conduct that are aligned with their personal values;
- recognize that business is not an isolated entity – it is interconnected with all other life and its actions affect all other life;
- encourage generosity;
- use right speech – truthful, helpful, timely, kind;
- listen carefully to others, both within and outside the company;
- tolerate ambiguity, not knowing, and paradox;
- encourage responsibility to those who work for and depend on the company – fair wages, health care, maternity/paternity leave, etc.;
- exercise humility;
- be compassionate and loving;
- create products that support life.

References

Confino, J. (2014). Thich Nhat Hanh: is mindfulness being corrupted by business and finance? *The Guardian*, March 28. Retrieved from www.theguardian.com/sustainablebusiness/thich-nhat-hanh-mindfulness-google-tech.

Duerr, M. (2004). *A powerful silence: the role of meditation and other contemplative practices in American life and work*. Retrieved from www.contemplativemind.org/admin/wp-content/uploads/2012/09/APS.pdf.

Duerr, M. (2011). *Assessing the state of contemplative practices in the U.S.* Kalamazoo, MI: Fetzer Institute. Retrieved from www.contemplativemind.org/admin/wp-content/uploads/ContemplationNation-2-Duerr.pdf.

Goldstein, J. (2013). *Mindfulness: a practical guide to awakening*. Boulder, CO: Sounds True.

Goleman, Daniel. (1998). *Working with emotional intelligence*. New York: Bantam Books.

Hochman, D. (2013). Mindfulness at every turn. *The New York Times*, November 3. ST2. Print.

Knowledge@Wharton (2012) Google's Chade Meng Tan wants you to search inside yourself for inner (and world) peace. April 25. Retrieved from http://knowledge.wharton.upenn.edu/article/googles-chade-meng-tan-wants-you-to-search-inside-yourself-for-inner-and-world-peace/.

Pew Research Religion and Public Life Project (2007). *U.S. religious landscape survey, summary of key findings*. Retrieved from http://religions.pewforum.org/reports#.

Tan, C.-M. (2012). *Search inside yourself: the unexpected path to achieving success, happiness (and world peace)*. New York: HarperOne.

15 | Teaching managers to manage themselves: mindfulness and the inside work of management[1]

JEREMY HUNTER

What is the relation of this [contemplation] to actions? Simply this. He who attempts to act and do things for others or for the world without deepening his own self-understanding, freedom, integrity and capacity to love, will not have anything to give others. He will communicate to them nothing but the contagion of his own obsessions, his aggressiveness, his ego-centered ambitions, his delusions about ends and means, his doctrinaire prejudices and ideas. There is nothing more tragic in the modern world than the misuse of power and action to which men are driven by their own Faustian misunderstandings and misapprehensions. We have more power at our disposal today than we have ever had, and yet we are more alienated and estranged from the inner ground of meaning and love than we have ever been.

Thomas Merton.

I have only three enemies. My favorite enemy, the one most easily influenced for the better, is the British Empire. My second enemy, the Indian people, is far more difficult. But my most formidable opponent is a man named Mohandas K. Gandhi. With him I seem to have very little influence.

Mahatma Gandhi.

Introduction

Contemporary management education has largely overlooked creating an educational process as systematic as accounting and financial

[1] I would like to thank Kirk Warren Brown, Christopher Lyddy and Ken McLeod for their generous input on improving this chapter, which is drawn from a forthcoming book in progress. I would also like to thank Jochen Reb for his boundless editorial patience and my wife Tomo Ogino for spending too many weekends alone while I wrote.

355

analysis for managing oneself. Students are left to fend for themselves to know how to skillfully handle and transform the inner forces of emotions, physical sensations, thoughts, and beliefs to produce elegant and effective results. The cost of this can been seen in leaders given enormous responsibilities to perform with few tools for managing the inevitable pressures that will come their way. This can lead to scattered, unfocused efforts, destructive actions misaligned to one's stated values, or habitual ways of perceiving that fail to adapt to changing circumstances (Hunter and Chaskalson 2013). Just as leaders need tools to manage external realities, they also need tools to manage the internal ones. Effectiveness starts inside.

This perspective builds on management philosopher Peter Drucker's observation that "you cannot manage other people unless you manage yourself first" (Drucker and Wartzman 2010). This work is aimed at a particular kind of person. The manager it addresses seeks to make a positive contribution through their work while also making a living. At the Drucker School where I teach, this is called "Doing good while doing well." Embedded in this notion is both a value for productive performance and a sense of personal responsibility to embody and express dearly held values through positive action in the world. However, these managers sense "something is off." Stress, tension, and distraction play too much of a role in their lives and they seek answers to remedy the pain they feel but cannot explain. They understand the fluid boundaries between the personal and the professional; and how tension in one area can detrimentally spill over into the other. They seek to be more effective in both arenas. They want greater balance, but do not know how to get it.

The goal of the chapter is to share my experience as a teacher, not a researcher or clinician, of mindfulness and allied awareness practices in a management school setting. The chapter describes the origins and methods of the Executive Mind/Practice of Self-Management courses I developed at the Peter F. Drucker School of Management in the early 2000s. It explores the motivation behind the creation of the courses and examines why a systematic method for self-management has not yet happened. What factors are different now compared to a century ago and why are they gaining traction now? The bulk of the discussion examines what instructional and learning methods are relevant and appropriate for executives. It will illustrate how these methods are used, drawing from the lives of working executives as well as lessons learned from my experience teaching executives. Finally, it will briefly explore what might be the future of mindfulness and management.

Why managers should manage themselves

For most of its modern history, management education has focused on systematic training in the external: accounting, finance, strategy, marketing, and all the important elements needed to manage an organization. Furthermore, educating managers in the United States has primarily been in the so-called "hard skills" of rational analysis and manipulating abstract symbolic systems, cultivating certain capacities of human ability but leaving others fallow.

Left out of the equation is systematic development of the perceptual, emotional, and somatic/embodied sensing qualities of managers. These are capacities that are simply taken for granted, ignored as irrelevant, or quietly derided as "soft." Because dominant managerial approaches assume that humans are conscious and rational, they underplay or ignore the reality that the vast majority of human functioning happens automatically and outside conscious awareness (Wilson 2002). This absence creates a vulnerability to the darker side of human nature.

There are costs to ignoring the non-conscious, emphasizing the external and not positively cultivating the internal. The most extreme example is toxic leadership where a leader's destructive qualities inflict "serious and enduring harm on their followers and organizations" (Lipman-Blumen, 2005, p. 18). The US Army describes them as having "a combination of self-centered attitudes, motivations, and behaviors that have adverse effects on subordinates, the organization, and mission performance. This leader lacks concern for others and the climate of the organization, which leads to short- and long-term negative effects" (Wilson 2014). Witness leaders with enormous power and responsibility who do not see how egocentric prejudices and projections distort their perceptions or how reptilian survival reactions distort their relationship to the world. They are blind to how reactive emotions such as anger or fear distort their actions.

Why does this matter? Consider the state of the world today. The reality of ecological, financial, and technological interconnectedness is now much more obvious, complex, and vulnerable. Actions seem able to travel further and faster. A rogue trader can send a market spiraling. Prolonged drought in California affects the food supply of the nation.

A nuclear accident shifts the environmental, political, and economic dynamics of an entire region. Can a leader act with skill and wisdom without first learning to deftly handle one's built-in but often inappropriate survival reflexes, cognitive biases, or emotional reactions? With institutions and communities reeling from economic, ecological, and social disruption, can they afford not to better manage themselves?

How can decision makers muster wisdom, ingenuity, and insight to make effective decisions and take effective action? Certainly, naturally talented individuals can arise to the occasion. However, it is more effective for leaders to systematically learn how to manage their own toxicity and cultivate their generative qualities to the benefit of themselves and their teams. Indeed research is beginning to demonstrate that a leader's quality of mindfulness influences employee experience and performance. Reb and colleagues (2014) found positive associations between a leader's trait-level mindfulness and greater employee job satisfaction, job performance, organizational citizenship behavior, and wellbeing. The employees of mindful leaders were less exhausted and enjoyed better work-life balance. Mindfulness training provides a developmental pathway for a capable leader.

Why has a systematic method for managing oneself not emerged before, and why now?

While mindfulness and meditation are often associated with Asia, the idea of developing attention for effective self-management is not a uniquely Asian idea. In addition to Drucker, the idea appears many times in Western thought. Adam Smith back in 1759 advocated cultivating an Impartial Spectator who could act as a witness to one's action to assess and guide moral behavior (Smith [1759] 1976). A century later, William James asserted a connection between disciplined perception and self-mastery and the essential need for developing attention:

> [T]he faculty of voluntarily bringing back a wandering attention, over and over again, is the very root of judgment, character and will. No one is *compos sui* [master of oneself] if he has it not. An education which should improve this faculty would be *the* education *par excellence*
>
> (James 1890.

Unfortunately, he did not have a practical method for realizing this ideal. In a sense, the West was "all talk and no action."

Years later, James, after hearing a Harvard lecture by Buddhist teacher Anagarika Dharmapala, stood up and declared that "This is the psychology everybody will be studying twenty-five years from now" (Fields 1981, p. 135). Unfortunately, while twentieth-century Western psychology created models of development that spoke to cognitive and emotional development (Piaget 1926), linguistic development (Vygotsky 1962), identity development (Erikson 1950), and moral development (Gilligan 1982; Kohlberg, Levine, and Hewer 1983; Piaget 1932) it never produced a model of attention development. It took nearly a century for James' vision to become a reality.

Efforts over the past four decades have slowly built a foundation of empirical evidence demonstrating the transformative capacity of contemplative practices. Many individuals and institutions have contributed to this effort. The Mind and Life Institute held its first public symposium at Massachusetts Institute of Technology (MIT) in 2003. This event occurred after years of dialogue between top Western scientists and "professional" contemplatives including the Dalai Lama. Under the theme of "Investigating the Mind," this event is considered a watershed moment in bringing scientific respectability to the study of inner transformation. Jon Kabat-Zinn of the University of Massachusetts created the mindfulness-based stress reduction (MBSR) program. This was the first systematic mindfulness tool to be delivered in secularized contexts and subject to rigorous research protocols (Kabat-Zinn 1990) Findings have shown that MBSR changes brain activity and structure, enhances emotional regulation, memory and perspective taking (Davidson *et al.* 2003; Hölzel *et al.* 2011). Others have found that mindfulness enhances cognitive functioning, including focused attention, working memory and unfocused sustained attention (Chiesa and Serretti 2010). Mindfulness has been associated with greater wellbeing, self-awareness, and self-regulatory measures as well as decreased negative affect (Brown and Ryan 2003); for a discussion of numerous other effects of mindfulness, see the other chapters in this volume or Brown, Creswell, and Ryan's (2015) *Handbook of Mindfulness: Theory, Research and Practice*.

Mindfulness at a management school

What is the intellectual foundation for why mindfulness and contemplative practices are relevant, if not essential, in a management education? How does this "woo-woo" stuff relate to the serious business of management? Why should a manager invest energy in learning a set of seemingly mystical practices associated more with ascetics than executives? How to discuss practices for inner development using everyday language so that they do not seem off-putting? What is needed is a rhetorical strategy so convincing that a hard-headed finance or engineering executive can embrace these practices as common-sense necessities. The answers I found to these questions came from different directions to cohere into a clear picture.

In the late 1990s and early 2000s, mindfulness, meditation, and allied practices were not on the cultural radar in the way they are today. The now growing body of science was still gestating. In large part, mindfulness and such things occupied a place in the public imagination somewhere on the incense-scented shelf between tarot cards and crystal healing. The essential relevance of these practices to effective management was not at all clear.

However, pioneers in the professions, like Jon Kabat-Zinn in medicine (1990), Ronald Epstein (1999) writing on mindfulness in the workplace, Len Riskin (2002) in law and even pro basketball coach Phil Jackson (Lazenby 2001) with the championship Chicago Bulls and LA Lakers, build a plausible case that managers might benefit from mindfulness. They demonstrated a clear relationship between quality of attention and quality of experience and performance. People who are present and aware function more effectively and they generally feel better in the process.

Another powerful block of evidence came from a project I was involved with that explored the relationship between contemplative practices and "good work" (Gardner, Csikszentmihalyi, and Damon 2002). The study consisted of a series of detailed interviews with successful professionals who were also long-term mindfulness practitioners. Study participants came from a variety of backgrounds and included healthcare executives, scientists, journalists, film producers and Fortune 500 CEOs (Hunter and McCormick 2008). From these conversations, a consistent picture emerged describing how mindfulness practice had deeply transformed these individuals' relationship to their work.

A few participants gave up unsatisfying, extrinsically-driven careers for more intrinsically meaningful livelihoods. One architect walked away from a glamorous global career for a more human-scaled, contemplative approach to work. Others discussed how the practice had saved them from a life driven by self-centered ruthlessness and led them down the path of compassionate action. Many described how mindfulness practice gave them solid ground to stand on in the face of complex and contradictory demands. Without fail, they all offered concrete examples of moving out of a narrow, selfish way of living to a larger reference point informed by a greater sense of service, even in traditional corporate contexts. They also described how they felt more effective at living, handled conflict better, skillfully managed difficult emotions, and made wiser, healthier decisions. "Productive" meant not just "getting things done," but doing the right things while living from a place of greater intrinsic meaning, personal responsibility and social contribution.

This study taught me how mindfulness creates choices for practitioners about how they take action in the world. Mindfulness helped me create choices too. For nearly a decade at that point, I had lived with a chronic, degenerative, and supposedly terminal autoimmune disease, and I relied on meditation and mindfulness to manage difficult emotions, focus my energy and, frankly, help me live day-to-day. It gave me tools to take responsibility for my own pain and suffering. Instead of projecting my suffering out into the world on innocent others or suppressing it out of my awareness, mindfulness gave me the ability to metabolize the energies of anger, fear, and anxiety. In so doing, I could make better choices and take wiser actions to live in a positive way.

An additional stream of support came from the research of my graduate advisor Mihaly Csikszentmihalyi at the University of Chicago. His writings on human development (Csikzentmihalyi and Csikszentmihalyi 1992; Csikszentmihalyi 1993) emphasized that human beings who better controlled their attention, their limited resources of psychic energy, were better equipped to control their own future. After all, our lives are what we attend to. Without conscious control of attention people are vulnerable to seduction from biological or cultural programs not of their own making or in their own interests. From Csikszentmihalyi's point of view, willfully controlling attention was the basis of the good life – it created the option to create options. To me, mindfulness is the clutch that moves us from habit to conscious choice.

A final thread comes from the writings of Peter Drucker. Critical that education focused too heavily on analysis, he claimed that in a dynamic environment it was also crucial to develop *perception*. In a world defined by knowledge, being able to perceive invisible configurations of meaning was essential to function and adapt in a changing world (Drucker 1989). Furthermore, he emphasized the necessity of "trained perception and disciplined emotion" to create mature human beings who are capable of functioning in the world (Drucker 1992, p. 319). Mindfulness trains perception to make more conscious invisible structures of meaning that drive action. It is an uncanny parallel.

The combined effect of experiences with mindfulness from other professions, the experiences of the study participants, my experience of mindfulness in relation to illness, Mihaly Csikszentmihalyi's connection between quality of attention and quality of life and Peter Drucker writing about the importance of cultivating perception and emotion created a compelling possibility. Mindfulness is deeply relevant to audiences outside Buddhist practice centers and monasteries. Mindfulness could form the foundation of a practice of self-management. The ability to "manage oneself" might be the basis of a "new" liberal art forming a vital part of any truly educated person's set of skills.

Developing *The Executive Mind* course: principles and practices

This section addresses how to implement a mindfulness course in a conservative management setting. The core strategy used in The Executive Mind course is to splice the DNA of mindfulness practice into a management environment without arousing an immune response. Because the needs of managers are (at least on the surface) different from those of medical patients or spiritual aspirants, the framing of mindfulness must shift to meet that circumstance. Special considerations need to be made about what is relevant and appropriate when introducing mindfulness into a management context. These include emphasizing action and results, familiar language, and practical and immediate value of the tools and frameworks.

Stress reduction is the starting point, not the aim of the work. The thrust of the course is not reducing stress but cultivating internal conditions that lead to effective action. Of course, having a calm, less-stressed mind is intrinsically important because it is healthier for the body. However, the course helps the participant cultivate the ability to make wiser, more effective, and compassionate choices for themselves and those they manage and live with. Enhancing their capacity to make choices emerges from them seeing how their mind is reacting to a situation. As the student observes this reaction that is normally hidden from view it becomes amenable to change. A person's mindful observation of the contents of their consciousness creates the possibility for transforming their results. A Buddhist might say the course transforms a person's *karma*, the genesis of their actions, to evince a positive shift in their *vipaka*, the fruits of their results. A later section will discuss the frameworks students use to implement this goal.

Natural language over spiritual jargon. Language is a key factor for creating willingness to try these practices. For managers who are comfortable in a world of rational analysis, asking them to dive into the pool of perception and emotion is a big, scary step. The rationalist may also bring a fair share of skepticism for this work. Language that can be alienating or off-putting detracts from learning the practice. To make the course as accessible as possible, I chose not to use Sanskrit or Pali terms or any other "spiritual" terminology. Words or phrases that sound out of place in a contemporary workplace or in competition with one's existing religious or spiritual commitments are not used. Depending on the circumstances, I even avoid the word "mindfulness" in favor of "enhancing attention and awareness." Even after a decade of teaching, some environments still see "mindfulness" as New Age frippery or faddish nonsense (a prime example is Luke Johnson's "Stoic response to the fad of meditation" in the *Financial Times*). The intention is not to "sell" an ideology of mindfulness but create a condition where a person experiences living in attention.

Incidentally, I have found that my most religious students find a complementary relationship between their faith commitments and cultivating greater attention and awareness. They consistently report that the tools help them to better enact their faith commitments in the world, and they often become the course's most enthusiastic supporters. Further examples of how language is used will be explored later in the chapter.

Moments as units of analysis. Every discipline needs a unit of analysis, a lens through which it sees the world. Mindfulness offers a powerful way of seeing the world: the unit of the moment. This is rather distinct because typical conversations about "managing oneself" happen at the level of a person, emphasizing personal traits, qualities, or habits: what are Rajiv's strengths and weaknesses or Sally's Myers-Briggs type? However, by focusing on the scale of the moment, mindfulness brings into view previously invisible factors affecting productive action.

Moments are the scale at which people experience the world. By directing attention to what is happening inside right now, a window opens to what is often unseen but not unfelt. New elements come into focus. Just as a movie is made up of the combination of light and sound, image and motion, our experience of life is made up of the combination of body sensations, emotions, and narratives and images (McLeod 2001).

The most concrete element of experience are sensations in the body. These can register as tensions, pressures, places of warmth or coldness, internal movements or qualities of space. Someone might notice tension in the jaw, an open feeling in the abdomen, a subtle vibration in the chest or a multitude of other possible sensations. A second character is emotion. Happy, fearful, strong, content, doubtful, curious, joyful, angry, irritable, enjoyment are only a few potential emotions. Often these intertwine with specific body sensations. The third category consists of inner narratives and images. These are the stories and pictures in one's head that form the running commentary to the flow of experience. These can be the thoughts, judgments, assumptions, expectations, explanations, preconceived notions that overlay what is happening right now. Managing oneself involves becoming aware of the contents of this flow and how they influence action in the moment.

Moments are also an unseen and unmeasured, but not unfelt, dimension of organizational life. Just as a TV screen is made up of thousands of pixels, organizational life is comprised of a web of momentary events. A manager sitting in a meeting has an impulsive thought to check her phone and reflexively steals a quick glance. This momentary distraction is interpreted by a colleague as a lack of interest. An off-hand comment is misinterpreted by an associate as a snub who then withdraws vital resources from the team. A manager looking over a faltering project feels a sense of panicked pressure in his forehead that leads to a sudden outburst, scaring people from bringing him bad news. These momentary actions ripple out into the workspace affecting the quality of interaction, commitment, and productive work. Mindfulness can shed light on these moments, raising awareness of previously unseen dynamics. Just as the invention of a microscope opened up a new previously unseen view on reality, mindfulness can help us see ourselves and our actions in a new way.

Focus on process and content of the immediate subjective experience. One danger of implementing a mindfulness course in an organizational setting is that it becomes a group therapy session. This can feel inappropriate in a professional context where one is surrounded by colleagues and potential career competitors. Therefore, the course is structured so that participants focus on the immediate internal processes of their experience. Discussing the process of how their mind worked in a situation rather than the larger narrative circumstances puts a tight focus on what gets aired. For example, Fred gets impatient in a meeting and loses his temper but discusses it as: "I heard a colleague say something that my mind registered as negative. I noticed there was a story in my head about how this wasn't going to work out well and I felt concerned. It reminded me of a past experience where something similar was being discussed and the outcome was a disaster. A bolt shot off inside me and before I knew it I was yelling at my colleague." We know exactly what was happening in Fred's head but the identities of the people being discussed, their personal histories, and the content of the meeting all remain out of the frame. By focusing on the process of experience, privacy and discretion can be maintained. It also holds a frame for Fred to be responsible for how he manages himself, rather than displacing blame to others, getting caught in a narrative about others and so on.

Emphasis on taking effective action. Because executives are defined by action and decisions, the class emphasizes action in life, not contemplation divorced from the mess of the world. Mindfulness practiced in a blissful retreat setting is not so helpful for the leader who needs to be mindful when the metaphorical bullets start flying. Instead, the mess of the world is embraced as an arena for training.

The course is oriented towards the student's life through exercises called "live-fire practices" nodding to military exercises where real, not rubber, bullets are used. Live-fire practices address an issue common to meditators: the "off-the-cushion dilemma." This occurs when the peace and calm of the meditation practice do not necessarily translate to peaceful, calm action in the world. By making the student's life the meditation hall participants practice in a much more demanding and intense way.

First-person case studies. No third person case studies are employed. By making their lives the case studied, a powerful set of personal insights arise from students' weekly investigations. By relying on the students themselves to observe and study their experience, they arrive at insights more immediately than if the course lecture had simply "told" them what the "right" answer is.

Consider the situation of Fatima, a manager at a large aerospace company. A direct report of hers sought her out for advice in dealing with a difficult client. Wanting to be helpful, Fatima fires off a checklist of what the younger associate needs to do. She notices the associate shut down and stop listening. Her initial reaction is to think the associate is ungrateful and wasting her time. However, she steps back and considers her own actions. She realizes that her voice was raised and her tone stern. Her "helpfulness" comes off as scolding and prickly. She reverses course and apologizes. She asks the associate more about the experience with the client and then brainstorms together different possible actions. The exchange becomes upbeat and positive. The associate leaves smiling with a list of action items. For Fatima, the exchange is a revelation. Her actions come across counter to her intentions to "help." She begins to be aware of how this pattern plays out elsewhere in her life. "No wonder my kids think I'm a Tiger mom!" She begins the patient process of creating a different pathway.

Let us turn toward a more practical and personal direction. The following sections will discuss how to practice mindfulness in action, including case studies followed by italicized prompts for inquiry. These practice prompts are ways to incorporate mindfulness in the moment.

Though the course includes regular meditation practices, what makes it unique is its systematic approach to action. The primary tool I use is a map, which forms the pillar around which the Executive Mind class is built. The map describes the mind's reactive process, drawn from the teachings of Ken McLeod, known for his modern interpretations of traditional Tibetan teachings (McLeod 2001). Developed in collaboration with McLeod and my colleague Scott Scherer (Hunter and Scherer 2009), the "Reactivity Map" (see Figure 15.1), or the "Moment Map", is used to help students understand their momentary and past automatic, reactive patterns, the results they bring about and how to transform them. The map provides a tool to "override the old connections between stimulus and response" (Csikszentmihalyi and Csikszentmihalyi 2006, p. 9).

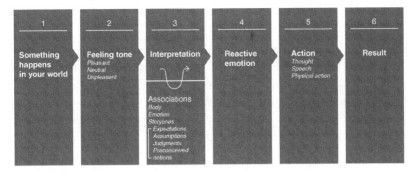

Figure 15.1 A map for managing the mind
Source: Based on McLeod (2001).

One pharmaceuticals executive confessed that at first, the process terrified him because he was used to a world of metrics, benchmarks, and processes. However, as he began to work with the map, he realized the "logic" of how the reactive process worked. Once he understood there were clear topographies in the map, he relaxed into the process. His "light bulb moment" came when he noticed he could manage his temper at work "because people can be less forgiving," but not so at home. There he expected his wife to understand and be forgiving. Seeing the imbalanced expectations in the two conditions through the map helped him embrace the tools.

One virtue of the map is that it makes space for a wider view of mindfulness than what is often presented in contemporary therapeutic literature as "present-moment, non-judgmental awareness," to include cognitive, evaluative dimensions as well as aspects of memory and body sensations (see Dreyfus 2013). Practitioners become familiar with how their minds work.

The map emphasizes the core essence of mindfulness: the ability of the mind to stay with an object and not get swept up in a reaction (McLeod 2001). Staying with an object, holding it in working memory, and not getting caught up in it yields an essential benefit: seeing or perceiving clearly. Clear perception allows the practitioner to see more deeply into the workings of the mind, recognize subtleties of the reactive process and make discernments about the causes and effects of these processes. The above example of the executive who expects forgiveness for his temper at home but not at work illustrates this. Otherwise, lacking mindfulness, one might be carried away by surface impressions, driven by short-sighted, knee-jerk reactions leading to potentially undesirable results. Practiced over time, one begins to see connections between past causes and future effects.

The map starts with taking in a sense impression ... something happens: a new email chimes, a balance sheet is full of red ink, the boss sighs during an important meeting. The sense impression is followed by one of three visceral feeling tones, pleasant, neutral or unpleasant – "I like it," "I don't like it" or "I don't feel strongly either way."

Pleasant sensations generally give rise to favorable, attractive interpretations, wanting more, "Who can resist just one potato chip?" Unpleasant sensations lead to avoidant or aversive stories, an email from a difficult colleague is a tiresome nuisance. The valence of this reaction connects to a story or interpretation. The stories trigger associations of past experiences bringing with them bodily and emotional reactions as well as narratives that could include judgments, expectations, or assumptions.

Memories arise of the last time the difficult colleague caused trouble, bringing on a sense of dread felt heavily in the stomach, and bring up the thought, "What does he want *now*?" This powers an emotional reaction, frustration, which leads to an action, <delete!>, which brings about a result. Six weeks later he asks why his email about buying Girl Scout Cookies from his daughter never got a response. No Thin Mints this year.

Working with reactive emotions. Let us start by working with reactive emotions and move backward through the map. This is helpful because reactive emotions like anger, fear, or disgust are often the most apparent for people to apprehend at an early stage of practice. The subtler aspects emerge as a person's capacity in attention increases.

Because they are unpleasant and sometimes dramatic, reactive emotions are often the first element in the reactivity map people become aware of. The reactivity can be so intense that the capacity to make mindful choices is impaired. Learning to pause and create distance between the reactive emotion and the action makes space for wiser choices.

Tracy is a senior administrator at a large hospital. She gets word that one of the hospital's nurses has tested positive on a random drug test. Instantly she feels a surge of energy course through her body. Her head pounds. Should she take quick action and make the call? Or should she wait to get a better sense of the situation?

"What were my choices? What was best to do? I had simultaneous conflicting feelings."

Part of her wants to sound the alarm that would involve several dozen agencies to inform them of the circumstances. However, this would subject the nurse to a public inquiry and the hospital to potential litigation. Another part of her thinks it is best to get a sense of the whole situation before taking action.

She takes a deep breath and counts to ten. The emotional wave peaks and passes away. A small space of calm opens up inside. She asks herself, "What actually happened? What are the facts? Are we jumping to conclusions without more information? As the lead, what am I responsible for?"

She decides to consult the ten supervisors involved in the situation to get their input. As it turns out the test result was false. However, Tracy found that by taking a moment to step out of the reactive emotion, she maintained a calm and collected demeanor:

I acted like an air traffic controller, and it actually became fun. I took myself out of the stress of the conflict and became completely impartial. This allowed me to gather the facts, assess the damage, address the situation in a more focused approach rather than an emotionally-driven shotgun approach. The calm way of doing things turned out to be particularly effective. My approach was solution-focused, I made thoughtful choices, which resulted in a win-win result.

Practice inquiry: Just because I feel X does not mean it has to drive my actions. What can I do to create space between emotion and action?

Working with interpretations and associations. Interpretations are the stories we create to make sense of a situation. People rely on past experience – associations – to make sense of things, a sort of mental shorthand (Bargh and Chartrand 1999). Associations are triggered because a situation resembles a previous experience and are imported onto, appropriately or inappropriately, the current circumstance (Ekman 2003).

When a person acts based on a past experience rather than the present circumstance trouble can arise from the mismatch. The phone rings and the caller ID reports the caller is your most difficult client. Your stomach ties itself into a knot and you brace for battle. However, no battle is happening other than the one you're remembering from the last time he called. If you pick up the phone with a terse and irritated tone, you may unintentionally create a self-fulfilling prophecy.

Associations may over-focus attention on one area and exclude other aspects of a situation or person or problem. For example, the founders of mindfulness based cognitive therapy for depression note that depressives habitually fall into a biased perception that emphasizes the negative aspects of a situation (Segal, Williams, and Teasdale 2001). Biased perception yields an incomplete picture and our actions may likely be inappropriate and the results undesired.

Sara works for a large entertainment firm as a contractor on a temporary project. Her boss is an intimidating, demanding figure. Whenever Sara spends time with her she feels nervous, pressured, and somewhat overwhelmed by the actions of her boss.

She notices the emotions she feels are influenced by the stories in her head. Sara examines the stories closely and realizes that she has thoroughly villainized the boss, creating a picture of a person with no redeeming qualities. Past memories feed into immediate circumstances, prejudging that the current situation will not go well, sending Sara into a tense reaction. The boss walks into Sara's office and senses the tension, which in turn raises her own discomfort with Sara. Their exchange is clipped and cool.

Sara realizes these associations are freezing her assessment of the boss into a no-win narrative. She makes an effort to become aware of and drop her habitual stories about the boss. She observes the boss as if it is the first time they have met and notices that the boss carries around her own set of anxieties and concerns. A crack appears in her narrative. The boss gradually becomes more human in Sara's eyes as she realizes the boss is not happy in her job. Sara's tension eases as she sees the boss simply as another human being. Gradually, after weeks of effort, the boss reacts to Sara's newly cultivated calm and begins to open to her as a peer, sharing her worries and fears. After a few months, the boss announces she is leaving the firm and, to Sara's astonishment, "she asked me to write a referral for her. It was amazing for me to see the change in our relationship that is no longer strained."

Practice inquiry: Just because this story appears in my head does not mean it's true. Just because my body reacts this way does not mean it is warranted. Are my judgments completely true? Are my expectations realistic or understood by the other? Am I harboring an unwarranted assumption? Are my preconceived notions freezing the possibilities of this situation?

Phil is a senior planner who must analyze a great deal of data in his work. Working through a routine but complicated spreadsheet analysis, he lets go of his old associations and imagines this task is new to him. He immediately notices a way to remove three steps from this cumbersome procedure. "This new process is much more efficient and now I spend more time analyzing the data instead of building the data."

During a session mentoring a younger colleague in a procedure new to her but old hat to him, Phil decided to step out of his "known world" and imagine the situation was new to him, side-stepping his associations, memories, and impatience:

I was able to see things from my colleague's point of view, as she had not run across this situation before. I really think this approach did two things for her. First it made approaching the problem less apprehensive for her. Seeing my humility made her feel at ease. Second, we were able to work all the way through the process. Before this exercise in this situation I would just tell her the answer, instead I showed her my thought process, which made her knowledgeable and more confident.

Through the process of shifting the experience from his point of view to the junior associate's he was able to more skillfully help her learn, build skills, and trust in her abilities. He enabled the colleague to engage in the process as an active learner rather than a passive recipient.

Practice inquiry: What if this was the first time I've seen this, been here or met this person? What is the other person experiencing?

Working with feeling tone. Moving through to the start of the map, feeling tones are the visceral of liking–neutral–disliking reactions that arise when encountering something. Feeling tones are the "spark" that light the flame of a reactive process. Pleasant feeling tones engender approach actions and unpleasant ones lead to aversive reactions. A useful frame to see this happen is watching reactions to the names of senders as new email is downloaded into one's inbox.

Miguel is a logistics supply chain manager for the West Coast division of a large materials company. He notices a strong sense of dislike when a certain name, let us call him "Eddie Lopez," shows up in his inbox. Eddie sent Miguel an email asking about a product line in which Miguel is an expert. What follows is the interaction between Miguel and me in response to Eddie's email:

Miguel: "When I see his name, my stomach turns into a knot!"

Me: "Why is that?"

M: "He's such a pain in the neck! He's one of our salespeople and is always pushy about what he needs. He frantically asks our team to get him information yesterday, but he takes his good old time to retrieve it from us. We're tired of being jerked around."

Me: "Sounds like he's frustrating you!"

M: "Yeah ... we really can't stand him."

Me: "So, in addition to the knot in your stomach, do you notice any other body sensations?"

M: "I feel this rapid heartbeat and an edgy part of me wants him to go away."

Me: "Can you sit with that edgy sensation of wanting him to go away?"

He closes his eyes and shifts his attention to the sensations in his body for a few moments. After a long pause, he takes a deep inhale and then exhales, opening his eyes.

M: "I feel calmer."

Me: "I'd like to ask about Eddie...is he a bad guy?"

Miguel thinks for a moment.

M: "No, he's not a *bad* guy, he's just a pushy guy."

Me: "Tell us about him, is he married? Does he have a family?"

M: "Yeah, he's married. I think his wife is expecting."

Me: "So what's your assessment about why he's so pushy? Why would somebody be insistent about getting information?"

M: "Well ... I know he's trying to land a big, new client ... but the thing is Eddie is on the East Coast and he should be interfacing with the East Coast team, not us!"

Me: "Ah. So, his coming to you seems like an intrusion, because he should be talking to someone else. But it also sounds like we've identified a management issue. Why isn't the East Coast team supporting him? Do you know?"

M: "That's right, it's an intrusion. I don't know why the other team isn't helping him, I just know he gets answers from us. I'm tired of solving his problems for him."

Me: "So, let's step back. We agreed that Eddie isn't really a bad guy. He's married and has a baby on the way, while at the same time he is trying to land a new client, but isn't getting the support he needs from the people that *should* be helping him and so he turns to you."

Miguel suddenly turns silent, looking down at his lap. He exhales deeply. When he finally speaks, it's in a whisper.

M: "Oh my God ... I created this problem. I created the negative relationship with Eddie because I only saw that his requests would mean more things for me to do. When in reality, I should be helping this guy, not judging him. I don't know everything that is going on with him and I might just be the only person he can turn to. I want to pick up the phone and reach out to him right now to get a sense of how things are going."

When the debrief started, Miguel's attention was hijacked by his own reactive emotions and judgmental storylines about his colleague Eddie, resulting in frustration and upset. Once he shifted attention to become mindful of what he was experiencing, starting with the negative feeling tone, the upset reaction began to subside. His mind cleared, allowing the possibility to shift his attention to Eddie's point of view.

By challenging his own assumptions about Eddie he became aware of a larger picture and saw a different world emerge, Eddie's world. Miguel noticed that his own concerns about being impinged upon by Eddie's needs clouded his understanding of the larger set of causes and effects that Eddie was experiencing. Suddenly, Miguel's awareness shifted with empathy towards a nervous expectant father eager to be a success with a large new client. A compassionate desire to help Eddie arose in the place of judgment and frustration.

For Miguel, this analysis of his reactive pattern proved to be a turning point in his managerial career. As time went on he began to notice more moments when an assignment would cross his desk and trigger the unpleasant feeling tone reaction of aversion. Like a scientist collecting data points, these accumulated moments revealed a consistent pattern. He noticed how his mind's knee-jerk resistance undermined his effectiveness and responsibility as a manager and set the wrong leadership tone for his team.

He began to see these new assignments were opportunities for his professional growth. Instead of resisting them, he began to embrace them; even to the point of thinking proactively about how he could be helping the company expand its presence. He realized that a neighboring firm needed one of his core products. He invited his counterpart there to lunch which ended with a new deal for Miguel.

There are other ways of working with feeling tone. Here mindfulness is a process of pausing. For example, when a sense of dislike arises the effort to make is to drop or step aside from the disliking and observe what is there. The phone rings again and you see it is a call from the same difficult but vital client, a sense of avoidance arises. Noting that, allowing it to be there without pushing it away, you take a deep breath and pick up the phone.

Practice inquiry: Just because it's unpleasant doesn't mean I have to move away. Just because it's unpleasant doesn't mean it's negative. (Think of a visit to the dentist where the sensations are unpleasant but the result is healthier teeth.)

Pleasant feeling tones are much more challenging to work with, because they feel good. They are harder to let go of or harder to perceive because we take them for granted. Lisa is always up for adventure and her job takes her to many places. When an invitation comes to go somewhere new, a sense of pleasantness and excitement arises. She feels attracted by the possibility of a novel experience and without thinking she agrees to take the assignment. However, her schedule is already packed, her body is tired from the wear and tear of travel, no matter how interesting the new prospect might be. She rechecks her calendar and begins to feel the anxiety of overload.

Practice inquiry: Just because it's pleasant doesn't mean I have to move toward it. Just because it's pleasant doesn't mean it's positive. (Think of the pleasant sensations offered by eating a large bag of potato chips, but also the resulting weight gain.)

Hopefully, by now it is clear how the map works. Practice develops the ability to see the elements of the map and how they correspond to experience. Practitioners begin to ask themselves: What is my objective? Where am I putting my energy? What do I see as my choices?

What am I actually doing? What happens as a result? Is this is a result that creates benefit or harm? Can I live with this? We can describe what mindfulness reveals with the model below:

Intention→Attention→Awareness→Choice→Action→Result

Intention creates conditions that influence what is sought and selected from experience. Intention shapes the placement of attention, our limited supply of mental energy. Attention brings information into awareness, interpreting experience through narratives as well as the body's somatic and emotional reactions. These reactions impact the menu of perceived choices, the array of potential actions and their corresponding results.

With time, practitioners begin to see the underlying stories and themes that drive their actions. Observing moments over time, patterns of thought, feeling, and action emerge. Practitioners begin to see the genesis of their problems, the underlying experiential components and, with a bit of trepidation, begin to address them. What seemed out of their control and hopeless becomes workable. They see life through a new lens and find an ability to create options where their mind said none existed before. They "unstick" themselves. Cynicism gives way to fresh possibility. Of course there are setbacks, frustrations, and aborted good intentions, but they become more willing to make the effort.

Lessons learned and some practical advice for teaching executives

After more than a decade of helping executives develop their capacity in mindfulness, here are a few lessons learned:

1. **Begin each semester/engagement with a dialogue about expectations.** The structure of the class is not a traditional "broadcast model" where the instructor "talks at" a group of passive students. It is more the creation of a community of learners. This dynamic must be consciously created. I have found that devoting part of the first session of a semester to discussing expectations the students have of the course, the teacher, and each other sets a positive frame for future learning. We come to agreement about sharing experience but not giving advice, holding course conversations in

privacy, not having crosstalk and not using electronic devices during class. I tell them my expectations that they will work hard, turn in material on time and they share expectations that I will push them into challenging territory and be a resource and support. This dialogue is essential to creating a community over the course of the semester. I also follow up with a mid-term review to ask them if their expectations are being met and what needs to be changed if not.

2. **Value is not the teacher talking, value is the experience the students are having.** One of my own assumptions that got imprinted early on in my teaching career is what the students experience is more valuable than the amount that I spoke in class. I try to keep my discussion limited to an hour in a two hour fifty minute class. Students also value in-class meditation exercises, mindfulness-in-action exercises and especially dialogue with one another. Learning from each other's experience is a powerful reassurance that they face common human problems and "aren't the only crazy one in the room." A typical 2 hour 50 minute class session breaks down like this:

   15 minutes: meditation practice
   5 minutes: discussing the practice as a group
   10 minutes: discuss with partner their lesson learned from the week's live-fire exercises
   60 minutes: collect and discuss insights and challenges from students and document on the board
   10 minutes: break
   25 minutes: lecture on the week's topic, covering scientific findings or mindfulness principles and weaving them into students' insights
   25 minutes: in-class activity to concretize the abstract
   10 minutes: discuss results of the activity
   10 minutes: check in, wrap up, and set up for next week
   The bulk of the class is not solely lecture, but a variety of experiences intended to emphasize the points for that week.

3. **Make everyday life the focus of the course with meditation as a support.** By equating mindfulness with mindfulness meditation one runs the risk of separating practice from living. As referenced earlier, a calm and peaceful meditator is not necessarily calm and peaceful on the streets. Bringing mindfulness into one's life is the purpose of the map.

It creates a framework for observing the mind in action and is the foundation for a variety of mindfulness exercises. One week practitioners may observe the feeling tone of liking and disliking as it arises in their working life. Another week may be spent examining storylines or judgmental patterns of thought and their affect on results. Students can practice letting go or not clinging to views or perspective and see how their actions and results change. At the same time, formal meditation practice builds strength and stability in attention to effectively use these skills. By emphasizing both formal meditation and live-fire meditation, the student receives a "full-body mindfulness workout."

4. **Aesthetic experiences are useful for bringing mindfulness to action.** Each semester, I hold one session at the Los Angeles County Museum of Art. The museum collection provides a number of opportunities to use art as a stage for mindfulness practice. For example, slowly walking the perimeter of Richard Serra's room-sized torqued steel sculpture Band[2] is an excellent tool for practicing mindfulness. Its undulations evoke a variety of reactions that help practitioners observe how physiological reactions frame their experience. Because the sculpture is divorced from their everyday experience it provides a "blank slate" to witness the mind in action.

5. **The instructor must have a robust mindfulness practice.** There is a direct correlation between the quality of my practice and the quality of my teaching. My ability to be present, empathic, and accepting of experience translates directly into the classroom experience, which student's detect. I also discuss my challenges and difficulties in practice to show that I struggle with the same things they do. A support system is essential. I meditate daily and do at least one extended retreat per year. I also have several seasoned teachers whom I consult.

6. **The class is an opportunity for the instructor to be mindful and practice equanimity and not clinging.** The relationship between student and instructor must be held in a field of non-judgment. A student's struggles are not for the teacher to "fix" or weigh in on with "the answer." Allowing students to face their lives with

---

[2] http://collections.lacma.org/node/214935.

unconditional support lets them know you are on their side. I ask questions to elicit thinking, but refrain from telling them what to do.

7. **Anticipate, screen for, and be ready to support students with unresolved life trauma.** I have discovered that students with unresolved trauma can have adverse experiences to meditation practices. It is also the case that such students seek out courses on how to manage themselves better. Before the class starts, students are asked to answer several questions about who they are, their work, their goals and interests for the class, and if they have a history of trauma. I let them know that the course might be challenging for them and to report to me if they have difficulty. I also let them know that I might suggest they seek out more professional help. I also received training in somatic experiencing, a body-based modality for healing trauma in case a student falls into a trauma-induced hyper-aroused state. I also keep a backbench of trauma therapists to whom I can refer students for deeper work. The good news is they almost always seek out therapy.[3]

Conclusion

I believe mindfulness in organizations will evolve through three distinct themes as practitioners mature. The first phase revolves around the most immediately obvious application: mindfulness as stress reducer. This theme has years of research behind it and it is likely that the vast majority of people who seek out mindfulness and similar methods do so because they need tools to address pain in their working lives.

The second theme, mindfulness as performance and productivity enhancer, emerges from the first. As people practice they see that mindfulness has other results that extend beyond reducing stress. Mindfulness gives tools to better manage attention in a distracted, multitasking environment. Skillfully handling emotional reactions affects the quality of their relationships and the possibilities that emerge out of them. Conversations become less contentious and more supportive. People work more harmoniously together and perform better.

The third stream, mindfulness as a tool for change and transition is emergent and represents a fuller flowering of the fruits of practice.

[3] See www.traumahealing.com/somatic-experiencing/practitioner-directory.html.

Fundamentally, mindfulness transforms one's relationship to change. It enables the capacity to let go of what no longer works and generate more effective options. My most recent course uses mindfulness to help executives navigate transitions. Why might this be important? Many executive students come to class having changes thrust upon them in the form of organizational merger, job loss, or retirement. They often lack tools for negotiating the inner shifts that happen because of outer changes. Mindfulness helps to mourn the losses faced when the old world, in the shape of a job, role, or organization, comes to end. It helps them move forward to explore new possibilities and shed old beliefs, identities, and assumptions, making space to create something new.

As I write this, multiple sources portend potentially troubling signs ahead. These crises in the making hold implications for the role mindfulness might play in organizational life. The January 18, 2014 issue of *The Economist* featured a cover story about the effects advanced artificial intelligence may have on the white-collar workforce. Service workers, like doctors, lawyers, and accountants, have previously been immune to technological shifts but increasingly sophisticated technologies are making these jobs vulnerable to disruption. What can be automated will likely be automated. The article cites an Oxford study that finds as many as 47 percent of today's jobs could be affected in the next twenty years.

At the same time, those left employed will perform functions that humans are uniquely suited to do: ideate, create, and innovate, manage complex interpersonal communication, and detect large patterns (Brynjolfsson and McAfee 2013). Here too mindfulness will play a valuable role because it enhances these capacities that cannot be reduced to algorithms.

In this emerging tumultuous condition, what could be more essential than a set of skills that help people to be calm and present, deal more effectively with their reactive emotions and make clearer, smarter decisions? Could it be possible that mindfulness might help workers constructively face widespread social disruption and suffering? Perhaps mindfulness can give people tools to more positively face and adapt to wrenching change? In a time where knowledge quickly becomes obsolete, mindfulness and managing oneself are skills that will become a necessary foundation for facing the future.

References

Bargh, J.A. and Chartrand, T.L. (1999). The unbearable automaticity of being. *American Psychologist*, 54, 462–79.

Brown, K. W., Creswell, D., and Ryan, R. M. (2015). *The handbook of mindfulness: theory, research and practice.* New York: Guilford Press.

Brown, K. W. and Ryan, R. M. (2003). The benefits of being present: mindfulness and its role in psychological well-being. *Journal of Personality and Social Psychology*, 84, 822–48.

Brynjolfsson, E. and McAfee, A. (2013). *The second machine age: work, progress, and prosperity in a time of brilliant technologies.* New York: W. W. Norton and Co.

Chiesa, A. and Serretti, A. (2010). A systematic review of neurobiological and clinical features of mindfulness meditations. *Psychological Medicine*, 40, 1239–52.

Coming to an office near you. (2014). *The Economist.* January 18. Retrieved from www.economist.com/news/leaders/21594298-effect-todays-technology-tomorrows-jobs-will-be-immenseand-no-country-ready.

Csikszentmihalyi, M. (1993). *The evolving self: a psychology for the third millennium.* New York: Harper.

Csikszentmihalyi, M. and Csikszentmihalyi, I. (1992). *Optimal experience: psychological studies of flow in consciousness.* New York: Cambridge University Press.

Csikszentmihalyi, M. and Csikszentmihalyi, I. (2006). *A life worth living: contributions to positive psychology.* New York: Oxford University Press.

Davidson, R. J., Kabat-Zinn, J., Schumacher, J., Rosenkrantz, M., Muller, D., Santorelli, S. F., … Sheridan, F. S. (2003). Alterations in brain and immune function produced by mindfulness meditation. *Psychosomatic Medicine*, 65, 564–70.

Dreyfus, G. (2013). Is mindfulness present-centered and non-judgmental? A discussion of the cognitive dimensions of mindfulness. In J. M. Williams and J. Kabat-Zinn (eds.), *Mindfulness: diverse perspectives on its meaning, origins and applications.* New York: Routledge.

Drucker, P. F. (1989). *The new realities.* Oxford: Butterworth-Heinemann.
   (1992). *The age of discontinuity: guidelines to our changing society.* New Brunswick, NJ: Transaction.

Drucker, P. F. and Wartzman, R. (2010). *The Drucker lectures: essential lessons on management, society and economy.* New York: McGraw-Hill.

Ekman, P. (2003). *Emotions revealed: recognizing faces and feelings to improve communication and emotional life.* New York: Henry Holt.

Epstein, R. (1999). Mindful practice. *Journal of the American Medical Association*, 282(9), 833–9.

Erikson, E. (1950). *Childhood and society*. New York: W. W. Norton and Co.

Fields, R. (1981). *How swans came to the lake: a narrative history of Buddhism in America*. Boston, MA: Shambhala Press.

Gardner, H., Csikszentmihalyi, M., and Damon, W. (2002) *Good work: when excellence and ethics meet*. New York: Basic Books.

Gilligan, C. (1982). *In a different voice*. Cambridge, MA: Harvard University Press.

Hölzel, B. K., Carmody, J., Vangel, M., Congleton, C., Yerramsetti, S. M., Gard, T., and Lazar, S. W. (2011). Mindfulness practice leads to increases in regional brain gray matter density. *Psychiatry Research: Neuroimaging*, 191, 36–42.

Hunter, J. and Chaskalson, M. (2013). Making the mindful leader: cultivating skills for facing adaptive challenges. In S. Leonard, R. Lewis, A. Freeman, and J. Passmore (eds.), *The Wiley-Blackwell Handbook of the Psychology of Leadership, Change & OD*. Chichester: Wiley-Blackwell, pp. 195–220.

Hunter, J. and McCormick, D. W. (2008). Mindfulness in the workplace: an exploratory study. In S. E. Newell (Facilitator), *Weickian Ideas*. Symposium conducted at the annual meeting of the Academy of Management, Anaheim, CA.

Hunter, J. and Scherer, J. S. (2009). Knowledge-worker productivity and the practice of self-management. In C. Pearce, J. Maciariello, and H. Yamawaki (eds.), *The Drucker difference: what the world's greatest management thinker means to today's business leaders*. New York: McGraw-Hill Professional.

James, W. (1890). *The principles of psychology*. New York: Dover.

Johnson, L. (2014). *Stoic response to the fad of meditation. Financial Times*, 13 May. Retrieved from www.ft.com/intl/cms/s/0/2995d74e-d9cf-11e3-b3e3-00144feabdc0.html.

Kabat-Zinn, J. (1990). *Full catastrophe living: using the wisdom of your body and mind to face stress, pain and illness*. New York: Delta.

Kohlberg, L., Levine, C., and Hewer, A. (1983). *Moral stages: a current formulation and a response to critics*. Basel, NY: Karger.

Lazenby, R. (2001). *Mindgames: Phil Jackson's long strange journey*. New York: McGraw-Hill.

Lipman-Blumen, J. (2005). *The allure of toxic leaders: why we follow destructive bosses and corrupt politicians – and how we can survive them*. New York: Oxford University Press.

McLeod, K. (2001). *Wake up to your life: discovering the Buddhist path of attention*. New York: HarperOne.

Piaget, J. (1926). *The language and thought of the child*. New York: Harcourt Brace.

Piaget, J. (1932). *The moral judgement of the child*. London: Routledge and Kegan Paul.

Reb, J., Narayanan, J., and Chaturvedi, S. (2014). Leading mindfully: two studies of the influence of supervisor trait mindfulness on employee well-being and performance. *Mindfulness*, 5(1), 36–45.

Riskin, L. (2002). The contemplative lawyer on the potential contributions of mindfulness meditation to Law students, lawyers, and their clients. *Harvard Negotiations Law Review*, 7, 1–66.

Segal, Z. V., Williams, J. M. G., and Teasdale, J. D. (2001). *Mindfulness-based cognitive therapy for depression: a new approach to preventing relapse*. New York: The Guilford Press.

Smith, A. ([1759] 1976). *The theory of moral sentiments*. New York: Oxford University Press.

Vygotsky, L. (1962). *Thought and language*. Cambridge, MA: MIT Press.

Williams, J. M. and Kabat-Zinn, J. (2013). *Mindfulness: diverse perspectives on its meaning, origins and applications*. New York: Routledge.

Wilson, D. S. (2014). Toxic leaders and the social environments that breed them. *Forbes*. January 10. Retrieved from www.forbes.com/sites/darwinatwork/2014/01/10/toxic-leaders-and-the-social-environments-that-breed-them/.

Wilson, T. (2002). *Strangers to ourselves: discovering the adaptive unconscious*. Cambridge: Belknap Press.

16 Mindfulness in coaching

LIZ HALL

Today we are so inter-dependent, so closely interconnected with each other, that without a sense of universal responsibility, a feeling of universal brotherhood and sisterhood, and an understanding and belief that we are really part of one big human family, we cannot hope to overcome the dangers of our very existence – let alone bring about peace and happiness.

The Dalai Lama (2006, p. 18)

Introduction

Coaching is a global phenomenon. In 2009, there were an estimated 43,000 business coaches worldwide (Bresser 2009), up from an estimated 30,000 business coaches in 2006 (International Coach Federation 2014). Executive coaching is informed by a broad range of theoretical frameworks (Passmore 2005) and, as coaching has become more established, the diversity of coaching forms has grown. In recent years, mindfulness has increasingly been used within coaching.

One reason for the rise in interest is the adaptation and introduction of mindfulness into varied secular settings, including politics, education, psychotherapy, and the workplace. The UK Government's National Institute for Health and Clinical Excellence's 2009 recommendation of mindfulness-based cognitive therapy (MBCT) for the treatment of recurrent depression has given mindfulness a stamp of approval that has influenced mindfulness-based coaching.

The expanding research highlighting an array of benefits to be gained from practicing mindfulness is naturally contributing to this growth in interest. Coaches seek to optimize clients' functioning and to help clients reach their full potential, so it follows that they will be interested in approaches and techniques that will support the achievement of these aims.

Meanwhile, mindfulness is being heralded by many as a welcome antidote to widespread mindlessness in these challenging and complex times (e.g. Cavanagh and Spence 2013). Many crises continue to play out; poor ethical behaviour is widespread (Chartered Management Institute 2013); stress levels are higher than ever (Chartered Institute of Personnel and Development 2013), and our mindless excessive consumption is threatening our very existence. Some see mindfulness as a means to promote sustainability (e.g. Ericson, Kjønstad, and Barstad 2014; Sheth, Sethia, and Srinivas 2011), and more ethical behaviour generally (Hall 2013).

Historically only a small number of authors and researchers have concerned themselves with mindfulness in relation to coaching (Cavanagh and Spence 2013; Collard and Walsh 2008; Hall 2013; Passmore and Marianetti 2007; Silsbee 2010; Spence, Cavanagh, and Grant 2008). This will hopefully change. In the meantime, there is much we can infer from existing coaching-related research including my own, and research in other arenas, including mental health, to inform a mindfulness-based coaching approach.

The chapter is divided into two parts, looking firstly at coaching mindfully and secondly at imparting mindfulness skills. The first part presents a model consisting of the four essential mindful coaching processes: focusing, exploring, embracing, and letting go/letting in (FEEL). The chapter examines common ground and potential differences/tensions between mindfulness and "traditional" coaching; and explores the impact of having a mindfulness practice on the coach's intrapersonal and interpersonal competences (including presence, empathy, and compassion). The second part examines the role of the coach in teaching/coaching mindfulness explicitly, highlighting issues with which mindfulness-based coaching is particularly suited to helping. It focuses in particular on how it can improve clients' resilience and ability to manage stress; and their ability to act and think ethically, responsibly and sustainably, suggesting that these can have a significant potential ripple effect on the wider system.

Coaching mindfully

FEEL model

I developed the FEEL model based on my research (Hall 2013) for self-coaching or coaching of others with mindfulness, explicitly or non-explicitly. It incorporates key components of mindfulness: attention

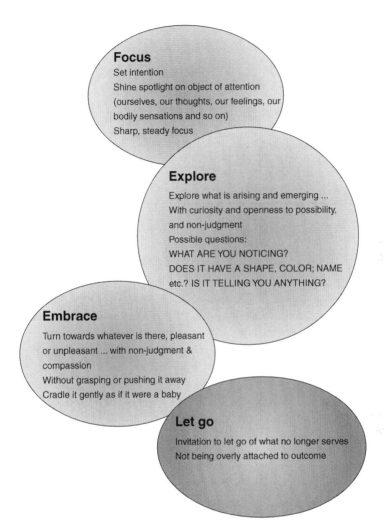

Focus
Set intention
Shine spotlight on object of attention
(ourselves, our thoughts, our feelings, our
bodily sensations and so on)
Sharp, steady focus

Explore
Explore what is arising and emerging ...
With curiosity and openness to possibility,
and non-judgment
Possible questions:
WHAT ARE YOU NOTICING?
DOES IT HAVE A SHAPE, COLOR; NAME
etc.? IS IT TELLING YOU ANYTHING?

Embrace
Turn towards whatever is there, pleasant
or unpleasant ... with non-judgment &
compassion
Without grasping or pushing it away
Cradle it gently as if it were a baby

Let go
Invitation to let go of what no longer serves
Not being overly attached to outcome

Figure 16.1 A fluid model for bringing in mindfulness
Source: Hall (2013).

to the present moment; attentional control; curiosity/enquiry; compassion (towards self and others); non-judgment; acceptance and letting go.

Rather like the GROW model (goals–reality–options–will/wrap-up) popularised by Whitmore (1992), within one session the coach might move through the model in a linear fashion or fluidly between the different parts, or stay within one or two parts of the model – spending a whole session "exploring," for example, or working on "letting go" (see Figure 16.1). Coaches can also use FEEL to tune into and explore what is happening within themselves, which may or may not at times be useful to share with the client.

FEEL stands for the following four essential mindful coaching processes: focusing, exploring, embracing, and letting go/letting in.

Focus This is about setting our intention and choosing our object of focus, just as we might choose to look at a flower through a magnifying glass. We may choose to focus on thoughts, feelings, or bodily sensations, or indeed an issue, just as we would normally do in coaching. The invitation – to ourselves if self-coaching, or to clients – is to focus steadily and concentratedly, but with a lightness of touch. We then expand to exploration.

Explore Still maintaining focus, we now gently explore whatever is arising and emerging, intentionally seeking to do so with compassion (or kindness for those clients who struggle with being self-compassionate), curiosity, non-judgment and openness to possibility. We may stay with the original topic/object, or work with whatever else comes to light. We continue to explore, without seeking to interpret or judge. We are seeking here to activate the "approach system," associated with a number of benefits, including creativity (Friedman and Förster 2001).

Questions to prompt curious, nonjudgemental exploration include:

What feelings are you noticing?
Where do you feel them in your body?
Are they familiar or new feelings?
Do they have a shape?
Do they have a color?
Do they have a name?
Are they telling you anything?
What else?

Embrace Here, whilst still maintaining focus and a sense of enquiry and exploration, we are turning towards *whatever* is there – unpleasant or pleasant – with non-judgment and compassion or kindness, without grasping or pushing away. Vietnamese Buddhist monk Thich Nhat Hanh suggests having in mind the image of gently cradling a baby. So, for example, if anger arises, we turn towards and lightly embrace the anger, rather than moving to evaluate and criticize. We are working with acceptance. We might label whatever it is, thus creating some distance, so that we are gently embracing rather than identifying with it or creating an unhelpful storyline about it.

Let go/let in Building on explore and embrace further, in let go, we are continuing to just witness and accept what is there without grabbing or rejecting, but we also open up to letting go. It can be hard to let go, of course, and may not always be appropriate. The idea is not to force anything, but to issue the invitation, noticing what is there and what can be let go of, what no longer serves, and making space for the new (letting in). When clients turn towards something with acceptance, they often see it dissipate of its own accord.

Some coaches – and clients – report that the letting go aspect of the model proved to be very powerful, bringing about meaningful shifts for the client. A handful of coaches participating in my workshop, however, struggled with this component, sharing that it felt inappropriate to encourage the client (in these cases, other coaches on the workshop) to let go. They wanted instead to move the client to action, resolution, and goal attainment. As we examine further on, coaching with mindfulness does not preclude working with goals. If an insight has arisen in the earlier stages around an issue or a goal identified in the coaching, it is of course appropriate to work with that, and it may be that letting go is inappropriate. Or that letting go precedes identifying actions, or comes after actions.

Coaches report using FEEL in a number of ways (Hall 2014). It lends itself well to exploring difficult feelings and issues, but also to exploring and embodying positive feelings, strengths, qualities, and affirmations, for example. One coach shared how they used FEEL to access "qualities people feel they have that could sustain their confidence and embracing them, and exploring their limiting beliefs and letting them go, then inviting the client to be truly present with their sustaining beliefs, nurturing them and drawing strength from them" (Hall 2014, p. 207).

Having presented a model for what coaching mindfully might look like, we now step back to analyze similarities and differences between practicing mindfulness and practicing coaching that emerged from my research. This research (Hall 2013) included an extensive literature review; fifty-one semi-structured and unstructured interviews with coaches, coaching psychologists, coach trainers, coaching clients, mindfulness practitioners/trainers, psychotherapists and

Table 16.1 *Where mindfulness meets coaching: some areas of common ground/desired outcome*

BELIEF		
Person is "whole"	Person is resourceful	We are inter-connected (systemic lens)
PERSPECTIVE/STATE		
Beginner's mind	Self actualization	Contemplation and reflection
Observer's/witness mind	Presence	
Metacognition		Curiosity and enquiry
QUALITY/ABILITY		
Compassion	Honesty	Wisdom
Empathy	Authenticity	Clarity and focus
Non-judgment	Intuitiveness	Co-creation
Trust (in oneself, others, and the wider system)		

neuroscientists, and an online survey of 156 self-selecting coaches in 10 countries via an online survey tool.

Similarities and differences between mindfulness and coaching

When considering how to coach mindfully, it can be helpful to have a sense of how much shared ground there already is between mindfulness and coaching – as behaviors, as sets of beliefs, and state and qualities/abilities aspired to, for example. That there is common ground between practicing both mindfulness and coaching is unsurprising. More surprising, perhaps, is the extent of the similarity between the two. Table 16.1 highlights some of this shared territory.

However, in my view, it is exploring potential areas of difference and resistance (see Table 16.2) that is most fruitful. Such an exploration touches on what it means to be human and how we make sense of our worlds, very much the territory of coaching. I examine mind modes; stance in relation to striving; attitude to goals; attitude to change; and stance in relation to attachment. These tensions sometimes create confusion and resistance to embracing mindfulness, particularly in a business setting, where there is an emphasis on getting things done and demonstrating return on investment as measured by output.

Table 16.2 *Areas of potential difference/tension between a mindfulness approach and "traditional" coaching*

Category	Mindfulness	Coaching
Temporal focus	Present moment	Future orientation
Degree of recognition of inter-connectedness	Sense of one-ness	Focus on individual agenda whilst considering the system
Number of people	Solitary (not always)	Involves two or more people (apart from self-coaching)
Activity/mind mode	Being and non-doing	Doing
Stance in relation to striving	Non-striving/letting go	Striving
Attitude to goals	Non-goal-oriented	Goal-oriented
Attitude to change	Accepting "what is"	Trying to change "what is"
Stance in relation to attachment	Non-attachment	Attachment e.g. to goal

Mind modes: being/non-doing and doing

"Non-doing has nothing to do with being indolent or passive. Quite the contrary. It takes great courage and energy to cultivate non-doing, both in stillness and activity" (Kabat-Zinn 1994, p. 44). Kabat-Zinn then describes how non-doing is about "letting things be and allowing them to unfold in their own way" (p. 45). The idea of letting go of "doing" can be frightening, for both coach and client. Reasons for this include widespread presenteeism (Johns 2009); a fear of what stopping might bring about; and polarized thinking.

People are valued, at work, in particular, for what they contribute. This is often measured by how *much* they do, as evidenced in the presenteeism that is so widespread these days. One client turned up to coaching after work on a cold evening, wearing no jacket. When asked by the coach whether they were cold, the client replied that they were indeed, but had left their jacket on the back of their chair so it appeared as if they were still in the office.

Many fear, on some level, that if they stop "doing," they will no longer exist. Action is how we get to experience ourselves (Langer 2005). People fear they will not like what they find when they stop. Keeping busy is a way of running away from ourselves. In addition, people can get caught in a trap of doing because they become hyper-vigilant towards threat.

Meanwhile, dualistic thinking around doing versus being/non-doing; striving versus non-striving and so on, fuels some coaches' and clients' resistance to mindfulness, including in coaching (Hall 2013; Malnick 2013). Yet it need not be either/or. Mindfulness is a state of being, of attentiveness and lively awareness. From this state springs a different way of doing, one in which we are no longer a slave to our automatic reactions (Williams and Penman 2011, p. 164), in which we can be adaptively responsive. When we practice mindfulness meditation, we may choose to rest in choiceful awareness, just observing from our cushion. We can choose to do nothing at all or we can respond and take action mindfully, as we do during a walking meditation. This is important to emphasize, particularly as coaching in organizations tends to focus on improving performance. The number one reason cited by coaching clients (42 percent) for seeking coaching was to optimize individual/team work performance (International Coach Federation 2014).

Mindfulness-based coaching does not (necessarily) advocate that clients drop all their activities for days on end. It promotes more "mindful doing." Mindfulness improves productivity and performance in many ways including enhanced emotion regulation and improved cognitive functioning (see for example Chapter 2 of this volume).

Explaining to clients how mindfulness will improve their performance can be very persuasive. However, perhaps the best gift a coach can offer the client is holding up a mirror and reflecting back when the client is doing too much, or consuming too much, and suggesting they take time out to "just be," asking them when will enough be enough?

Own goals?

Traditionally, coaching has been strongly associated with goal setting and goal achievement, with the goal-oriented GROW being one of the most widely used coaching models. Yet Clutterbuck, Megginson and David (2013) and others suggest that in our complex and rapidly changing world, specific, measurable and time-bound, challenging goals can be inappropriate and even potentially dangerous, and that there is a place for goal-free coaching.

Mindfulness, with its qualities of acceptance and non-attachment to outcome, is well-suited to goal-free or "goal-lite" coaching. Being more open to whatever emerges and not so wedded to goals can uncover a trove of hitherto hidden treasures, helping clients sit with "not knowing." This can be what is needed in an ambiguous world. Such a stance can be particularly helpful for leaders, who more than most, perhaps, are expected to be decisive, to lead, to *know*. In trying to preserve a façade of being all-knowing, they can shut themselves down to a host of interesting possibilities. As Williams and Penman (2011, p. 163) point out, "acceptance in the context of mindfulness is not the passive acceptance of the intolerable" and "mindfulness is not about detachment."

In addition to helping clients accept what is, mindfulness-based coaching helps clients identify what truly matters to them, in line with their values (Cavanagh and Spence 2013; Hall 2013), which in turn can be seen as higher order goals (Grant 2013). And as Grant argues (p. 64), self-congruent and self-concordant goals are more likely to engage the client, meaning they are more likely to put in effort to achieve them. So in that sense mindfulness promotes goal attainment. It also helps clients resist the temptation to sabotage progress toward goals (e.g. Spence, Cavanagh, and Grant 2008).

Mindfulness also appears to positively impact goal-directed behavior via improvements in self-efficacy (e.g. Cavanagh and Spence 2013). The higher someone's self-efficacy is, the higher their motivation, effort, performance, and achievement will be (Bandura and Locke 2003). Improved, positive self-regulation via mindfulness appears to be key too. Effective self-regulation positively impacts goal-attainment (Carver and Scheier 1998) and mindfulness helps people self-regulate, perhaps due to the combination of attentional control and reduced emotional reactivity (Cavanagh and Spence 2013).

Future research should further study both similarities and differences of mindfulness and coaching. In practice, coaches are already working with mindfulness, using models such as FEEL. Below, we take a closer look at how coaches work with mindfulness.

Table 16.3 *Ways to use mindfulness in coaching*

1. Coach benefits personally from practicing mindfulness regularly (preferably daily), promoting self-awareness, self-care and resilience, creativity, and happiness (which has a positive impact on how they coach)
2. Coach uses mindfulness techniques to prepare for sessions, so they are more resourceful, creative, and present from the outset
3. Coach uses mindfulness techniques within sessions, enhancing their ability to be intuitive, to notice and regulate their emotions, and distinguish between theirs and the client's issues
4. Coach uses mindfulness techniques for reflection post-session, enhancing their ability to notice and capture data, and spark insights, for example
5. Coach works with a mindfulness-informed coach supervisor to further support a mindful approach
6. Coach uses mindfulness-informed approaches such as the FEEL model to foster mindfulness in the client
7. Coach shares core mindfulness training/sharing mindfulness practices explicitly with the client within coaching sessions or as "homework," helping the client be more resourceful, and to address specific issues/goals

Working with mindfulness

Table 16.3 lists some ways in which mindfulness can be used in coaching. These include heightened emotional intelligence, enabling the coach to be more present for, attune to, and resonate with the client, improving their ability to be empathic and compassionate towards the client. We examine these aspects below.

In relationships

How a coach "shows up" impacts whether or not a client will engage the coach and the coaching's effectiveness, amongst others. The coaching relationship is the only genuinely effective ingredient we can influence (de Haan 2008). Practicing mindfulness develops the four pillars of emotional intelligence: self-awareness, self-management, social awareness and relationship management (e.g. Boyatzis and McKee 2005). It makes perfect sense for coaches and others working in helping professions, in which relationships are so key, to underpin their practice with mindfulness.

The highest-rated characteristic coaching buyers look for in external coaches is "personal chemistry" (Ridler and Co 2011). When pushed to elaborate, organizations cited "listening well" (97 percent) and "coming across as open and sincere" (89 percent) (Ridler and Co 2013). Once coaching has started, the strength of the relationship between coach and client is what makes the most difference in determining the coaching outcome (de Haan and Page 2013). The term "presence" can be used to encapsulate all that we mean when we think of how an excellent coach shows up.

Presence

The importance of presence in coaching and other helping professions is emphasized widely, and is explicit in the core coaching competencies of professional coaching bodies including the Association for Coaching and the International Coach Federation. The Federation defines it as "the ability to be fully conscious and create a spontaneous relationship with the client, employing a style which is open, flexible and confident" (International Coach Federation, 2014) while Siegel (2010, p. 13) writes that "being present with others involves the experience of openness to whatever arises in reality." The more present the coach is, the more they engender trust and confidence in the client, and the more open they are "to the unfolding of possibilities" (Siegel 2010, p. 34), which in turn helps the client access multiple perspectives and options.

Despite the widespread emphasis on the importance of presence, there is little in the coaching literature regarding how to develop it. Mindfulness is increasingly being acknowledged as an effective means to develop presence (e.g. Hall 2013; Siegel 2010, Silsbee 2010). It does this through helping coaches (and clients) monitor and modify their internal world (Siegel 2010), increasing emotional self-awareness (Creswell *et al.* 2007), and promoting self-management and self-regulation (e.g. Boyatzis and McKee 2005).

Some 65 percent of respondents to the Mindfulness in Coaching survey (Hall 2013) reported practicing mindfulness to become more present for clients. Other reasons included to help themselves "be more self-aware" (73 percent); "live more in the moment" (74 percent); to manage/prevent stress (67 percent); focus (64 percent); relax (63 percent); "not get too caught up in thoughts" (57 percent); be more resilient (53 percent); manage reactions/responses (49 percent), and prepare for coaching sessions (47 percent).

We can be present when we are alone but I believe that when we talk about presence in coaching, we actually mean presence plus attunement and resonance. Attunement requires presence, but is "a process of focused attention and clear perception ... moving presence into the social sphere of taking in another's internal state for interpersonal attunement" (Siegel 2010, p. 35). To attune to the client, the coach also needs to tune into their own internal shifts. The more aware we become of our own emotional and bodily states through mindfulness, the more our insula and anterior cingulated cortex activate and the better we are at reading others (Singer *et al.* 2004). Furthermore, mirror neurons appear to play a vital role in how we attune to others' internal states (Iacoboni 2008).

Being able to empathize with the client is key to successful coaching relationships. Mindfulness and meditation training are associated with increased empathy, in particular with lower levels of personal distress and higher levels of perspective taking (e.g. Atkins 2013). Farb and colleagues (2007) showed that after just eight weeks of mindfulness training, participants had increased empathy, with higher levels of insula activation, key in mediating empathy (Singer *et al.* 2004). It is important, though, to avoid over-identification, and mindfulness can help the coach remain emotionally detached (e.g. Passmore and Marianetti 2007). It can help them manage psychoanalytic processes such as transference and counter-transference, which otherwise can threaten the relationship and effectiveness of coaching outcomes. Effectively managing adverse reactions is positively associated with psychotherapy outcome (Hayes, Gelso, and Hummel 2011), which logically is likely to be the case in coaching too. A study by Scheick (2011) points to how developing "self-aware mindfulness" can help in the management of countertransference within relationships with clients (in this case, nurses). The depth and accuracy of self-assessment is directly proportional to the present level of self-awareness, and requires introspection to appraise one's emotions.

Interlude: personal reflection on "tuning in"

A client shared how they had recently suffered a work-related trauma. As they described their sadness and fears, I became aware of tightness in the stomach, and I felt choked, almost unable to speak. Waves of compassion for this person washed over me and I noticed a very strong urge to help, which I reflected I would need to monitor, as it could easily get in the way of empowering the client to find their own answers. I shared with my client some of what I was feeling, including profound sadness, a tight throat, and sense of paralysis. My client valued this sharing, saying that they were indeed feeling paralyzed, and that they had been silenced somehow by the trauma.

We set the intention of compassionately and nonjudgmentally turning towards her difficult feelings, using the FEEL model, and she was able to gently sit with these feelings, giving them a name, and giving them permission to go. She turned towards other feelings also present, including a sense of calmness, and that everything would be all right, but also that it was okay to feel sad and scared. After the coaching, I reflected how mindfulness has greatly enhanced my ability to notice and to feel compassion for others but that it is important not to get overly emotionally entangled, as this can get in the way of good coaching outcomes, making collusion more likely, for example. I reflected how important it is to maintain a balance in order to be at our most resourceful, being able to observe and manage emotions rather than get overtaken by them, and to accept whatever arises. To make best use of ourselves as "instruments" in a professional capacity, we need to be able to self-manage and self-regulate, not wallow in a sea of feelings.

For a "mindful coach," curiosity, openness, and acceptance come together in a "healing form of love" (Siegel 2010, p. 55), what we might think of as loving-kindness. I believe there is most definitely a place for love and compassion within coaching. In this final section exploring how mindfulness can enhance the coaching process, I examine how mindfulness can develop compassion, and how this enhances coaching.

Compassion

All bar one (who was unsure) of a group of fourteen coaches I polled agreed that compassion is central to coaching (Hall 2013). I defined compassion as: "The motivation to empathise with another, to feel what they're feeling, to care deeply about their wellbeing, happiness and suffering, and to act accordingly ... and the heartfelt emotions evoked within us when this motivation is activated" (Hall 2013, p. 70).

Mindfulness helps develop compassion (e.g. Atkins and Parker 2012). Developing the mental expertise to cultivate positive emotion alters the activation of circuitries previously linked to empathy and theory of mind in response to emotional stimuli (Atkins 2013; Lutz *et al.* 2008).

Adopting a compassionate coaching approach has been linked to better coaching outcomes, according to Boyatzis (2010), who researched clients' neural reactions to "compassionate" and "critical" coaching approaches. A compassionate coaching style was one where the coach intentionally encourages a positive future to arouse a positive emotional state, while a critical coaching style focuses on failings and what the person should do. With a compassionate approach, clients are more likely to learn and make behavioural changes: in the brains of those coached by compassionate coaches, a week or so later, the parts of their brain associated with visioning, a critical process for motivating learning and behavioral change, were activated, according to the research.

Imparting mindfulness skills

Having explored how coaching mindfully can enhance the coaching process, I now explore how actually teaching mindfulness to clients can enhance outcomes in coaching. Although coaching is typically non-directive, there can be a place for coaches imparting expertise where appropriate, with the client's permission. Passmore and Marianetti (2007) highlight teaching mindfulness as one of four areas where mindfulness can help in coaching (the other areas are preparing for coaching, maintaining focus in the session, and remaining "emotionally detached").

So, for example, if a client is suffering from pre-presentation nerves, or reports experiencing overwhelm, or cognitive overload, or a leader wishes to "be more authentic," the coach may decide to explicitly teach the client some mindfulness practices which may be of help – either within the session or as homework. The appropriateness will depend on factors including the client's presenting issues and objectives, and the context in which the coaching is taking place. Below we focus on some of these issues before looking at context.

Mindfulness training within a coaching intervention can be very effective in addressing a wide range of client issues and goals and

Table 16.4 *Applications of mindfulness-based coaching to specific client issues*

Applications to client issues

Stress management and resilience	Functioning and performance	Interpersonal
Enhance ability to recognize, slow down, or stop automatic and habitual reactions	Increase working memory capacity, planning and organization	Increase emotional intelligence, including empathy, emotional regulation, and social skills
Be more self-accepting and self-compassionate	Improve clarity, focus/concentration	Enhance awareness of others
Manage mild depression	Enhance problem-solving ability	Resolve/manage conflict
Become calmer/tackle stress, anxiety, overwhelm, burnout	Enhance ability to make decisions	Develop authentic leadership
Have higher self-esteem/self-confidence	Be more intuitive	Improve ability to communicate
Increase health and wellbeing	Improve creativity	Develop greater presence
Manage anger	Identify values/find "meaning and purpose"	Improve difficult relationships
Enhance self-awareness	Be more aligned with values	Achieve better work-family balance
Live more "in the present"	Deal with change and complexity	
Accept how things are	Improve strategic thinking	
Tackle sleeping problems	Be better able to think medium- and long-term	
Improve resilience		

Table 16.4 lists some of these. In the remainder of this section, I will focus on some applications of mindfulness training that can be particularly beneficial.

Stress management and resilience

Numerous studies underline the positive impact of mindfulness on wellbeing, resilience levels, and the ability to manage stress (e.g. Chiesa and Serretti 2009). It is arguably in this arena where mindfulness-based coaching can make one of the most significant contributions in the workplace. Nearly half (42 percent) of employers have seen an increase in stress-induced absenteeism (Chartered Management Institute 2013). Stress management is a common health goal in coaching and even if a client does not explicitly state stress management as a goal, they will often talk about increasing their resilience or improving their work-life balance, for example. Some 27 percent of coaching clients cited managing work-life balance as their reason for seeking coaching (International Coach Federation 2014).

Role modelling a mindful way of being – curious about what life has to offer, calm and grounded, responsive rather than reactive, for example – can inspire the client to change their own way of being. It can be fruitful to explore with the client when they feel they are operating from a being or doing mode, looking at what nourishes them, and what depletes them. However, at times, what is most helpful is to explicitly impart mindfulness skills. Some 55 percent of coaches who use mindfulness with clients do so to help their clients with stress, according to the Mindfulness in Coaching survey (Hall 2013). Other related reasons for introducing mindfulness include helping clients to improve their wellbeing (45 percent), be calmer (59 percent), and manage reactions (51 percent). The top reason was to help clients become more self-aware (70 percent).

Helping the client realize that they are not their thoughts and can choose whether or not to run with unhelpful storylines can be enormously powerful. One way to do this is by sharing mindfulness techniques. The meta-cognitive mode of mindfulness helps bring about a shift from a "stress appraisal" to a positive reappraisal, enabling an appreciation that thoughts are transient, psychological events rather than the truth (e.g. Garland, Gaylord, and Park 2009).

Ethics, responsibility, and sustainability

Mindfulness-based coaching has much to offer in helping humanity tackle its biggest challenges, which include unethical behavior in the workplace (Chartered Management Institute 2013; Institute of Leadership and Management 2013) and widespread mindless consumption.

One study (INSEAD 2008) suggested that managers exposed to mindfulness-based coaching programs were more likely to act in socially responsible ways, leading to greater levels of corporate social responsibility, whereas standard executive education failed to shift behavior.

Based on my own limited research too (although this is an area crying out for empirical and conceptual research), I propose the following ways in which mindfulness-based coaching can contribute to ethical, sustainable, and responsible thinking and behaving:

1. boosting clients' self-awareness and awareness in general (e.g. Creswell *et al.* 2007) so that more ethical behavior ensues (e.g. Amel, Manning, and Scott 2009);
2. helping clients operate from an approach state so they can be more resourceful and more courageous, standing up for what they truly believe, and to be more creative (e.g. Colzato, Ozturk, and Hommel 2012);
3. helping the coach be grounded and highly present for the client, offering a safe and nonjudgmental space in which to explore and challenge attitudes and behaviors, including mindless consumption and frenetic busyness;
4. helping clients be more comfortable with ambiguity and complexity, and more able to stay with not knowing;
5. helping clients be more aware of the "interconnectedness" between them and the wider system;
6. promoting systemic and strategic thinking in clients;
7. fostering compassion to self and others in clients;
8. loosening clients' tendency towards polarized thinking;
9. helping clients be more curious and enquiring about the world around them;
10. helping clients get in touch with and act according to values;

11. helping clients be more content with what they already have (e.g. Brown *et al.* 2009);
12. helping clients turn towards and stay with what is difficult, including overwhelm and fear when faced with threats to the environment.

Below, I examine three of the aforementioned potential contributions towards promoting more ethical behavior: boosting self-awareness, helping clients be content with what they have, and interconnectedness.

Self-awareness

Ruedy and Schweitzer (2010) argue that a number of causes of unethical behavior – self-serving cognition, self-deception, and unconscious biases – are exacerbated by a lack of attention and awareness, and thus insufficient mindfulness may explain the ubiquity of unethical behavior. They find that individuals high in mindfulness report that they are more likely to act ethically and are more likely to value upholding ethical standards.

Acting with awareness is significantly positively associated with self-reported sustainable behaviour (Amel *et al.* 2009). The other mindfulness factors the researchers explored, such as observing sensations, did not predict behavior.

Wanting what we have

Buddhist teachings have long encouraged mindfulness practitioners to explore the natural human tendency to want what we do not have, only to lose interest once we attain it. Seeking to reach a place of no desire – as some Buddhist literature encourages – will not be for everyone. However, there is a place, I believe, for humankind in general, including within organizations, to seek to be more content with what we have already and to tackle the addictive cycle of excessive consumption. "Mindful" coaches can explore the nature of desire with clients, challenging clients when they are very driven to keep attaining more and more. Such an exploration dovetails comfortably with exploring being/non-doing and doing modes, and goals, as examined previously. Sometimes the right question for the coach to ask the client is "When is enough enough?" Mindfulness closes the aspiration gap between current and desired states, associated with poorer subjective wellbeing, by helping people want what they have, independent of financial status (e.g. Brown *et al.* 2009).

Another study, by Sheth *et al.* (2011) makes the business case for "mindful consumption," a concept premised on caring for self, community, and nature which translates behaviorally into tempering the self-defeating excesses associated with acquisitive, repetitive, and aspirational consumption (p. 1).

Interconnectedness

That we are interconnected is becoming much more evident through the spread of social media and the far-reaching impact of environmental and economic crises, among others. Interconnectedness is a common theme in some of the mindfulness literature, some of which is Buddhist. However, one reason why mindfulness training is spreading far and wide is because it is being made accessible outside a spiritual framework. And it seems that regardless of whether we set out to experience interconnectedness, practicing meditation can lead to a sense of the dissolving of the self/non-self boundary and a feeling of one-ness with the universe, attributable to the left and right orientation and verbal-conceptual association areas of the brain becoming "switched off" (Nataraja 2009). I have mixed feelings about this. On the one hand, I rejoice in the increasing accessibility to mindfulness and do believe that promoting it within a secular setting is absolutely the right thing. On the other hand, however, I believe many of the threads running through traditional mindfulness teachings, including impermanence and interconnectedness, have so much to offer all of us, and arguably hold the key to a sustainable future. If through mindfulness meditation we come to realize deeply that all is impermanent and that we are all interconnected, we are much more likely to think and act ethically and sustainably. This is the "enlightened self-interest" the Dalai Lama talks about.

Adapting mindfulness training to individual clients

We have examined how a mindfulness-based approach might explicitly be brought into coaching around two areas, stress management/

resilience, and ethics and sustainability, and Table 16.4 lists other issues to which mindfulness-based coaching is particularly suited. However, it is not just a question of which issue presents itself in the coaching but of the context too.

The importance of context

Explicit mindfulness training/coaching for mindfulness needs to be fit for the client's purpose, culturally relevant, and explored with suitable language.

Intentions to be in the present and to attain a higher state of awareness are common across many spiritual traditions, including Christianity, Taoism, and Sufism.

Mirdal (2012) laments the lack of Islamic thought in much of the development of mindfulness, despite similarities in philosophy and the growing need for mental health support among Muslim populations. Mirdal suggests that Sufism, in particular Rumi's teachings, can offer a meaningful alternative to Buddhist-inspired practice. When working with Christian clients, we might want to reference Christian meditators such as St Teresa of Ávila, the sixteenth-century mystic, for example.

It is often more appropriate, however, to look at mindfulness through a secular lens, talking about strategies to build resilience or emotional intelligence. Yet, a secular approach does not guarantee cultural accessibility. In New Zealand, one Māori local government manager ended the coaching relationship because his coach suggested mindfulness as a stress reduction measure, instead of working with a Māori model of health and wellbeing such as Te Whare Tapa Whā, which includes attention to the extended family, for example (Stewart, 2012).

Future research directions

The whole area of how mindfulness enhances coaching is ripe for exploration. How can mindfulness training be combined with coaching and how does coaching offered by "mindful coaches" differ from that delivered by "non-mindful" coaches? This chapter draws from existing research to suggest that mindfulness-based coaching can build coaches' competence in a number of areas including presence, and can help clients address a range of issues. It would be fruitful to investigate the impact of mindful coaching on client issues we might expect to be impacted by mindfulness, such as creativity, emotional intelligence, stress management, and coping/flourishing in times of organizational change.

This chapter presented the FEEL model, which is an evolving model for coaching with mindfulness. Feedback from coach users so far has included that it is particularly helpful for turning towards difficult emotions and to help clients access sustaining, nourishing, and empowering qualities within themselves. The "letting go" aspect has proved challenging for some. However, no formal evaluation has been carried out, and no client feedback gathered. Research is recommended into the effectiveness of this model and into other frameworks and models to aid coaches and clients to coach/self-coach mindfully.

This chapter has suggested a number of areas of common ground and potential tensions between mindfulness and coaching. This too might be fertile ground to explore in more depth both conceptually and empirically.

I distinguish between coaching mindfully, in which case the client will very likely benefit from the coach having a mindfulness practice but this may not be explicit, and the explicit sharing of mindfulness techniques. In other words, clients will not always know they are being coached mindfully. That said, it would be interesting to explore when mindfulness is and is not appropriate and helpful in coaching. Are there clients for whom mindfulness is inappropriate, for example, those who may be averse to what they might see as an approach developed for a Western culture or for people with certain religious beliefs and affiliations? Attention to client context is always going to be important. This is an area that would benefit enormously from empirical research, if only to lay concerns to rest, and potentially offering new insights into adapting mindfulness-based coaching to individual clients.

Conclusion

Mindful coaching is an emerging approach. Despite the huge amount of interest in mindfulness within the coaching profession and elsewhere, it is still early days in terms of shaping what mindful coaching looks like and understanding exactly what it can offer coaches and their clients – individuals and organizations. However, this chapter has sought to shed some light on these areas, and to inspire others to explore too.

I distinguished between coaching mindfully and mindfulness training/coaching for mindfulness, suggested a model for mindful coaching, and highlighted some benefits for the coach and client, including increased self-awareness, presence, compassion, resilience and ethics.

I suggested that the practices of mindfulness and coaching have much in common, including the aspired-to perspectives/states of beginner's mind and non-judgment, and the belief that people are resourceful and that we are all interconnected. I also explored potential differences between the practices of coaching and mindfulness, with a particular focus on the elements of non-striving/striving, goal setting/non-attachment to goals, and being/doing, concluding that although at first glance these may seem to be opposed, they, in fact, complement one another and are fruitful areas of exploration, particularly in the frenetic, consumerist world in which so many coaches and organizations operate. Mindfulness is a way of doing as well as a way of being/non-doing. Mindfulness-based coaching offers an antidote to some of the frenzy and mindlessness, yet supports goal identification and achievement in alignment with true values, and improves performance.

Drawing on the wealth of existing mindfulness research, the chapter proposed that mindfulness-based coaching (incorporating coaching mindfully and the sharing of mindfulness practices/coaching for mindfulness) can deliver direct benefits to individual clients and sponsoring organizations, improving emotional intelligence, resilience, cognitive functioning, and ethical behavior, among others. However, more research is needed.

Although it is important for coaches to ensure that being explicit about mindfulness is appropriate for their clients, it seems likely that *all* clients will benefit from working with a coach who practices mindfulness. I hope that readers will be inspired by this chapter to carry out research in this burgeoning, highly promising field, and if they are not already doing so, to commit to a regular mindfulness practice, thus reaping the numerous benefits this can bring, including renewed joy in precious daily life.

References

Amel, E. L., Manning, C. M., and Scott, B. A. (2009). Mindfulness and sustainable behavior: pondering attention and awareness as means for increasing green behavior. *Ecopsychology*, 1(1), 14–25.

Atkins, P. W. (2013). Empathy, self-other differentiation and mindfulness training. In K. Pavlovich and K. Krahnke (eds.), *Organizing through empathy*. New York: Routledge, pp. 49–70.

Atkins, P. W. and Parker, S. K. (2012). Understanding individual compassion in organizations: the role of appraisals and psychological flexibility. *Academy of Management Review*, 37 (4), 524–46.

Bandura, A. and Locke, E. A. (2003). Negative self-efficacy and goal effects revisited. *Journal of Applied Psychology*, 88 (1), 87–99.

Boyatzis, R. E. (2010). Coaching with compassion: an fMRI study of coaching to the positive or negative emotional attractor. Academy of Management Annual Conference. Montreal: Academy of Management, pp. 1–2.

Boyatzis, R. E. and McKee, A. (2005). *Resonant leadership: renewing yourself and connecting with others through mindfulness, hope, and compassion*. Boston, MA: Harvard Business Review Press.

Bresser, F. (2009). *Global Coaching Survey 2008/2009*. Germany: Frank Bresser Consulting.

Brown, K. W., Kasser, T., Ryan, R. M., Linley, P. A., and Orzech, K. (2009). When what one has is enough: mindfulness, financial desire discrepancy, and subjective well-being. *Journal of Research in Personality*, 43(5), 727–36.

Carver, C. S. and Scheier, M. F. (1998). *On the self-regulation of behavior*. Cambridge University Press.

Cavanagh, M. J. and Spence, G. B. (2013). Mindfulness in coaching: philosophy, psychology or just a useful skill? In J. Passmore, D. Peterson, and T. Freire (eds.), *The Wiley-Blackwell handbook of the psychology of coaching and mentoring*. New York: Wiley-Blackwell, pp. 112–34.

Chartered Institute of Personnel and Development (2013). *Absence Management 2013*. London: Chartered Institute of Personnel and Development.

Chartered Management Institute (2013). *Managers and the Moral Maze*. London: Chartered Management Institute.

Chiesa, A. and Serretti, A. (2009). Mindfulness-based stress reduction for stress management in healthy people: a review and meta-analysis. *The Journal of Alternative and Complementary Medicine*, 15(5), 593–600.

Clutterbuck, M. D., Megginson, M. D., and David, M. S. (eds.). (2013). *Beyond goals: effective strategies for coaching and mentoring*. Surrey: Gower Publishing.

Collard, P. and Walsh, J. (2008). Sensory awareness mindfulness training in coaching: accepting life's challenges. *Journal of Rational-Emotive and Cognitive-Behavior Therapy*, 26(1), 30–7.

Colzato, L. S., Ozturk, A., and Hommel, B. (2012). Meditate to create: the impact of focused-attention and open-monitoring training on convergent and divergent thinking. *Frontiers in Psychology*, 3, 116.

Creswell, J. D., Way, B. M., Eisenberger, N. I., and Lieberman, M. D. (2007). Neural correlates of dispositional mindfulness during affect labeling. *Psychosomatic Medicine*, 69(6), 560–5.

Dalai Lama. (2006). *Mindful politics: a Buddhist guide to making the world a better place*, ed. M. McLeod. Somerville, MA: Wisdom Publications.

De Haan, E. (2008). *Relational coaching*. Chichester: Wiley.

De Haan, E. and Page, N. (2013). Outcomes report: conversations are key to results. *Coaching at Work*, 8(4), 10–13.

Ericson, T., Kjønstad, B. G., and Barstad, A. (2014). Mindfulness and sustainability. *Ecological Economics*,104, 73–9.

Farb, N. A., Segal, Z. V., Mayberg, H., Bean, J., McKeon, D., Fatima, Z., and Anderson, A. K. (2007). Attending to the present: mindfulness meditation reveals distinct neural modes of self-reference. *Social Cognitive and Affective Neuroscience*, 2 (4), 313–22.

Friedman, R. S. and Förster, J. (2001). The effects of promotion and prevention cues on creativity. *Journal of Personality and Social Psychology*, 81(6), 1001.

Garland, E., Gaylord, S., and Park, J. (2009). The role of mindfulness in positive reappraisal. *Explore: The Journal of Science and Healing*, 5(1), 37–44.

Grant, A. M. (2013). New perspectives on goal setting in coaching practice: an integrated model of goal-focused coaching. In S. David, D. Clutterbuck, and D. Megginson (eds.), *Beyond goals: effective strategies for coaching and mentoring*. Farnham, England: Gower Publishing Limited.

Hall, L. (2013). *Mindful coaching: how mindfulness can transform coaching practice*. London: Kogan Page.

   (2014). Mindful coaching. In J. Passmore and J. Passmore (eds.), *Mastery in coaching: a complete psychological toolkit for advanced coaching*. London: Kogan Page, p. 197.

Hayes, J. A., Gelso, C. J., and Hummel, A. M. (2011). Managing countertransference. *Psychotherapy*, 48(1), 88–97.

Iacoboni, M. (2008). *Mirroring people: the new science of how we connect with others*. New York: Farrar, Straus and Giroux.

INSEAD (2008). *An overview of CSR practices response benchmarking report*. France: INSEAD.

Institute of Leadership and Management (2013). *Added values: the importance of ethical leadership*. London: Institute of Leadership and Management.

International Coach Federation (2014). *About: 2014 ICF global consumer awareness study*. Retrieved from http://coachfederation.org/consumerstudy2014.

Johns, G. (2009). Presenteeism in the workplace: a review and research agenda. *Journal of Organizational Behavior*, 31 (4), 519–42.

Kabat-Zinn, J. (1994). *Wherever you go, there you are: mindfulness meditation for everyday life*. New York: Hyperion.

Langer, E. J. (2005). *On becoming an artist: reinventing yourself through mindful creativity*. New York: Ballantine Books.

Lutz, A., Brefczynski-Lewis, J., Johnstone, T., and Davidson, R. J. (2008). Regulation of the neural circuitry of emotion by compassion meditation: effects of meditative expertise. *PLoS one*, 3(3), e1897.

Malnick, T. (2013). Curiosity, enquiry and non-judgement. In L. Hall (ed.), *Mindful coaching: how mindfulness can transform coaching practice*. London: Kogan Page, p. 80.

Mirdal, G. (2012). Mevlana Jalāl-ad-Dīn Rumi and mindfulness. *Journal of Religion and Health*, 51(4), 1202–15.

Nataraja, S. (2009). *The blissful brain: neuroscience and proof of the power of meditation*. 2nd edn. London: Gaia Books Limited.

Passmore, J. (ed.) (2005). *Excellence in coaching: the industry guide*. London: Kogan Page Publishers.

Passmore, J. and Marianetti, O. (2007). The role of mindfulness in coaching. *The Coaching Psychologist*, 3(3), 131–7.

Ridler and Co. (2011). *Ridler Report 2011: trends in the use of executive coaching*. London: Ridler and Co.

Ridler and Co. (2013). *Ridler Report 2013: trends in the use of executive coaching*. London: Ridler and Co.

Ruedy, N. E. and Schweitzer, M. E. (2010). In the moment: the effect of mindfulness on ethical decision making. *Journal of Business Ethics*, 95(1), 73–87.

Scheick, D. M. (2011). Developing self-aware mindfulness to manage countertransference in the nurse-client relationship: an evaluation and developmental study. *Journal of Professional Nursing*, 27(2), 114–23.

Sheth, J. N., Sethia, N. K., and Srinivas, S. (2011). Mindful consumption: a customer-centric approach to sustainability. *Journal of the Academy of Marketing Science*, 39(1), 21–39.

Siegel, D. J. (2010). *The mindful therapist: a clinician's guide to mindsight and neural integration*. New York: W. W. Norton and Company.

Silsbee, D. (2010). *The mindful coach: seven roles for facilitating leader development*. 2nd edn. San Francisco, CA: Jossey-Bass.

Singer, T., Seymour, B., O'Doherty, J., Kaube, H., Dolan, R. J., and Frith, C. D. (2004). Empathy for pain involves the affective but not sensory components of pain. *Science*, 303, 1157–62.

Spence, G. B., Cavanagh, M. J., and Grant, A. M. (2008). The integration of mindfulness training and health coaching: an exploratory study. *Coaching: An International Journal of Theory, Research and Practice*, 1(2) 145–63.

Stewart, L. (2012). We say Kia Ora? *Coaching at Work*, 7(6), 44.

Whitmore, J. (1992). *Coaching for Performance*. London: Nicholas Brealey Publishing.

Williams, M. and Penman, D. (2011). *Mindfulness: a practical guide to finding peace in a frantic world*. London: Piatkus.

Index

Made in the USA
San Bernardino, CA
27 August 2019